D1391081

Plate I *General view of Room 2 looking towards Room 3, showing painted scheme as reconstructed from in situ and fallen plaster fragments*

THE ROMAN HOUSE WITH BACCHIC MURALS AT DOVER

(The discovery, excavation, preservation and detailed analysis of a substantially complete Roman house (popularly known as the Painted House) containing large areas of *in situ* and fallen painted wall-plaster, together with related structures and finds, forming part of the *extra-mural* settlement of the *Classis Britannica* forts at Dover.)

BY

BRIAN PHILP

With other contributions by:-
Joanna Bird, Katherine Hartley, Christine Molenkamp, Wendy Williams, Peter Keller, Graham Morgan, Keith Parfitt and John Willson.

FIFTH RESEARCH REPORT IN THE
KENT MONOGRAPH SERIES (ISSN 0141–2264).

Published by:-

Kent Archaeological Rescue Unit
CIB Headquarters, Dover Castle, Kent.

1989

Dedicated to

the memory of the late

JAMES IRVINE

WALTER SCOTT

(GEOFFERY) ALAN DALE

whose hard work, enthusiasm and genuine interest in the Roman 'Painted House' and Dover's buried heritage (often contrasting with official and financial interests) is continued by kindred spirits.

ISBN 0 947831 06 1

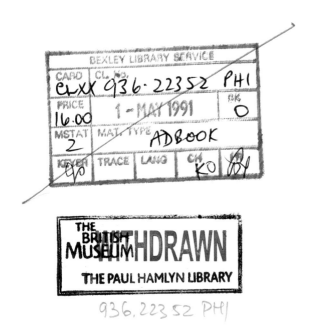

Produced for the Unit by Alan Sutton Publishing Limited, Gloucester.
Printed in Great Britian

The Unit is greatly indebted to the **HISTORIC BUILDINGS AND MONUMENTS COMMISSION (ENGLISH HERITAGE)** for a substantial grant towards the cost of this publication. The Unit also gratefully acknowledges financial contributions from the **COUNCIL FOR KENTISH ARCHAEOLOGY** and the **KENT ARCHAEOLOGICAL TRUST.**

CONTENTS

LIST OF FIGURES

LIST OF PLATES

COLOUR PLATES

ABOUT THIS REPORT

This report is the fifth in the Kent Monograph Series. It largely follows the pattern set by the four previous volumes which were:

Vol. I Excavations at Faversham, 1965 (published in 1968 by the C.K.A.).

Vol. II Excavations in West Kent, 1960–1970 (published in 1973 by the Kent Unit).

Vol. III The Excavation of the Roman Forts of the Classis Britannica at Dover, 1970–1977 (published in 1981 by the Kent Unit).

Vol. IV Excavations in the Darent Valley, Kent (published in 1984 by the Kent Unit).

As with those Reports the entire proceeds from sales go to covering the costs of printing this volume, or into a fund for the publication of subsequent volumes. Other Reports are already in preparation.

The subject matter of this second Report on the Dover excavations is about work by the unit on two adjacent sites (Painted House and Bingo Hall sites), at intervals between 1970 and 1977, that revealed an exceptionally well-preserved Roman town-house, now known as the Roman "Painted House". This work, in an area of the extra-mural settlement north of the *Classis Britannica* naval fort found by the Unit in 1970–1, also revealed several other important Roman and later structures. Only those relating to second and third century Dover, classified within eight periods, are dealt with in this Report.

Apart from the exceptional quality of the Roman House, the two sites also produced an unparalleled collection of related Roman wall-plaster, both *in situ* and fallen. This is discussed in detail together with coins, stamped tiles, small finds, samian, mortars, coarse pottery and box-flue tiles. Due to the level of funding, both in preparation and publication, no attempt has been made to carry out a detailed pottery fabric or environmental analysis and the illustrated material is largely confined to the main dating evidence. The small amount of vessel-glass from the site is mostly being held over for future publication.

As with previous Reports in this series, footnotes have been excluded and the Bibliographical references, numbered progressively throughout the text, are listed in that order at the back. These show as numbers placed in round-brackets and prefixed by the letters Ref. (e.g. Ref. 147). Similarly, the illustrated finds are also numbered progressively through the text, this time prefixed by the letters No. or Nos. so as to eliminate recurring finds-numbers and thus hopefully avoiding confusion. Coins (not illustrated) are noted in the text by a unique number (e.g. Coin 15) which refers to the number in the table of coins in the appropriate specialist section. References in the text to drawn sections and layers are shown in brackets, prefixed by the letters S. and L. respectively, (e.g. S.H, L.18). As with other Kent Monographs the main text is set in 11 on 12 point Bembo typeface, at about 800 words to a page.

FOREWORD

In welcoming this fifth major volume of the Kent Monograph series, I am very pleased to have the opportunity of paying tribute to the author, Brian Philp and all those who have worked with him so assiduously to excavate and un-cover the remarkable Roman Painted House at Dover and then to turn the site into one of the most important heritage attractions in Kent today. It is a record of much painstaking and patient archaeological rescue work over nearly two decades, starting in 1970 when the Roman House was discovered during a routine archaeological rescue assignment ahead of redevelopment and culminating with this scholarly account of what has been found there.

Nowhere else north of the Alps has such a large area of Roman painted plaster survived, making this an excavation of exceptional importance, thoroughly justifying the delicate care and precise recording applied to the task by Brian Philp and his Unit. Equally noteworthy is the way in which the Unit took the initiative and went on to devise a scheme of preservation and presentation so that the site and its unique treasures could be opened to public access as a museum. This meant establishing a Trust, raising the finance and physically undertaking a substantial amount of building and graphical display work – activities normally well beyond the conventional duties of archaeologists but without which this unique find would have remained buried and largely forgotten.

The success of the venture is shown by the constant stream of visitors, both experts and tourists. Since 1977 when the Museum was first opened to the public, on time and within budget, more than 300,000 people have been to see this fine Roman masonry building with its many rooms and superbly painted walls, probably part of a Mansio or hotel once used by Roman travellers entering and leaving Britain. So effective is the presentation that the Unit has received the accolade of no less than four national awards, for outstanding contribution to tourism, the best presentation of an archaeological site to the public, the team with the greatest initiative and the Museum of the Year.

Nevertheless, it is this Kent Monograph compiled with great care over many years and containing contributions of outstanding quality both by Brian Philp and by other members of his Unit that the detailed historical, technical and structural information resulting from this important excavation is now made available to other researchers, historians and students. Its publication marks the end of the beginning of what looks like being an even larger enterprise as the Unit now implements its plans to extend the Painted House scheme at Dover to take in a neighbouring Roman military bath-house, the Norman Church of St. Martin-le-Grand and a long lost Saxon Church.

Kent County Council is proud to have been associated with the Roman Painted House project and wishes Brian Philp and the Unit continued success in their future endeavours.

A.H. Hart
Leader
Kent County Council

CHAPTER I.

INTRODUCTION

SUMMARY

A continuous programme of large-scale rescue-excavation by the Kent Archaeological Rescue Unit from 1970–1977, ahead of extensive town-centre redevelopment, located a succession of Roman buildings on two sites north of the *Classis Britannica* naval fort discovered by the Unit in 1970–71. These formed part of a substantial *extra-mural* settlement, or *vicus*, that covered an area of at least 5 hectares. These buildings underwent a series of substantial changes throughout most of the second and third centuries, largely reflecting the frequent changes within the adjacent fort. Collectively, the fort, *vicus*, flanking harbour and twin lighthouses probably constituted the *Novus Portus* of Ptolemy, which by the mid-second century had become the Gateway of Roman Britain.

Three small ditches (Period I) across part of the sites probably served both as boundary and drainage ditches during the late-first or early-second centuries. These were superceded (Period II) by a large rectangular enclosure, nearly 42 by 39 m., with rammed-chalk foundations that was probably never finished. Its intended function is not clear, but it seems to correspond with the unfinished *Classis Britannica I* fort, tentatively dated to A.D. 117.

The first full development of the sites (Period III) came in A.D. 140–160 and corresponded with the initial occupation within the completed *Classis Britannica* II fort. A major military bath-house (not covered by this Report) covered most of the Period II enclosure, but a Flint Walled Enclosure was built on the northern limit of the site. Only a small part of this was found, but a possible southern entrance could suggest a rectangular enclosure, again of uncertain function, some 40 to 45 m. in width and length.

Major rebuilding (Period IV) took place north of the bath-house about A.D. 160–180, which corresponded with the rebuild of the *Classis Britannica* II fort (there Period II). Two new buildings, both with mortared tufa block walls, but not aligned with each other, were built with one sealing the demolished walls of the Period III enclosure. One, unheated, consisted of three rooms with earth floors and some internal painted surfaces, was 11.50 m. by 9.00 m. The second, (the Tufa Block Building) of which only the extreme south end was found, had a pillared hypocaust and seems to have formed the end of a major north-south range, mostly beyond the limits of the excavation. Both buildings were probably domestic.

About A.D. 180–200 (Period V) an additional range (the Buttressed Building) was butted to the east wall of the Tufa Block Building, probably to create the southern side of a major court-yard building conjectured marginally further north. Unusually, it had a central nave with matching internal buttresses and at least a south aisle, a total width of 7.50 m. and a minimum length of about 24 m. A conjectured north aisle would balance the building structurally and increase the overall width to about 9.70 m. to create a basilican-type building, perhaps an elaborate means of access eastwards from the Tufa Block Building. This work corresponds with the rebuilding of the *Classis Britannica* II fort (there Period III).

About A.D. 200 another major programme of rebuilding (Period VI) removed the Buttressed Building (C8) and the detached domestic building (C7) to its south, but again left intact the Tufa Block Building on the west side. To this was built an elaborate east-west range, some 28 m. long, with an overall width of 12 m. and butting to the south wall of the pre-existing hypocausted building. This was a grand, official two-storied masonry building (now known as the Painted House), with a north passage and at least six rooms, four heated by channelled hypocausts. Its

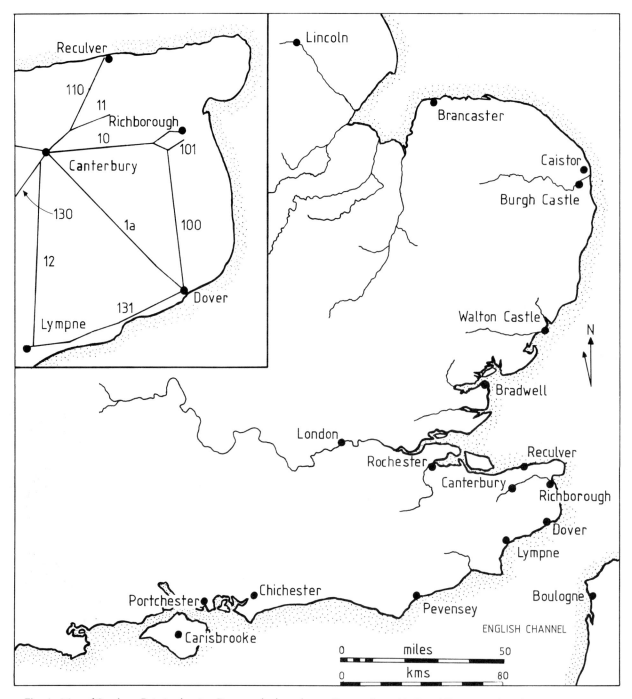

Fig. 1. *Map of Southern Britain showing Dover and other relevant Roman sites with (inset) Roman roads and major sites in East Kent.*

ceiling and walls were elaborately decorated with painted plaster, much of the latter still *in situ*. The scheme, a grand three-dimensional framework of coloured aediculae, compare with those of major buildings in Rome and Ostia. The design incorporated numerous colour-bordered panels and specific Bacchic motifs set on a foreground stage. The building also seems to correspond with the Period III occupation inside the *Classis Britannica* fort. Again the implications are that the Tufa Block Building was a paramount north-south range, to which the Painted House block and similar rooms found later to the east, formed an east-west range some 60–65 m. long. It seems likely that the two ranges were part of a major courtyard building, perhaps an official *mansio*, some 60–65 m. square overall and perhaps 40–45 m. square internally. This building, like the *mansio* at Richborough also over-built by late-Roman shore-fort fortifications, probably formed a major port-of-entry link in the *cursus publicus*.

About A.D. 210–230 (Period VII) the angle formed by the Painted House and Tufa Block Building was infilled by an unpretentious single-storey timber building with clay walls and floors. This was at least 12 by 7 m. and had at least three rooms and two corridors, all with simple painted geometric designs. Two phases of rebuilding took place before about A.D. 270. The building was constructed after the abandonment of the naval fort (in A.D. 208) and probably served to compensate for the loss of offices, or accommodation, caused by this event.

About A.D. 270 (Period VIII) army units moved into Dover and constructed a large new fort as a defensive measure against growing Saxon raids. The construction of its western defences resulted in the partial demolition of the Tufa Block Building and the Painted House range, though substantial parts of three rooms of the latter were preserved beneath the rampart behind the fort wall.

A. THE SITE (Figs. 1, 2 and 3).

The town of Dover has for 20 centuries provided the natural Gateway to Britain, thanks largely due to its unique geographical position. Not only is it the nearest point of Britain to the Continent, but the town occupies the only gap in twenty kilometres of high chalk cliffs, at a point where the English Channel funnels into the Straits of Dover (Fig. 1). These factors have made Dover pre-eminent as the main British port-of-entry throughout the ages, though the decision in January, 1986 to build a Channel Tunnel from France to Folkestone, could well deprive it of its primary, historic role.

The Roman settlement at Dover (the *Dubris* of the *Notitia Dignitatum*) was largely established on the west bank of a small estuary which occupied the Dover Gap and which was probably tidal for two or three km. inland (Fig. 2). In Roman times the estuary was probably about 200 m. wide at high tide, but due to the post-Roman marine transgression and massive river silting, the present River Dour is barely 5 m. wide along most of its length. Subsequently, the medieval town spread across the silted estuary and these events have created archaeological deposits up to a depth of about 8 m. (25 ft.).

The Dour valley cuts north-west into the North Downs, perhaps originating in the now dry Alkham Valley and draining smaller valleys on its way to the sea. In general it is a steep-sided valley which in Roman times had little if any flood-plain. At the site of the Roman settlement the slopes reached right down to the estuary banks requiring most of the buildings to be terraced and framed between the 3 m. and 15 m. contours. On both sides of the valley the ground rises to a height in excess of 100 m. thus giving dominant views of the Roman settlement, the estuary, the Channel and occasionally the coast of Gaul. More particularly the Roman settlement sat on the lower slopes of a broad spur, now known as The Western Heights, largely centred on Queen Street (N.G.R. TR. 319.413) and the area to its north. Another very minor spur may exist almost opposite on the line of the present-day Castle Hill, although there is so far little meaningful evidence of Roman settlement on the east side of the estuary. Geologically the site sits on a coombe deposit of chalk debris and shattered flints, in part capped by brickearth and in turn overlying the eroded Middle Chalk that formed the main part of the valley sides.

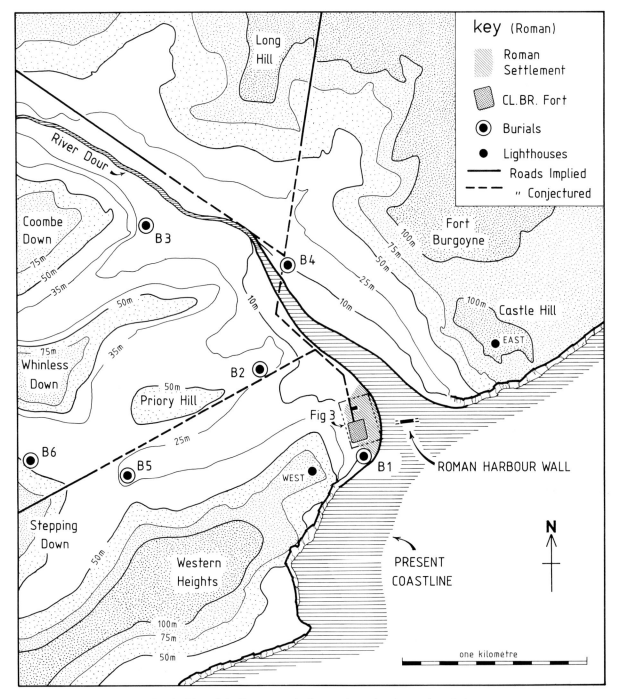

Fig. 2. *Map of the Dover area in Roman times showing roads and sites.*

Excavations by the CIB teams from 1970 onwards have demonstrated that in the early-second century the site was selected as a major naval base and port for the *Classis Britannica*, the Roman fleet in British waters. It then became the principal Channel port, superceding Richborough (Ref. 1) and almost certainly to be identified as the *Novus Portus* of Ptolemy (Ref. 2). The principal land structure was a large 1 hectare (2½ acres) naval fort discovered and excavated by the team in 1970–1977 and published by it in 1981 (Ref. 3). This contained at least 20 major buildings. Continuing excavations have shown that many prime Roman buildings survive on the north and north-east sides of the fort, including the now famous Roman 'Painted House'. Together with other Roman buildings on the east and south sides of the fort an extensive extra-mural settlement is indicated, mainly of second century date (Fig. 3). The settlement was supplemented by a large harbour in the estuary that was protected on the seaward side by a substantial timber-framed sea wall, found in 1855 (Ref. 4). In addition, each of the flanking chalk headlands was provided with tall masonry lighthouses, one of which still stands some 14 m. high within the grounds of the much later Dover Castle.

Roman roads led from the settlement area towards Richborough (*Rutupiae*), Canterbury (*Durovernum Cantiacorum*) and Lympne (*Portus Lemanis*) and several small Roman cemeteries in the adjacent rural area probably reflect small farmsteads.

B. THE PROGRAMME AND ITS AIMS.

The threat from massive road-building and re-development across the centre of ancient Dover was recognised in 1969 both locally, through the New Dover Group and at county level by the Council for Kentish Archaeology (C.K.A.). In the general absence of full-time teams in Britain at that time the response was for the Reculver Excavation Group to cancel its 1970 excavation inside the shore-fort of Reculver and to transfer all its equipment, manpower and resources to Dover. The ensuing excavation, under the umbrella of the C.K.A. and with the support of several of its affiliated groups, ran through 1970 and 1971. The prospects of even larger excavations over even bigger areas for many years ahead, in Dover and throughout Kent, saw the formation of the full-time Kent Archaeological Rescue Unit (K.A.R.U.), at the end of 1971, drawn largely from the Reculver and West Kent Groups (C.I.B. teams), both founded and directed by the writer.

The prime purpose of all the work at Dover was to record the maximum amount of archaeological evidence in the available time. The roadworks and redevelopment schemes covered an almost continuous area of eight acres of modern Dover, that lay directly over deep deposits of Roman and medieval date. The task of dealing with all this work was formidable and remains so as new sites are threatened with development.

Most sites only became available after demolition of standing buildings and often only some weeks before the intended date of reconstruction. This called for a considerable degree of organisation, non-stop work and a very flexible approach. Mechanical aids were essential, as were trained personnel and good site discipline. By 1985 some 46 sites had been dealt with in this way of which 17 are now substantially published and the others are in preparation.

The broad opening strategy and methods have stood the test of constantly changing threats and time-scales and also uncertain funding. Retrospectively, the main disadvantage was that most sites had to be tackled individually rather than as part of a pre-planned 15 year programme of work. This resulted in some duplication of effort, a somewhat staggered advance through the town-centre and considerable hardship during severe weather. Nonetheless, the basic research problems listed at the outset in 1970 have provided a sound basis for the work and the resolution of most has made considerable advances in knowledge at local, regional and national level. Even so, new problems continue to be identified and examined as the large-scale excavations continue. It was also possible to carry out several preservation schemes within the broad rescue framework as and when circumstances allowed.

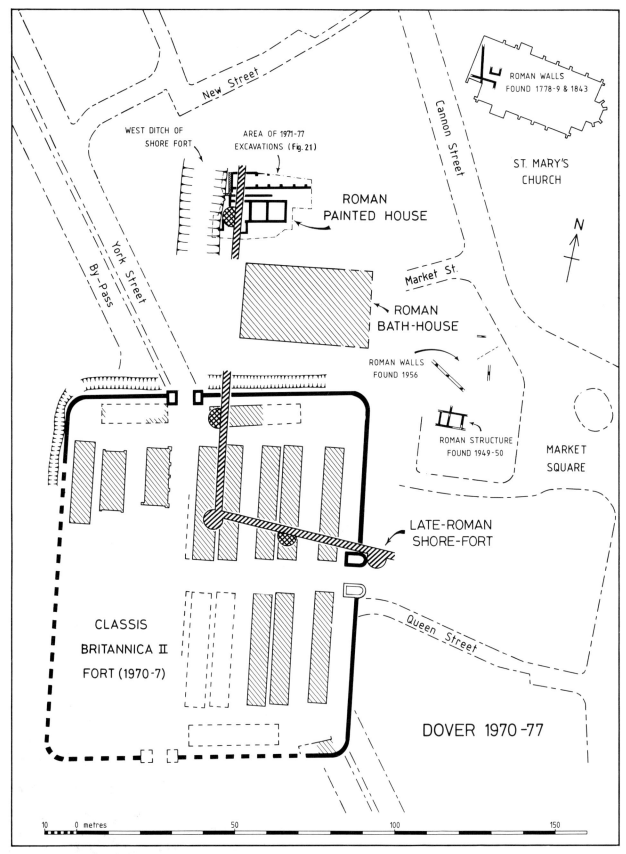

Fig. 3. *Plan showing the Classis Britannica fort, the site of the Painted House and Bingo Hall excavations and some of the adjacent Roman buildings.*

Even with the completion of the excavation, recording and preservation aspects of the work the total task was far from complete. Every object had to be cleaned, coded, stored and studied. As with most rapidly expanding schemes the facilities were always far behind the requirements. At the very beginning they were virtually non-existent. All the post-excavation work for the 1970 excavations had to be carried out by the writer almost single-handed, in his own time and where it could be done. In 1973 limited facilities were obtained to allow a start on the long process of study and writing. These were substantially improved in 1975 when a building in Dover Castle was renovated and work, punctuated by numerous and urgent rescue-excavations in many parts of the County, has continued more or less continuously since then.

C. DISCOVERY, EXCAVATION AND PRESERVATION OF THE PAINTED HOUSE.

During the first campaign of urgent rescue-work on the York Street Bypass in 1970, which covered four large sites, a single trial-trench was also excavated in July on the north side of Market Street. This was dug across the projected line of the west wall of the late-Roman shore-fort, which had been revealed in a large excavation to the south. The area was then abandoned gardens and a temporary car park (Plate II) behind derelict houses and had been designated as the site of a multi-storeyed carpark. This excavation produced the first evidence of *in situ* wall-painting, from which the name 'Painted House' was eventually coined.

In view of the certain threat to the site a large-scale excavation was undertaken on this site in 1971 (Market Street Site 1971) as part of a much larger programme of rescue-work. A metal-framed plastic tent was erected across site to provide protection. This major excavation revealed four rooms of a very substantial masonry town-house, exceptionally well-preserved, complete with fine concrete floors, elaborate hypocausts and brilliantly painted walls. In eight weeks it was possible to excavate part of Room 1 and all of Rooms 2, 3 and 4 and to remove hundreds of boxes of fallen plaster, all carefully coded. The discovery aroused great local interest and Dover Corporation readily agreed to reposition the intended carpark and to actively consider creating a major tourist attraction, roughly estimated to cost £100,000 (in 1971). Whilst deliberation continued at all levels after the excavation, the Roman House was at risk from vandalism, bad weather and frost. Rather than let this situation continue indefinitely the Unit reburied the Roman House under tight control and with the use of muslin, hessian, wooden shutters, plastic covers, soil and a protective metal roof.

In 1972, ahead of further threat from development, another large excavation (Market Street Site 1972) completed a wide area immediately west and south-west of the Roman House. This located Rooms 5 and 6, a large section of the later west wall of the shore-fort, its corresponding defensive ditch and also a massive, added bastion. Similarly, another large area, immediately east and south of the Painted House was excavated in 1973 (Paint Shop Site 1973) and this located adjacent Roman masonry structures of considerable size. Both sites were backfilled on completion.

By the end of 1973 it was clear that the Painted House site and very large areas on all four sides were to be developed as part of a major town-centre proposal. Within this the Painted House was to be protected, but no funding was provided for any degree of preservation or public presentation.

By 1975, when most of the Roman House had been buried for more than three years, there was considerable doubt as to the condition of the painted walls. The town-centre scheme had not started and officers of the new Dover District Council costed a preservation scheme at about £440,000, a figure well beyond local resources at a time of financial stringency. The solution to these problems was a project devised by the Unit which entailed the re-excavation of Rooms 2, 3 and 4 and the excavation of narrow strips of ground on the south and west sides that had previously been unavailable.

To this was linked a grand 'open month' (August 1975) which was widely advertised as being the last opportunity for the public to see the painted walls before final reburial. The Unit completed the difficult re-excavation on 31st July (in four weeks) and the public was admitted on 1st August for just four weeks. The response was spectacular and more than 18,500 paid for guided tours, the revenue from which paid for the total re-excavation. A 'Friends of the Roman Painted House' scheme was launched in the first week and about 800 people soon enrolled, at £5, or more, per head, to launch a complete preservation scheme, with a target of £90,000. The Dover District Council soon agreed a contribution of £25,000 and the Kent County Council a generous grant, also of £25,000. Much later the Department of the Environment agreed a contribution of £12,500 and the Pilgrim Trust another £2,000 and eventually a total of about £74,500 was raised.

By November, 1975 a special charitable trust (Dover Roman Painted House Trust) had been set up; by December architects had been appointed and in January, 1976, planning consent for a full preservation scheme was speedily passed. Tenders for the construction work from four building contractors arrived at the end of March, but alarmingly all were some £30,000 *over* the architects estimated costs. In a last desperate bid to save the scheme from financial collapse, the Unit agreed to the architects suggestion that the Unit should work as the main contractor. This it did for the next 13 months, largely unpaid, during which time it supervised and completed not only the whole building programme, but also laid out the forecourt, installed all the services, galleries and bridge, designed the layout of all the displays, completed the basic conservation work on the Roman House and numerous other duties. The whole programme lasted 404 days, almost non-stop and was completed within one week of the originally projected date. The final cost of the structure, materials and sub-contracting labour was only £74,000, well within the target figure. This would normally have been greatly extended by inflation, then running at about 30% and by essential changes to the original plans. All the additional costs were offset by the huge voluntary input by the K.A.R.U., which with an estimated finished value of £250,000, thus saved about £180,000.

The preservation scheme was finally opened on 12th May, 1977 when all the Friends were invited for free guided tours. The scheme later won four national awards, including in 1978 'The Best Presentation of an archaeological site to the public in Britain'. It has been open to the public for about 200 days each year since 1977, mostly staffed by volunteer members of the Unit. By 1988 nearly 300,000 people, from 160 different countries, had paid the nominal admission charge to see the Roman House.

The preservation scheme was preceded by the total excavation of a long strip of ground on the north side of the Painted House that was planned to provide a pedestrian access as part of the intended town-centre redevelopment scheme. This site also lay alongside the old Metropole Hotel, then in constant use as a major Bingo Hall and for this reason the site was identified as the Bingo Hall site, 1975–6.

The excavation-archive for the total Painted House and Bingo Hall sites (1970–1977) consists of 12 site-plans, 84 sections, 579 recorded contexts, about 179 long-bone boxes of pottery and bone, 28,938 fragments of wall-plaster, 472 listed small-finds, 671 photographs and 4 site-folders.

Of these only those specifically relating to Roman Periods I–VIII are included here. These are 18 site-plans, 33 sections, 59 drawings and 440 objects including 18 coins, 37 stamped tiles, 23 small-finds, 152 samian sherds, 5 mortars, 197 coarse pots and 8 flue tiles. The wall-plaster from the Painted House and Bingo Hall sites is treated in considerable detail for it seems to constitute the largest collection of Roman wall-plaster so far found in Britain.

The post-excavation archive contains the analysis and summary of features, contexts and finds. The complete archive is stored in the Kent Unit's security controlled Headquarters in Dover Castle where it is being used to help update subsequent and continuing work. The finds and archive will eventually be placed in a secure local depository where they can be available, under tight control, to scholars and the public. – The Painted House was eventually scheduled as an Ancient Monument (Kent No.301) and the surrounding area still awaits development (in 1988).

ACKNOWLEDGEMENTS

The writer gratefully acknowledges the large number of people who helped make the various programmes of excavation, post-excavation, preservation and presentation of the 'Painted House' site, such a success. Of the large work-force, numbering more than 400 people, the following deserve a special word of thanks for their efforts over a substantial period of time. In particular thanks are due to the excavation supervisors, Edna Mynott, Gerald Clewley, Gerald Cramp, Howard Davies, John Gaunt, Alan Gidlow, Wesley Harcourt, Ralph Mills, Jim Williams and John Willson. Special thanks are also due to the main-core of diggers including:- Mrs Winifred Berry, Frances Brennan, Thora Clitheroe, Margot Ferguson, Joan Nelson, the late Nellie Roberts, Wendy Williams; Misses Alison Borthwick, Angela Cott, Jean Taylor; Messrs. Timothy Allen, David Bolton, the late John Bray, Peter Cauldrey, the late Douglas Crellin, Trevor Dennis, Anthony Emms, Mark Errington, Derek Garrod, the late Ray Gierth, Maurice Godfrey, Nigel Gore, Peter Grant, Duncan Harrington, Gordon Hutchinson, the late James Irvine, Peter Keller, Andrew Mills, Patrick Mungovan, Robert Moon, Keith Nicol, Keith Parfitt, Ray Perkins, the late Bill Ramsey, Christopher Reed, Ben Stocker, Edmund Tullett and Jack Verrill.

Apart from the author who worked unpaid for 13 months on the building-works, particular thanks are due to the building supervisor, Peter Keller and to the main building workers, Mrs Winifred Berry, Mrs Wendy Williams, Miss Angela Cott; Messrs. Anthony Emms, the late Ray Gierth, Peter Grant, Wesley Harcourt, the late James Irvine, Robert Moon, Keith Nicol, Ben Stocker and John Willson. Maurice Godfrey and the late Wally Scott gave much help and technical advice, the latter visiting the site-works on more than 100 days.

Access to the sites was readily given by Ian Gill of Dover Corporation and by Mr. D. Bird of Maybrook Properties Ltd. The Painted House scheme received considerable *gratis* support from John Lansdowne of Turner, Lansdowne and Associates (architects) and Powell-Tolner and Associates (structural engineers), for all of which the Kent Unit is much indebted.

The Department of the Environment (now Historic Buildings and Monuments Commission) kindly and wisely provided the bulk of the excavation and post-excavation funding, mainly through the good offices of Dr. G. Wainwright and Dr. C. Young under their budget for rescue-archaeology. Some additional funds for the excavation were kindly supplied by Dover Corporation, the Pilgrim Trust and the Marc Fitch Fund and various other institutions and individuals, in addition to the major input from the Unit. Again the Unit wishes to express its thanks to all concerned.

The funding for the Painted House programme came spontaneously from the Dover District Council, the Kent County Council and the Pilgrim Trust and individuals and later from the Department of the Environment towards the conservation aspects of the work. Good support for all the operations came from the Council for Kentish Archaeology, under the chairmanship of Mrs. Rosalind Johnson and from many of the affiliated local groups, notably those from Dover, Reculver and West Kent.

In addition strong moral support was at all times given by the various members of the initial steering-committee and eventual trustees of the Dover Roman Painted House Trust, which is here gratefully acknowledged, notably from Mrs. Jane du Boulay, Dr. M. Apted, Mr. Harold Dennard, Mr. I. Killbery, Mr. Alastair Lawton, Mr. Dickie Newman, Mr. George Ruck and Mr. Philip Wilson-Haffenden.

Of specialist help with this report thanks are particularly due to Mrs. C. Robertson, Miss Frances Brennan, Mr. Peter Keller and Mr. Ralph Mills for their detailed work on the Painted House plaster and to Mrs. Wendy Williams for her work on the Bingo Hall site plaster. Mrs. Joanna Bird has kindly reported on the samian ware; Mrs. Katherine Hartley on the mortaria; Dr. John Kent on the Roman coins; Mr. John Willson has reported on the Roman coarse pottery and the flue-tiles; Mr. Keith Parfitt has reported on the small-finds and Mrs. Christine Molenkamp on the stamped tiles.

Mr. Michael Dutto and Mr. Trevor Woodman drew all the site-plans and sections for publication from the original site drawings; Mrs. Wendy Williams and Mr. Graham Welstead provided all the drawings of small finds and tile-stamps; Mrs. Wendy Williams, Mr. Graham Welstead and Mr. John Willson have drawn the coarse pottery; Mr. John Willson has provided the drawings of the flue-tiles; Mrs. Pam Barrett did most of the typing at all stages and Mrs. Christine Molenkamp and Miss Alison Borlase carried out all the editorial and many other duties. Finally, Mrs. Wendy Williams completed the very many drawings of the painted plaster, both that *in situ* and that reconstructed that are a major feature of this Report. To all these staff, supporters and official bodies the writer offers his sincere thanks.

CHAPTER II.

THE EXCAVATED STRUCTURES.

The area on the north side of Market Street generally contained a depth of 5 m. of archaeological deposits, over an orange brickearth, in turn overlying the natural chalk coombe rock. These undisturbed natural soils formed the tail end of the Western Heights and slope sharply down to meet the valley bottom no more than 90 m. east of the site.

The primary soils contain late-Neolithic flints and potsherds and these are everywhere sealed by prolific Romano-British deposits of second to fourth century date, mostly to a depth of about 2.5 m. The succeeding Anglo-Saxon deposits probably occupy less than 50 cm.; the medieval and later deposits mostly about 1 m. and the modern debris, rubble and garden soil, the upper metre.

The Roman structures in this area mostly related to the *Classis Britannica* fortified base established at Dover in the first half of the second century (Ref. 5). They formed part of the extensive civil settlement, or *vicus*, that lay north and east of the fort. The buildings are everywhere sealed by defensive structures and soil deposits relating to the late-Roman shore-fort constructed across the area at about A.D. 270 and probably occupied until about A.D. 400. The structures relating to the *Classis Britannica* were mostly built of masonry, on a large scale and it is these, in a compact area north of Market Street, that form the substance of this Report (Fig. 3). The precise site considered here covers an area about 27 m. east-west and 21 m. north-south and it forms only about a quarter of the total area so far excavated on the north side of Market Street. The centre of the site lies 130 m. north-west of the Market Square. It is flanked on the north side by the Metropole Bingo Hall and on the west side eventually by the York Street Bypass.

The ditches and buildings in the area under consideration fall into a fairly clear sequence and these have been divided into eight periods. These are dealt with in chronological order, as follows:-

PERIOD	STRUCTURE	CODE	DATE
I	The Early Ditches	C1–C3	Late-first century/early-second century
II	The Rammed Chalk Enclosure	C4	Opening decades second century
III	The Flint Walled Enclosure	C5	A.D. 140–160
IV	a) The Tufa Block Building	C6	A.D. 160–180
	b) The Building beneath the Painted House	C7	A.D. 160–180
V	The Buttressed Building	C8	A.D. 180–200
VI	The Painted House Range	C9	A.D. 200
VII	The Clay Walled Building	C10	A.D. 210–270
VIII	The Demolition for the Shore-fort	–	A.D. 270

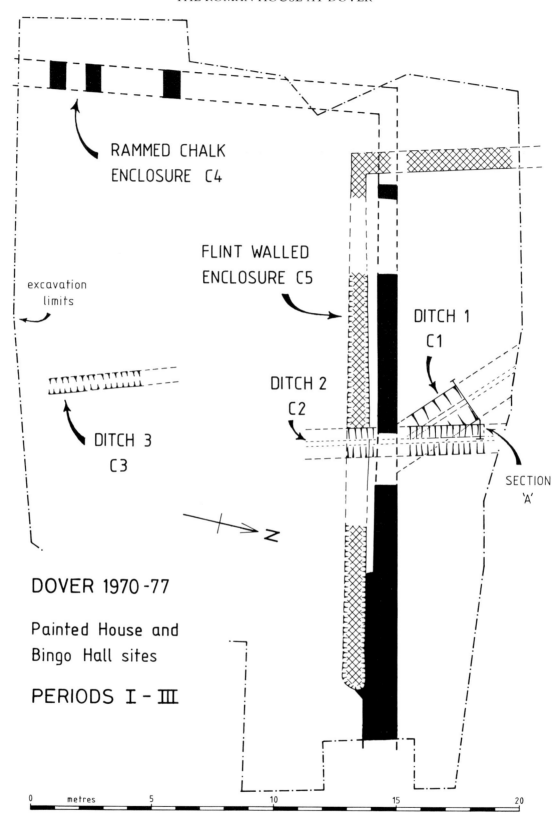

RAMMED CHALK
ENCLOSURE C4

FLINT WALLED
ENCLOSURE C5

DITCH 1
C1

excavation
limits

DITCH 2
C2

DITCH 3
C3

SECTION
'A'

N

DOVER 1970-77

Painted House and
Bingo Hall sites

PERIODS I – III

0   metres   5   10   15   20

Fig. 4. *Outline plan showing Roman ditches C1–C3 (Period I) and structures C4 and C5 (Periods II and III).*

PERIOD I – THE EARLY DITCHES (Figs. 4 and 21).

The earliest features on the two sites reported here were three small ditches, of which only short lengths were seen. One was found in 1975 projecting from beneath the south wall of the Painted House and the other two were found on the Bingo Hall site in 1976. None could be examined in much detail owing to the presence of large amounts of extant Roman masonry, intrusive features and safety baulks.

DITCH 1. (C1), Section A (Fig. 5) and Section H (Fig. 22).

This ditch was located on the Bingo Hall site where a length of only 2 m. could be traced, running on a north-west by south-east axis. Here it was about 1.70 m. wide, about 1.30 m. deep and had a V-shaped profile and a cupped base. It was cut through the natural brickearth soil and also through a marked layer of dark brown loam (S. A, L.9) mostly found over both sites and containing flints and pottery of Neolithic date. This layer is regarded as the pre-Roman topsoil which can be traced across a wide area.

The lower filling of the ditch consisted of a brown clay-loam with chalk specks and this seems to represent natural silting (S.A., L.6–8). This was cut away on one side by a small V-shaped feature, that could represent a partial recut. This was filled with a mottled grey-brown clay (S.A., L.5) and the remainder of the ditch with orange-brown clay, perhaps a deliberate backfill (S. A. L. 3–4).

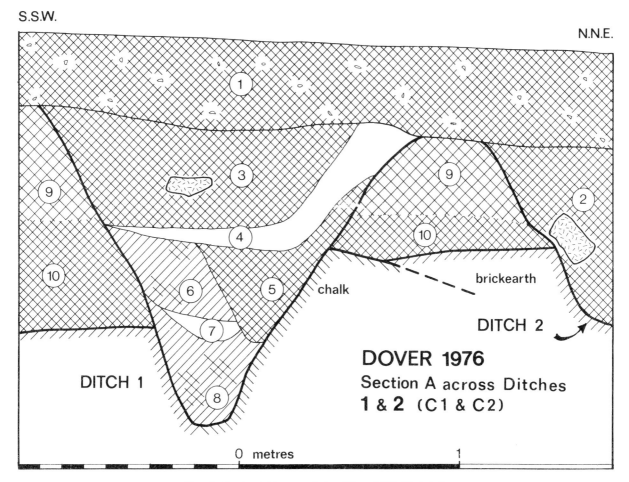

Fig. 5. *Section 'A' across ditches C1 and C2 (Period I).*

The short section examined contained no dating evidence, but the ditch was completely sealed by a thick layer of dark-brown loam and chalk specks (S.A., L.1). This layer occurred widely across both sites and seems to represent the upcast soil from the excavation of adjacent foundation-trenches. The filling of this ditch was also cut through by Ditch 2 in one place, the Rammed Chalk Enclosure (Period II) and the Flint Walled Enclosure (Period III).

DITCH 2. (C2), Section A (Fig. 5) and Section H (Fig. 22).

This was located close to Ditch 1, which it appeared to cut across. It was traced for only 1.85 m. on a north-south axis and had a depth of about 80 cm. Only the west side of the ditch was revealed during the excavation and from this it is likely that the ditch was about 1.00 m. wide. It, too, had been cut through the brickearth and the pre-Roman topsoil. Its filling, however, consisted of a mottled orange clay (S.A., L.2) that contained pieces of cut chalk and tufa blocks and also a sherd of a late-first century carinated beaker (No. 79). This ditch was also sealed by the layer of upcast, or dumped soil and cut by the Rammed Chalk Enclosure and the Flint Walled Enclosure.

DITCH 3. (C3).

This ditch was found extending southwards from under the south wall of the Painted House for a minimum distance of 3.45 m. It appears to have had a north-south axis, a U-shaped profile and a cupped base. It was at least 60 cm. wide at its top and about at least 45 cm. deep. Its filling consisted of a mottled orange-brown clay containing chalk specks (S.A., L.2) and two potsherds. One was the rim of a samian Form 18 of Flavian-Trajanic date and the other the rim of a bowl (No. 80) of the same date. On this evidence Ditch III is unlikely to have been dug and filled much before the end of the first century and more probably somewhere in the range A.D. 90– 120. It had been cut through the natural brickearth and the pre-Roman soil and was again sealed by a third deposit of upcast soil. It was later cut through by the foundations of the building beneath the Painted House (Period IV) and of the Painted House itself (Period VI).

These three small ditches may form part of a limited network of linear ditches that cross part of the overall site. These are considered in the discussions (p. 273).

PERIOD II – THE RAMMED CHALK ENCLOSURE (C4), (Figs. 4, 10 and 21).

Two long lengths of rammed-chalk foundations were found in different years, the west one on the Market Street site in 1973 and the north one on the Bingo Hall site in 1975–6. Their identical construction and relative position in the chronology of the overall site, strongly suggests that they formed part of a single scheme. Indeed their projected ends would have met together at an angle of about 94° beneath the later Tufa Block Building (C6), though the exact corner had been removed by the excavation of the great West Ditch of the much later shore-fort.

The north foundation cut through both Ditches I and II (Period I), but was in turn overlaid by parts of the foundations of the Flint Walled Enclosure (Period III). For these reasons the Rammed Chalk Enclosure is here regarded as a well-defined Period II.

The west foundation consisted of large, irregular lumps of chalk packed tightly and then rammed into a trench about 1.10–1.20 m. wide and 1.20 m. deep. This was traced for a distance of 19.10 m. to where it passed beneath Room 6 of the later Painted House. From there onwards it had been removed, but in another 8.00 m. it would have joined with the northern foundation at what is presumed to have been a corner.

The north foundation was traced for a distance of 21.67 m., but again the west end had been destroyed and another 3 m. would have created a near right-angled corner with the west foundation. The north foundation did, however, change its character abruptly at a point 18.42 m. from the conjectured corner (Plate III). Whereas the western 15.42 m. was of rammed-chalk placed in a foundation-trench generally 90–115 cm. wide and 80 cm. deep (S.C. Fig. 10 and S.G. Fig. 22), the eastern 6.25 m. had increased in width to a massive 2.45 m.! This clearly marked a major change in the structure which suggests the need for a greatly increased wall thickness. Of special interest here was a thin skin of gritty white mortar still sticking to the top of the Rammed Chalk foundation. Clearly, mortared masonry had been built directly onto this broad foundation and very thoroughly robbed along the entire lengths. The north foundation likewise consisted of two layers of large chalk-rubble blocks, in total some 31–35 cm. thick, which had been rammed hard to form the surface for the masonry. In addition the 'broad foundation' was sealed by a 5 cm. layer of grey silt, which appears to have been washed in immediately after the robbing took place.

What also seems clear is that the upcast soil from the excavation of these foundations, mostly the dark brown loam representing the pre-Roman soil, had been spread across part of the site and in the process sealed Ditches I and II (S.A., L.1). No finds could be specifically identified from this layer, but Periods I and III considered, these foundations should have been laid sometime in the opening decades of the second century A.D.

On their own merits these two linear foundations should represent boundary walls, or even two sides of a rectangular enclosure. This in fact was proved to be the case for in 1977 the corresponding south foundation was found, actually joining the continuation of the west foundation. In 1983 a long length of the east foundation was found and this too was found to join the south foundation. The enclosure so described measured about 41.70 m. by 38.50 m., but as only the north and west foundations are dealt with here the other two foundations will be covered by a subsequent report (see discussion).

PERIOD III – THE FLINT WALLED ENCLOSURE (C5), (Figs. 4 and 22).

Evidence for two varying lengths of flint foundation were found on the Bingo Hall site in 1975–6. The longest had been built east-west across the site, whilst the shortest had been built north-south. They joined each other roughly at right-angles (91°) under the east wall of the later Tufa Block Building and were of integral build. These foundations cut across two of the early ditches (Period I) and also across part of the Rammed Chalk Enclosure (Period II). As they were sealed by all the later structures identified as Periods IV to VIII this Flint Walled Enclosure is shown here as Period III.

In detail the west foundation was traced northwards for 6.57 m. before it disappeared under the side of the excavation. It was 67 cm. high, 83 cm. wide and constructed of five courses of flint and tufa fragments set in tufa-mortar and brown clay (S.H. Fig. 22). The south wall had only survived for 1.00 m. at its extreme west end where it joined the west wall, the rest having been robbed out. The robber-trench was generally 95–100 cm. wide, 38–60 cm. deep and had mostly vertical sides and a cupped base (S.G. Fig. 22). It was filled with a mixture of brown clay and loam, and contained chalk and flint. The robber-trench was traced for 19.60 m., thus giving a total length of 20.60 m. for the south foundation. It ended in a gentle curve, not apparently against any obvious feature.

What is clear is that these flint foundations totally superceded those of the Rammed Chalk Enclosure. This suggests a major change of plan and it seems highly probable that the total robbing of the four walls of the Rammed Chalk Enclosure and the construction of these flint foundations formed part of the same major scheme. The robber-trenches which removed the masonry over the chalk foundations contained mixed soils (S.G., L. 61) and also a small quantity

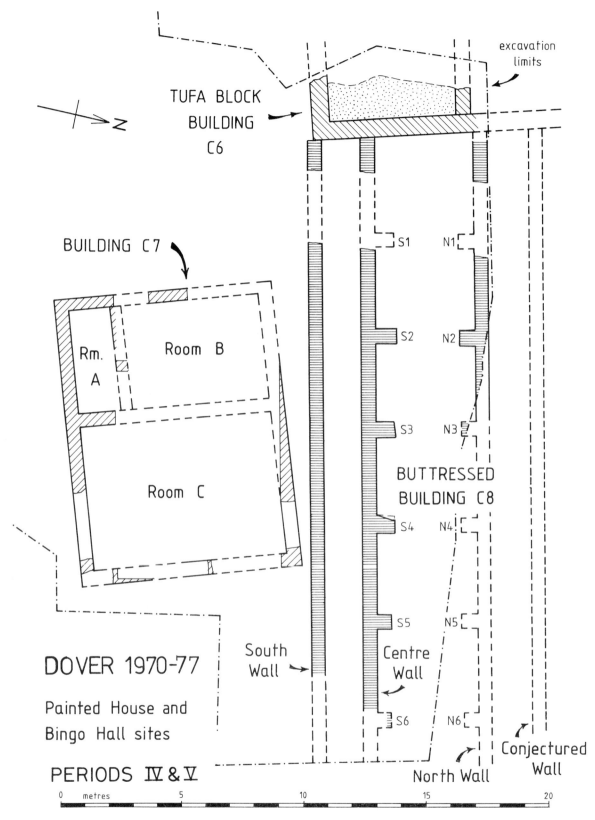

TUFA BLOCK
BUILDING
C6

excavation
limits

N

BUILDING C7

Rm.
A

Room B

Room C

S1   N1

S2   N2

S3   N3

BUTTRESSED
BUILDING C8

S4   N4

S5   N5

South
Wall

Centre
Wall

DOVER 1970-77

Painted House and
Bingo Hall sites

PERIODS IV & V

S6   N6

Conjectured
Wall

North Wall

0   metres   5   10   15   20

Fig.6. *Outline plan showing Roman structures C6, C7 and C8 (Periods IV–V).*

of pottery. This included four samian vessels, a Form 18, a Form 42 and a cup, all of Flavian date and a Form 18/31 of Hadrianic date. Some 93 coarse sherds (Nos. 81–93) were also recovered from the robber-trenches and although these include one or two vessels of first century date the majority belong to the second century and include some that could be dated as late as A.D. 160. It seems clear from this evidence that the robbing could not have taken place before about A.D. 130 and more probably at about A.D. 140–160. This agrees well with the evidence from Ditches II and III and also from later deposits.

As regards function it is significant that no internal or external foundations, walls or floors were found directly associated with these two flint foundations at any point. It seems probable, therefore, that these joining masonry foundations represent boundary walls enclosing two sides of an area centred to the north-east and therefore largely untouched by excavation. In all probability the area enclosed was rectangular and, if so, then identical, or similar foundations, probably existed on the other two (north and east) sides. The ending of the south wall about 21.50 m. from the south-west corner of such a four-sided enclosure could mark an entrance, which if central and about 2 m. wide, could suggest an enclosure about 45 m. wide or even 45 m. square. Significantly, or not, this is only slightly larger than the Period II enclosure with the Rammed Chalk Foundations, which it replaced.

PERIOD IV – THE TUFA BLOCK BUILDING. (C6), (Figs. 6, 7, 8 and 21).

This building was found at the west end of the Bingo Hall site in 1975– 6. Only parts of its south and east walls survived and it contained substantial traces of a pillared hypocaust. It formed a major element in the development of the site for it overlay the robbed foundation of the Rammed Chalk Enclosure (Period II), the Flint Walled Enclosure (Period III) and thus indirectly the two early ditches (Period I). In addition both the Buttressed Building (Period V) and the Painted House (Period VI) had subsequently been built against it. Similarly, its east wall later served as the west limit of the Clay Walled Building (Period VII). Towards the end of the third century it was largely destroyed by the excavation of the great West Ditch of the shore-fort (Period VIII) and what survived was buried beneath the berm between the fort wall and the inner lip of the ditch (Plate IV).

In detail the east wall was traced for 6.70 m. within the excavation and the south wall for 2.27 m. before being cut by the fort ditch. The walls were built integrally and stood five courses high above an external offset course 10 cm. wide (S.B. Fig. 8 and S.H. Fig. 22). The facing was mostly squared tufa blocks with occasional greensand and flint, but it had a flint core with all being set in a creamy white mortar. Both walls were 94 cm. wide, had survived to a height of about 98 cm. and stood on an unmortared flint foundation about 30 cm. deep. Significantly, the line of the new south wall followed exactly the projected line of the largely destroyed south wall of the Flint Walled Enclosure and the new east wall largely sat along the line of the west wall of the enclosure.

Much of the sequence of events was recorded in a single vertical section (Fig. 8), where the primary deposits (L. 112 and 113) were cut into by the Flint Walled Enclosure (C5) and a large pit of uncertain function, perhaps contemporary (L. 110). Both the pit and the partially robbed flint wall of the Enclosure were sealed by levelling layers (L. 107–109), into which the foundations of the east wall of the Tufa Block Building (C6) had been cut. The tufa demolition layer (L. 104) of the Buttressed Building (Period V) clearly overlay the foundation offset, which in turn was sealed by the layers (L. 102–103) relating to the Clay Walled Building (Period VII) and its eventual demolition (L. 94, 95 and 98).

The area bounded by the east and south two walls had been subdivided by the insertion of an east-west cross-wall some 54 cm. wide and surviving for a length of only 1.08 m. (Fig. 7). It was built of flints set in a grey-white mortar and butted to the original east wall. It survived to a

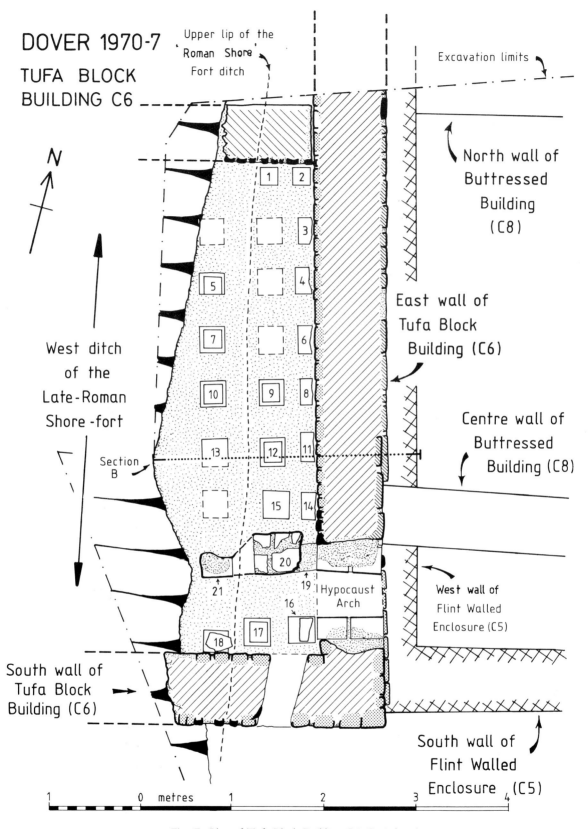

Fig. 7. *Plan of Tufa Block Building C6 (Period IV).*

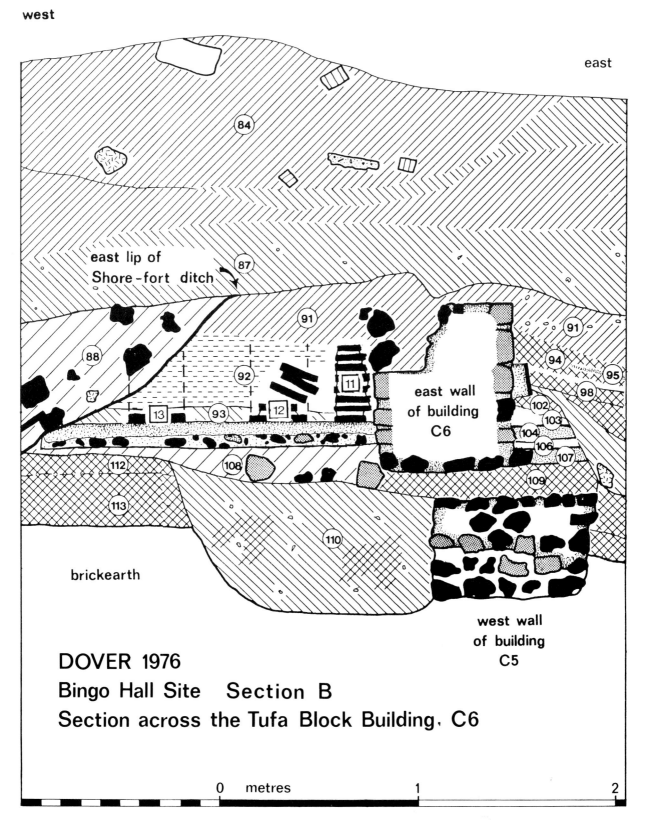

west

east

84

east lip of
Shore-fort ditch

87

91

88

91

92

94

95

11

98

13

12

east wall
of building
C6

102

93

103

104

106

112

108

107

113

109

110

brickearth

west wall
of building
C5

DOVER 1976
Bingo Hall Site   Section B
Section across the Tufa Block Building, C6

0   metres   1   2

Fig. 8. *Section 'B' across the Tufa Block Building C6 (Period IV).*

height of only 15 cm. Presumably it served as an internal wall and divided the room into at least two parts. Of the other internal arrangements nothing more can be said.

The internal floor of this building was made of *opus signinum* concrete of grey-white mortar, containing tile chips and small pebbles. This was 13 cm. thick and had been laid on a bedding of chalk and flint about 7 cm. deep. The floor supported the pillars of a substantial hypocaust which had been substantially robbed (Plate V). Parts of 21 pillars survived to varying heights of between 4 and 40 cm. and consisting of 1–8 courses of tiles laid horizontally (Fig. 7, Nos. 1–21). The tiles were mostly 20 by 20 by 4 cm., but in six cases the base tile was larger and normally 28 by 28 by 4 cm., though one was 36 by 36 by 4 cm. There had been nine rows of pillars on the north-south axis and at least three rows on the east-west axis, hence an absolute minimum of 27 pillars in all, but many more must have once existed. Originally, these probably rose to a height of at least 60 cm. and supported a suspended floor of which no trace survived, either *in situ* or as demolition rubble. No trace of a furnace for this hypocaust was found and it is likely that it had been on the west or north sides. Nor was any trace found of *in situ* flues for ducting the hot air up inside the walls and these must have been at a higher level. Several fragments of box-flue tile were, however, found in the rubble in the partially demolished hypocaust. These included fragments of a voussoir (No. 276) and parts of at least two box-flue tiles (Nos. 277 and 278). None was stamped, nor was the fabric of known *Classis Britannica* type. The single voussoir is not sufficient to suggest that this room had been vaulted.

It is clear that the hypocaust underwent a major change when a new furnace arch was inserted at the south-east corner. It seems likely that this was done when the internal wall was added and this suggests that the original furnace was then only serving the northern part of the divided room and that the southern part required the new furnace!

The construction of the new south-east furnace required an opening to be made in the east wall, some 86 cm. wide at the base and rather wider higher up. In this opening were built the furnace walls, consisting of large tile fragments set in pink *opus signinum* mortar. The south side survived nine courses high, the north side seven courses high and the space between them measured 46 cm. The north wall was continued into the room for a distance of about 1.25 m. and was clearly laid over three of the original pillars which had been deliberately reduced for this purpose. The walls had a maximum width of 20 cm. It seems likely that this new furnace had been serviced from the south corridor of the Clay Walled Building (Period VII), though no trace of burning was found.

The rubble fill of this room and its partially robbed hypocaust, contained 160 fragments of painted wall-plaster. Two designs seem to be represented (not illustrated). The main design (87 fragments) consists of a deep pink, marbled dado, beneath a broad yellow dado-band, surmounted by white panels. The latter are bordered by a dark red stripe and lined internally with a black line. The second design (nine fragments) may represent a series of white octagons with square interspaces, bordered in red and green. As these two precise coloured designs are not known in either the Painted House or the Clay Walled Building, it seems probable that these represent the internal decoration of this room of the Tufa Block Building.

The Dating Evidence for Period IV

As regards dating there is generally more evidence than for the earlier periods. Some twelve sherds of pottery were found in the dumped soil beneath the floor (S. B, L. 108 and 112) and all were of first or second century date and none later than Antonine. They included a samian Form Curle 11 of Flavian date and a coarse ware straight sided dish (No. 94). In addition it is certain that this building was constructed after Periods I, II and III with the latter dating from about A.D. 140–160. Some allowance must also be made for the use of the Period III Flint Walled Enclosure which, even if very short, probably had a life of at least ten years. The evidence also shows that the subsequent Buttressed Building (Period V) was constructed towards the end of the second century. On the small amount of pottery and also the circumstantial evidence, therefore, the Tufa Block Building was probably constructed at about A.D. 160–180.

The primary ash and carbon fill of the hypocaust (S. B, L. 93) contained coarse pottery that included three vessels (Nos. 95 to 97) almost certainly dating from the first half of the third century. This suggests a date for the final use of the hypocaust before the insertion of the furnace near the south-east corner. The rubble representing the final demolition (S. B, L. 92) of the building contained 17 sherds including another third century vessel (No. 98).

It is clear that the construction of the Tufa Block Building marked another major phase in the Roman history of the site. It clearly required the removal of the Flint Walled Enclosure above the ground. This suggests a major structure, for a smaller one could have been built to avoid the Flint Enclosure by a matter of only half a metre! By far the greater part of this building must have been built beyond the limits of excavation, but there is some likelihood that much of this was also destroyed by the digging of the later shore-fort ditch. Its exact function is not clear, but it contained at least one heated room and therefore some domestic element seems to be implied (discussion on page 277).

PERIOD IV – THE BUILDING (C7) BENEATH THE PAINTED HOUSE (Figs. 9 and 21).

This building was found on the Painted House site in 1971 and 1972 and was strangely not parallel to any other Roman structure in the area. Its axis had been swung about 6° south-west of the other buildings. The greater part of it still remains buried beneath the extant floors and walls of Rooms 1 and 2 of the Painted House. Most of its south wall was revealed, but only varying lengths of the north, east and west walls were seen at different times (S. D Fig. 20 and F Fig. 22). A short section of the west wall was found under the door-opening between Rooms 2 and 3 of the later Painted House (S. E Fig. 22) and much of the outer side of the north wall could be seen projecting from beneath another wall. Only one internal north-south cross-wall (between Rooms A and C) was found, but the corresponding east-west wall of Room A could be seen just extending from beneath the later south wall of the Painted House.

Clearly, the best exposed section of masonry is on the south side where some 8.00 m. of the south wall can still be seen by visitors to the Painted House. Here, too, the other three walls of Room A can be seen, partly extending under the south wall of the Painted House. The north wall of Room A is largely masked by the later masonry, but it is clearly separated from it by a thin band of soil (Fig. 16, No. 5). Its south wall overlay Ditch 3 (Period I) and its foundations appear to have cut through the various dumps covering both the foundations of the Rammed Chalk Enclosure (Period II) and the Flint Walled Enclosure (Period III). Its west wall lay 4m. east of the corner of the Tufa Block Building and was broadly similar in construction. It is here regarded as contemporary with it (hence both Period IV).

It lay, however, less than half a metre south of the Buttressed Building (Period V), which is unusually close and in sharp contrast to the sensible planning elsewhere on the Dover sites. This suggests that these two buildings were not built as part of a single scheme. In addition it seems unlikely that Building C7 would have been deliberately constructed so close to the Buttressed Building, had the latter pre-existed, when more ground was readily available. The most likely solution is that Building C7 already existed when the Buttressed Building was constructed, for the latter had no scope to allow a sensible distance as its position was pre-determined by the south end of the pre-existing Tufa Block Building. Hence, the circumstantial evidence favours a Period IV construction, which happily agrees with the evidence of the broadly similar structural details. Either way, both Building C7 and the Buttressed Building were swept away in Period VI, when the Painted House itself was constructed. All this suggests that Building C7 was constructed about A.D. 160–180 and destroyed no later than about A.D. 200.

The building was laid out as an approximate rectangle, with the north and south sides each being about 11.40 m. in length. However, the west wall at 9.00 m. was some 17 cm. shorter than the east wall (at 9.17 m.) and the average width was thus about 9.10 m. It was divided into at least

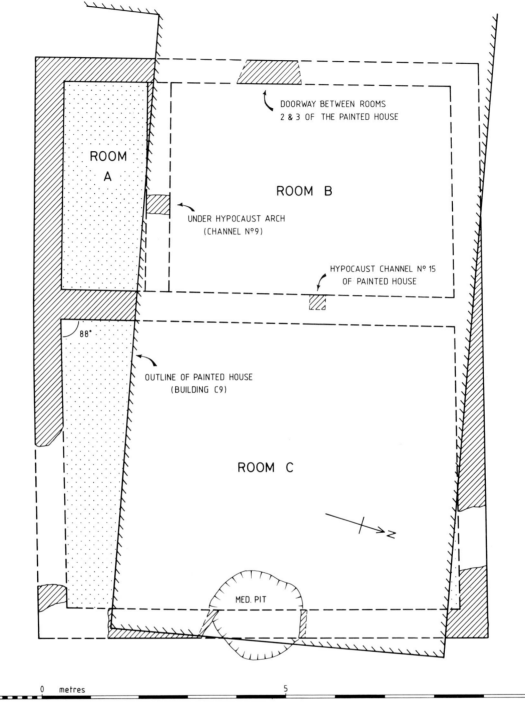

ROOM
A

DOORWAY BETWEEN ROOMS
2 & 3 OF THE PAINTED HOUSE

ROOM B

UNDER HYPOCAUST ARCH
(CHANNEL N°9)

HYPOCAUST CHANNEL N° 15
OF PAINTED HOUSE

88°

OUTLINE OF PAINTED HOUSE
(BUILDING C9)

ROOM C

→ z

MED. PIT

1   0   metres   5   10

Fig. 9. *Plan of Building C7 (Period IV).*

three rooms (Rooms A–C), but it is just possible that other internal walls could exist out of sight under the later Painted House. No internal walls were found projecting eastwards from beneath the partially removed floor of Room 1 of the Painted House, but it is just possible that the construction of the hypocaust could have removed a wall here. Room A measured 4.12 m. by 1.70 m. internally and Room B, 5.65 m. by 4.12 m. internally. The remaining area, designated Room C, was about 8.00 m. by 5.65 m. internally and about twice the size of Room B!

In detail all four external walls had foundations of large unmortared chalk blocks, about 48 cm. wide and 20 cm. deep set in a broad U-shaped foundation-trench. On these sat a wall-footing, some three courses high, of large flints set in a white mortar containing small blue and orange grits. This increased the width to about 60 cm. and raised the height by another 54 cm. roughly level with the surface of the dumped deposit over the site. On this the wall proper had been built, though of this only parts of a single course survived owing to the very thorough demolition for the Painted House scheme. This wall was built of large flints, chalk and tufa blocks set in a similar mortar as the wall-footings. The tufa blocks appeared to form an external skin for the external walls though very few of these actually survived.

Of the internal walls, both appeared to have a single course of chalk-rubble foundation and at least two courses of flint-footings of similar size to the external walls. At least two courses of tufa above the footing appear to represent the wall proper and on the west face of Room C where a rendering of mortar had been painted white, which shows that this was an exposed surface.

There was no trace, or suggestion, that this building had stone floors or any form of heating. The floor surfaces appear to have been of trodden soil. Nor is it completely certain that the entire superstructure was stone-built. Certainly there was no trace of substantial rubble and mortar demolition material here that could relate, but this could have been totally removed. One small area of demolition material which was revealed, however, lay in Room C between two of the heating channels of Room 1 of the later Painted House. This consisted mainly of clay and fragments of red and white plaster. From this it seems clear that at least part of Building C7 had clay walls and, if so, it is likely that these were internal partitions. Nor did any evidence survive of the means of roofing.

In contrast to the successive buildings in the adjacent Bath House area, the site occupied by Building C7 (Period IV) seems to have been largely vacant prior to its construction. The site lay just within the north-west corner of the Rammed Chalk Enclosure (Period II) and just outside the Flint Walled Enclosure (Period III). Hence, other than Ditch 3 (Period I) the first structure on this particular site was built in Period IV!

It is difficult to identify the precise function of this building. Its incomplete plan makes specific comparisons difficult, but at least the traces of painted plaster show internal decoration and suggest either a small house or a building of some refinement. The fact that it was replaced directly by the Painted House could suggest that it had served a similar function, but this is only one of several possibilities (discussion page 277).

The Dating Evidence

Thirteen small sherds of coarse pottery were found in what seems to have been a localised, primary occupation level associated with this building. Of these, two vessels (Nos. 99 and 100) are of mid-second century date.

The dating evidence for this building is very limited owing to the fact that so much of its structure and the deposits which they seal, still remain buried by the extant Painted House building. It seems likely, however, that Building C7 was cut through the same dumped deposits as the Tufa Block Building and was also of the same date. This suggests a construction date of about A.D. 160–180 and certainly it was substantially demolished when the Painted House was built about A.D. 200.

PERIOD V – THE BUTTRESSED BUILDING (C8), (Figs. 6, 10 and 21).

At some point subsequent to the completion of the Tufa Block Building (Period IV), a major new building was added to its south-eastern corner. This was also found during the excavation of the Bingo Hall site in 1975–76. Its main axis lay east-west along the length of the excavation and it clearly extended beyond the excavation limits to the east. Directly related structures could exist to the north in an area never touched by excavation. Nothing of the superstructure of this building remained and only the massive mortared flint foundations of three east-west walls and seven integral buttresses, were located (Fig. 6).

The construction of this large building involved the removal of the surviving foundations of the underlying Flint Walled Enclosure (Period III). This was done almost entirely with the exception of the final west end of the south wall of the enclosure and at least part of its west wall, both of which lay safely buried beneath the walls and floors of the Tufa Block Building (Period IV). This localised survival is useful evidence that the enclosure foundations generally were not removed during Period IV.

It is clear that both the robbed foundation-trenches of the Rammed Chalk Enclosure (Fig. 10, S.C.L. 30–32) and the Flint Walled Enclosure (L. 29) were buried by thick layers of dumped soil (L. 27–28), which had also been spread to the north (L. 35 and 38). It is likely that much of this soil was derived from the construction of the adjacent Period IV buildings. Certainly the centre wall of the Buttressed Building cut through them all leaving a well-defined vertical column of trench backfill (L. 37) to show from what level its trench had been cut. More soil (L. 35) had then been spread north of the foundation to bring the area up to a fairly constant level. The three foundations also cut across the two Period I ditches on this site and also partially through the fill of the robbed Period II Rammed Chalk Enclosure (L. 30–32).

The south foundation also overlapped the surviving west wall of the Flint Walled Enclosure (Period III) and butted to the east wall of the Tufa Block Building (Period IV), to which it was clearly added. Nor were the parallel foundations of the Buttressed Building laid out at right-angles to the Tufa Block Building for they joined at an angle of about 93°. The three walls are discussed in detail below.

North Wall.

This ran under the northern limits of the excavation and could not be examined across its full width. A total length of 11.80 m. was seen from where its west end butted to the Tufa Block Building to a point where it disappeared under the side of the very deep excavation. It seems highly likely that it ran also for 23.60 m. or more, thus corresponding to the south wall with which it clearly formed a pair. Of the length found some 2.95 m. had been cut away by the foundation-trench for the late-Roman fort wall, thus leaving only 1.62 m. to the west and 7.23 m. to the east. Even part of the latter was masked by the side of the excavation, but the presence of the two rectangular buttresses demonstrated its minimum length.

In detail the foundations had been laid in a vertical-sided foundation-trench at least 42 cm. wide and probably 64 cm. deep if this matched the south wall. The foundation was at least 51 cm. deep and generally consisted of two courses of roughly laid flints set in a creamy mortar, over a dump of flints mostly 32 cm. deep. The two buttresses were of an integral build, with Buttress N2 being 62 cm. wide and 67 cm. long. Buttress N3 was 65 cm. wide and probably about 70 cm. long.

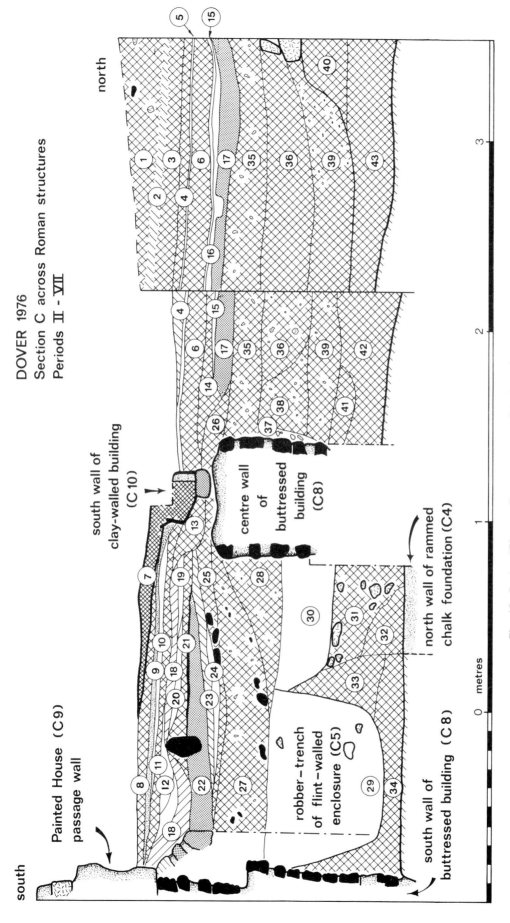

DOVER 1976
Section C across Roman structures
Periods II - VII

south

north

Painted House (C9)
passage wall

south wall of
clay-walled building
(C10)

centre wall
of
buttressed
building
(C8)

north wall of rammed
chalk foundation (C4)

robber-trench
of flint-walled
enclosure (C5)

south wall of
buttressed building (C8)

metres

0   1   2   3

Fig. 10. *Section 'C' across Roman structures C4, C5 and C8–C10 (Periods II–VII).*

Centre Wall (Figs. 10 and 22).

This ran almost down the centre of the excavation and it was thus possible to trace it for 23.62 m. from where it butted the Tufa Block Building to a point where it passed beyond the east end of the excavation. Again some 2.95 m. had been removed by the construction of the later fort wall with only 1.52 m. remaining on the west side of the fort wall. The long length running on the east side incorporated five largely rectangular buttresses (S2–S6).

In detail the foundations were of almost identical construction to the north wall, but were mostly 55 cm. deep and 64 cm. wide. The buttresses (Plates VI and VII) were again of integral construction and the dimensions and spacing are given in the table below. From the more or less uniform spacing it seems highly probable that a pair of opposing buttresses (N1 and S1) was removed when the fort wall was built. Both are included in the table.

	Spacing	Buttress width	Buttress length
Space to Tufa wall	= 3.70 est.	–	–
Buttress S1–N1 (missing)	= –	.65 est.	.70 est.
Space	= 3.30 est.	–	–
Buttress S2 and N2	= –	.62 est.	.80
Space	= 3.10	–	–
Buttress S3 and N3	= –	.65	.75
Space	= 3.08	–	–
Buttress S4	= –	.72	.75
Space	= 3.30	–	–
Buttress S5	= –	.63	.60
Space	= 3.27	–	–
Buttress S6	= –	.60	.25 (min.)
Totals	19.75 m	3.87 m	
Total length of wall	= 23.62 m		

Table of the internal dimensions of the centre wall.

South Wall (Figs. 10 and 22).

This was traced with difficulty along most of the excavation, for it lay beneath the wall of the North Passage of the Painted House which had used it as a foundation. It butted to the south-east corner of the Tufa Block Building and ran down the site for at least 21.10 m. before disappearing under the eastern (low-level) limit of the excavation.

Again a section about 3.20 m. in length had been cut away by the construction of the west wall of the shore-fort and it seems likely that its superstructure was removed for the construction of the Roman Painted House. Its foundations, where examined, were about 40–50 cm. deeper than the foundations of the two adjacent buttressed walls and this suggests that it was intended to carry more weight. In detail the foundations had been laid in a vertical-sided trench some 65 cm. wide and 1.15 m. deep. It was mostly built of flint, with occasional lumps of tufa and chalk, all set in a creamy-yellow mortar.

DISCUSSION.

The construction of this long building (over 23.00 m. in length) and its peculiar arrangements, strongly suggests yet another major phase of building that required the removal of the south wall of the Flint Walled Enclosure. Its effect was to create a long south-range, that extended from the Tufa Block Building, which itself may have constituted a west-range of a larger complex. Exactly what function the Buttressed Building served is not yet clear for the pairs of opposing buttresses are highly unusual, yet clearly constructed for some specific functional purpose. If each buttress supported a vertical pier, or column, as seems likely then a narrow, double-colonnaded passageway is suggested. If so, it could have provided access from the Tufa Block Building, eastwards to another important structure beyond the limit of the excavation. It had no heated rooms, no drains, no plastered walls and its general massiveness suggests a simple functional use. In addition there was no trace of floor material, nor of fragments of decorated stone or fine finishes.

If the building had been a double-colonnaded structure, then a balancing fourth wall would be required to the north just beyond the limit of the excavation. This would then create a structure with side aisles and a narrow central 'nave' and increase the internal width to about 8.40 m. and the overall width to about 9.70 m.

The north-south (width) measurements of the structure would then be as follows:-

south wall	=	65 cm. wide
south aisle	=	155 cm. wide
centre wall	=	62 cm. wide
centre nave	=	400 cm. wide
north wall (estimated)	=	64 cm. wide
Conjectured north aisle	=	155 cm. wide
Conjectured north wall	=	65 cm. wide
Total		9.66 m.

The level of the floor must have been related carefully to that of the Tufa Block Building, as it seems very likely that one gave access to the other. The raised floor of the Tufa Block Building above its hypocaust suggests the controlling level, which would either have required a level in the Buttressed Building some 50–80 cm. higher than the surviving masonry, or else several steps down. Any door-treader here, whether original or added, would have been set some 20–30 cm. higher than the surviving masonry. Presumably, if such existed, it was removed during the demolition of the building during the fort-construction period. Sometime after the construction of the Buttressed Building, yet earlier than the construction of the Painted House (Period VI), a water-pipe was carefully laid in the narrow space between the Buttressed Building and Building C7. This was traced for a distance of only about 1.5 m. and was evidenced by a single iron water-pipe collar, about 10 cm. in diameter, set in a small trench running roughly east-west (Fig. 20, S.D., L. 8). It was not possible to locate this elsewhere on the site, mainly due to the presence of extensive Roman masonry, but it seems probable that it carried water from the aqueduct some 90 m. west of the site, to a building east of the excavation. This could have been by one of several possible routes, either straight, diagonal or branched.

The Dating Evidence for Period V.
The dating evidence for Period V, is much more abundant than for any earlier period. It includes a large group of pottery from the extensive dumped layers across the site sealed by the floor levels of the Buttressed Building; it includes another large group of material from the fill of the robber-trench of the Flint Walled Enclosure which preceded it; it contains a small amount of pottery from the actual foundation-trenches of the Buttressed Building (S.C, L. 37) and even two sherds from a localised occupation layer buried by the demolition debris of the building.

In total this material includes two coins (Coin Nos. 1 and 2), 76 sherds of samian (Nos. 57 to

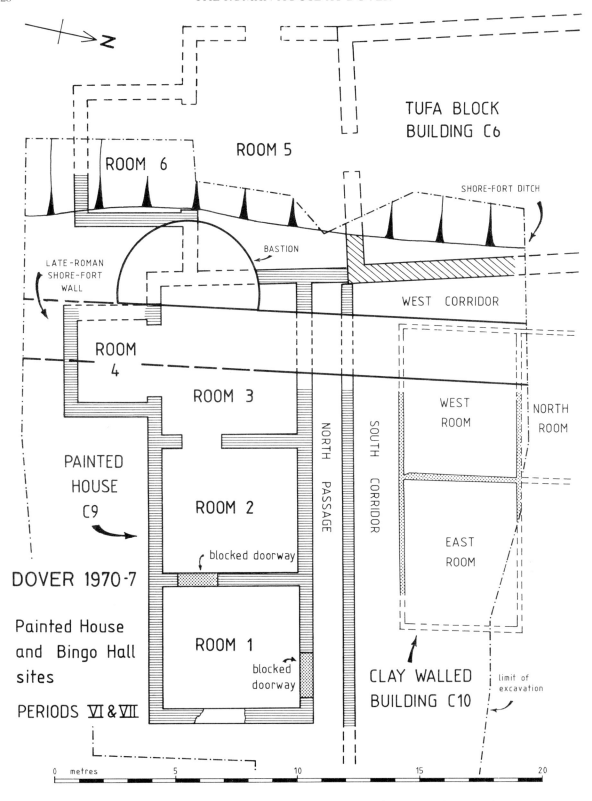

N

TUFA BLOCK
BUILDING C6

ROOM 5

ROOM 6

SHORE-FORT DITCH

BASTION

LATE-ROMAN
SHORE-FORT
WALL

WEST CORRIDOR

ROOM
4

ROOM 3

WEST
ROOM

NORTH
ROOM

PAINTED
HOUSE
C9

NORTH PASSAGE

SOUTH CORRIDOR

ROOM 2

DOVER 1970-7

blocked doorway

EAST
ROOM

Painted House
and Bingo Hall
sites

ROOM 1

blocked
doorway

CLAY WALLED

BUILDING C10

limit of
excavation

PERIODS VI & VII

0   metres   5   10   15   20

Fig. 11. *Outline plan showing Roman structures C6, C9 and C10 (Periods VI–VII).*

66), one mortarium (No. 74), 1373 sherds of coarse pottery (Nos. 101–161) and seven small-finds (Nos. 34–37, 45–46 and 55). The coins are both of Hadrian (A.D. 117–138). The samian includes 33 vessels that date from the second half of the first century, eleven vessels that date from the early to mid-second century and 25 vessels that are mid to late-second century. Similarly, about five of the coarse pottery vessels are of first century date, at least twenty are of early to mid-second century date and at least twenty more are of mid to late-second century date, mostly Antonine. The earlier pottery must represent material thrown up when the foundations of the Buttressed Building cut through earlier deposits, but clearly the latest vessels are most significant. The Antonine period is strongly represented by both samian and coarse wares. Although several vessels are dated mid to late-Antonine there is nothing here that need be later than A.D. 180. Exclusively late-second century types are missing, although these occur commonly on Dover sites. Allowing for a large amount of residual material this evidence suggests that the Period V Buttressed Building was constructed about A.D. 180 and this neatly fits the evidence for both Periods IV and VI.

PERIOD VI – THE 'PAINTED HOUSE' (C9), (Figs. 11 and 21).

This major building was discovered in 1970, partially excavated in 1971 and 1973 and completed in 1975. It lay on an east-west axis right across the site and forms the principal building in this report. Part of it clearly over-rode Ditches 1, 2 and 3 (Period I), the Rammed Chalk Enclosure (Period II), Building C7 (Period IV) and the south wall of the Buttressed Building (Period V). It missed the Flint Walled Enclosure (Period III) and very clearly butted up to the Tufa Block Building (Period IV). From this it is clear that only the Tufa Block Building survived this major building programme, but that its contemporary Building C7 was totally demolished for the construction of the Painted House.

It is now clear, thanks in part to a much later excavation on a large site to the east, that the Painted House formed part of a very large range with an east-west axis. This probably formed the south range of a large building complex to the north, beyond the limits of all excavations. The fact that this new large building was butted to the pre-existing Tufa Block Building (C6), strongly suggests that the Tufa Block Building was itself part of a major range, perhaps the original west range of the suggested complex to the north.

The Painted House was clearly a good quality building (Plates VIII and IX) and was laid out with some precision. It effectively joined the earlier Tufa Block Building at an angle of 93° and in turn lay only some 3° off the axis of the underlying Building C7. These differences are clear on most plans. The new range also sat fairly well over the earlier foundations, for Rooms 1 and 2 together almost exactly fitted the east-west length of the earlier building (C7). In addition the north walls of Rooms 1 and 2, largely followed the lines of the north wall of the demolished building, whilst the new south wall largely followed the internal wall of the earlier building.

The new building seems to have consisted of six rooms, all constructed in a uniform manner and of integral build, with a narrow passage on the north side (Fig. 11). Although the west end of the building had been destroyed by the ditch of the late-third century shore-fort, no trace of it existed beyond the ditch and this proves that the building could not have extended as far as that. In plan Rooms 1, 2 and 3 were clearly intended to be about the same size, but it is likely that Room 5 was much larger. Rooms 4 and 6, however, were extensions of Rooms 3 and 5, respectively, with which they were connected by full-width openings and in effect created double-rooms.

From what survived of Room 6 it is clear that it was about 1.4 times larger than the corresponding Room 4. Accordingly, the former has been shown larger on the plan and if it had been placed symmetrically along the south wall of Room 5, as seems likely, then Room 5 would have been the largest in the new building. The overall length of the building, as found, was about 21.80 m., but allowing for the missing west end the original length was probably about 27.70 m.

The width of the building was mostly 8.50 m., but with the south extensions this increased to a maximum of 12 m. The following table gives the dimensions of each room:-

Room	east-west length (metres)	north-south width (metres)	openings
1	4.80	5.63 (no plaster)	north and west
2	4.85	5.57 (plaster)	west and east
3	5.95	5.57 (plaster)	east and south
4	3.20	3.45	north
5	9.20 estimated	6.12	south and west (?) and north (?)
6	4.50 estimated	3.86 (plaster)	north

Table of the internal dimensions of each room.

As regards access it seems that only Room 1 was entered from the north passage, but it was linked to Room 2 by a doorway (later blocked) near its south-west corner. Room 2 was linked by opposing doorways with both Rooms 1 and 3. Room 3 was thus linked with Room 2 and it also shared a wide opening with Room 4. However, the presence of vertical wall flues in both Rooms 3 and 5 preclude an opening in their only common wall and it must be that these rooms were not connected. This suggests that the double Rooms 5 and 6, clearly integral, may have joined with the hypocausted room at the south end of the Tufa Block Building by means of an opening subsequently destroyed. An external door may also have existed in the west wall of Room 5. Room 3 could also have been linked with the north passage, but, if so, any opening was entirely removed when the fort wall was built. Notional doorways for Room 5 are shown on the plan.

1. THE STRUCTURE (Figs. 12 and 16).

The almost total uniformity of walls, floors and heating systems clearly demonstrate that all the rooms of the Painted House were constructed as part of a single comprehensive scheme. This is supported by the absence of any evidence of additions or alterations to the main structure, other than very minor repairs to the wall-plaster or changes during the final demolition.

(a) The Foundations.

The foundations generally consisted of flint rubble, with a few fragments of tufa and chalk, packed into a foundation-trench about 30 cm. deep and 70–80 cm. wide. The trench for these generally cut through all the underlying deposits either to the natural brickearth or the natural chalk wash. The south wall of Room 2, however, was built largely along the top of what remained of one of the internal walls (Fig. 16, No. 6) of the earlier building.

(b) The Walls.

The wall proper (Fig. 16, No. 1) sat on a broader wall-footing (Fig. 16, Nos. 2 and 3), which in turn sat neatly on the rubble foundations (Fig. 12 and Fig. 16, No. 4). The wall-footing consisted of two or three courses of flint set in a creamy-white mortar. These were generally 60–70 cm. wide and about 30–60 cm. high. The wall itself had a reduced width, of only 60 cm., thus creating small internal and external offsets (Fig. 16, No. 2). The wall was built largely of selected flints set in even courses in a white mortar. At a point some four or five flint courses (50 cm.) above the footing were two courses (12 cm.) of red bricks laid horizontally. Above this were at least another seven courses (86 cm.) of coursed flints though, as on many other Romano-British sites, it is highly likely that double courses of bonding bricks occurred at regular intervals to the top of the structure. The bricks were all the standard building brick mostly 45 by 30 by 4 cm., no roofing tile being included.

The highest point of surviving masonry was 1.75 m. above internal floor-level and about 2.40 m. above external ground-level. With an average height of the surviving walls of Rooms 1, 2, 3 and 4 about 1.30 m. internally and 1.70 m. externally the Painted House represents one of the most complete examples of a Roman town-house anywhere in Britain. The height of the rooms to ceiling-level would probably have been about 3 m. and this agrees with the suggested reconstruction of the painted plaster (page 114). It seems probable that the building had a second storey and this is generally supported by the thickness of the walls, which seem excessive for a single-storey structure. Just possibly some of the fallen wall-plaster could have come from such a second storey.

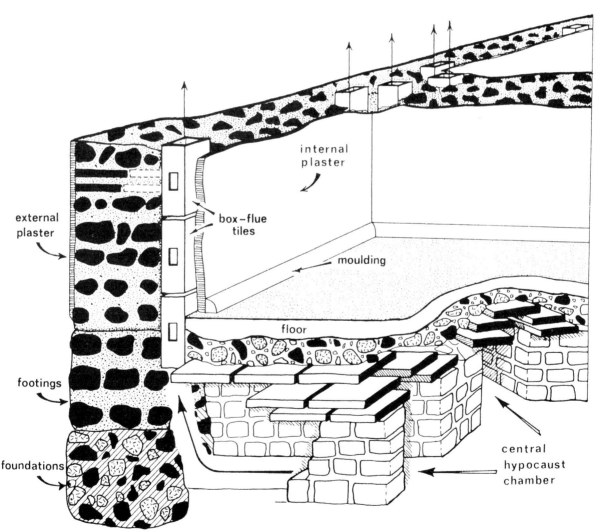

Fig 12. *Diagrammatic drawing showing the underfloor channels and vertical wall-flues of the hypocaust system of the Painted House, C9.*

(c) The Roof.

As regards the roof the only materials surviving were small fragments of the typical tegulae and imbreces found in the demolition rubble inside the building. It must be that the building was totally roofed and that almost certainly this consisted of tiles laid on a substantial wooden frame. It is possible that it had a low, single pitched roof following the east-west axis of the range and giving a fall to the south or north. More likely, however, the roof consisted of a two-sided pitch with a central ridge running the length of the building and ending in plain gables. What complicates this elemental arrangement are Rooms 4, 5 and 6. The two smaller rooms (4 and 6) project well beyond the main south wall of the range and clearly some alteration of the roof-line is implied. If these two rooms were each only a single storey in height then a low-level roof butting straight to the external walls could have been constructed. It seems that Room 5 could not be covered under this arrangement for it was offset about 2.00 m. to the north. It is much more likely that the axis of the roofs of Rooms 5 and 6 was north-south and that it joined a pre-existing north-south roof over the Tufa Block Building to which Room 5 was clearly added. In this case it would have been joined at right-angles by the east-west roof covering Rooms 1–3. In the absence of further evidence there is little that can usefully be added. The absence of large quantities of roof tile in the Painted House, either broken or complete, demonstrates that these were mostly systematically removed during the demolition work.

(d) The Windows.

As regards window openings, there is also very little evidence. Nothing survived *in situ* and only very small fragments of angled plaster, painted dark red, could suggest the jambs of window openings (Figs. 87– 89).

It is clear that the great majority of Roman houses had window openings and that these were normally small and placed at a high level in the rooms. Many had small glass panes inserted in them, but no glass was found at Dover though it seems likely that any openings would have been glazed. Presumably the glass was carefully removed ahead of the demolition.

(e) The Floors.

Of floors in the Painted House there is ample evidence surviving in some detail. All six rooms, but not the north passage, were provided with solid floors of pink-red concrete (*opus signinum*). The overall uniformity and quality of these implies that they too formed part of a single scheme and indeed were very probably the work of a single group of craftsmen. In all cases the floors were laid on a foundation bed of flints and chalk rubble about 8–12 cm. deep, compacted down over both the levelled demolition of the earlier building and the hypocaust channels. The floors were made of an admix of crushed tile fragments and tile dust, thoroughly mixed with a white mortar, to a thickness of about 10 cm. The finished surfaces were hard, smooth and mostly perfectly flat over the full lengths exposed. Taking the sizes of all six rooms, as given in the table (above), a total of about 170 sq. mts. of floor were laid. With an average thickness of 10 cm. this would have required some 17 cu. mts. of *opus signinum* which could probably have weighed some 20 tonnes. No trace of any flooring was found in the passage and it must be that this simply had a trodden earth floor. The floors of any second storey would, for reasons of weight, have been wooden boards laid on joists.

The floors in the rooms were good quality and quite in accord with the importance of the building. That mosaic panels were not incorporated is readily explained, for in Roman Britain the great majority of floor mosaics were laid in the late-third or fourth centuries (Ref. 6), by which time the Painted House had been largely demolished and buried.

It is clear that the walls were built before the floors were laid, for in each room the floor and its sub-base can be seen to butt to the already existing masonry. With the floors laid and the wall-renderings applied the final finish was the insertion of a fine quarter-round moulding, or fillet, over the joint formed by the horizontal floor and vertical wall. Made of *opus signinum* the mouldings were mostly 6 cm. high and 8 cm. wide and these had been painted red to match the floors.

(f) Wall and Ceiling Renderings.

The main walls of the Painted House structure were mostly 0.60 m. thick as built, but with internal and external renderings this was increased to about 0.64 m. The thick internal renderings in each room consisted of a 3 cm. layer of good lime mortar very similar in composition to the mortar used in the actual walls. This masked the flints and brickwork in the wall and provided a solid backing and a good flat surface for the plaster and the paint layers. Detailed descriptions of this final plaster layer (Fabric Type A) and of the grand painted scheme employed throughout the Roman House are given below (pages 143 and 114, respectively). In all some 61 sq. mts. of painted plaster remained *in situ* on the walls and over 20,000 fragments were found in the rubble layers over the floors.

Although no large articulated masses of fallen ceiling-plaster were found in the Painted House, smaller groups and fragments were located in the primary soil layer directly on the floors. This plaster anyway contrasts sharply with that on the extant walls, being much thinner and finer (Fabric B, p. 144) and there can be little doubt that this came from the ceilings. The painted designs were also distinctive and these are discussed below (p. 220).

The external surfaces of the walls were mostly found unpointed, though clear evidence of trowelling survives on parts of the south wall. Although only small areas of external rendering were found it is highly likely that all the outer walls were originally plastered over. This either happened at the time of the original construction, or some years later. Nor was much of this external plaster found on the site and it must be that it had weathered off over several years and been taken away before the major demolition took place.

In detail this rendering consisted of a 2 cm. layer of poor quality clay-chalk mortar (Fabric Type C – see page 144) which had originally been painted plain red. Only two areas of this had survived totalling, in all, just over 2 sq. m. One patch survived on the external face of the south wall of Room 2 and the other on the external face of the east wall of Room 4.

(g) The Door-openings and Finishes (Figs. 13–14).

Of the five presumed door-openings in the section of the Painted House so far excavated, three survive in part, a fourth is implied and the fifth is conjectured. Each of the three surviving openings had originally been provided with massive sills, but all three had been removed at the time of the demolition. Later blocking masked the two associated with Room 1, but that on the west side of Room 2 remained open and has provided important information. Here, a deep lateral socket beneath each adjacent wall, showed that the sill had been rectangular in section, some 2.47 m. in length, about 44 cm. in width and 13 cm. in depth. It had certainly been built into the structure as an integral part of it and its subsequent removal could only have been achieved by smashing its centre. It is just possible that this sill consisted of a large wooden beam, but the greater probability is that it was a shaped stone sill, in one or two parts. The doorway here had a maximum width of 1.60 m.

Of the doorway linings some interesting detail had survived in the opening between Rooms 2 and 3 (Fig. 14). Here it is clear that the sillstone had been laid along the top of the underlying wall of Building C7, thus causing it to lie on the west side of the opening and not at its centre. It is also clear that a vertical door-frame (now gone), of wood or stone, had been erected on top of the sillstone and this built-in as the flanking walls were laid against it (Plate X). The masonry forming the south jamb had a fine vertical line of mortar projecting marginally, some 7 cm. from the south-west corner. This suggests the lining here had consisted of two parts, a main central section and a narrow side section perhaps 7 cm. wide. A pair of corresponding vertical lines of mortar was found on the wall faces inside Room 3, each some 10–12 cm. from the corner of the door-opening. These suggest that at least part of the door-lining was returned around the corners a small way into the room. The most probable arrangement is that some sort of wood or stone, architrave or corner pilaster was built on to each of the four corners of the door-opening. If such corner pieces were each of a similar size, then the central upright lining of the doorway would have been about 44 cm. wide in a wall just 58 cm. in width.

The same door-opening also exhibited some more detail of equal interest. At all four corners of the doorway the original floor and part of the original quarter-round moulding had been badly repaired with a poor quality *opus signinum*. Close examination showed that the four holes, of varying sizes, had been made in the floor at the corners of the doorway and had thus also removed some of the mouldings. It seems likely that this was done to remove the conjectured corner architraves, or pilasters, for the underlying masonry, which had not initially been plastered or painted, was made good, after the alterations took place. This was done with an

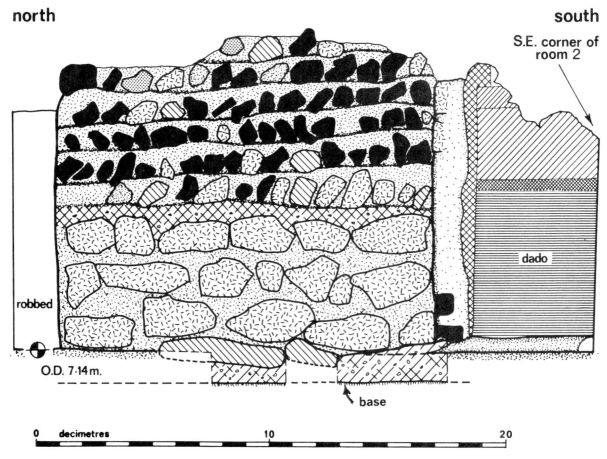

Fig 13. *Detail of blocked doorway between Rooms 1 and 2 of the Painted House, C9.*

uneven and poor quality chalk-wash mortar, to which was applied an off-red paint that in places overlapped the original red paint and provided a rough frame for the altered door-opening. The need to damage the floor in such a way suggests that these corner linings had also been built-in below floor-level and required considerable work to free them! This then required the floors and parts of the mouldings to be repaired! One other suggestion needs to be considered and that is that the damage to the floors and mouldings was caused by the removal of the sillstone, perhaps after it had become very worn. However, the cuts through the floor on the east side of the door-opening did not penetrate through the wall to the face of the sillstone and could thus not have served such a purpose.

Of special interest is the way in which the two door-openings in Room 1 had been blocked. This must have been done at the time of the demolition of the Painted House when the shore-fort was constructed. The sillstones were removed from each and mixed soil and rubble was allowed to collect in the cavities. That on the north side was then blocked with at least three courses of chalk blocks with some tile and greensand stone set in white mortar, still some 48 cm. high. That between Rooms 1 and 2 (Fig. 13) still survives to the remarkable height of 1.30 m., some nine courses in all and 50 cm. wide. It was clearly built in two stages, with a layer of brown clay separating the upper and lower sections. The bottom three courses contain large, irregular chalk blocks set in a hard, white mortar that had been pointed from inside Room 2. Clearly, this low section was built free-standing, probably as a kerb to retain the tail of the rampart. Indeed, the capping layer of brown clay could have been rampart material. Either way, the clay band was eventually capped by the upper section of wall, consisting of six courses of angular flints that include occasional chalk blocks and tile fragments. This material is bonded with a distinctive white mortar containing numerous small pebbles. This had been pointed from inside Room 1, but the face inside Room 2 is very irregular and was presumably built overhand. It seems likely that the rampart needed retaining to at least this height.

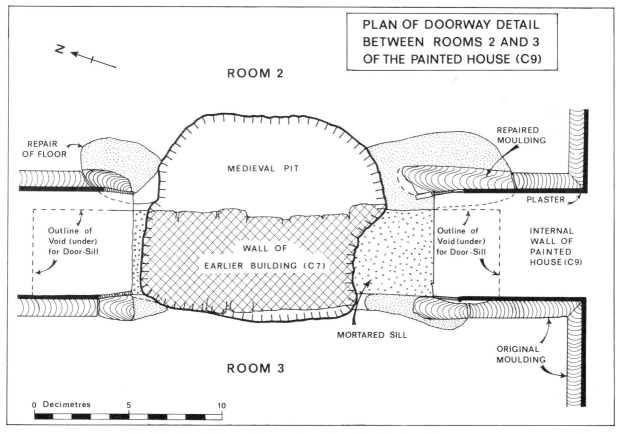

Fig 14. *Plan of doorway between Rooms 2 and 3 of the Painted House, C9.*

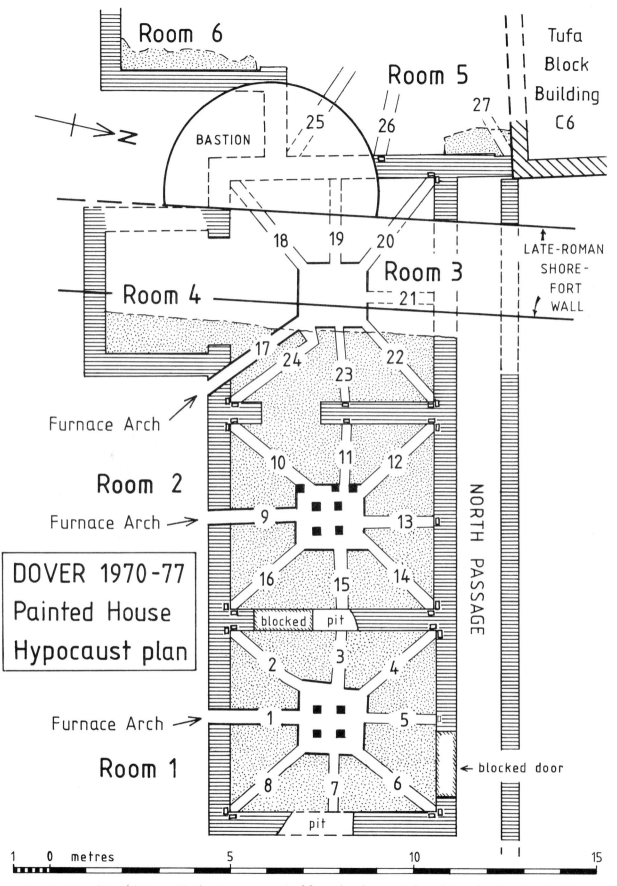

Room 6

Tufa
Block
Building
C6

Room 5

N

25

26

27

BASTION

18 19 20

LATE-ROMAN
SHORE-
FORT
WALL

Room 4

Room 3

21

17

24

22

23

Furnace Arch

10 11 12

Room 2

9

13

Furnace Arch

DOVER 1970-77
Painted House
Hypocaust plan

16 15 14

blocked pit

2 3 4

Furnace Arch

1 5

Room 1

blocked door

8 7 6

pit

NORTH PASSAGE

1 0 metres   5   10   15

Fig. 15. *Plan of Painted House C9, showing arrangement of flue-arches, hypocaust channels (numbered) and vertical flues.*

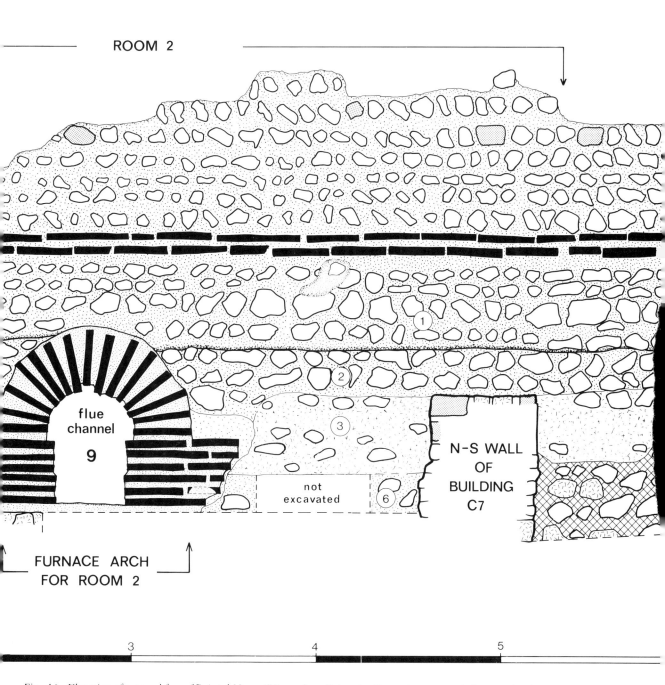

ROOM 2

flue
channel
9

FURNACE ARCH
FOR ROOM 2

not
excavated

N-S WALL
OF
BUILDING
C7

3   4   5

Fig. 16. *Elevation of external face of Painted House C9, south wall showing flue-arches, external plaster and earlier Building C7.*

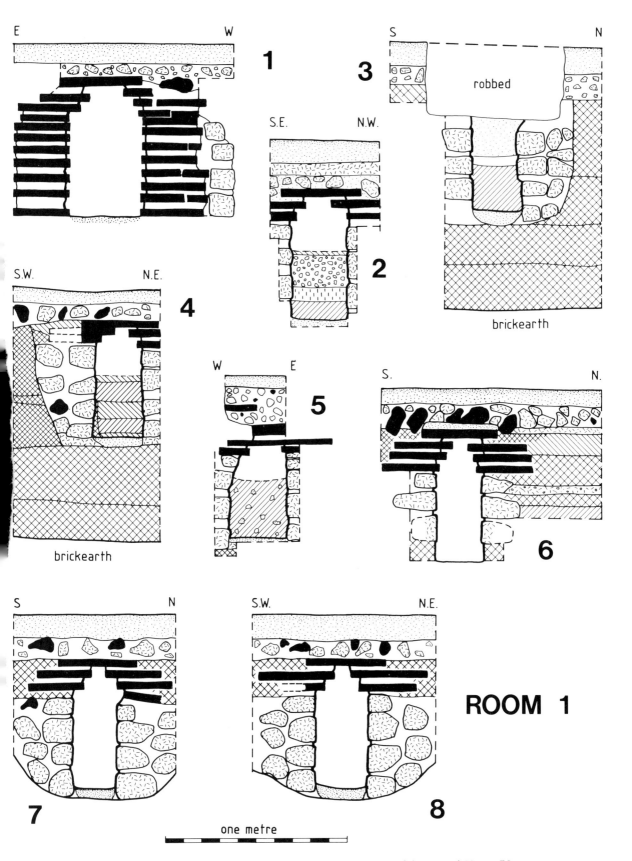

E W

1

S.E. N.W.

2

S N

3

robbed

brickearth

S.W. N.E.

4

brickearth

W E

5

S. N.

6

S N

7

S.W. N.E.

8

ROOM 1

one metre

Fig. 17. *Sections through hypocaust channels in Room 1 of the Painted House C9.*

ROOM 1 →

east

O.D. 7·88m.

③

④

flue
channel

1

FURNACE ARCH
FOR ROOM 1

6   7   8   9

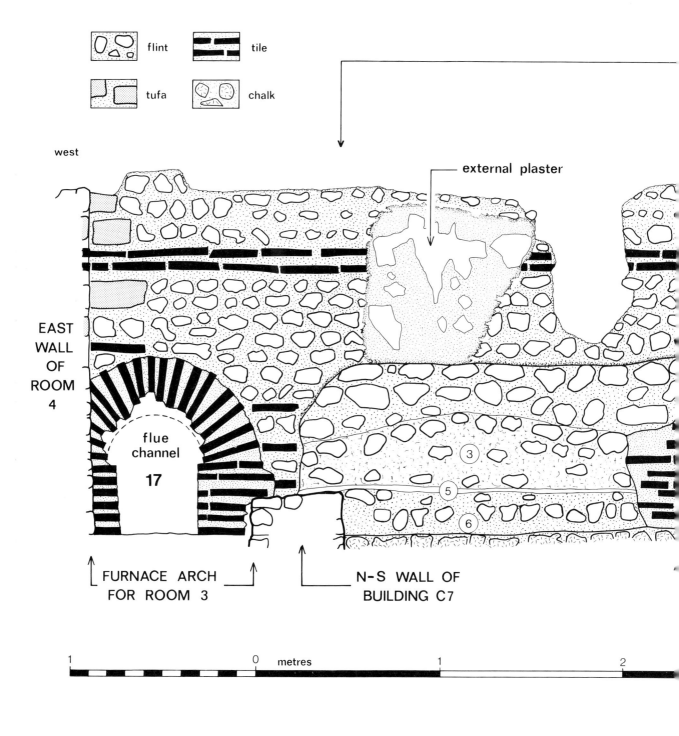

flint

tile

tufa

chalk

west

external plaster

EAST
WALL
OF
ROOM
4

flue
channel

17

③

⑤

⑥

↑ FURNACE ARCH ↑
FOR ROOM 3

↑ N–S WALL OF
BUILDING C7

1   0   metres   1   2

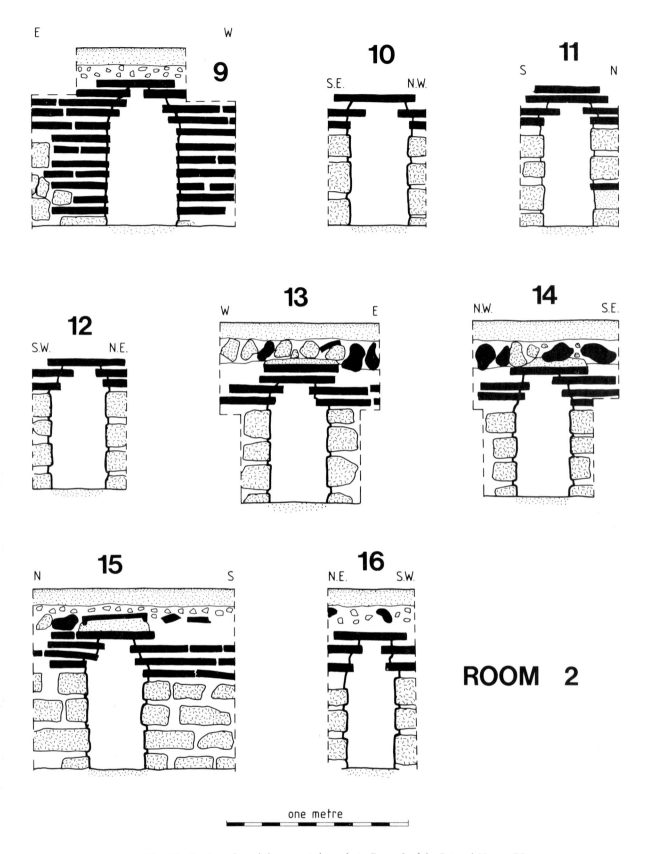

Fig. 18. *Sections through hypocaust channels in Room 2 of the Painted House C9.*

(h) The Heating System (Figs. 12 and 15–19).

The four main rooms (Nos. 1, 2, 3 and 5) of the Painted House were provided with underfloor and wall-heating of standard hypocaust type, as frequently employed in the finer buildings of the Roman World. Virtually identical and complete systems survived in Rooms 1 and 2 and what survived in Rooms 3 and 5 suggests the same basic arrangement. Rooms 4 and 6 do not appear to have been heated directly though they shared wide open bays with Rooms 3 and 5, respectively, and this must have provided indirect heat.

The basic arrangement in each case was for the heat to come from a separate source outside each room. The point of entry was a large arched flue (Fig. 16) in an external wall below floor-level, which provided an opening about 0.60 m. high and 0.40 m. wide (Plate XI). The arch was turned in large Roman tiles, generally 15 to 17 in number, set in a hard pink mortar. The side jambs, also of brick, set in *opus signinum*, consisted of six bricks laid flat on each side.

The three arched flues here were fed, probably with only small quantities of wood to supply a moderate heat, from the south side. Here there may have been light timber structures that provided cover for the fire and the fuel, but no trace survived. The floor of the south-west corner room of the underlying building was dug away to create a small oval stoke-hole for the flue-arch of Room 2 and a short length of north-south wall built to protect the east side of the flue-arch of Room 1. The flue-arch for Room 3 (Plate XII) fitted neatly between the wall of Room 4 and the surviving foundations of the west wall of the underlying building (C7).

The heat passed through the arched flues into wide channels (Figs. 17– 19, Nos. 1, 9 and 17) to the centre of the rooms. Here was a square chamber, generally 1.80 m. by 1.80 m. A series of seven more channels radiated outwards from the central chamber to the four corners of the room and to the centre of the three remaining sides (Plate XIII). These channels were smaller in section than the main entry-channel and each was deliberately tapered at its extreme end to help induce the hot air along to the vertical wall-ducts (Figs. 18 and 19). The wall-ducts consisted of a series of box-flue tiles (Nos. 279–283), mostly about 36 cm. high, placed one above the other to create a vertical duct from just beneath floor-level to the roof outlet. These averaged about 17 by 13 cm. in section and about 2 cm. thick. Each flue tile had two of its external surfaces combed during manufacture to provide a keying for the mortar. They also had a small rectangular vent in each of their two lateral sides, a device mainly intended for iron clamp-nails, or to facilitate air circulation in a multi-flue system, such as employed in the hot-room of a bath-house. Apart from serving to help to key the mortar these side vents were largely superfluous in the Painted House. The ducts had been built into the walls of the room, a pair at each corner and one in the centre of each of three sides, giving a total of eleven ducts per room. The wall plaster covered the box-flue tiles so that they were completely concealed within the walls, though clearly the surface over them would be considerably hotter than the remaining parts of the wall. Indeed this has caused long cracks in the surface plaster in front of several of the ducts.

In detail the underfloor channels were generally 0.65 m. high and 0.24–0.30 m. wide. They had been constructed in deep cuts made into the underlying deposits and lined with mortared chalk blocks, mostly 18–26 cm. in length, 14 cm. in width and 11 cm. deep and three or four courses high (Figs. 17– 19). The channels were capped by corbelled arches consisting of bricks, or brick fragments, laid in three of four courses. The topmost course served to cap the channels and also to form a strong, firm bed for the sub-base and floor above. The floors were carried across the central chambers on a special bed of large bridging tiles, laid as blocks of nine tiles. These tiles were mostly 59 cm. square, of which parts of six survive in Room 1 and parts of seven in Room 2. These were in turn supported on small, free-standing pillars (*pilae*), normally placed at the junction of the bridging tiles and mostly measuring 22 cm. by 22 cm. (Fig. 15). Here the treatment of Rooms 1 and 2 varied.

In Room 1 there had been four pillars, of which three survive complete, each consisting of twelve tiles set in brown clay. These are corbelled above with two larger tiles and closed over by the bridging tiles. In Room 2, however, there had been seven pillars (of which five survive) with the extra three on the west side being inserted very much as an afterthought. Clearly, the central

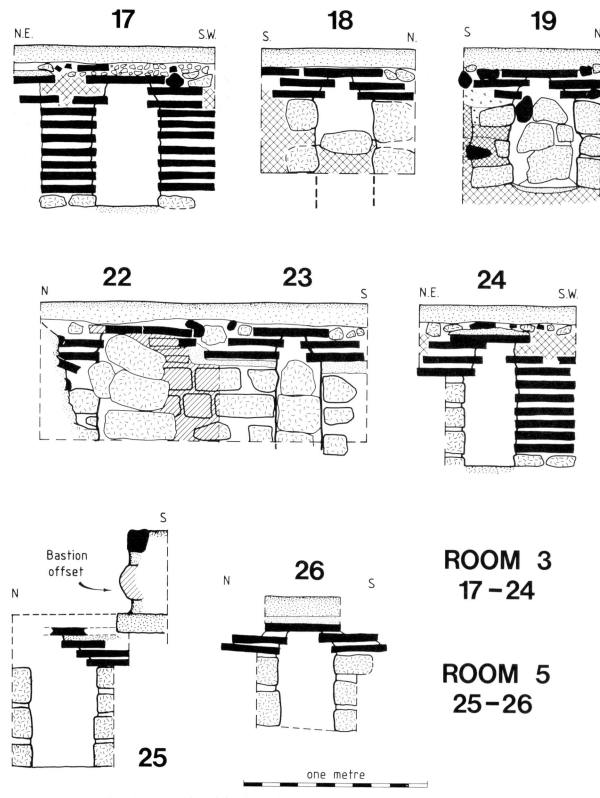

Fig. 19. *Sections through hypocaust channels in Rooms 3 and 5 of the Painted House C9.*

chamber here had been built rather too large and the bridging tiles on the west side could not reach the support provided by the flanking channels. In addition, the pillars here each consisted of 13 tiles. All the pillars and bridging tiles are shown on the main site-plan (Fig. 21). The base of both the central chambers and all the channels had been surfaced with a thin spread of mortar. The central chamber in Room 3 had been substantially destroyed when the foundations for the later fort wall had been dug. Its faint imprint could still be seen, however, with five of its radiating flue channels surviving in part. All of these had been plugged with large chalk blocks to seal the voids (Plate XIV).

The maximum height of surviving wall-flues is 1.45 m. above the floor in Room 2 and this consists of a vertical column of four and a half box-flue tiles springing from a point about 20 cm. below the floor surface. It must be that these wall-flues ran to at least ceiling-level or, as is probable, out to roof-level though the precise outlet arrangements seem to be largely unknown. As the box-flue tiles were mostly cased in mortar it was impossible to see if all had been stamped. Three flue-tiles removed from Room 1, however, were stamped CLBR the insignia of the fleet (Fig. 24, Nos. 26, 27 and 33) and it seems likely that all or most of the others would have been stamped too. In addition, at least five of the bridging tiles from the hypocausts in Rooms 1 and 2 revealed stamps (Fig. 24, Nos. 28– 32), but the others could not be examined owing to their inaccessibility.

2) THE DESCRIPTION OF THE ROOMS

Room 1.

This room survived in a rather damaged state and its painted designs are now almost totally missing. Parts of its north, west and south walls survive to a height of about 1.40 m. but barely two courses of its east wall survived. The east wall was also cut by two large medieval pits, the north wall by the cut-out for an Anglo-Saxon hut and the west wall by another pit. The centre of the room was also cut by two medieval pits which removed large areas of the floor and also parts of the hypocaust system. The bad state of this room, with its lack of painted plaster and badly pitted floor, mainly reflects its use long after the other rooms had been buried (see page 49). The continued wear and tear and no doubt some weathering caused the plaster to fall off the walls, all save very small patches of the red dado on the north and west walls. The large quantity of missing plaster was not found on the floor and it must have been removed in Roman times, showing that the room continued to be used. The same factors probably caused the damage to the surface of the floor. It is estimated that originally this room probably had 18 painted panels (see below).

At the time of the demolition of the Painted House, in about A.D. 270, the west and north door openings were both blocked. So, too, were several of the hypocaust wall-flues blocked, either at floor-level or a little higher, some of the box-flue tiles having been first removed. It seems clear from this that the hypocaust system was not then required and that the openings were deliberately blocked, perhaps to discourage vermin, or to avoid draughts, or both. This also suggests that Room 1 continued in use after A.D. 270, though access must have been from another opening, perhaps in the damaged south wall. About one third of what survived of the eastern half of this room had to be removed by excavation ahead of the construction of the cover-building.

The stratification within Room 1 had been largely removed by a series of medieval pits, some of which cut through parts of the west wall, the east wall and the floor and also removed sections of the underlying hypocausts. What little stratification survived clearly post-dated the construction of the shore-fort wall and is thus beyond the scope of the present report.

Room 2.

This is the best preserved room in the Painted House. All the walls stand to a height of at least 1.50 m. whilst the south wall attains a maximum height of 1.70 m. and the north-east corner 1.75 m. Only three cuts appear in the line of the walls, two being the medieval pits on the east side and the other being a deep slot through the south wall, perhaps cut in late-Roman times. The floor is in very good condition except near its centre where another medieval pit has cut it away and exposed part of the central hypocaust chamber beneath. Several small black patches on the floor, mainly on the north and west sides, may mark where braziers or small fires were placed either during the use of the building, or subsequently.

The heating system beneath Room 2 survived substantially intact. Most of the wall-flues remain in place, though the pair in the north-east corner were destroyed by a medieval pit. Several remain largely choked by rubble from the demolition. The east doorway contains the late-Roman blocking and the west doorway was slightly damaged by another medieval pit which descended to just below the doorsill.

Two minor repairs were detected on the west side of this room. A small piece of floor was replaced close to the south jamb of the doorway and a small area of plaster, close to the floor and covering the central wall-flue, was replaced and repainted dark green to match the dado. It seems likely that the heat from the flue had caused the plaster to crack and fall away.

The floor moulding in Room 2 had been painted red. Above this the walls had been painted to ceiling-level with a bold three-dimensional design (see page 108), including a dark green dado.

The stratification within this room was largely intact being cut by only four medieval pits (S. E Fig. 22, L. 34–46 and S. F, L. 2–14 and 46–56). As stated a small pit had cut away some of the masonry at the north-east corner and another cut down into the west doorway. The other two medieval pits cut through the centre fill of the room with one cutting through the actual floor and into the central chamber of the underlying hypocaust.

The *opus signinum* floor of Room 2 was covered throughout by a layer of orange-brown loam, crumbled mortar and fragmentary painted plaster (S. E, L. 55 and 88 and S.F, L. 62) mostly to a depth of 2 to 5 cm. This must represent the primary decay of the building after its abandonment. Most of the plaster from this layer was thin and finely made (Fabric Type B) and contrasted sharply with the thick, coarser wall-plaster (Fabric Type A) still *in situ*. It seems very likely that this finer plaster had lined the ceiling and that it had fallen before the main demolition began and an elaborate design has been identified (see page 220).

Across the western half of Room 2, the primary layer was sealed by a great wedge-shaped mass of clean rubble, mortar fragments and painted plaster, the latter (S.E, L. 54 and S.F, L. 61), all similar to that remaining *in situ* on all four walls. This contained no soil and it seems clear that it represents clean demolition rubble derived mostly from the west, south and north walls of the room and probably totalling some 7 tonnes in all (Plate XV). Significantly, there was little rubble on the eastern side of the room. The main rubble layer contained several thousand fragments of fallen wall-plaster. The rubble was itself sealed by dipping layers (S. E, L. 49–53 and S. F, Fig. 22, L. 17, 39–45 and 57–60) of loam and clay that were clearly tipped in from a high point on the west side. Some of the layers extended across the east wall of the room. Collectively, these layers formed part of the rampart-bank placed behind the fort wall (Period VIII) and as such are not considered here.

A coin of Julia Paula (Coin No. 10) of A.D. 218–222, was found in the primary layer in Room 2 and four more 3rd century coins (Coin Nos. 15–18) were found at the junction of the dumped soil and the rubble in Room 3 (see below).

Room 3.

A large part of this room had been removed during the construction of the west wall of the late-Roman shore-fort. This left a width of about 1.75 m. on the east side and a width of about 0.70 m. on the west side. Again where the walls survive they still stand about 1.40 m. above the floor on the east side, but much less on the west side where they were cut down by the builders of the later Roman bastion. The north-west corner had been largely destroyed, but has since been partially rebuilt for the preservation scheme. The floors and mouldings, where these survive, are generally in excellent condition. Two small holes cut in the floor near the north-east and south-east corners are deliberate cuts, probably made at the time of the fort building programme.

The heating system only partially survives. Almost all the central chamber was removed by the fort wall builders, but substantial parts of five under-floor flue channels survive. The pattern of these differs slightly from that of Rooms 1 and 2. The main flue ran from the large arch near the south-east corner into the central chamber and then radiated outwards in the normal way. There was not, however, a channel for the centre of the south side owing to the presence of the wide bay joining Rooms 3 and 4. The channel to the centre of the north wall had been removed by the fort wall, but elsewhere three of the vertical wall-flues survive.

The floor moulding had also been painted red and again the internal wall surfaces had been painted with a three-dimensional design to ceiling level (see page 114), almost identical to that in Room 2, but including a dado.

The stratification in this room had been substantially removed by a very large medieval pit (S.E., L. 31–32) and a major robber-trench that had been dug to remove much of the adjacent fort wall (S. E., L. 27–30). Otherwise the sequence was similar to that as in Room 2. The floor was again totally sealed by a thin layer of loam and crumbled mortar. This was in turn sealed by a deep layer of rubble and painted plaster, mostly 60 cm. deep, but again devoid of soil. This was found across most of Rooms 3 and 4 and indeed still remains intact, in part, beneath the later Roman bastion on the west side. This rubble also matched the *in situ* masonry and plaster and it must represent the demolition of part of the superstructure of the Roman House. These two rooms probably contained another eleven tonnes of building debris.

The rubble here was similarly sealed by layers of loam and clay which again must represent dump for the rampart-bank. These mostly joined with the corresponding layers in Room 2.

Of special interest here is the fact that the demolition rubble in the north-east corner of Room 3 actually lay against the inside face of the fort wall! Although it is certain that the fort wall had been built in a large trench cut through the centre of Rooms 3 and 4, it seems clear that at least part of the Painted House structure was left intact until at least part of the fort wall was completed. Perhaps the section left standing provided the fort wall builders with protection against the elements for at least some, or all, of the work. Either way, the final demolition caused the rubble to pile against the wall's inner face, though the published section shows only the fill of a medieval robber-trench at the critical point (S. E, L. 27–30). Some 2–4 m. to the north the Clay Walled Building had clearly been demolished before the foundation-trench of the fort wall was dug (S. H, Fig. 22, L. 37–39).

Room 4.

This small room was largely removed by the builders of the fort wall. Only the east wall and a joining section of the south wall survive (Plate XVI). Its west wall was totally removed, but a small stub of the foundation of its north-west respond survived to show its original limits. In general where the wall survives it stands to a height of about 1.20 m. A thin strip of floor survives along the east side where, owing to the wide bay between Rooms 3 and 4, the floor forms a continuous strip through the two rooms for a distance of about 9.03 m. As in Room 3 a pair of small holes had been punched through the floor at the south-east corner. This room was not heated directly, but as it inter-connected with Room 3, no doubt warm air circulated freely between the two. The floor moulding had been painted red and this room had been decorated (see page 111) in the same style as Rooms 2 and 3, but with a green dado.

The absence of a north wall to this room required a variation in the structural arrangements. Instead, a short respond, about 0.68 m. wide and projecting some 0.22 m. into the room, was built on each side as an integral part of the structure. This created an opening about 2.76 m. wide, in effect leaving Room 4 as a vestibule to Room 3. Clearly, some form of strong lintel would be required across the bay, supported on each side by the responds, to hold the roof. Whether this took the form of a brick arch or a straight wooden lintel is not known.

Only a small area of stratified soil had survived in this room, due to the construction of the fort wall and later pits. The rubble layer extended from Room 3 and again it contained wall plaster matching that still *in situ*. The overlying layers had mostly been removed.

Room 5.

The greater part of this room was destroyed during the excavation of the great West Ditch of the shore-fort and only sections of the east, south and north walls survive. Short sections of the north-east and south-east corners still stood three or four courses high, the latter being largely concealed by the later Roman bastion. A short length of the south wall, 13 tile courses high, projects from beneath the bastion (Plate XVII) and also marks the junction with Room 6. A small section of its north wall, mainly of tufa blocks, originally formed part of the Tufa Block Building to which the whole range had been added.

Only small sections of the *opus signinum* floor had survived, one in the north-east corner and another larger area projecting from beneath the bastion. The heating system seems to have been identical to those in Rooms 1, 2 and 3 though only parts of three of the main underfloor channels survive. A single vertical wall-flue survives in the centre of the east wall and there is the prospect that another survives in the south-east corner right underneath the bastion. The moulding and the dado were painted red and it is likely that this room was also painted to its full height (see page 112).

Little of the original stratification had survived in Room 5, for it lay outside the fort wall where most of it had either been cut away to create a wide berm, or removed by the excavation of the great fort ditch. A primary loam on the floor contained small fragments of ceiling plaster (Subjects 29 and 32, see below, p. 193), and this was sealed, as in Rooms 2, 3 and 4, by clean rubble from the demolition of part of the superstructure.

Room 6.

By far the greater part of this room had been destroyed by the excavation of the shore-fort ditch. All of the east wall survived to a height of about 0.60 m., but otherwise only a short stub of the south wall remained to a similar height (Plate XVIII). A thin strip of the *opus signinum* floor survived in fair condition along the east side, but there was no trace of any heating ducts or channels and it seems probable that this room was not heated. What is significant is the position of this room in relation to Room 5. It seems likely that, as in the case of Room 4, it formed a vestibule and this tends to be partly confirmed by the absence of evidence of heating in Room 6. The floor moulding was painted red and the dado green and it seems probable that this room was also decorated to its full height (see page 112). Very few stratified deposits relating to this room had survived, the great majority having been removed by the excavation of the fort ditch.

North Passage

This ran along the north side of Rooms 1, 2 and 3 for a distance of about 17.40 m. to a point where it stopped against the east wall of Room 5. It was mostly 1.17 m. wide and must have had a trodden earth floor. The shared wall on the south side was solidly built and some 64 cm. (with plaster) wide, but its north wall was poorly built, generally only 48–52 cm. wide, it tapered upwards and was far from straight. It had anyway been built along the top of the partially demolished south wall of the Buttressed Building (C8). At its highest point, about 1.20 m. above the presumed floor-level, an imprint of a flat brick was found set at an angle of about 30°. This suggests a structural variation at this point, perhaps the sill of an external window opening.

The precise function of this passage is not entirely certain. It clearly provided access from Room 1 through its north doorway, but it did not connect with either Room 2, Room 3 or Room

5, unless Room 3 had been provided with a north doorway later removed by the fort wall. It is possible that it contained a wooden stairway at its western end, that could have given access to the projected upper storey. No evidence for this was found in the ground, but the critical area had been largely destroyed.

A small gully found, in four places, along the centre of the passage seems to have served as a simple drain flowing eastwards. It was unlined, U-shaped in profile, about 47–60 cm. wide and 15–25 cm. deep. It must have had a cover of some sort to prevent problems of access along the passage. What it served is not known, though with its origin at the west end of the passage it may have carried roof-water away from the internal corner of the south and west ranges. Its silt filling contained a few indeterminate sherds, probably of second century date.

At the extreme east end of the passage a large drain, lined with chalk blocks and flints, had been constructed close to the north doorway of Room 1, flowing eastwards (S. D, Fig. 20, L. 4). This respected both walls of the passage, but was stratigraphically later than the south wall of the Buttressed Building, the north wall of Building C7 and also the low-level waterpipe. It was rectangular in section, about 60 cm. wide internally and about 50 cm. deep. The recorded section suggests a recut, but this was not established. It was eventually partially robbed, filled with soil and small rubble and then sealed by a thick layer of *opus signinum* concrete (L. 3) where it passed

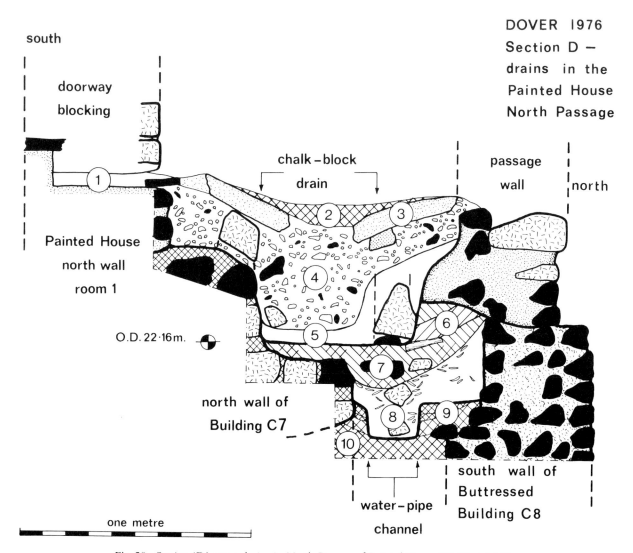

Fig 20. *Section 'D' across drains in North Passage of Painted House C9 (Period VI).*

in front of the north doorway of Room 1. This concrete had eventually split when the underlying fill of the drain had contracted and a plug of clay (L. 2) was then inserted to maintain a reasonable level. The drain contained a quantity of domestic rubbish, including two coins and pottery of second and third century date (see below p. 56). From this it is clear that the drain had not been filled before about the middle decades of the third century A.D.

The precise function of this large drain is not clear, but presumably it related in some way to the north doorway of Room 1 from where it started. This suggests it took waste water from the room itself, or perhaps even roof-water from the east end of the range. Exactly how the small gully running eastwards along the passage linked with this drain is not clear, as the critical point of intersection had been removed by a large pit and the base-levels do not conform.

The Dating Evidence for Period VI.

The dating evidence for the Painted House consists of pottery and coins from several deposits and also the construction and occupation dates of earlier and later structures. It is certain that the Painted House was constructed after the demolition of Building C7 (Period IV) and the Buttressed Building (Period V), both of which it superceded, the latter being constructed about A.D. 160–180 (see above). It is also clear that the Painted House was already in existence when the Clay Walled Building (Period VII) was added to it and again the construction of the latter has been dated to about A.D. 210–230. These dates set the overall limits for the construction of the Painted House, but allowing for at least a short period of use for the Buttressed Building (Period V), a date of about A.D. 200 is the most likely for Period VI.

This date is supported by the material evidence from the site, that was recovered either from the dumped soil over the demolished Buttressed Building, the demolition of Building C7, or from deposits relating to the construction of the Painted House itself. An illegible bronze coin (Coin No. 3) came from the construction layers of Room 3 and another (Coin No. 4) of Commodus (A.D. 176–7) was found in soil upcast from the foundations on the south side. Twelve sherds of samian (No. 67) ware from these deposits include four of first century date, five of the first half of the second century and three of mid-second century and A.D. 150–190, respectively. Some 127 sherds of coarse pottery also came from these deposits (Nos. 162–172). Most seem to date from the first half of the second century and must be derived from earlier deposits, but two are certainly Antonine. The coins, samian and coarse pottery are generally in good accord and confirm a date not earlier than the end of the second century for the construction of the Painted House. Third century types are absent!

There were also two deposits which relate to the occupation of the Painted House. One was the filling of a drain at the east end of the North Passage and the other the primary ash and soil in the stoke-hole area, just outside the south wall. The drain fill contained two coins (Coin Nos. 5 and 6), five samian sherds (Nos. 68 and 69), two mortaria (Nos. 75 and 76) and 192 coarse potsherds (Nos. 173–187). The coins are both bronze, one being of Severus (A.D. 193–211) and the other being illegible. The samian is mostly Hadrian to late-Antonine and one mortar is of 3rd century date.

The stoke-hole contained material including a bone pin (No. 47), one samian sherd of first century date and 70 sherds of coarse pottery (Nos. 188–190), the latter mostly Antonine, but including at least three of early to mid-third century date. This material all collected during the occupation of the Painted House though it does include some of earlier date. However, at least five vessels are of third century date and thus fit comfortably into the overall dates of the House ending at about A.D. 270.

PERIOD VII – THE CLAY WALLED BUILDING (C10), (Figs. 11 and 21).

This structure was found along most of the length of the Bingo Hall site in 1975–6. It consisted of at least three rooms (East, West and North Rooms) with a corridor on the south side and probably another corridor on the west side. More rooms may exist beyond the north edge of the excavation. All the walls had been built of an orange clay, probably held within a wooden frame and all had been plastered and painted. One main wall had been rebuilt and in places two or three thin clay or mortar floors, each with a corresponding thin covering of soil, may be regarded as three distinct phases (Phases I–III) in the history of the building.

In terms of the history of the site it is certain that the building was constructed over the tufa demolition rubble of the Buttressed Building (Period V); against the east wall of the Tufa Block Building (Period IV) and also against the north wall of the Painted House (Period VI). It was thus deliberately constructed in the otherwise open area in the angle formed at the internal junction of the Tufa Block Building and the Painted House. In effect, it created a second east-west range parallel to Rooms 1, 2 and 3 of the Painted House. It was in turn cut through by the later fort wall (Period VIII) and also partly buried beneath the rampart-bank.

In detail this structure was traced for an east-west length of at least 12.50 m., from the Tufa Block Building to a point where it was cut away before the east end of the excavation. Its north-south width was at least 6.85 m. and clearly the North Room extended for some distance beyond this.

The main east-west walls of the building clearly lay along the approximate centres of the foundations of the robbed Buttressed Building (Plate XIX). Similarly, the one known internal north-south wall ran from buttress (S2) to buttress (N2), even if somewhat diagonally, of the same building (Plate XX). Logically, the builders of the Clay Walled Building should have been unaware of the presence of the robbed Buttressed Building, for the two events were separated by many years. Either, there were indications of the buried building now not visible, or this was largely coincidental. It is equally possible that the use of standard units of measurement caused building lines to coincide, even if the corresponding structures were of widely differing periods. Either way, there was little scope for putting in vertical posts to support the Clay Walled Building and it seems that its walls rested almost directly on the top of the truncated masonry.

It seems likely that the structure was of only one storey and no direct evidence of windows, doors or roof was found. Certainly the general absence of broken tiles in association with the structure, suggests a light roof, whilst the absence of window glass could be due either to its non-existence or its subsequent careful removal. It is clear that when the demolition took place much of the superstructure was removed, that some of the clay walls were knocked down in an irregular manner over the latest floors and the stubs of many of the walls left in place. Each room is described below.

East Room.

A section of the north wall of this room survived to a height of 84 cm., but only stubs of the south and west walls, about 20 cm. high remained. The east wall appears to have been totally removed. The internal north-south width was 4.52 m., whilst the minimum east-west length was about 5.75 m. The walls were mostly 20–28 cm. thick including the plaster but insufficient survived to establish the details of any containing wooden frame. Two distinct floors (S. G. Fig. 22, L. 36 and 38) could be traced over much of the room and the original south wall (S.G. L. 46) had been removed and rebuilt (Phase II) marginally further north (S. G. L. 32), from where it had subsequently fallen (S. G. L. 31).

Faint traces of plaster were found on all the surviving walls, notably at the north-west corner where a substantial painted section survived *in situ* (Plate XXI). This showed a bottom dado zone, 20 cm. high, consisting of grey-green flecks of paint over a mottled red-white background to create a marbled effect (Figs. 96–98). Along the top edge of this was a broad grey-green band, from which sprang two vertical lines in yellow and red. The former began some 9 cm. from the corner of the room and seems to have formed the outer border of an upright, rectangular white panel at least 60 cm. high. The many fallen fragments of plaster recovered from the floor of this room suggest a series of matching upright panels, with outer borders in yellow and inner borders in red and perhaps 1.75 m. or more high above the dado. The upper corners of the panels were decorated with groups of five to seven pellets in red. A broad zone of pink-red plaster seems to have formed a ceiling band above the panels. It seems likely that the west wall would have contained four panels, or only three if a door opening linked the East and West Rooms (see below), each with an overall width of about 1.02 m.

West Room.

Only parts of the north, south and east walls of this room were found and it seems likely that the west wall was destroyed when the later fort wall was built, for no trace of a continuation of this room was found west of the fort wall. The north-south width of the Room was again 4.52 m. and its east-west length has been estimated at about 5.70 m. allowing for the south corridor returning on the west side. The walls were 20–30 cm. thick and mostly survived to a height of about 20–30 cm. Again there were two floors (Fig. 22 S. H., L. 69, 75, 70–72) and two thin corresponding soil deposits (S. H., L. 68–73, 58–60), suggesting two phases. As with the East Room the south wall had been rebuilt in Phase II. Slight traces of circular voids, which probably represent upright wooden posts, were noted in the north and east walls of this room, but the unstable nature of the surviving clay made precise details uncertain. Six were found in the east wall, where they were generally 10 cm. in diameter and mostly spaced at intervals of about 30 cm. centre to centre. A similar one was found in the north wall. There was no trace that such posts had been driven into the ground and anyway this would have been difficult due to the presence of the underlying buttresses. No certain trace of a door-opening was found, but a missing section of the east wall of this room, about 1.82 m. wide, could mark a doorway joining the East and West Rooms.

The internal wall faces were all lined with the same thick layer of plaster and this painted. Lengths of plaster survived *in situ* on both the east and south walls and these showed a low-level dado with yellow and black splashes on a cream background, at least 16 cm. high. The fallen sections of plaster found on the clay floor showed the dado to have been at least 24 cm. high and to have had at least one vertical black stripe. Above the dado was a black band 6 cm. wide, from which sprang vertical yellow and green stripes. These marked the outer and inner frames, respectively, of a series of upright, rectangular white panels. These were enclosed within a thin red frame, itself below a high-level grey-green band. The upper corners of the frames were decorated with groups of green pellets (Figs. 99–101) and a broad grey-green band above the panels appears to have been a ceiling band.

It is clear that the dado and its upper band were at least 30 cm. high and the panels are estimated at about 1.75 m. high above these, with a ceiling height of about 2.20–2.50 m. The exact width of the panels is not known, but allowing for the overall red frame a panel width of about 1.00 m. seems likely and this would allow four or five panels on the respective walls. Any door-opening, estimated at about 85 cm. in width, would effectively have reduced the number of panels to three of four per wall, respectively.

North Room.

This room lay almost entirely outside the limits of the excavation and only one small cut was made to find the thickness of the north wall of the West Room and the floor of any room beyond.

This located a small quarter-round moulding of poor quality mortar, about 7 by 7 cm., over a clay floor. The internal face of this room had been rendered with two thin bands of plaster, both painted red. Nothing more can be said about this room or its decoration, other than that the moulding may indicate a rather elaborate or more important room.

The South Corridor.

This was traced for a minimum length of 12.15 m. from the east wall of the Tufa Block Building eastwards, to a point where it had been destroyed. Its width was generally 1.81 m. Its south wall was formed by the pre-existing masonry north wall of the Painted House passage and its north wall was also the south (clay) wall of the East and West Rooms. Three distinct floors (S. G., L. 49–52, 45 and 43) were found and three corresponding soil deposits, (S. G, L. 48, 44 and 42), suggesting three phases. The rebuild of the north wall of the corridor (see above) had taken place during Phase II, but the plastering of its south wall appears to have taken place during Phase III.

Both north and south walls retained long lengths of *in situ* plaster to a maximum height of 22 and 51 cm., respectively. This showed that the masonry wall and also the clay wall had both been rendered with thick layers of identical white mortar, between 1–6 cm. in thickness, strongly suggesting that they had been treated as part of a single operation. Both walls showed slight traces of two layers of plaster within this thickness, but the very variable surfaces of each wall demanded generous applications of plaster at many points.

Both walls had then been painted with a pale yellow background speckled with red splashes to give a mottled effect and this must represent the dado. At regular intervals along both walls were pairs of nearly vertical lines in red, mostly 1 cm. wide, 21–30 cm. apart and each pair some 80–89 cm. from the next. The technique is similar to that used in the Painted House dados.

The *in situ* plaster in the corridor shows that the dado, some 48 cm. high, was bordered along its top by a dark red band about 2 cm. wide. Above this were upright, rectangular white panels outlined on three sides by two coloured stripes.

The large area of fallen plaster (Plate XXII) from the masonry wall displayed three-sided panels in three different colour schemes, running in a repeated series. One panel had a broader green stripe enclosing a thin red stripe; the next panel had a broader red stripe enclosing a thin yellow stripe and the third panel had a broad yellow stripe enclosing a thin green stripe. The upper corners of each panel were decorated with groups of studs, each group taking the colour of the thin inner stripe (Figs. 92– 94).

If the pairs of red lines on the dado marked the inner frames of adjacent panels, then the panels were probably about 97 cm. in overall width and thus there could have been at least eleven down each side of the corridor. A broad red band found near the west end of the corridor may have framed a door-opening in the missing section of the south wall, but this remains uncertain.

The West Corridor.

No certain trace of a presumed West Corridor was found, but the circumstantial evidence suggests that it had existed. In particular no evidence of the West Room was found west of the fort wall, nor any trace there of the continuation of the north wall of the West Corridor. It is thus difficult to offer any other solution than that there was a West Corridor, linking with the long South Corridor and accordingly it has been shown as of similar width on the reconstructed plan. Its width is shown as about 1.80 m., and its minimum length as 6.55 m.

This area also showed traces of three floors, of clay or mortar and also the three corresponding soil layers, again indicative of three phases, though most of these had been removed by later features. The west wall of this presumed corridor supported one small patch of *in situ* plaster and this had been painted on a rendering of white mortar like that used in the South Corridor. The plaster overlapped the Phase I and the Phase II floors and again clearly related to Phase III. Some 200 fragments of plaster were found in the area of the supposed West Corridor. These suggest that it had a white dado flecked in red and panels with yellow or green stripes.

A small circular pit (S. H., L. 100) had been cut through the Phase I and II floors (S. H., L. 103 and 104), probably at the end of Phase III when it was sealed by the overall demolition layers. It was 72 cm. in diameter, 53 cm. deep, bowl-shaped in profile and filled with black-brown loam.

The Dating Evidence for Period VII.

The dating evidence for this building is fairly substantial. The circumstantial evidence is particularly significant for it provides date-limits at both ends. Clearly, the Clay Walled Building was added after the completion of the Painted House complex (Period VI) dated to about A.D. 200 (see above) and thus it could not have been constructed before the beginning of the third century. Similarly, the Clay Walled Building was demolished for the construction of the shore-fort (Period VIII), probably built at about A.D. 270. It seems clear from this, therefore, that the three phases identified within the Clay Walled Building must all lie within the date-range of A.D. 200–270.

Happily, the material evidence from the building agrees well with this dating. In total it comprises two coins, 14 sherds of samian ware, two stamped tiles and 357 sherds of coarse pottery, of which 29 vessels have been drawn (Nos. 191–219). Whilst this material falls into some eight small groups these may usefully be considered under three main headings.

The first group consists of material from the Phase I floors and the Phase I occupation deposits. These include a bronze fitting (No. 38), four small samian sherds, of which three are Antonine and one Flavian. In addition there are 122 sherds of coarse ware of which 12 vessels are described and illustrated (Nos. 191–202). Two of these vessels, probably of first century date or a little later, were found in the Phase I floor and were probably derived from nearby when the floor was laid. The rest include three straight-sided dishes, five bead-rim dishes and two cooking-pots with outcurved rims. Most of these vessels are common in late-second and early-third century deposits. Some occur in the *Classis Britannica* Fort, Period III (A.D. 190–208) and also in the soil over its demolition rubble (A.D. 210–270). Here most of these vessels probably date from the first quarter of the third century, with the small samian sherds perhaps derived from elsewhere on the site. On the material and circumstantial evidence Phase I has been assigned to about A.D. 210–230.

The second group consists of material from the Phase II walls, the Phase II floors and also the Phase II occupation. This consists of one coin, two small finds (Nos. 52 and 53), five mostly small sherds of samian ware, including Forms 18, 18/31, 37 (No. 70) and Curle 15, of which three are again Antonine and a fourth first century. In addition there are 39 coarse ware potsherds of which three are drawn (Nos. 203–205). Of these one is a straight-sided dish and two are dishes with bead rims. Again these seem common in late-second and early-third century deposits. The most significant object here is certainly the coin (No. 7) actually found inside the Phase II (replacement) wall. This is a little-worn denarius of Severus Alexander (A.D. 222–235) which is unlikely to have been discarded much before about A.D. 230–240, allowing for minimal circulation. It provides a most important *terminus post quem* for the Phase II wall which, allowing for a span for both the preceding Phase I and the succeeding Phase III, is likely to have been built close to about A.D. 230–250. The samian is again rather too early whilst the coarse wares could mostly date from the second quarter of the third century. On this evidence the Phase II rebuilding has been tentatively assigned to about A.D. 230–250.

The third group consists of material from the Phase III occupation deposits and the final demolition layers. This consists of one coin (No. 8) and five sherds of samian ware, including

Forms 31, 37, 42 and Curle 21 (?), two of which are Flavian, two are Antonine and another late-second century to mid-third century. In addition there are two stamped tiles (Nos. 12 and 15) and 196 coarse ware sherds of which 14 (Nos. 206–219) have been drawn. These include three cooking-pots with outcurved rims, and four dishes with bead rims all of which could date from the late-second century or early-third century. However, the two upright dishes with bowed, thickened sides; one jar with a cavetto rim and three rather coarse flanged dishes, generally appear in mid to late-third century contexts. The coin is a worn sestertius of Hadrian (A.D. 117–119) and was clearly at least a century old when lost. This group clearly contains a quantity of earlier material, but the latest six vessels could all date to the third quarter of the third century and thus pre-date the suggested demolition in about A.D. 270. On this evidence the modest relaying of floors representing Phase III has been assigned to about A.D. 250–270.

It also seems clear that the Painted House must have remained in full, or at least partial, use for most of Period VII (A.D. 200–270), for quite clearly it was still in remarkably good condition when it was substantially demolished. Traces of minor repairs were found in Rooms 2 and 3, where the plaster over the lowest parts of two wall-flues seem to have been replaced and repainted. The thin band of soil and plaster on the floors of Rooms 2, 3 and 4 probably represent the initial decay of the structure during a period of disuse. To judge by the massive rubble layers sealing this soil it must have been formed just before the demolition took place and may represent a period of no more than a few months, or perhaps a year or two at the most.

PERIOD VIII – THE DEMOLITION FOR THE CONSTRUCTION OF THE LATE-ROMAN SHORE-FORT (Fig. 22).

The next event in the development of the sites under consideration here was clearly the most dramatic and significant event in the later history of Roman Dover. This was the construction of a massive masonry army fort across about four acres of the settlement. The construction formed part of the late-third century expansion of the chain of Roman coastal forts built to defend the South East shipping-lanes and shores against Saxon raids (Ref. 7). The forts at Reculver, Brancaster, Caistor and probably Carisbrooke formed the original early-third century scheme (Phase I), whilst the forts at Dover, Burgh Castle, Richborough, Bradwell, Portchester and probably Walton Castle formed the late-third century expansion (Phase II).

Only at Dover and Richborough (Ref. 8) were there substantial earlier Roman buildings and at both sites the new forts resulted in large-scale clearance. At Dover, the shore-fort effectively destroyed much of the north-east area of the second century *Classis Britannica* II fort, the latter by then in considerable decay after an abandonment lasting at least 60 years (Ref. 9).

On the Painted House and Bingo Hall sites the effect was clearly devastating, for both lay on the line of the proposed western defensive wall and ditch. The surviving north-south range of the Tufa Block Building (Period IV) was substantially demolished and what little survived was largely cut away by the great ditch of the shore-fort. The east-west range of the Painted House (Period VI) was smashed through for the construction of the fort wall across much of Rooms 3 and 4. Room 2 and the east sides of Rooms 3 and 4 then became buried beneath the internal rampart-bank and Rooms 5 and 6 were reduced and then substantially destroyed by the shore-fort ditch. Only Room 1 survived the destruction for it seems clear that it remained in use for some years after the construction of the fort wall. The Clay Walled Building (Period VII) was largely demolished and then deeply buried beneath the rampart.

The details of the shore-fort, its defensive walls, ditches and bastions and also its internal arrangements are not considered here, but will form the subject of a subsequent report. However, the dating evidence from the Painted House and Bingo Hall sites for its construction also represents the effective end of Period VII and is thus relevant here.

The Dating Evidence for Period VIII

The dating evidence itself comes from four main sources. First, from the thin layers of soil accumulating over the floors of the Roman House. Second, from the massive deposits of demolition debris from the upper part of the house itself. Third, from the fillings of the partially robbed hypocaust channels and lastly from the dumps of soil and debris which formed the base of the rampart-bank that backed the internal face of the fort wall.

In addition it is worth recalling the large quantity of material evidence recovered from deposits relating to Periods I–VII that were also totally sealed by the demolition debris and rampart. The latest coin in Period VII was a denarius of Severus Alexander (A.D. 222–235), found in the wall of the Clay Walled Building (Phase II) and probably deposited at about A.D. 230–250. Several coarse pottery vessels from the same structure probably dated from about A.D. 250–270 (Period VII, Phase III).

The primary soil deposits on the floors of most of the rooms and the North Passage of the Painted House produced only two coins (Coin Nos. 9 and 10) and eight coarse potsherds. The coins are of Trajan (A.D. 98–117) and Julia Paula (A.D. 218–222), the former apparently having been in circulation for at least 100 years! The later coin proves that these deposits could not have formed before about A.D. 220 and although it could have been dropped at any time after this date, allowing for a period of circulation, a decade of two later is in fact more likely.

The demolition layers of rubble both inside and outside the Painted House and also over the Clay Walled Building, produced three more coins (Coin Nos. 11–13), twelve stamped tiles (Nos. 1, 2, 4, 5, 10, 11, 17, 18, 19, 20, 21 and 25), 21 sherds of samian ware, two mortaria (Nos. 77 and 78) and 282 coarse ware potsherds of which 20 vessels (Nos. 220–239) are illustrated. One coin is of Hadrian (after A.D. 132), one is of Antoninus Pius (A.D. 138–161), but the other is a denarius of Julia Mamaea (A.D. 222–235) which was found with the clay demolition material above the destroyed Clay Walled Building. The samian is mostly Antonine to mid-third century and the mortars are both third century types. The coarse pottery includes three flanged dishes, four straight-sided dishes, two bead rim dishes, two cavetto rim cooking-pots and fragments of at least three colour-coated vessels. Whilst some of these vessels probably date from the early-third century the majority seem consistent with a mid to late-third century date.

Only a small amount of material was recovered from the hypocaust channels. This included one coin (Coin No. 14), four sherds of samian ware (No. 71), 26 sherds of coarse pottery (No. 240) and two stamped tiles (Nos. 6 and 22). The coarse pottery is mostly Antonine, the samian all late-second to mid-third century, but the coin is badly corroded and cannot be identified.

The dumped soil sealing the demolition rubble and forming the base of the rampart-bank produced 13 sherds of samian ware (Nos. 72 and 73), 290 sherds of coarse pottery of which 35 vessels (Nos. 241–275) are illustrated and nine stamped tiles (Nos. 3, 7, 8, 9, 13, 14, 16, 23 and 24). Most of the samian is Antonine to mid-third century. The coarse pottery includes one flanged dish, eight straight-sided dishes, seven bead rim dishes, four cavetto rim cooking-pots and at least three colour-coated wares. Whilst several of the vessels are of second or early-third century date, the majority are again consistent with a mid or late-third century date.

In addition four more coins (Nos. 15–18) were found together in Room 3. Unfortunately, these came from a minor collapse of a soil section, during one night, so their precise location cannot be determined. The cause of the collapse was the loose nature of the mortar and plaster in the rubble layer. The coins were found, together with a small amount of soil and rubble, on the cleaned floor of Room 3. It seems certain, however, that they came from the interface between the underlying loose rubble and the layer of dumped soil above (S. E, Fig. 22, L. 61 and L. 64). The fact that they were all found together in an area otherwise largely devoid of coins and small finds suggests that they may have been held within a small container, since perished. It also seems certain that these must have been dropped by someone involved in either the demolition or the building work. The close date-range of the coins also suggests a group of current coins, such as may have been carried in a purse.

One coin (Coin No. 15) is of Pupienus (A.D. 238), two more (Coin Nos. 16 and 17) are of

Severus Alexander (A.D. 222–235) and the latest one (Coin No. 18) is of Gordianus III (A.D. 238–244).

Richard Reece has kindly commented that these coins were almost certainly minted c. A.D. 230–244 and that, due to the general absence from circulation of good silver coins after about A.D. 253, it seems likely that they were brought together during the years A.D. 240–253. He has also added that on their merits the coins were more likely to have been deposited (here lost) in A.D. 240–253, with a rapidly decreasing chance after that date. If, however, the coins were being carried about in a purse by a workman on the site in the form of a mobile hoard, then it is possible that they were lost at any time between A.D. 240–270, but hardly later.

In summary, the direct evidence for the destruction of the Painted House (in Period VIII) consists of ten coins, 37 samian vessels and 606 coarse potsherds, of which 56 are illustrated. Of the coins one is corroded, two are early-second century, one is mid-second century and six date between A.D. 218–244, with the latest being that of Gordianus III (A.D. 238–244). Whilst a little of the samian is exclusively second century the greater part is Antonine to mid-third century. Similarly, whilst some of the coarse pottery is late-second to early-third century the bulk must date to about the middle to later third century. The total evidence is thus generally in good accord. Clearly the demolition of the Painted House and the formation of the lower part of the rampart which sealed the rubble could not have taken place before about A.D. 240 and a date-range of A.D. 250–270 is the most likely. This also agrees well with the evidence from the preceding Period VII where the latest coin in Phase II (the second of three phases) was of Severus Alexander (A.D. 222–235).

INTERPRETATION OF MAJOR SECTIONS (All on Fig. 22).

SECTION E. West–East Through The Painted House

LAYER	DESCRIPTION	INTERPRETATION
1	Brown loam	Modern disturbance
2–9	Grey and brown loams	Medieval and later
10	Light brown loam	Medieval pit
11	Flint and tufa rubble	Bastion decay
12–13	Brown loams	Saxon dump
14–18	Grey and brown loams	Fill of late-Roman Shore-fort ditch
19	Orange-brown loam	Pre-Painted House deposit
20	Mortar and plaster rubble	Painted House demolition rubble in Room 3
21–23	Flint, tufa and chalk	Late-Roman Shore-fort wall
24–25	Chalk, tufa and flint rubble	Late-Roman Shore-fort wall foundation
26	Grey and brown loams	Post-Medieval disturbance
27–30	Clays, loams and mortar	Fill of Medieval robber-trench
31–32	Orange-brown clays and loams	Medieval pit
33	Brown loam	Medieval deposit
34–46	Loams, clays and ash	Medieval pit
47	Mortar and gravel	Late-Roman dump
48	Flint, chalk and tile rubble	Late-Roman gully
49–53	Mixed loams and clays	Late-Roman Shore-fort rampart dump
54	Mortar, plaster and flint	Painted House demolition rubble
55	Orange-brown loam and mortar	Primary decay in Painted House, Room 2
56–61	Brown loams and mortar	Late-Roman Shore-fort rampart dump

62	Brown loam and mortar	Primary decay in Painted House, Room 3
63	Brown loam and orange clay	Late-Roman Shore-fort rampart dump
64	White mortar and flint	Painted House demolition rubble
65	Brown loam and mortar	Primary decay in Painted House, Room 3
66–77	Carbon and ash	Late-Roman pit
78–83	Loam, clay and mortar rubble	Late-Roman Shore-fort rampart dump
84	Chalk rubble	Painted House demolition
85–87	Rubble, carbon, ash	Late-Roman Shore-fort rampart
88	Orange-brown loam	Primary decay in Painted House, Room 2
89	*Opus signinum*	Painted House floor, Room 2
90	Flints and chalk rubble	Foundation bed for floor
91	*Opus signinum*	Consolidation over bridging tiles of central hypocaust chamber
92	Mortar	Foundation bed for pilae stacks in central hypocaust chamber
93	Brown clay	Pre-Roman soil
94	Flints and chalk rubble	Foundation bed for floor
95	*Opus signinum*	Floor repair
96–97	Clay and pebble layers	Levelling for Painted House construction
98	Crushed mortar	Building C7 floor levels (Room B)
99	Brown loam and mortar	Building C7, west wall foundation trench
100	Brown clay + chalk and carbon	Roman dump
101	Brown clay	Pre-Roman soil
102	Orange clay	Brickearth – natural deposit
103	Grey and brown loam	Medieval pit
104	Grey loam and clay	Post-Roman deposit
105	Mortar rubble and plaster	Late-Roman decay
106–108	Burnt red and brown clays	Late-Roman deposits

SECTION F. South–North Through The Painted House

LAYER	DESCRIPTION	INTERPRETATION
1		Modern disturbance
2–14	Clays, loams and mortar	Medieval pit
15	Dark brown loam	Modern disturbance
16	Fine, light brown loam	Post-Roman hill-wash
17	Orange clay and flints	Late-Roman Shore-fort rampart bank (upper sealing)
18–19	Clay and loam	Late-Roman Shore-fort rampart dump
20	Brown clay	Late-Roman Shore-fort rampart bank (lower sealing)
21–25	Rubble and *opus signinum*, clays and loams	Late-Roman Shore-fort rampart dump
26	Rubble	Painted House demolition
27–30	Dark grey and brown loams	Late-Roman Shore-fort rampart dump
31–32	Rubble	Painted House demolition
33–35	Grey-brown loam, carbon and mortar	Fill of stoke hole for Room 2
36	Dark brown loam and mortar	Stoke hole
37–38	Dark and light brown loams	Fill of ditch C3

39–42	Clay loam and mortar	Late-Roman Shore-fort rampart dump
43–44	Orange clay	Late-Roman Shore-fort rampart bank (lower sealing)
45	Grey ash	Late-Roman Shore-fort rampart bank
46–56	Clay, loam and rubble	Medieval pit
57–60	Loam and rubble	Late-Roman Shore-fort rampart bank
61	Mortar and rubble	Painted House demolition
62	Clay and crushed plaster	Primary decay in Painted House, Room 2
63	*Opus signinum*	Painted House floor, Room 2
64	Flints and chalk rubble	Foundation bed for floor
65	*Opus signinum*	Consolidation over bridging tiles of central hypocaust chamber
66	White mortar	Foundation bed for pilae stacks in central hypocaust chamber
67	Brown clay	Pre-Roman soil
68–71	Brown clays and loams	Late-Roman dumps
72	Orange clay	Floor?
73	White plaster and mortar	Painted House construction-level
74–75	Brown clays	Levelling for Painted House construction
76	Grey-brown clay-loam	Fill of gully in Painted House passage
77	Orange clay	Dumped soil
78	Brown clay	Pre-Roman soil
79	Cream clay	Natural deposit

SECTION G. North–South Through The Bingo Hall Site

LAYER	DESCRIPTION	INTERPRETATION
1–24	Clays and loams	Late-Roman Shore-fort rampart bank and later deposits
25–26	Mortar + clay plaster	Painted House demolition
27	Orange clay	Late-Roman Shore-fort rampart bank
28–31	Orange and brown clays	Clay Walled Building (C10) demolition
32	Light orange clay	Collapsed south wall of Building C10 (PII)
33	Black loam	PII occupation, Building C10
34–35	Orange-brown and grey clays	Collapsed south wall of Building C10 (PI)
36	Orange clay and mortar	PII floor of Building C10 (= collapsed PI wall)
37	Black loam	PI occupation, Building C10
38	Orange clay	PI floor, Building C10
39	Black loam	PI occupation, Building C10
40–41	Orange-brown clay	Clay Walled Building (C10) demolition
42	Black loam	PIII occupation, Building C10
43	Orange clay	PIII floor, Building C10
44	Black loam and mortar	PII occupation, Building C10
45	Yellow mortar	PII floor, Building C10
46–47	Orange clay	Collapsed south wall of Building C10 (PI)
48	Black loam	PI occupation, Building C10
49–51	Orange and grey clays	PI floor, Building C10
52	Tufa and mortar	Demolition of Buttressed Building (C8), = PI floor of Building C10

53–54	Orange clay and brown loam	Levelling layers
55	Tufa, mortar and rubble	Demolition of Building C8, = PI floor of Building C10
56	Orange clay	Levelling layer
57–58	Dark brown clay	Upcast soils
59	Orange-brown clay	Upper fill of robber-trench of Flint Walled Enclosure (C5)
60	Dark grey clay-loam	Fill of Ditch C2
61	Dark grey clay-loam	Fill of robber-trench of rammed chalk foundation (C4), north wall
62	Mottled orange clay	Fill of Ditch C2

SECTION H. West–East Through The Bingo Hall Site

LAYER	DESCRIPTION	INTERPRETATION
1	Grey clay and rubble	Medieval pit
2–36	Grey and brown clays and loams	Late-Roman Shore-fort rampart bank
37	Flint and chalk rubble + mortar	Late-Roman Shore-fort construction level
38–39	Grey and brown clay-loams	Fill of Shore-fort wall foundation trench
40	Brown loam	Tread layer over Shore-fort foundation
41–54	Mixed clays and loams	Upcast from Shore-fort foundation trench
55–57	Mottled orange-brown clay	Demolition of Clay Walled Building (C10)
58–60	Grey-brown clay-loams	PII occupation of Building C10
61–62	Mortar and orange clay	PII floor (and PI demolition) of Building C10
63	Black loam	PI occupation of Building C10
64–66	Orange clay	PI floor of Building C10
67	Orange clay and chalk	Demolition of Buttressed Building (C8), = PI floor
68	Black loam	PI occupation of Building C10
69	Crushed tufa	PI floor of Building C10
70–72	Orange clay	PII floor of Building C10
73	Black loam	PI occupation of Building C10
74	Black loam	Pre-Clay Walled Building occupation
75	Cream tufa mortar	PI floor of Building C10
76–79	Orange-brown clays	Upcast soils
80	Dark-grey clay-loam	Fill of Ditch C2
81	Orange-brown clay and loams	Fill of Ditch C1
82	Dark brown clay	Pre-Roman soil
83	Cream clay	Natural deposit
84–85	Black and brown loams	Post-Medieval disturbance
86	Grey-brown loam	Post-Medieval deposit
87	Brown loam	Medieval hill-wash
88	Grey loam and flint debris	Fill of late-Roman Shore-fort ditch
89–90	Brown loams	Cut-out for Shore-fort wall
91–92	Mortar debris	Demolition of Tufa Block Building (C6)
93	Black-brown ashy loam	Carbon deposit in hypocaust
94–98	Orange clays and loams	Demolition of Clay Walled Building (C10)
99–100	Clay-loam and plaster	Roman pit fill
101–103	Clays and carbons	Floors and occupation levels of Building C10

104	Burnt mortar	Demolition of Buttressed Building (C8) and floor of Building C10
105–108	Clay-loam and mortar	Levelling layers
109	Orange clay	Upcast from levelling layers
110	Orange-brown clay-loam	Fill of pit or robber-trench
111–112	Brown clay-loam	Upcast soils
113	Dark brown clay	Pre-Roman soil
114	Cream clay	Natural deposit

CHAPTER III

THE EXCAVATED OBJECTS

A. THE ROMAN COINS.

Although more than 200 Roman coins were found on the Painted House and Bingo Hall sites during the various excavations, the great majority relate to shore-fort deposits and are thus beyond the scope of this Report. Only 18, which relate directly to Periods I – VIII, are included here and these have kindly been identified by Dr. John Kent, of the Department of Coins and Medals at the British Museum.

Coin No.	Obverse	Date A.D.	Denom. and R.I.C. Number (Ref. 134)	Context and Period	Deposit	Key-Find No.
1	Hadrian	118	Sestertius	PV. Dump Layers	DV–3078	4371
2	Hadrian	117–136	Bronze	PV. Robber Trench	DV–9941	4271
3	Illegible		Bronze	PVI. Const. Layers, PH Rm. 3.	DV–9662	4061
4	Commodus (as Caesar)	176–177	Denarius	PVI. Upcast from const. of PH.	DV–9613	4002
5	Illegible		Bronze	PVI. Upper drain in PH passage	DV–3047	4345
6	Severus	193–211	Bronze	PVI. Drain fill, PH passage	DV–3010	4347
7	Severus Alexander	222–235	Denarius	PVII. Inside Phase II wall	DV–3049	4348
8	Hadrian	117–119	Sestertius	PVII. Phase III, Demo. layer	DV–3060	4355
9	Trajan	98–117	Dupondius	PVIII. Primary on floor	DV–2337	678
10	Julia Paula (Elagabalus)	218–222	Denarius. 214	PVIII. over Floor	DV–2310	671
11	Hadrian	After c. 132	Sestertius	PVIII. Demo.	DV–1189	662
12	Antoninus Pius	138–161	As.	PVIII. Demo.	DV–1111	323
13	Julia Mamaea	222–235	Denarius	PVIII. Demo.	DV–3034	4336
14	Illegible		Bronze	PVIII. Hypocaust	DV–4205	1059

Coin No.	Obverse	Date A.D.	Denom. and R.I.C. Number (Ref. 134)	Context and Period	Deposit	Key-Find No.
15	Pupienus	238	Denarius. 4★	PVIII. Dump.	DV–2348	731
16	Severus Alexander	222–235	Denarius. cf. 70★	PVIII. Dump.	DV–2348	731
17	Severus Alexander	222–235	Denarius. 55★	PVIII. Dump.	DV–2348	731
18	Gordianus III	238–244	Antoninianus, 2★	PVIII. Dump.	DV–2348	731

B. THE STAMPED TILES (Figs. 23 and 24, Nos. 1–33).

by Christine Molenkamp, B.A.

A total of 37 Roman tiles, stamped with the letters CLBR or a variation of this stamp, was found on the Painted House and Bingo Hall sites. Of these, 20 (including four unclassified) were published in 1981 in the Classis Britannica Report (Ref. 10, Table A). The remaining 17 were not included in that study and are published here for the first time. This brings the total number of published stamped tiles from the Dover excavations (888 were published in 1981) to 905. All 33 (Nos. 1–33) of the classifiable stamps are catalogued and illustrated here and those which were previously published are marked with an asterisk. These include stamps on three box-flue tiles (Nos. 279–281).

Groups and Types.
At Dover, 13 main groups of tiles (Groups A to M) were identified in 1981, representing a minimum of 55 different dies. A maximum of eight of these groups (a maximum of 15 dies) is represented by the 33 illustrated tiles (Nos. 1–33) and these are catalogued below (Table A). No new tile-stamps were recognised. As in 1981, Types F1 and H1 are the most numerous.

Fabrics.
In the 1981 Survey, two fabric types were represented:-
Fabric 1: From a source near Boulogne, a hard, fairly uniform buff (Munsell 5YR 7/6) coloured fabric.
Fabric 2: From a source in the Sussex Weald or from Romney Marsh, a reddish pink (Munsell 2.5YR 6/8) coloured fabric, relieved by streaks, lenses and swirls of creamy-white clay.

From a brief visual examination of the illustrated stamped tiles, no new fabrics were recognised and only one (No. 2★) was of Fabric 1, the rest were all of Fabric 2.

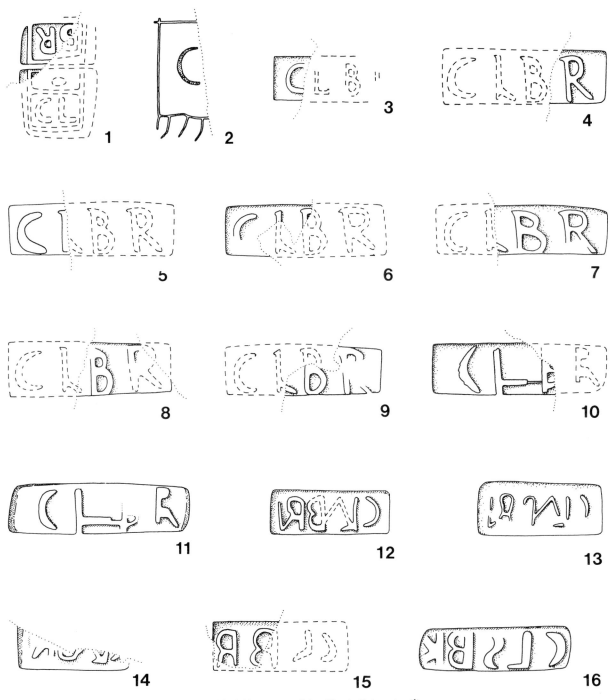

Fig. 23. *Tile-stamps of the Classis Britannica* ($\frac{1}{2}$).

No.	Group and Type	Length and width of stamps in mm.	Fabric colour and surface	Tile Type	Thickness mm.	DV–	KF–	Context
1.	A5	32 x 31+	OF & S	Flat	34	9608	4013	PH'75 P.VIII Demo. ★
2.	B3	29+ x 50	RPF & S	Imb.	19	1111	324	PH'70 P.VIII Demo. ★
3.	D1	21+ x 23	OF & S burnt	Imb.	20	9619	4130	PH'75 P.VIII Dump.
4.	F1	30+ x 29	OF & S	Imb.	17	2308	–	PH'71 P.VIII Demo. ★
5.	F1	33+ x 28	pale OF & S	Imb.	16	9608	4015	PH'75 P.VIII Demo. ★
6.	F1	45+ x 28+	PF & PS	Imb.	16	9707	4127	PH'75 P.VIII Hypo.
7.	F1	60+ x 26+	PF & PS	Imb.	18	9619	4129	PH'75 P.VIII Dump.
8.	F1	40+ x 30	OF & OS	Imb.	20	3074	4372	B.Hall P.VIII Dump.
9.	F1	53+ x 27	OF & OS	Imb.	20	9611	4009	PH'75 P.VIII Dump. ★
10.	F2	69+ x 28	RF & GS	Imb.	19	1111	325	PH'70 P.VIII Demo. ★
11.	F2	98 x 27	ORF & S	Imb.	20	9608	4014	PH'75 P.VIII Demo. ★
12.	G1	65 x 23	PF & S	Imb.	20	3031	4344	B.Hall P.VII Phase III
13.	G1	68 x 27	PF & GS	Imb.	20	3071	4368	B.Hall P.VIII Dump.
14.	G1	61+ x 20+	OF & S	Imb.	16	9611	4005	PH'75 P.VIII Dump. ★
15.	G3	35+ x 25+	OGF & GS	Imb.	20	9824	4238	B.Hall P.VII Phase III
16.	G5	84 x 24	ORF & S	Flat	30	9611	4007	PH'75 P.VIII Dump ★
17.	H1	55+ x 37	RF & PS	Flat	18	9819	4261	B.Hall P.VIII Demo.
18.	H1	51+ x 35+	OF & S	Flat	15	1188	641	PH'71 P.VIII Demo. ★
19.	H1	95 x 30+	OF & S	Flat	18	1188	642	PH'71 P.VIII Demo. ★
20.	H1	58+ x 35+	scorched GF & S	Flat	18	1189	657	PH'71 P.VIII Demo. ★
21.	H1	69+ x 37	OF & S	Flat	21	9608	4016	PH'75 P.VIII Demo. ★
22.	H1	95 x 35+	PF & RGS	Flat	35	9707	4128	PH'75 P.VIII Hypo.
23.	H1	59+ x 25+	OF, G scorched S	Flat	18	9619	4045	PH'75 P.VIII Dump. ★
24.	H1	42+ x 36	OF & S	Flat	16	9611	4008	PH'75 P.VIII Dump.★
25.	H3	43+ x 25	OF & S	Imb.	14	1188	640	PH'71 P.VIII Demo.★
26.	M5/K1	65 x 24	RPF & S	Box	20	3064	–	PH Rm 1 P.VI in situ
27.	K1	63 x 25	RPF & S	Box	20	3064	–	PH Rm 1 P.VI in situ
28.	K4	75 x 25		Bridge	50	–	–	PH Rm 1 P.VI in situ
29.	K4	77 x 25		Bridge	50	–	–	PH Rm 1 P.VI in situ
30.	K5	27+ x 22		Bridge	50	–	–	PH Rm 1 P.VI in situ
31.	K5	80 x 25		Bridge	50	–	–	PH Rm 2 P.VI in situ
32.	K5	86 x 25		Bridge	50	–	–	PH Rm 1 P.VI in situ
33.	K7	60+ x 24	RPF & S	Box	20	3064	–	PH Rm 1 P.VI in situ

Table A. Classification, dimensions and context of the illustrated stamped tiles.

Abbreviations

Bridge	=	bridging-tiles	★	=	published in the 1981 survey (Ref. 10)
Imb.	=	Imbrex	PH'70	=	Painted House site 1970
Box	=	Box-flue	PH'71	=	Painted House site 1971
O	=	orange	PH'75	=	Painted House site 1975
R	=	red	B. Hall	=	Bingo Hall site 1976
P	=	pink			
F	=	fabric			
S	=	surface			
G	=	grey			

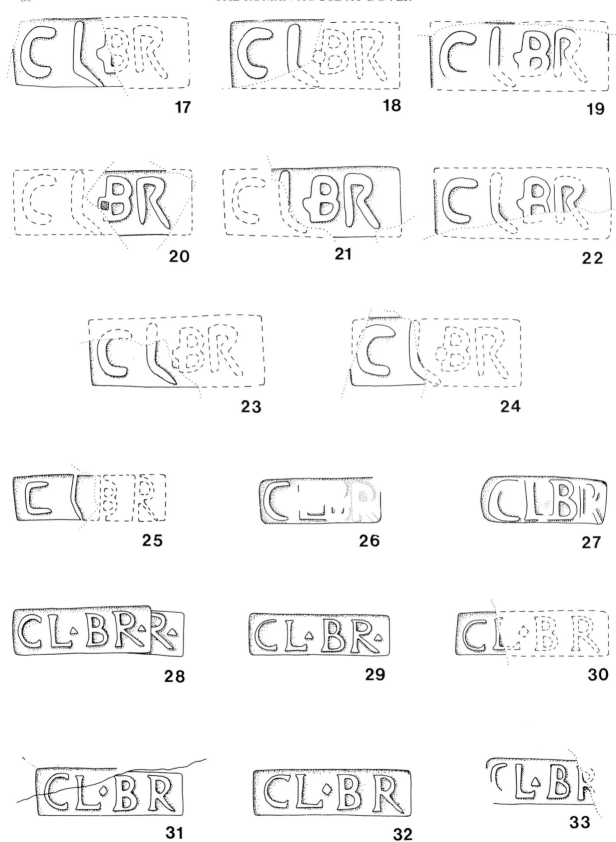

Fig. 24. *Tile-stamps of the Classis Britannica* ($\frac{1}{2}$).

Chronology

A study of the context of each of the stamped tiles from the Painted House site shows that the 37 tile stamps, representing some 15 of the identified dies, were found in stratified deposits (Table B). Interestingly, no stamps were found in Period I–V contexts predating the construction of the Painted House. Nine, however, relate to Period VI of which eight were found *in situ* in the Painted House structure. Two stamps were found in Period VII contexts and may be residual, whilst the remaining 26 stamps were found in Period VIII demolition and dumped deposits across the site.

stamp type	PVI in situ	PVI	PVII Phase III	PVIII Primary	PVIII Demo.	PVIII Hypo. fill	PVIII Dump	Total
A5					1			1
B3				1				1
D1							1	1
F1					2	1	3	6
F2				1	1			2
G1			1				2	3
G3			1					1
G5							1	1
H1					5	1	2	8
H3					1			1
M5/K1	1							1
K1	1							1
K4	2							2
K5	3							3
K7	1							1
Unassigned		1			1		2	4
Totals	8	1	2	2	11	2	11	37

Table B. Tile-stamp types from stratified deposits

C. THE SMALL FINDS (Figs. 25 and 26).

by Keith Parfitt, B.A., M.I.F.A.

Of the many and varied small finds from the two main sites represented by this Report, only 23 are described and illustrated here. These are mainly objects from stratified deposits relating to Periods I–VIII, as later objects are beyond the scope of this Report. The finds described include copper-alloys, bone, shale and glass.

Objects of copper alloy (Fig. 25, Nos. 34–44).

	Deposit	Site	Period	Context
No. 34 Annular ring, with a sub-rectangular cross-section and two slight ridges on the exterior. Internal diameter 17 mm. This appears to be a finger ring.	DV–9622	PH 75	PV *c.* A.D. 180–200	Dumped deposits

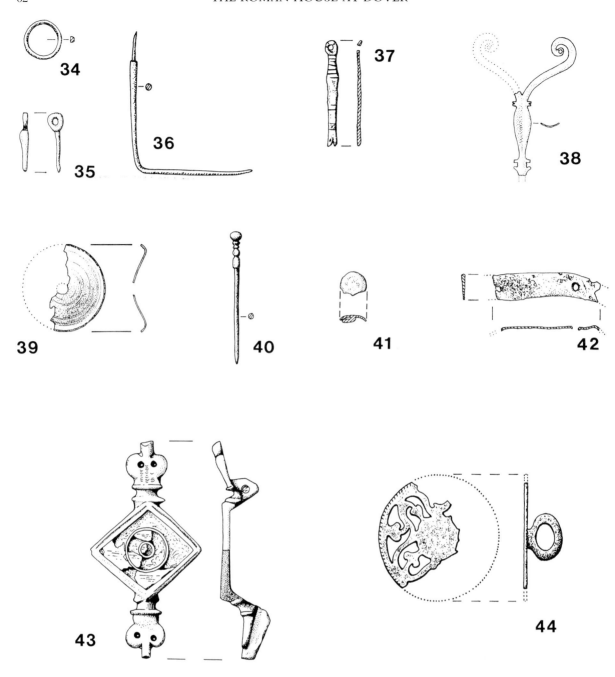

Fig. 25. *Objects of copper alloy* ($\frac{1}{2}$), *No. 43* ($\frac{1}{1}$).

No. 35 Central pin from a fairly large buckle. The main shaft of the pin is rectangular in cross-section and tapers to a rounded point. At the other end a circular eye has been formed to allow attachment to the main body of the buckle. Length of the pin is 23mm.	DV–9935	BH	PV *c.* A.D. 180–200	Robber-Trench deposits
No. 36 A writing stylus, with circular cross-section. The object is now bent and the writing tip has broken away. An iron example of similar form, without a flat head for erasing, comes from London, (Ref. 11, Pl. XX p. 58).	DV–9935	BH	PV *c.* A.D. 180–200	Robber-Trench deposits
No. 37 Nail cleaner with a suspension loop at the upper end in the same plane as the blade. The lower end is forked and there are incised horizontal lines decorating one side. Length is 55mm.	DV–9941	BH	PV *c.* A.D. 180–200	Robber-Trench deposits
No. 38 Carefully made decorative fitting of sheet metal. A probable rivet, or nail-hole, exists at the end of a curving tendril. The surviving tendril appears to be one of a matching pair.	DV–9896	BH	PVII *c.* A.D. 210–230	Phase I deposits
No. 39 About half of a disc, with a central perforation. The central part of the disc is concave and the outer edge is turned down. The purpose of the object is not clear but it may be some sort of harness mount. Diameter is 46mm.	DV–9824	BH	PVII *c.* A.D. 250–270	Phase III deposits
No. 40 Complete short pin, with ornamented head, consisting of two beads then two reels surmounted by a flattened sphere. This piece falls into N. Crummy's metal pin Type 2. Finds from Colchester suggest an early-second to third century date for the production of these objects. (Ref. 12). Length 70mm.	DV–3060	BH	PVII *c.* A.D. 250–270	Phase III deposits
No. 41 Small stud with a domed head. The shaft is now bent 1 to one side. The piece is poorly preserved. Diameter of the head is 14mm.	DV–1189	PH71	PVIII *c.* A.D. 270	Demolition deposits
No. 42 Strip of sheet bronze with two small punched holes for attachment. Probably some sort of binding or edging. Width is 11–14mm. Surviving length is 59mm.	DV–9819	BH	PVIII *c.* A.D. 270	Demolition deposits
No. 43 Decorated brooch, originally with a hinged pin (now missing). The head and foot of the brooch are similar and possibly represent stylised animal heads. In the centre of the brooch is a	DV–9819	BH	PVIII *c.* A.D. 270	Demolition deposits

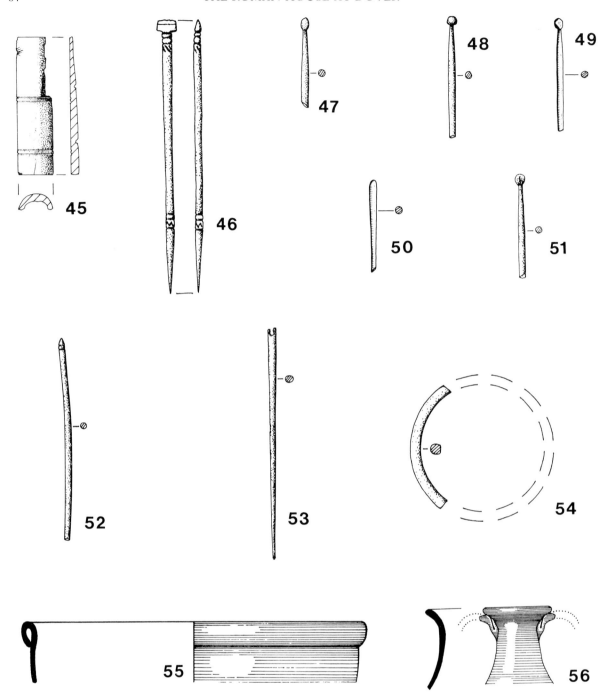

Fig. 26. *Objects of bone (½); shale (½); and glass (½).*

lozenge which contains traces of much-decayed enamel. Two concentric ribs of bronze within the lozenge divide it into three zones, probably each containing a different colour enamel, originally. The whole of the brooch was cast as one, with the pin forming a separate addition. There has been some damage to the brooch and the head has been bent forward.

A very similar brooch comes from Lombard Street in London (Ref. 13) p. 90, Fig. 24, 8.

No. 44 About a quarter of a large mount with a curving open-work design, in the form of ivy leaves, surrounding a plain central area. The edge of the piece is decorated with small incised grooves. There is a large oval loop on the back for attachment. Broadly similar to an example from Richborough (Ref. 14).
DV–3072 BH PVIII *c.* A.D. 270 Dumped deposits

Objects of Bone (Fig. 26, Nos. 45–53).

No. 45 About half a handle, decorated with two pairs of incised lines. Two small holes have been drilled on the inside but these do not go all the way through. The full lenght of the piece survives: 73mm.
DV–9622 PH 75 PV *c.* A.D. 180–200 Dumped deposits

No. 46 Complete decorated, writing stylus. Such items are more usually made from iron or bronze. In this bone example the broad upper end, used for erasing when writing in wax, is rather short, but there is no doubt that it was completely serviceable. Length is 145mm.
DV–9935 BH PV *c.* A.D. 180–200 Robber Trench deposits

No. 47 Pin with small ovoid head. The shaft tapers towards both ends, although the point is broken away. Surviving length: 48mm. This pin belongs to N. Crummy's Type 3 (Ref. 15) which has been tentatively dated to the third to fourth century A.D.
DV–9621 PH 75 PVI *c.* A.D. 190–208 Stokehole fill

No. 48 Pin with a small spherical head. The shaft tapers towards the head and the point has broken away. Surviving length: 64mm. N. Crummy's Type 3, third to fourth century A.D.
DV–9877 BH PVII *c.* A.D. 250–270 Phase III deposits

No. 49 Pin with small ovoid head. Shaft tapers towards the head and the point is broken away. N. Crummy's Type 3. Surviving length: 60mm. — DV–2309 — PH 71 — PVIII *c.* A.D. 270 — Demolition deposits

No. 50 Pin with a plain rounded head. The shaft has a circular cross-section and tapers towards the point, which has broken away. Surviving length: 49mm. N. Crummy's Type 1 (Ref. 16), dated later-first to earlier-third century A.D. — DV–1179 — PH 71 — PVIII *c.* A.D. 270 — Demolition deposits

No. 51 Pin with a small spherical head. The shaft tapers towards the head and the point has broken away. Surviving length: 55mm. N. Crummy's Type 3, dated third to fourth century A.D. — DV–3074 — BH — PVIII *c.* A.D. 270 — Dumped deposits

No. 52 Simple pin with two grooves cut below a conical head. The shaft has a circular cross-section and the point is broken away. Surviving length 107mm. N. Crummy's Type 2 (Ref. 17) dated first to earlier-third century A.D. — DV–9829 — BH — PVII *c.* A.D. 230–250 — Phase II deposits

No. 53 Long needle with the head and part of the eye missing. The shaft is circular in cross-section and tapers towards the point. It is broken into three pieces but has an overall length of 123mm. — DV–9971 — BH — PVII *c.* A.D. 230–250 — Phase II deposits

Objects of Shale (Fig. 26, No. 54).

No. 54 About one third of a plain shale bracelet with an oval cross-section. The internal diameter of the piece is about 67mm. — DV–9890 — BH — PVII *c.* A.D. 250–270 — Phase III deposits

Objects of Glass (Fig. 26, Nos. 55 & 56).

No. 55 Fragment of a bowl of light olive green glass, with a slightly outcurved flattened tubular rim, folded outwards and downwards. — DV–9941 — BH — PV *c.* A.D. 180–200 — Robber-Trench deposits

No. 56 Rim and neck of a bottle of light olive green glass, with traces of two opposed handles just below the rim. Outcurved rim folded upwards and inwards. Surfaces irridescent and pitted. — DV–3034 — BH — PVIII *c.* A.D. 270 — Demolition deposits

D. THE SAMIAN WARE (Figs. 27 and 28, Nos. 57–73).

by Joanna Bird, B.A., F.S.A.

The samian examined from the Painted House sites consists of a maximum of 229 identifiable vessels. These include some 54 decorated bowls (including three stamped or signed in the mould) and a further 15 stamped plain vessels. The comments in the following paragraphs are based on these 69 pots, though only the samian from Periods I–VIII is included in the catalogue.

The South Gaulish ware includes only one decorated bowl, a Dr. 29, which could be of pre-Flavian date, a second 29 of early Flavian date and 13 Flavian-Trajanic Dr. 37s, including a signed bowl probably of T. Flavius Secundus (Fig. 27). Trajanic samian from Les Martres-de-Veyre is uncommon, comprising four decorated sherds; there is a decorated bowl and a plain stamp of the later Martres potter Cettus. Lezoux samian of Hadrianic to mid-Antonine date forms the bulk of the stamped and decorated bowls, though the Sacer-Attianus group, Cinnamus and X–6 are the only potters certainly represented by more than one vessel. Apart from stamps of Genitor and Maccalus, a bowl attributed to Casurius and one which may be by Paternus II, the later Antonine potters are absent, suggesting a fall in the use of samian on the site after c. AD 180.

The stamped and decorated East Gaulish wares date from the Hadrianic period to the first half of the third century. The largest number (four) comes from the Argonne, and includes a stamped Dr. 37 by Pacus, a potter not previously known to have made decorated bowls, a bowl in the style of Germanus, and a stamp of Bracisillus. These, and perhaps also the bowl assigned to Censor of Trier, are likely to be of Antonine date, while the unidentified stamp attributed to Chémery or La Madeleine is probably Hadrianic or early Antonine. Only two of the decorated bowls were made at Rheinzabern, by Helenius and perhaps by Comitialis V, and these are probably to be dated within the first half of the third century rather than very much earlier.

The date range indicated by the stamped and decorated samian is confirmed by the plain wares. There is only one definitely pre-Flavian form, a Ritt. 12, and little Les Martres ware; the commonest Central Gaulish form is Dr. 37 (a maximum of 31 sherds), followed by Dr. 18/31 (19), 31 and 33 (18 each). Mid to-late Antonine forms were relatively uncommon: a maximum of three examples of Walters 79, four of Dr. 31R, and two of Dr. 45. East Gaulish plain ware formed only 5% of the total, the most frequent form found being Dr. 45: at least two of the eight examples recovered were in Argonne ware. Among the less common forms present was at least one two-handled beaker with barbotine decoration, probably of form Dr. 53, from Rheinzabern.

The notes on the potter's stamps, including those on decorated vessels, are by Brenda Dickinson and B.R. Hartley.

PERIOD I, Ditch 3. Painted House 1975, (DV–9631).

Dr. 18, South Gaul, Flavian-Trajanic.

PERIOD III, Robber Trench deposits. Bingo Hall (DV–9907, 9953 and 3040).

Dr. 18/31, Central Gaul, Hadrianic.
Dr. 42 dish with barbotine decoration, South Gaul, Flavian.
Dr. 18, South Gaul, Flavian.
Worn South Gaulish cup sherd, second half C1.

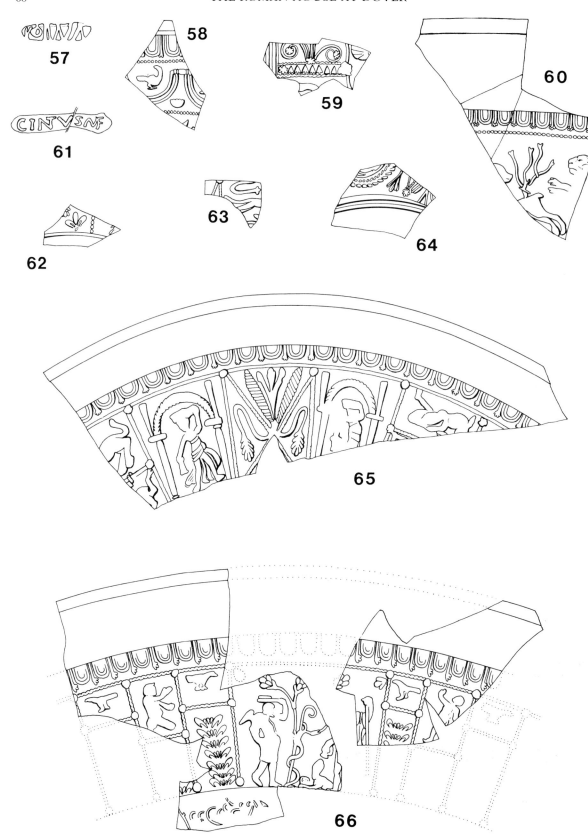

Fig. 27. *Samian; potters stamps Nos. 57 and 61 ($\frac{1}{1}$); decorated sherds ($\frac{1}{2}$).*

PERIOD IV, Tufa Block Building. Bingo Hall, (DV–9875).

Curle 11, South Gaul, Flavian.

PERIOD V, Dumped deposits. Painted House 1975, (DV–9615, 9622 and 9672). Bingo Hall 1976, (DV–3025, 9832, 9948, 9973 and 9976).

Dr. 18/31, Central Gaul, early C2.
Dr. 45, East Gaul, early-mid C3.
Dr. 27, South Gaul, later C1.
Dr. 18, South Gaul, Flavian.
Curle 11, Central Gaul, early-mid C2.
Dr. 18/31, Central Gaul, Hadrianic-early Antonine.
Two Central Gaulish dish sherds.
Dr. 37, Central Gaul; panel design, including festoon above a hare flanked by short leaves. Early-mid Antonine.
No. 57. Dr. 33a, stamped VOMVA Die 2a, Vomuanus (?) of La Graufesenque. (Kiln-site inferred on fabric, distribution etc.) This is clearly by a potter whose other stamp, VOMVN or VOMVAN, appears on vessels at Rottenburg and Wiesbaden. The lettering on the two dies is very similar, but they are almost certainly different, even allowing for the mis-stamping of the Dover piece. If he was literate at all, which is open to doubt, his name must have been Vomuanus, rather than Vomunus, as the Dover stamp shows. The fabric and slip of this cup belong to the Flavian-Trajanic period.
Dr. 37, Central Gaul, later C2.
Closed form, probably Déch. 67, South Gaul, Flavian.
Dr. 27, South Gaul, Flavian-Trajanic.
Dr. 27, South Gaul, Flavian-Trajanic.
Dr. 18/31R or 31R, Central Gaul, mid-later C2.
Dr. 27, South Gaul, Trajanic probably.
Dr. 37, South Gaul. Saltire panel with trifid and corded motifs, basal wreath of palmettes. Later Flavian-Trajanic.
Ritt. 12, South Gaul, Neronian.
Dr. 36 or 42, South Gaul, Flavian.
Dr. 18, South Gaul, Flavian-Trajanic.
Dr. 18/31, Central Gaul, early C2.
Dr. 37 foot, South Gaul, Flavian.
Dr. 18, South Gaul, Flavian-Trajanic.
3 x Dr. 27, South Gaul, Flavian-Trajanic.
2 x South Gaulish cup sherds.
Curle 11, hooked flange, South Gaul, probably Trajanic.
No. 58. Dr. 37, Central Gaul, in the style of Sacer. The ovolo is shown on Stanfield & Simpson (Ref. 18) 1958, pl. 84, No. 15. pl. 82, No. 3, has the bird and festoon, with what is probably the same foliage in its lower frieze as that on this bowl. c. A.D. 125–150.
Dr. 27, South Gaul, later C1.

Period V, Robber-Trench deposits. Bingo Hall 1976, (DV–9935, 9941, 9954, and 9996).

No. 59 Dr. 37, South Gaul. Scroll of deeply toothed leaves; the arcades contain 'spectacle' scrolls over a line of darts, above a small animal. The individual motifs are too common among Flavian potters for certain attribution, but cf. Patricius (Knorr 1952,

taf. 50 top), (Ref. 19) for the leaves and small scroll, and two bowls attributed to
Meddillus or Quintus for similar arcades (Hartley 1972b, Nos. D77–78); (Ref. 20);
Hermet 1934, (Ref 21), pl. 81, No. 7, is the closes parallel for the arcade. *c.* A.D. 75–90.

Dr. 37, South Gaul, with paws of animals at the base. Flavian-Trajanic.

Dr. 27, probably one of the early East Gaulish factories such as La Madeleine;
Hadrianic-early Antonine.

Dr. 18/31, Central Gaul, Hadrianic-Antonine.

Dr. 33 probably, South Gaul, Flavian; burnt and worn.

South Gaulish sherd.

No. 60   Dr. 37, Central Gaul. The motifs all occur on bowls attributed to Donnaucus of Les
Martres-de-Veyre: the ovolo and tree on Stanfield and Simpson (Ref. 18) 1958, pl. 47,
No. 555, the lion and deer on pl. 47, No. 558. *c.* A.D. 100–125.

Dr. 27, South Gaul, Flavian; the stamp has worn away.

Dr. 37, South Gaul; the gladiator is apparently a small version of Oswald 1936–37 (Ref.
22), No. 1088, Flavian.

Dr. 31, stamped [CIИИ]ΛMVƧ. Die 6b', Cinnamus ii of Lezoux. Other dies of the potter
have been found at the pottery but not this one. Die 6b, of which this is probably a
surmoulage, was used on Dr. 27 and 18/31R, and is probably to be dated *c.* A.D.
140–170; a similar date is likely for this.

Dr. 27, Central Gaul, Hadrianic-early Antonine.

Dr. 27, probably one of the early East Gaulish factories such as La Madeleine;
Hadrianic-early Antonine.

Dr. 18 probably, South Gaul, Flavian.

Dr. 38, Central Gaul, mid C2.

Dr. 33, Central Gaul, Antonine.

Dr. 18, South Gaul, Flavian.

Central Gaulish cup sherd.

Central Gaulish dish sherd.

No. 61   Dr. 18/31R stamped CINTVSMF Die 4a, Cintusmus i of Lezoux (other dies have been
found at the pottery). One of his earlier stamps, which appears in the Rhineland, in
the Castleford Pottery shop of A.D. 140–150, and on form 27. His later work occurs
in the Pudding Pan Rock wreck. *c.* A.D. 145–160.

No. 62.   Dr. 37, Central Gaul. Beads and leaf used by X–6 (Stanfield & Simpson 1958 (Ref. 18),
pl. 74, No. 11). *c.* A.D. 130–150; burnt.

Dr. 27, no g, South Gaul, later C1.

Dr. 37, Central Gaul. The ovolo is incomplete, but may be Rogers 1974 (Ref. 23), B15,
used by Drusus II. Hadrianic-early Antonine.

3 x Dr. 33, Central Gaul, Antonine.

Curle 15 or 23, Central Gaul, Antonine.

2 x Dr. 27, Central Gaul, early C2.

Curle 11, Central Gaul, early C2.

No. 63.   Dr. 37, South Gaul, panel with saltire, panel with hound and bud.
Flavian.

No. 64.   Dr. 29, South Gaul. Basal panels with wreath medallion, scrollery and foliage motifs
and a saltire with triple leaf. *c.* A.D. 60–80.

No. 65.   Dr. 37, South Gaul. Four-pronged ovolo tongue, coarse wavy line borders. Panels
containing (a) a lion, probably, above (b) a panther eating its prey, Hermet 1934,
(Ref. 21) pl. 25, No. 33; (c) a maenad, Oswald 1936–37 (Ref. 22) No. 371, in a wreath
arcade supported on columns; (d) a large saltire with triple poppybuds, corded motifs
and toothed leaves; (e) a satyr, Hermet 1934 (Ref. 21), pl. 19, No. 81, in an arcade as
(c); (f) panther as (b), above (g), lost. The arcading is characteristic of late South
Gaulish ware (eg. Holt: Grimes 1930 (Ref. 25), Fig. 38, No. 54; *cf.* Hermet 1934 (Ref.
21), pl. 86, for closely similar vessels. *c.* A.D. 90–110.

Dr. 27, South Gaul, Flavian.

Dr. 31, Central Gaul, tip of stamp]I; Antonine.

Dr. 31, Central Gaul, Antonine.

2 x Dr. 18/31, Central Gaul, Trajanic.

5 x Dr. 18/31, Central Gaul, Antonine.

Dr. 18/31R, Central Gaul, Antonine.

Dr. 31R, Central Gaul, mid-later Antonine.

No. 66   Dr. 37, South Gaul with a cursive signature Şiicunduş] retrograde below the decoration. The reading seems virtually certain, despite the rather straight initial letter. Of the various South Gaulish Secundi, neither Şecundus i (Tiberio-Claudian) nor Secundus ii (Neronian-Vespasianic) fit the decoration. L. Ter(tius?) Secundus, although of the right date, is not known to have made decorated ware, but T Fl(avius) Sec(undus) of La Graufesenque did (Hermet 1934, pl. 24, Nos. 278–279) (Ref. 21) and probably worked at the right period. Further, the ovolo on this bowl is recorded on a mould and on a bowl fragment, both bearing the stamp OFTFLSEC (retrograde) in the decoration (Vernhet and Vertet 1976, Pl. II), (Ref. 24).

Trident-tongued ovolo above panel design: (a) a bird to left, above (b) possibly column of grass tufts, as (i); (c) pan (Hermet 1934, pl. 19, No. 94) (Ref. 21), above (d), probable column of grass tufts; (e) bird to right, above (f) column of grass-tufts; (g) satyr (pl. 19, No. 82) (Ref. 21) and Bacchus with leopard (pl. 19, No. 70) (Ref. 4) separated by a tree; (h) = (a), above (i) = (f); (j) small satyr (pl. 18, No. 42) (Ref. 21) above (k), lost. Other sherds show the satyr from (g) with a tendril above, and a second pair of panels containing columns of grass tufts.

All the figures are on bowls at La Graufesenque, the Bacchus and larger satyr on form 37 (pl. 86, No. 3) (Ref. 21). The pan and smaller satyr on form 78 (pl. 92, No. 13). This assemblage recalls the work of Germanus i, whose characteristic grass tuft, here used in vertical series, confirms the link. Bowls by potters using the Germanus repertoire, and sometimes with vague reminiscences of his style, are not uncommon in the Flavian-Trajanic period. The pendant leaves in the top corner of panel (g) are often used by such potters c. A.D. 90–110.

PERIOD V Wall of Buttressed Building. Bingo Hall 1976, (DV–3057).

Dr. 27, South Gaul, Flavian-Trajanic.

PERIOD VI Painted House 1975, (DV–9613, 9621, 9688). Bingo Hall 1976, (DV–3010, 3038, 3047).

No. 67.   Dr. 37, Central Gaul. The frieze is probably the scroll attributed to Donnaucus (Stanfield & Simpson 1958, pl. 45, No. 517) (Ref. 18). The ornament is Rogers 1974, Q32, (Ref. 23) the figure probably Apollo, Oswald 1936–37, No. 77 (Ref. 22). c. A.D. 100–125.

Dr. 27, Central Gaul, Hadrianic.

Dr. 37, South Gaul, Flavian-Trajanic.

Dr. 18/31, Central Gaul, Trajanic.

Central Gaulish platter sherd.

Dr. 30 or 37, Central Gaul. Cinnamus group ovolo 3a or 3b, finely beaded border. c. A.D. 140–170.

Dr. 18/31 or 31, Central Gaul, C2.

Curle 11, South Gaul, Flavian; the flange has apparently been ground off.

Dr. 33, Central Gaul, Hadrianic.

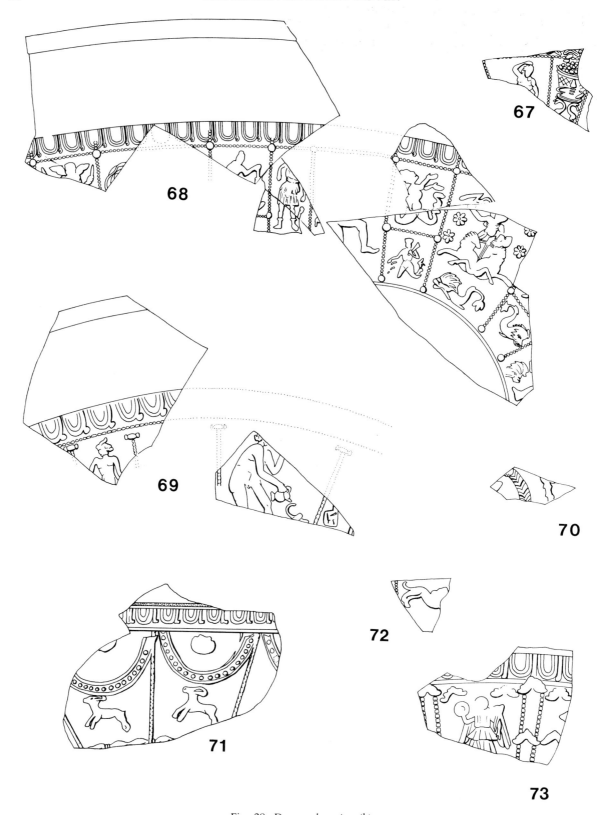

Fig. 28. *Decorated samian* ($\frac{1}{2}$).

Dr. 18, South Gaul, second half C1.
Dr. 27, Central Gaul, Hadrianic.
Dr. 31, Central Gaul, mid C2; slightly burnt.
No. 68. Dr. 37, Central Gaul. Some of the motifs were shared by several Lezoux potters, notably Paternus II, Albucius and Q I Balbinus: the ovolo (Rogers 1974 (Ref. 23), B104 or 105), the rosette (Rogers C144), the amor (Oswald 1936–37, No. 450) (Ref. 22), and the male figure (Oswald No. 650, probably). The tritons are Oswald Nos. 25 and 30, the Diana with bow No. 111 variant, the Diana No. 116, Diana/Luna No. 117 variant, and the dolphins Nos. 2383 and 2394A. *c*. A.D. 150–180.
No. 69. Dr. 37, in the style of Cettus/Satus of Les Martres-de-Veyre. The ovolo, leaf, astragali and Bacchus are shown on Terrisse 1968, pl. 22, No. 521, (Ref. 26), the pan on Stanfield & Simpson 1958 pl. 144, No. 49, (Ref. 18). The fragmentary figure may be a standing Bacchus. *c*. A.D. 135–160.
2 x Dr. 18/31, Central Gaul, mid C2.
Dr. 31, Central Gaul, later Hadrianic-Antonine.
Dr. 18/31, South Gaul, late Flavian-Trajanic.

PERIOD VII Bingo Hall (DV–9858, 9859, 9830, 9986, 9827, 3059, 3032, 9971, 9972, 9824, 3022)

Central Gaulish dish sherd, probably Antonine.
Dr. 31, Central Gaul, Antonine.
Small closed form, Central Gaul, mid C2.
Platter base, South Gaul, Flavian probably.
Dr. 37 probably, Central Gaul, Antonine.
Central Gaulish sherd.
Dr. 18, South Gaul, second half C1.
Curle 15, Central Gaul, Hadrianic-Antonine.
Dr. 18/31, or 31, Central Gaul, Antonine.
Base, large bowl (possibly Curle 21), Central Gaul, Antonine.
No. 70. Dr. 37, South Gaul. Wreath used by Germanus, who also used the small pan (Hermet 1934 pl. 19, No. 94; pl. 102, Nos. 40, 52, 55) (Ref. 21). *c*. A.D. 70–90.
Dr. 31, Central Gaul, Antonine.
Dr. 42, dish with barbotine leaves, South Gaul, Flavian.
Rim, probably from a mortarium or related large bowl; East Gaul, later C2-mid C3.

PERIOD VIII, Demolition deposits. Painted House 1970 and 1971, (DV– 1105, 1189, 2306). Painted House 1975, (DV–9608, 9707, 9711). Bingo Hall 1976, (DV–3005, 9819, 9836, 9887).

Curle 11, hooked flange, Central Gaul, Hadrianic.
Dr. 27, South Gaul, probably Trajanic.
Dr. 33, Central Gaul, Antonine; burnt.
Central Gaulish sherd.
Dr. 18/31, Central Gaul, first half C2.
Platter/dish foot, East Gaul (Argonne), later C2-C4.
Central Gaulish sherd, Hadrianic.
Dr. 31, Central Gaul, Antonine.
Dr. 30, possibly, Central Gaul, Antonine.
Dr. 31R, Central Gaul, mid-later Antonine.

Dr. 33, East Gaul, later C2–mid C3.

2 x Dr. 31, Central Gaul, Antonine; one slightly burnt.

Central Gaulish sherd.

Dr. 37, Central Gaul. Part of large vine leaf, probably from a scroll frieze. Antonine.

Dr. 44 or 38, Central Gaul, Antonine.

Dr. 31R/Lud Sb, East Gaul, later C2-first half C3; burnt.

Mortarium, Central Gaul, late C2.

Mortarium, East Gaul (Argonne), late C2-early C3.

Central Gaulish sherd.

Dr. 37, Central Gaul. The leaf is smaller than Rogers 1974 (Ref. 23), H74, the closest parallel for the shape. Early-mid Antonine, probably.

Dr. 45, East Gaul (Argonne), later C2–C3, probably.

Dr. 37, East Gaul, later C2-mid C3; burnt.

No. 71 Dr. 37, Trier. The ovolo, festoons and astragalus border occur on stamped bowls of Censor (Fölzer 1913, taf. 16, Nos. 11, 12, 20, 26, 27) (Ref. 27). The round motif is probably a large rosette (taf. 16, No. 24). The deer is taf. 30, type No. 621. Later C2-early C3.

Dr. 37, East Gaul (Rheinzabern), late C2–mid C3.

PERIOD VIII, Dumped deposits, Painted House 1971, DV–2371, Painted House 1975, DV–9616, 9619, Bingo Hall, DV–3070, 3072, 3074, 3076

Probably a two-handled vase, as Dr. 53 and Lud VMe (Oswald and Pryce 1920 (Ref. 28), pl. 81) decorated with barbotine ivy leaves. Rheinzabern, later C2-first half C3.

Dr. 33, East Gaul, later C2-early C3.

Dr. 31, Central Gaul, Antonine.

Mortarium, East Gaul, late C2–mid C3; heavily worn.

Mortarium, East Gaul, late C2–mid C3; apparently unworn.

Dr. 31R/Lud Sb, East Gaul, later C2-mid C3.

Dr. 33, Central Gaul, Antonine.

Dr. 37, Central/East Gaul, later C2.

Beaker (as Oswald and Pryce 1920, pl. 79), (Ref. 28) Rheinzabern, later C2-mid C3.

No. 72 Dr. 37, Central Gaul, small lion in panel. Antonine.

No. 73 Dr. 37 in the style of Germanus of Lavoye. The ovolo, double beadrows and foliage motif are shown on Oswald 1945, Fig. 7, No. 7, (Ref. 29). The line beneath the ovolo is on Fölzer 1913, taf. 28, No. 465 (Ref. 27). The victory is apparently a new figure. Mid-late Antonine probably.

Dr. 18/31, South Gaul, Flavian-Trajanic.

Dr. 33, Central Gaul, Antonine.

E. THE MORTARIA, (Fig. 29, Nos. 74–78).

by Katherine Hartley, B.A., F.S.A.

Five mortars were recovered from stratified layers within the Painted House site. These are described and illustrated below. Four fabrics were identified:-

FABRIC 1.
Oxford (Cowley, Headington, Sandford etc.) (Ref. 30). Slightly sandy, off-white fabric occasionally with pink core: The very distinctive trituration consists entirely of mixed pink, brownish and transparent quartz. The texture of this fabric varies according to the amount of tempering: mortaria *c.* A.D. 100–140 have so much, that the fabric can be indistinguishable from the normal one associated with the Verulamium region: some mortaria may be in this fabric up to A.D. 240, but most are in the fine-textured fabric normal in the later period when little or no tempering was the norm.

FABRIC 2.
Probably Kent. Hard, very slightly micaceous, creamy-brown fabric with ill-sorted quartz inclusions: trituration consists of flint, quartz and occasional black (? iron rich) material.

FABRIC 3.
Slightly granular, orange-brown fabric with abundant well-sorted, mainly quartz inclusions: trituration consists of grey flint with occasional quartz and red-brown material.

FABRIC 4.
Import. Very hard, fine-textured, pinkish-brown fabric with mostly quartz inclusions: trituration probably mostly or entirely quartz.

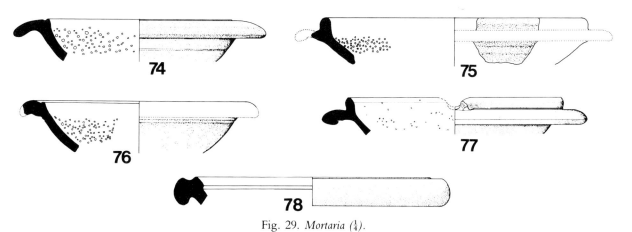

Fig. 29. Mortaria ($\frac{1}{4}$).

Unstamped Vessels

PERIOD V, Dumped deposits. (DV–9976)

No. 74 Fabric 3, a mortarium of Kentish origin, dateable to the very late-first or early-second centuries. Manufacture in Kent was more common in the Antonine period than at any other time but this could be an early rim-form.

PERIOD VI, (Both DV–3047)

No. 75 Fabric 1, an incomplete rim made at Oxford. Form M18/22, dated to A.D. 240–400.
No. 76 Fabric 2, an incomplete rim probably made in Kent, perhaps in the first century but more probably in the second century A.D.

PERIOD VIII, Demolition deposits. (Both DV–1189)

No. 77 Fabric 1, Oxford. Form M18, dated A.D. 240–300.
No. 78 Fabric 4, probably imported from Gallia Belgica within the period A.D. 180–250. Form, Bushe-Fox 26–30 (Ref. 31).

F. THE COARSE POTTERY (Figs. 30–37, Nos. 79–275).

by John Willson, M.I.F.A.

This catalogue contains illustrations and descriptions of 197 pottery vessels from the excavation of the Roman Painted House and the Bingo Hall sites at Dover, excluding either samian or mortaria which are discussed elsewhere in the report.

Of a total of about 2,900 coarse pottery sherds recovered from the stratified deposits under consideration here, just 197 vessels have been selected. These are generally representative of the majority of the significant types and forms recovered from the deposits that relate to some eight main periods. No attempt has been made here to produce a definitive fabric-analysis as this will be the subject of a later study, covering a whole range of Roman pottery from the extensive excavations at Dover, when adequate resources are available (Ref. 32).

The dating of this coarse pottery is largely provided by the associated samian and coins, but also by its relationship to the main periods of occupation of the site. It starts with the first settlement on the site in the late-first century A.D., followed by the contemporary occupation of the adjacent forts of the *Classis Britannica* during the second and very early-third centuries and ends with the demolition and preparation of the site for the construction of the late-Roman shore-fort *c.* A.D. 270. The great majority of the pottery is therefore dated to the second and third centuries with a 'terminal date' of *c.* A.D. 270.

Parallels have been drawn from 26 publications dealing with Roman coarse pottery from many British sites, both local and distant and also including some continental sources, where applicable. The overall date-range for each individual type is generally given, though clearly at Dover a more precise dating is determined by the stratification and related finds.

Abbreviations

The following terms have been used in the following catalogue to identify pottery types of similar form:

RICHBOROUGH I	Nos. (Ref. 33)
SOUTHWARK	Forms/Nos. (Ref. 34)
CANTERBURY (1946)	Nos. (Ref. 35)
DOVER	Nos. (Ref. 36)
COLCHESTER	Form. (Ref. 37)
GILLAM	Types (Ref. 38)
BOULOGNE	Nos. (Ref. 39)
RICHBOROUGH III	Nos. (Ref. 40)
RICHBOROUGH IV	Nos. (Ref. 41)
ANDERSON	Nos. (Ref. 42)
CANTERBURY (1956)	Nos. (Ref. 43)
FAVERSHAM	Nos. (Ref. 44)
RECULVER	Nos. (Ref. 45)
DARENTH	Nos. (Ref. 46)
VERULAMIUM I	Nos. (Ref. 47)
FISHBOURNE	Type (Ref. 48)
HIGHAM	Nos. (Ref. 49)
BRIXWORTH	Nos. (Ref. 50)
RICHBOROUGH II	Nos. (Ref. 51)
CAMULODUNUM	Cam. (Ref. 52)
BILLINGSGATE, LONDON	Nos. (Ref. 53)
NEW FRESH WHARF, LONDON	Nos. (Ref. 54)
LYMPNE	Nos. (Ref. 55)
PORTCHESTER	Types. (Ref. 56)
VERULAMIUM II	Nos. (Ref. 57)
OXFORDSHIRE	Type (Ref. 58)

PERIOD I, Ditch 2 (Fig. 30, No. 79). Bingo Hall 1976, (DV–9839).

No. 79   Carinated beaker with an outcurved rim of fine sandy ware. Grey-brown fabric and a grey surface with traces of burnishing on neck. A similar vessel from Richborough I (Pit 11) is dated to the first half of the second century A.D. The form, however, is generally dated to the late-first century.

PERIOD I, Ditch 3 (Fig. 30, No. 80). Painted House 1971, (DV–2312).

No. 80   Carinated bowl with a reeded flanged rim of sandy ware. Dark grey fabric and surface with a single groove on body. Similar to Southwark Form IV.A.3, dated there to A.D. 80–110.

PERIOD III, Robber-Trench deposits, (Fig. 30, Nos. 81–93). Bingo Hall 1976, (DV–3040, 9907, 9921, 9953 and 9997).

No. 81   Jar with a recessed rim of sandy ware. Light grey fabric and a grey surface. Similar vessels from Canterbury (1946, Nos. 60 and 72) are dated to A.D. 90–120.

No. 82   Lid with an angular rim of sandy ware. Pink fabric and a cream surface.

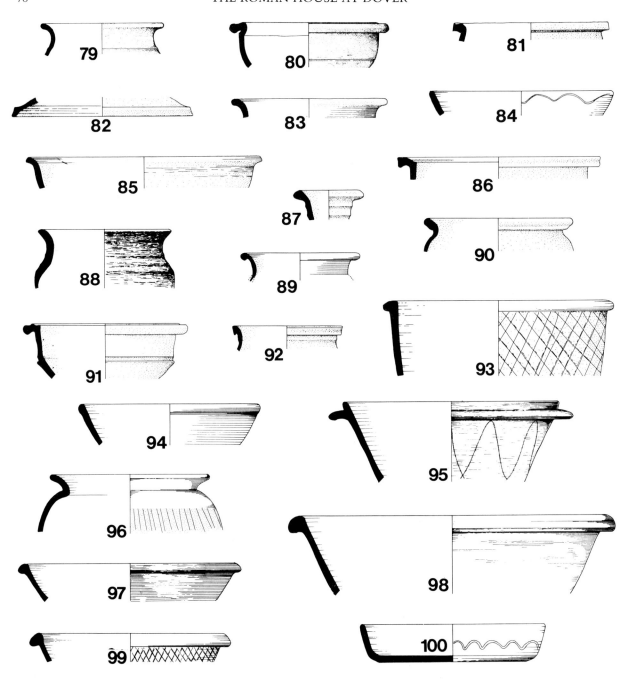

Fig. 30. *Coarse pottery* ($\frac{1}{4}$), *from Periods I, III and IV*.

No. 83 Jar with an outcurved rim of sandy ware. Dark grey fabric and a brown surface with burnishing to neck and inside rim.

No. 84 Shallow dish with straight sides and a plain rim of sandy ware. Grey fabric and surface, burnished all over and is decorated with a wavy line to exterior. B.B.2. Similar vessels from Southwark (Form IV.J.2) are dated to *c.* A.D.140 + but probably more common in the later Antonine period.

No. 85 Bowl with an outcurved rim of slightly gritted sandy ware. Dark grey fabric with a dark grey interior and a buff coloured exterior. Burnishing on inside of rim and a burnished horizontal band on exterior.

No. 86 Bowl with a horizontal reeded rim of sandy ware. Creamy-buff fabric and surface. Probably a Canterbury product dating to the early-second century A.D.

No. 87 Flagon with a triangular rim and a ring neck of sandy ware. Orange-buff fabric and surface. Similar to Southwark (Form I.B.2) dated Flavian-early Hadrianic.

No. 88 Hand-made carinated jar with an outcurved rim of slightly grog-tempered ware. Black fabric and surface with burnishing to exterior and inside of rim. A local copy of a carinated beaker typical of the second half of the first century A.D.

No. 89 Jar with an outcurved slightly rolled rim of sandy ware. Dark grey fabric and surface with burnishing to neck and inside rim. Probably dated to the late-first and early-second centuries A.D.

No. 90 Jar with an everted, thickened rim of slightly gritted, sandy ware. Grey fabric and surface.

No. 91 Carinated bowl with a horizontal reeded rim of sandy ware. Pinkish-buff fabric and surface with a groove and a cordon below, at the carination. Similar vessels at Boulogne (Nos. 45 and 46) are dated from *c.* A.D. 70–120.

No. 92 Jar with a slightly outcurved, squared rim of smooth sandy ware. Buff fabric and surface. surface.

No. 93 Deep dish with a heavy bead rim of sandy ware. Dark grey fabric and surface. Black burnished all over with acute lattice pattern decoration to exterior. B.B.2. Similar to Southwark (Form IV.H.4) *c.* A.D. 130–140+, but probably more common in the later-Antonine period.

Period IV, Tufa Block Building, (Fig. 30, Nos. 94–100). Painted House 1975, (DV–9645). Bingo Hall 1976, (DV–3023, 9866, 9870, 9875).

No. 94 Dish with an upright grooved rim of sandy ware. Dark grey fabric and surface, black burnished all over. B.B.2. These straight-sided dishes occur frequently in association with both bead rim dishes (as No. 97) and the everted rim jar/cooking-pots (as No. 96), in Kent at Reculver, Faversham, Darenth and Dover in second and third century contexts. They appear at Colchester (Form 40), dated A.D. 130 and onwards; at Southwark (Nos. 1677 and 1696) dated to the late-second to early-third centuries. In Northern Britain they are dated A.D. 140–200 (Gillam Type 234).

No. 95 Dish with a flanged rim of slightly gritted sandy ware. Dark grey fabric with some small white grit inclusions and a dark grey surface. Burnished black all over and decorated with intersecting arcs. B.B.1. Similar vessels from Dover (No. 447) in contexts dated *c.* A.D. 240–250; Colchester (Form 305) where they are dated *c.* A.D. 240–400 and in Northern Britain (Gillam Type 228) A.D. 290–370. Clearly at Dover these vessels appear between the mid to late-third century.

No. 96 Cooking-pot with an everted rim of sandy ware. Dark grey fabric and surface. Burnished black to rim and shoulder and decorated with diagonal burnished lines on body. B.B.2. These everted rim jars/cooking-pots are often found directly associated with bead rim dishes (as No. 97) and straight-sided dishes (as No. 94), in Kent at Reculver, Faversham, Darenth and Dover in mid-second and early-third century contexts. They appear at Southwark (Form II.F.6 and II.F.7) during the late-second century. In Northern Britain they are dated to A.D. 160–280 (Gillam Type 143/144).

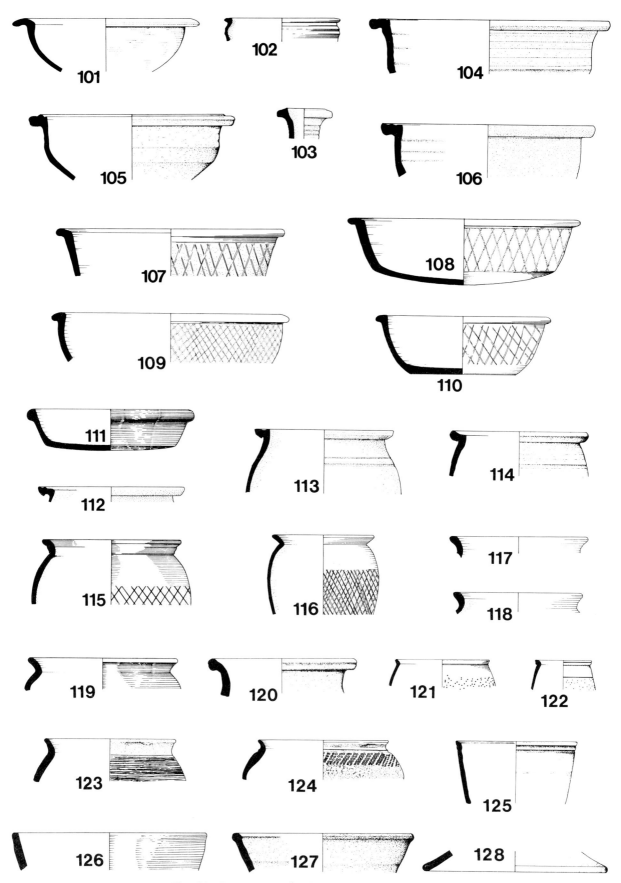

Fig. 31. Coarse pottery (¼), from Period V dumped deposits.

No. 97 Dish with a bead rim of sandy ware. Dark grey-black fabric and black burnished all over. B.B.2. The bead rim pie dishes were introduced early in the second century, consisting of both decorated and undecorated forms. The vessels tend to become coarse, plain, thicker and with much more pronounced rims by the end of the century. They are often found in association with the straight-sided dish (as No. 94) and the everted rim jar/cooking-pots (as No. 96). In Kent at Reculver, Faversham, Darenth and Dover they are found in mid-second and early-third century contexts. This particular vessel can be paralled at Southwark (Form IV.H.6) and is dated to the late-second century A.D.

No. 98 Dish with a heavy bead rim of sandy ware. Grey fabric and surface, burnished black all over. B.B.2. Similar to vessels from Dover (No. 525) dated A.D. 200–250 and Southwark (Form IV.H.7) where they are dated to the later-second century A.D.

No. 99 Dish with a bead rim of sandy ware. Grey fabric and surface. Burnished all over and decorated with acute lattice pattern. B.B.2. Similar to vessels from Dover (No. 553) and Southwark (Form IV.H.2) dated *c.* A.D. 130–140+.

No. 100 Straight-sided dish with an upright rim and a chamfered base of sandy ware. Dark grey fabric and surface. Burnished all over and decorated with wavy line pattern to exterior. B.B.2. Southwark (Form IV.J.2) dated *c.* A.D. 120–130+.

PERIOD V, Dumped deposits (Fig. 31 Nos. 101–128). Bingo Hall (DV– 3025, 9832, 9948, 9976, 9999). Painted House 1975 (DV–9615, 9622, 9672, 9686).

No. 101 Dish with an outcurved rim of sandy ware. Dark grey fabric and grey surface with faint traces of burnishing all over. A similar range of vessels from Richborough III (Nos. 214–221) are dated from the mid-first to the early-second centuries A.D.

No. 102 Small squat bowl with a horizontal triangular rim of fine smooth sandy ware. Grey fabric and surface. Decorated with cordons and grooves around girth and burnishing to exterior. Probably dated to the second-half of the first century A.D.

No. 103 Ring-necked flagon with a slightly downturned horizontal rim of hard sandy ware. Buff-red fabric and surface, the vessel is covered in a creamy-yellow slip. The style of a heavy rim with faint rings on the neck is a late feature in ring-neck flagons and would appear to be of Hadrianic date. The fabric and creamy slip indicates that the vessel may be a product from the Verulamium region.

No. 104 Bowl with a reeded flanged rim of sandy ware. Creamy-white fabric and surface with a faint carination towards the base of the vessel. Similar vessels from Southwark (Form IV.A.3) are dated *c.* A.D. 80–110.

No. 105 Bowl with a reeded flanged rim of sandy ware. Cream-buff fabric and cream surface. A similar vessel from Boulogne (No. 47) is dated *c.* A.D. 80–150.

No. 106 Bowl with a reeded flanged rim of sandy ware. Grey fabric and dark grey surface. Similar to Southwark (Form IV.A.5) where they are dated A.D. 115–150.

No. 107 Dish with a slightly hooked rim of gritty sandy ware. Black fabric with small sub-angular flint grits, brown interior and a grey-black exterior. Burnished all over with a lattice decoration to exterior. B.B.1. Southwark (Form IV.G.2) A.D. 120–150+.

No. 108 Dish with a slightly hooked rim of gritty sandy ware. Grey-black fabric with small sub-angular flint grits and black surface. Burnished black all over with lattice pattern decoration to body. B.B.1. Similar to No. 107 dated A.D. 120–150+.

No. 109 Dish with a bead rim of sandy ware. Dark grey-brown fabric and surface. Burnished all over, black internally and black-brown externally. Decorated with acute lattice pattern. B.B.2. Similar to No. 99, dated to A.D. 130–140+.

No. 110 Dish with a beaded rim and a chamfered base of slightly gritted sandy ware. Dark grey fabric and brown surface. Black burnished all over and decorated with acute lattice pattern to body. B.B.2. Similar to No. 99 dated *c.* A.D. 130–140+.

No. 111 Shallow dish with a large beaded rim of sandy ware. Dark grey-brown fabric and dark grey surface with traces of black burnishing all over. Similar vessels from Dover (No. 423) were found in contexts dated *c.* A.D. 150–180, at Southwark (Form IV.H.5) is dated to the late-second century A.D.

No. 112 Jar with a horizontal reeded rim of hard sandy ware. Dark grey fabric with a blue-grey surface. Similar vessels from Canterbury (1946), No. 83 and Dover (No. 463) are dated *c.* A.D. 100–150.

No. 113 Jar with a recessed rim of hard granular sandy ware. Dark grey fabric and surface with two horizontal grooves on shoulder. Similar vessels from Canterbury (1946 No. 71) and Dover (No. 710) date to A.D. 100–150.

No. 114 Jar with a recessed rim of slightly gritty sandy ware. Grey fabric and surface. Similar to No. 113 dated A.D. 100–150.

No. 115 Cooking-pot with an outcurved and thickened rim of sandy ware. Light grey fabric and grey surface. Burnishing to rim and shoulder with burnished acute lattice pattern to body. Similar vessels from Dover (No. 572) and from Northern Britain (Gillam Types 125–129) are dated to A.D. 120–180.

No. 116 Jar with an everted rim of sandy ware. Dark grey fabric and interior whilst the exterior is brown. Burnishing to shoulder, neck and inside rim and is decorated with lattice pattern on body. B.B.2. Similar to Southwark (Form II.F.12) where it is dated *c.* A.D. 120–200.

No. 117 Jar with an outcurved rim of slightly gritted sandy ware. Black fabric and burnished black to exterior and inside rim. Heavily sooted. Dated from the mid to late-second century A.D.

No. 118 Jar with an outcurved thickened rim of sandy ware. Creamy-grey fabric and a dark grey-black surface with burnishing to exterior and inside rim. Dated to the mid-second century A.D.

No. 119 Cooking-pot with an everted rim of sandy ware. Dark grey fabric and a black-brown surface with black burnishing to rim and shoulder. Similar to No. 96, dated to A.D. 160–280.

No. 120 Cooking-pot with a heavy outcurved grooved rim of sandy ware. Dark grey fabric and surface.

No. 121 Rough-cast beaker with an angular rim of fine ware. White fabric with a 'metallic' grey-brown surface slip. It has a plain zone below the rim, followed by a zone of rough-cast decoration to the body. Probably a Nene Valley product similar to Dover (No. 769) generally dated to the second century and on.

No. 122 Rough-cast beaker with a grooved rim of fine sandy ware. Hard red fabric with a 'metallic' grey colour-coated surface. Plain zone below the rim followed by a groove and rough-cast decoration to the body. Similar vessels from Colchester (Form 391A) date from A.D. 120+ and at Dover (No. 414) from contexts dated A.D. 150–180.

No. 123 Cooking-pot with a slightly outcurved thinned rim of grog-tempered ware. Dark grey fabric with grey grog inclusions and a dark grey-black surface. Burnishing to neck and inside rim with horizontal combing to shoulder. A copy of a native ware type and bears some similarities to a vessel from Dover (No. 581), which was found in contexts dated A.D. 160–180.

No. 124 Cooking-pot with a slightly outcurved rim of grog-tempered ware. Light grey fabric with grey grog inclusions and dark grey-black surface. Traces of burnishing to neck with a zone of stick-stabbing to shoulder. A similar ware and vessel to No. 123. Probably a native product or copy.

No. 125 Beaker with an upright grooved rim of fine sandy ware. Buff-orange fabric and surface, decorated with two grooves below the rim and a further faint groove on the body.

No. 126 Dish with a plain upright rim of grog-tempered ware. Dark grey fabric with off-white and grey grog inclusions and a dark grey surface. Black burnished exterior with an uneven surface finish.

No. 127 Dish with an upright and slightly thickened rim of sandy ware. Whitish-grey fabric and a light grey surface.

No. 128 Pot-lid of sandy ware. Grey-brown fabric and a dark grey surface.

PERIOD V, Robber Trench deposits, (Fig. 32, Nos. 129–158). Bingo Hall 1976, (DV–9923, 9935, 9941, 9954, 9996).

No. 129 Miniature dish with a horizontally flanged rim of soft sandy ware. Light grey fabric and grey surface. A similar vessel from Richborough IV (No. 452) is dated to A.D. 75–100.

No. 130 Dish with a bead rim of sandy ware. Buff-brown fabric and surface. A similar vessel from Richborough I (No. 86) is dated to the first century A.D.

No. 131 Dish with a bead rim and chamfered base of sandy ware. Dark grey fabric and surface. Burnished black all over and decorated with acute lattice pattern. B.B.2. Similar to Dover (No. 507) dated A.D. 70–170.

No. 132 Dish with a bead rim of sandy ware. Black fabric and surface. Black burnished and decorated with acute lattice pattern. B.B.2. Similar to Dover (No. 504) and Southwark (Form IV.H.1) dated c. A.D. 130 and on.

No. 133 Dish with a bead rim of sandy ware. Grey fabric and dark grey surface. Burnished all over and decorated with acute lattice pattern. B.B.2. Similar to No. 132 dated c. A.D. 130 and on.

No. 134 Dish with a bead rim of sandy ware. Black fabric and surface. Black burnished and decorated with acute lattice pattern. B.B.2. Similar to No. 132, c. A.D. 130 and on.

No. 135 Dish with a bead rim and a chamfered base of sandy ware. Dark grey fabric and surface. Black burnished all over and decorated with acute lattice pattern. B.B.2. Similar to No. 132. Dated c. A.D. 130 and on.

No. 136 Deep dish with a bead rim and a chamfered base of sandy ware. Black fabric and surface. Black burnished all over and decorated with acute lattice pattern. B.B.2. Similar to Southwark (Form IV.H.4) dated c. A.D. 140+ but probably more common in the later-Antonine period.

No. 137 Dish with a bead rim and chamfered base of sandy ware. Light grey fabric and surface. Burnished all over and decorated with vertical line pattern. B.B.2. Similar to Dover (No. 431); Southwark (Form IV.H.1) and in Northern Britain (Gillam Type 310) date range A.D. 130–210.

No. 138 Dish with a plain slightly inturned rim of sandy ware. Grey fabric and buff surface with mica-dusted finish. Southwark (Form IV.J.3) dated to the first half of the second century A.D.

No. 139 Rough-cast beaker with a cornice rim of Castor ware. White fabric, surface coated with a grey-brown 'metallic' colour-coat with rough-cast decoration to body. Similar to Dover (No. 417) where it was found in contexts dated c. A.D. 150–180.

No. 140 Rough-cast beaker with a cornice rim of Castor ware. White fabric with small quantities of red ironstone inclusions. Brown-red colour-slip on surface, with a plain zone between rim and rough-cast. Similar to No. 139 dated A.D. 150–180.

No. 141 Rough-cast beaker with a cornice rim of Castor ware. White fabric, surface coated with a grey 'metallic' colour-coat. Rough-cast decoration to body. Similar to No. 139 dated A.D. 150–180.

No. 142 Beaker with a grooved rim of fine ware. Orange-grey fabric coated with a dark grey 'metallic' colour-slip. Source uncertain but probably British. Similar to Colchester (Form 391A) where it is dated A.D. 120 and on.

No. 143 Rough-cast globular beaker with a high outcurved rim of colour-coated fine ware. White fabric with a 'metallic' dark grey surface with rough-cast decoration to body. Probably imported from the Lower Rhineland see Anderson, (Fig. 8, No. 2) dated c. A.D. 130–180.

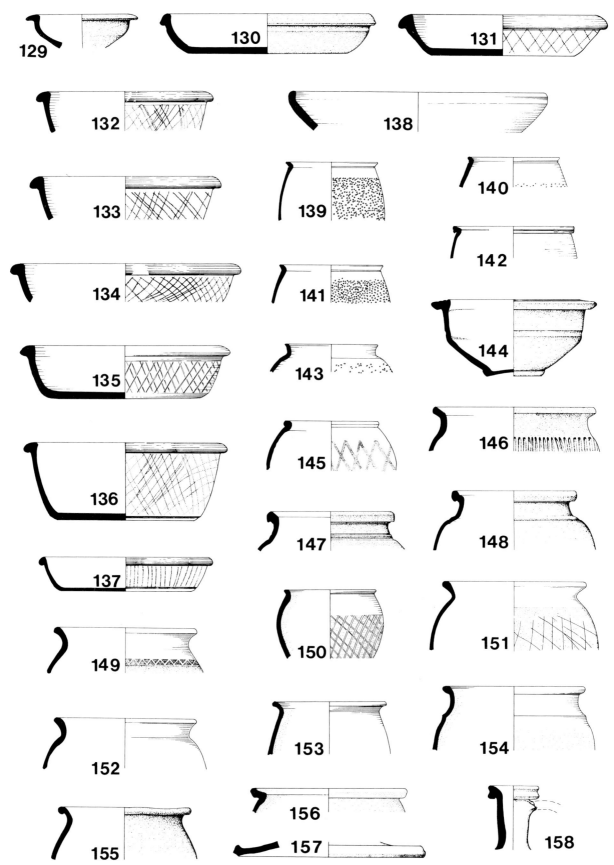

Fig. 32. Coarse pottery ($\frac{1}{4}$), from Period V robber-trenches.

No. 144 Carinated bowl with a reeded flanged rim of sandy ware. Grey fabric and surface with a groove on body above carination. Similar to Southwark (Form IV.A.6) dated to *c.* A.D. 120–150.

No. 145 Squat jar with a bead rim of sandy ware. Light grey fabric and dark grey surface with burnishing to rim, shoulder and body and decorated with lattice pattern. Probably a product from the North Kent Marsh/Upchurch Marsh kilns, and dating from the late-first to early-second centuries A.D.

No. 146 Cooking-pot with a bevelled rim of sandy ware. Grey fabric and dark grey surface. Burnished neck and rim with vertical tooling on shoulder. Similar vessels from Dover (No. 723) and Boulogne (Type 75) are dated from the late-first to mid-second centuries A.D.

No. 147 Cooking-pot with a bevelled rim of sandy ware. Dark grey fabric and surface with two grooves on neck.

No. 148 Cooking-pot with an outcurved recessed rim of sandy ware. Dark grey fabric and surface with a cordon on the shoulder. Heavily sooted.

No. 149 Jar with an outcurved rim of sandy ware. Grey fabric and dark grey surface with burnishing to rim and shoulder with a thin zone of zig-zag decoration. Probably dates from the early to late-second century A.D.

No. 150 Small jar with an outcurved rim of sandy ware. Dark grey fabric and surface with burnishing to shoulder and inside rim and lattice decoration to body. B.B.2. Southwark (Form II.A.17) dated *c.* A.D. 130–200.

No. 151 Jar with an everted rim of sandy ware. Grey fabric and surface with burnishing to rim and shoulder with a crude zone of lattice pattern decoration to body. Similar to Dover (No. 752) and Gillam (Type 139). Date range A.D. 150–250.

No. 152 Jar with an everted rim of sandy ware. Grey-brown fabric and surface with burnishing to rim and shoulder. Similar to No. 151. Dated A.D. 150–250.

No. 153 Jar with an outcurved rim of sandy ware. Dark grey fabric and grey surface with burnishing to exterior and inside rim. A similar vessel from Dover No. 674 was found in contexts dating to the late-second to early-third centuries A.D.

No. 154 Cooking-pot with an outcurved rim and cordon on shoulder of sandy ware. Dark grey fabric and surface with burnishing on shoulder, neck and inside rim.

No. 155 Jar with an outcurved rolled rim of sandy ware. Grey fabric and dark grey surface.

No. 156 Jar with a recessed rim of sandy ware. Dark grey fabric and surface. Similar to Dover (No. 711) where it is dated from the late-first to early-second centuries A.D.

No. 157 Pot-lid of sandy ware. Grey-brown fabric and surface. Similar to Dover (No. 882) probably Antonine.

No. 158 Single-handled flagon with a collared rim of fine soft ware. Buff-white fabric and surface. Stub of handle immediately below rim. Similar vessels were being produced at the Whitehall Garden kilns at Canterbury *c.* A.D. 130–160 (Canterbury (1956) No. 5); at Boulogne (Type 13) similar vessels also date to the mid-second century A.D.; at Dover (No. 848) a similar vessel was found in contexts dated A.D. 160–210.

PERIOD V, from Walls and Occupation deposits, Buttressed Building, (Fig. 33 Nos. 159–161). Bingo Hall (DV–3054, 3057, 9871).

No. 159 Jar with an everted rim of sandy ware. Dark grey fabric, grey-brown interior and dark grey-black exterior. Black burnishing to shoulder and inside rim with lattice decoration to body. B.B.2. Southwark (Form II.F.10) dated *c.* A.D. 120–200.

No. 160 Dish with a bead rim of sandy ware. Grey fabric and grey-brown surface with a burnished black exterior and decorated with lattice pattern. Similar to Dover (No. 507). Dated A.D. 70–170.

No. 161 Straight-sided dish with a plain upright rim of sandy ware. Dark grey fabric and surface and black burnished all over. Similar vessels at Colchester (Form 40), are dated after A.D. 120.

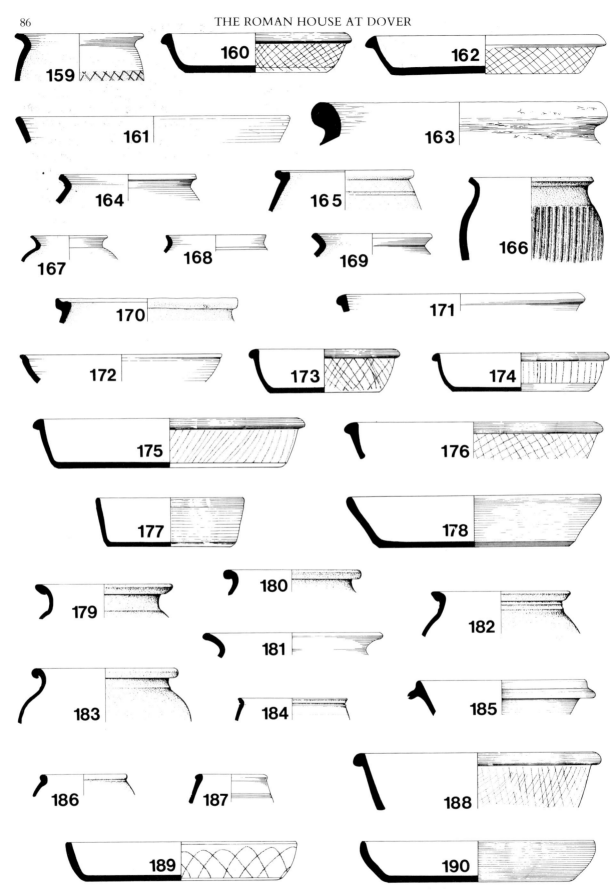

Fig. 33. *Coarse pottery (¼), from Period V Buttressed Building and Period VI deposits.*

PERIOD VI, (Fig. 33, Nos. 162–190). Painted House 1975, (DV–9613, 9620, 9622, 9669). Bingo Hall 1976, (DV–3038, 3047).

No. 162 Shallow dish with a bead rim of sandy ware. Dark grey fabric and surface. Black burnished all over and decorated with lattice pattern. B.B.2. Similar to No. 132 above, dated A.D. 130+.

No. 163 Storage jar with a heavy rolled rim of grog-tempered ware. Buff-brown fabric and surface with a lightly burnished or smoothed finish.

No. 164 Jar with an everted rim of sandy ware. Grey-brown fabric and dark grey-black surface with burnishing to exterior and inside rim. Dated probably second century A.D.

No. 165 Jar with a recessed rim of granular sandy ware. Brown fabric and dark grey surface. It has a horizontal groove on the body. Similar to No. 113, dated A.D. 100–150.

No. 166 Cooking-pot with a bevelled rim of sandy ware. Grey fabric and dark grey surface. Burnished on neck and rim with vertical tooling on body. Similar to No. 146 dated late-first to mid-second centuries A.D.

No. 167 An ovoid beaker with an outcurved rim with a small groove at neck. Smooth sandy ware with a grey-brown fabric and grey surface, light burnishing to shoulder and inside rim. A similar vessel from Dover (No. 477) was found in contexts dated A.D. 150–200.

No. 168 Globular beaker with a high outcurved rim of colour-coated fine ware. White fabric and 'metallic' grey colour-slip surface. A similar vessel from Dover (No. 835) was found in contexts dated A.D. 160–210. Probably imported.

No. 169 Jar with an everted rim of hard sandy ware. Orange-buff fabric and dark brown-grey surface. Burnished to exterior and inside rim. Probably dated mid-second to mid-third centuries A.D.

No. 170 Jar with a recessed rim of coarse sandy ware. Grey fabric and dark grey granular surface. A similar vessel from Canterbury (1946) (No. 72) is from contexts dated to A.D. 100–150.

No. 171 Dish with a bead rim of sandy ware. Dark grey fabric and surface and burnished all over. B.B.2. Similar to No. 97, dated to the late-second century A.D.

No. 172 Shallow dish with a slightly beaded rim of sandy ware. Grey fabric and surface and burnished silver-grey all over. A similar vessel from Southwark (No. 1403) is dated to the first century A.D.

No. 173 Dish with a bead rim of sandy ware. Light grey fabric and grey surface. Burnished grey all over and decorated with acute lattice pattern. B.B.2. Similar to No. 132 dated A.D. 130 and on.

No. 174 Dish with a bead rim and chamfered base of sandy ware. Light grey fabric and surface. Grey burnished all over and decorated with vertical line pattern. Similar to No. 137, dated A.D. 130–210.

No. 175 Dish with a bead rim and chamfered base of sandy ware. Dark brown fabric and dark grey surface. Black burnished all over and decorated with diagonal line pattern. B.B.2. Similar vessels from Dover (No. 390) and Southwark (Form IV.H.3) are dated A.D. 140–180.

No. 176 Dish with a bead rim of sandy ware. Light grey fabric and grey surface. Burnished grey all over and decorated with acute lattice pattern. B.B.2. Similar to No. 99 above dated *c.* A.D. 130–140+.

No. 177 Dish with an upright, slightly grooved rim and a chamfered base of sandy ware. Dark grey fabric and surface. Burnished all over with a dark grey interior and a grey-brown exterior. B.B.2. Similar to Dover (No. 474) dated A.D. 140–200.

No. 178 Deep dish with a plain upright rim and a chamfered base of sandy ware. Dark grey fabric and a grey-brown surface, burnished all over. B.B.2. Similar to vessels from Dover (No. 670) from contexts dated A.D. 190–208.

No. 179 Cooking-pot with an outcurved slightly rolled rim of sandy ware. Grey-brown fabric and dark grey surface. Similar vessels from Dover (No. 470) and Faversham (No. 248) are dated from the late-second to early-third centuries A.D.

No. 180 Jar with an outcurved, slightly rolled rim of sandy ware. Grey fabric and dark grey surface.

No. 181 Cooking-pot with a cavetto rim of sandy ware. Grey-brown fabric and surface with burnishing to exterior and inside rim. B.B.1.? Similar vessels from Dover (No. 542) and from Colchester (Form 279B) are dated *c.* A.D. 200–300. Here an early to mid-third century date seems likely.

No. 182 Jar with an angular rim of sandy ware. Dark grey fabric and surface with two small cordons on neck.

No. 183 Cooking-pot with a rolled rim of sandy ware. Grey-brown fabric and dark grey surface with a faint cordon on neck. Similar vessels from Reculver (No. 3) and Dover (Nos. 440–443) are dated generally from the mid-second and third centuries A.D.

No. 184 Beaker with a cornice rim of fine ware. White fabric and a 'metallic' grey slip. Probably imported, generally dated to the Antonine period.

No. 185 Dish with a downturned flanged rim of sand, grit and grog-tempered ware. Dark grey fabric with brown and black grog inclusions and some fine brown grits. Dark grey-black surface and a black burnished finish. These flanged rim dishes first start appearing in the middle of the third century, becoming common by the late-third and throughout the fourth centuries A.D. Typical examples can be compared from a wide area, for example Darenth (No. 191); Southwark (No. 1281); Verulamium I (Nos. 1162–1169) and Fishbourne (Type 356). At Higham (Nos. 22–28) similar vessels were probably manufactured there at or about *c.* A.D. 240.

No. 186 Small jar with a bead rim of sandy ware. Grey fabric and surface with burnishing to rim and exterior and is probably a North Kent Marsh or Upchurch Marsh product. A similar vessel from Canterbury (1946), No. 95, is probably dated to the late-first century A.D.

No. 187 Beaker with a slightly beaded rim of fine sandy ware. Pale orange fabric and surface. Grey metallic colour-slip all over with two grooves around the body.

No. 188 Dish with a bead rim of sandy ware. Grey fabric and surface, burnished all over with acute lattice design to body. B.B.2. A similar vessel from Dover (No. 540) was found in contexts dated A.D. 210–270 and at Brixworth (No. 35) where it is dated A.D. 150–250.

No. 189 Dish with an upright rim of slightly gritted sandy ware. Dark grey fabric with some white grit inclusions and a grey-brown surface. Burnished all over and exterior decorated with intersecting arcs. B.B.1. These dishes appear at the end of the second century and are common on many sites over a wide area for example: At Dover (Nos. 499 and 637) they were found in deposits dated A.D. 210–270. At Southwark (Form IV.J.1) a date range of A.D. 190–340 is given, whilst in Northern Britain (Gillam Type 329) they are dated A.D. 190–340. Here they were found in deposits dated *c.* A.D. 200–250.

No. 190 Dish with curved sides and a plain pointed rim of sandy ware with some grog inclusions. Grey fabric and surface, burnished all over. Dated by association to *c.* A.D. 200–250.

PERIOD VII, (Clay Building), (Fig. 34, Nos. 191–219). Bingo Hall 1976, (DV–3001, 3021, 3035, 3036, 3043, 3049, 3059, 9824, 9837, 9858, 9859, 9864, 9865, 9877, 9893, 9896, 9972, 9982, 9998).

No. 191 Dish with a slightly flanged beaded rim of sandy ware. Light grey fabric and grey surface. Black burnished all over and decorated with lattice pattern. B.B.1. This vessel is a variant of Southwark (Forms IV.G.1/IV.G.2) where they are dated to A.D. 120–150+.

No. 192 Dish with a bead rim of sandy ware. Dark grey fabric and brown surface, black burnished all over. B.B.2. Similar to No. 97 above, dated from the late-second century A.D.

No. 193 Dish with a bead rim and a chamfered base of sandy ware. Dark grey-brown fabric and surface with black burnishing all over. B.B.2. Similar to No. 98, dated from the late-second century to *c.* A.D. 250.

No. 194 Dish with a bead rim of sandy ware. Brown-black fabric and surface, burnished all over. B.B.2. Similar to No. 98 dated from the late-second century to *c.* A.D. 250.

No. 195 Dish with a bead rim of sandy ware. Dark grey fabric and grey-brown surface, burnished all over. B.B.2. Similar to No. 97 dated from the late-second century A.D.

No. 196 Straight sided dish with a plain upright rim and a chamfered base of sandy ware. Dark grey fabric and surface, burnished all over and decorated with two rows of wavy line pattern to the exterior. B.B.2. Similar vessels at Verulamium I (Nos. 735 and 1007) are dated *c.* A.D. 130–160 and at Southwark (Form IV.J.2), *c.* A.D. 120–130+.

No. 197 Dish with an upright grooved rim and a chamfered base of sandy ware. Dark grey fabric and a grey-brown surface, black burnished all over and decorated with curvilinear line pattern. B.B.1. Similar vessels from Fishbourne (Type 201.3) and Southwark (No. 1286) are dated to the late-second and third centuries A.D. At Dover (No. 578) they appear in contexts dated A.D. 160–180.

No. 198 Straight-sided dish with a plain upright rim and a chamfered base of sandy ware. Dark grey fabric and surface, burnished all over. B.B.2. Similar to No. 178 dated at Dover to A.D. 190–208.

No. 199 Dish with an upright rim and slightly curved sides with a thickening at the internal junction of the wall and base, of Pompeian Red ware. Buff-brown fabric with red grit inclusions and buff-brown surface. Inside and over the lip of the rim the vessel is coated with a dark red colour-slip. These vessels are usually found on military sites such as Richborough II (No. 161) and Camulodunum (Cam. 17) also at Fishbourne (Type 2) where it is the most common imported platter type. Most were found in pre- A.D. 75 contexts, but the type continued in use into the beginning of the Flavian period.

No. 200 Large bowl with an outcurved rolled rim of sandy ware. Grey fabric and dark grey surface, with burnishing to exterior and inside rim. Probably dated to the late-first to mid-second centuries A.D.

No. 201 Cooking-pot with an outcurved, slightly beaded rim of sandy ware. Grey fabric and dark grey surface. Decorated with burnished horizontal bands on the neck and a cordon on the shoulder. Similar to Southwark (Form II.G.2) where it is dated A.D. 100–150.

No. 202 Flagon with an outcurved beaded rim of fine grog-tempered ware. Light grey fabric, coated with a creamy-buff slip.

No. 203 Deep dish with a bead rim of sandy ware. Dark grey fabric and surface, black burnished all over. B.B.2. Similar to No. 98 dated from the late-second century to *c.* A.D. 250.

No. 204 Dish with a plain upright rim of soft sandy ware. Creamy-buff fabric and surface. Decorated with two external grooves.

No. 205 Dish with a bead rim and chamfered base. Sandy ware with a dark grey fabric and a grey-brown surface. Burnished all over and decorated with diagonal line pattern. B.B.2. Similar to No. 137, dated to A.D. 130–210.

No. 206 Amphora with a downturned rim of fine hard granular ware. Creamy-buff fabric and surface. Camulodunum (Cam. 186). Similar vessels at Billingsgate, London (No. 8) and at Verulamium I (No. 13) are dated *c.* A.D. 80–130.

No. 207 Bowl with an angular rim of North Gaulish ware. Sandy grey fabric and surface with burnishing to rim and bands around body. Imported ware from Northern Gaul. Similar examples can be compared from London, New Fresh Wharf (Fig. 1 Nos. 1–4), where they were found in contexts dated from the mid-second to early-third centuries A.D. and at Boulogne (Types 40 and 41), dated to the second century A.D.

No. 208 Cooking-pot with a cavetto rim of sandy ware. Grey fabric and dark grey surface. Burnished black on rim and shoulder and decorated with lattice pattern on body. B.B.1. These late cooking-pots first appear at Dover (No. 542) in contexts dated A.D. 210–270. At Fishbourne (Type 329) and in Northern Britain (Gillam Type 146) where they are dated *c.* A.D. 260–350.

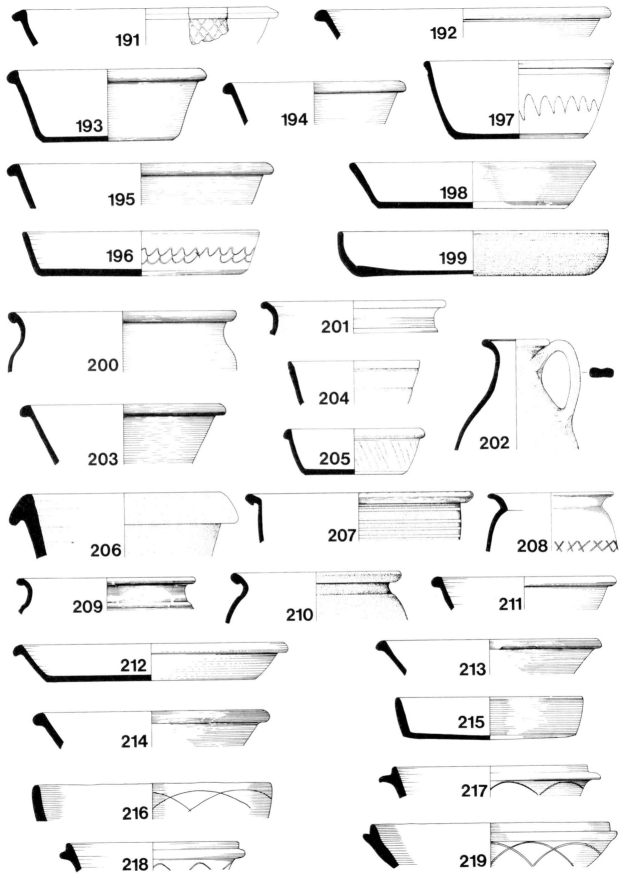

Fig. 34. *Coarse pottery* ($\frac{1}{4}$), *from Period VII deposits.*

No. 209 Jar with an outcurved rim of sandy ware. Grey fabric and grey-brown surface with a burnished black exterior and inside rim, with cordon on neck. Similar in form to Southwark (Form II.G.2) where it is dated A.D. 100–150. This vessel is however, of a North Kent marsh fabric.

No. 210 Jar with an outcurved rolled rim of sandy ware. Brown fabric and grey-brown surface.

No. 211 Dish with a bead rim of sandy ware. Grey-brown fabric and dark grey surface. Burnished silver-grey all over. B.B.2. Similar to No. 98 dated from the late-second century to c. A.D. 250.

No. 212 Dish with a bead rim and a chamfered base of sandy ware. Light grey fabric and dark grey surface, black burnished all over. B.B.2. Similar to No. 111 above, dated A.D. 150–180.

No. 213 Dish with a bead rim of sandy ware. Dark grey fabric and surface, burnished black all over. B.B.2. Similar to No. 111 above dated A.D. 150–180.

No. 214 Dish with a bead rim of sandy ware. Dark grey-brown fabric and surface, burnished black all over. B.B.2. Similar to No. 97 above, dated to the late-second century+.

No. 215 Dish with a plain upright rim of sandy ware. Grey fabric and surface burnished all over. This is a later type of straight-sided dish than No. 178, the wall is thicker near its junction with its base and there is no chamfer. Similar vessels appear at Dover (No. 501) in contexts dated A.D. 210–270 and at Southwark (Nos. 1800 and 1846); Verulamium I (Nos. 1066 and 1129) and Brixworth (No. 16), they generally appear to range in date from about A.D. 200–350. Here they are from contexts dated to the mid to late-third century.

No. 216 Hand-made dish with a plain upright rim of sand, grog and grit tempered ware. Dark grey fabric heavily tempered with grog, mudstone and white grit inclusions. Brown surface which is burnished all over and decorated with intersecting arcs to exterior. This ware appears to be indigenous to late-third and fourth century sites in East Kent, East Sussex and Hampshire and several production centres have been suggested. The ware first appears at Dover during the late-third century and parallels at Lympne (No. 46), Portchester (Type 107) and Richborough I (No. 106) also seem to appear c. A.D. 270–280 and continue in use until about the mid-fourth century. Here these vessels appear in contexts dated c. A.D. 250–270.

No. 217 Dish with a slightly downturned flanged rim of slightly gritted sandy ware. Dark grey with some small white grit inclusions, dark grey surface, burnished all over and decorated with intersecting arc pattern on body. B.B.1. Similar to No. 95, broadly dated A.D. 240–400, but here they are clearly confined to mid to late-third century contexts.

No. 218 Dish with a flanged rim of slightly gritted sandy ware. Dark grey fabric with some small white grit inclusions, and dark grey surface. Burnished all over and decorated with intersecting arc pattern on the body. B.B.1. Similar to No. 95, broadly dated A.D. 240–400, but here they are clearly confined to mid to late-third century contexts.

No. 219 Hand-made dish with a slightly upturned flanged rim of sand, grog and grit-tempered ware. Dark grey fabric heavily tempered with grog, mudstone and white grit inclusions. Brown surface which is burnished all over and decorated with intersecting arcs to exterior. Same fabric as No. 216 and probably manufactured at the same production centre. The ware appears indigenous to late-third and fourth century sites in East Kent, East Sussex and Hampshire. The ware first appears at Dover during the late-third century and parallels at Lympne (No. 45) and Portchester (Type 86), also seem to appear c. A.D. 270–280 and continue in use until about the mid-fourth century. On this particular site the ware appears in contexts dated to the mid to late-third century A.D.

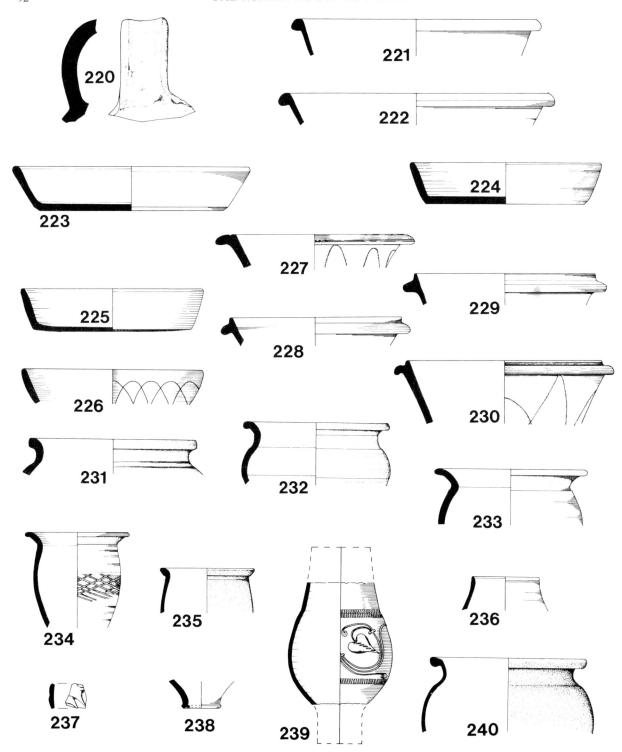

Fig. 35. *Coarse pottery* ($\frac{1}{4}$), *from Period VIII demolition deposits.*

PERIOD VIII, Demolition deposits, (Fig. 35, Nos. 220–240). Painted House 1970 & 1971, (DV–1105, 1179, 1188, 1189, 2306, 2309, 2331). Painted House 1975, (DV–9608). Bingo Hall 1976, (DV–9819, 9836).

No. 220 An amphora handle (body missing) of fine soft ware. Pinky-buff fabric and cream surface.

No. 221 Dish with heavy bead rim of sandy ware. Grey fabric and surface and burnished dark grey-black all over. Similar to No. 98 above dated to the late-second to mid-third centuries A.D.

No. 222 Dish with a heavy bead rim of sandy ware. Grey fabric and surface, burnished black all over. Similar to No. 98 dated from the late-second century to *c.* A.D. 250.

No. 223 Dish with a plain upright rim and a chamfered base of sandy ware. Grey fabric and surface, black burnished all over. B.B.2. Similar to No. 178 dated A.D. 190–208.

No. 224 Dish with a plain upright rim of sandy ware. Dark grey-brown fabric and surface. Burnished black all over. Similar to No. 215, dated A.D. 210–270.

No. 225 Dish with a plain upright rim of sandy ware. Dark grey fabric and grey-black surface. Black burnished all over. Similar to No. 215, dated *c.* A.D. 210–270.

No. 226 Dish with an upright rim of slightly gritted sandy ware. Dark grey fabric with some fine white grit inclusions and a black surface. Burnished all over and decorated with intersecting arcs. B.B.1. Similar to No. 189 dated *c.* A.D. 210–250.

No. 227 Dish with a flanged rim of sandy ware. Dark grey fabric and surface. Burnished black all over and decorated with intersecting arcs. B.B.1. This form of flanged rim vessel appears to be of third century date and can be paralleled at many sites: at Dover (No. 505) in contexts dated A.D. 210–270; at Southwark (Nos. 1697 and 568) they date from the early to late-third century; at Fishbourne, (Type 220.2) and in Northern Britain (Gillam Type 227) they are dated *c.* A.D. 200–300.

No. 228 Dish with a flanged rim of sand, grog and grit-tempered ware. Grey-brown fabric and dark grey surface, burnished all over. Similar to No. 185, dated to the mid-third and fourth centuries A.D., but here in late-third century contexts.

No. 229 Dish with a flanged rim of sand, grit and grog-tempered ware. Black fabric and dark grey surface. Burnished black all over. Similar to No. 185, dated to the mid-third and fourth centuries A.D., but here in late-third century contexts.

No. 230 Dish with a down-curved flanged rim of sand, grog and grit-tempered ware. Dark grey fabric heavily tempered with grog and quartz grit inclusions and a grey-black surface. Burnished black all over and decorated with intersecting arcs on the body. This grog and grit-tempered ware appears to be indigenous to late-third and fourth century sites in East Kent, East Sussex and Wessex. Several production centres are suggested. The ware can be found in dog-dishes as No. 254, cavetto rim cooking-pots as No. 269 as well as flange rim dishes. This particular vessel can be paralleled with vessels from Dover (No. 506), Lympne (No. 44) and Verulamium I (Nos. 1103 and 1172), where their date range is *c.* A.D. 270–350. Here, however, they are confined to late-third century contexts.

No. 231 Cooking-pot with an outcurved thickened rim of sandy ware. Brown fabric and grey-brown surface with two burnished bands on the neck. This vessel would appear to be a survival piece as such forms are normally confined to the first century. At Verulamium I (Nos. 69–72) similar vessels are found in contexts dated A.D. 49–60.

No. 232 Cooking-pot with an outcurved rim of sandy ware. Grey fabric and dark grey surface. Burnishing to rim and shoulder with a faint groove on shoulder. Vessels of a similar type from Colchester (Form 299) are common from *c.* A.D. 150–350. Here at Dover they are from late-third century contexts.

No. 233 Cooking-pot with a cavetto rim of sandy ware. Grey fabric and surface. Burnished black exterior and inside rim. Similar to No. 208 above, broadly dated A.D. 210–350, but here are from late-third century contexts.

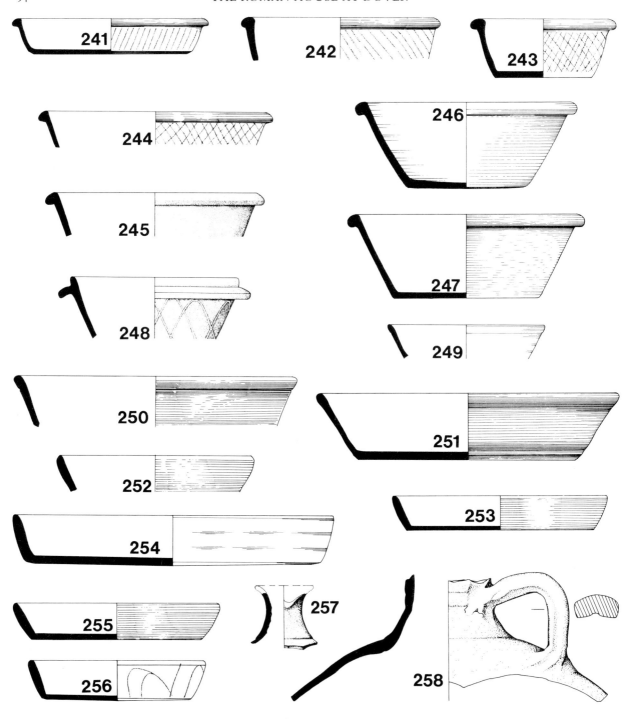

Fig. 36. *Coarse pottery* ($\frac{1}{4}$), *from Period VIII dumped deposits.*

No. 234 Cooking-pot with a cavetto rim of sand, grog and grit-tempered ware. Grey fabric and grey-brown surface, burnished black exterior and decorated with a zone of lattice pattern on the body. B.B.1. This is a typical ultimate version of the wide cavetto rim of the cooking-pot. Examples from Southwark (Nos. 561 and 1870); Fishbourne, (Type 385.2) and Gillam (Type 147) are dated from c. A.D. 270–350. At Dover these vessels appear in contexts dated to the late-third century.

No. 235 Beaker with a small outcurved rim of sandy ware. Grey fabric and dark grey surface with burnishing to rim and neck. Probably of third century date.

No. 236 Narrow-mouthed beaker with a plain grooved rim of fine sandy ware. Grey-brown fabric and dark grey surface and black burnished exterior. Probably a North Kent Marsh/Upchurch ware product. A similar vessel from Dover (No. 701) was found in contexts dated c. A.D. 150–208.

No. 237 Wall sherd of a Hunt cup of Castor ware (rim missing). White fabric, grey 'metallic' slip on surface with applied decoration depicting an animal running. A typical Nene Valley product dated by Anderson (Fig. 14, No. 3) to A.D. 160–180. At Dover (No. 415) a similar vessel was found in contexts dated A.D. 150–180.

No. 238 Base of a beaker (rim not seen) of fine sandy ware. Orange-buff fabric with some ironstone inclusions. Orange-brown slip on surface. Probably dated to the late-third century A.D.

No. 239 Beaker (rim missing) of colour-coated ware. Fine grey-buff fabric with a purple interior slip. The vessel has an exterior of purple-grey 'metallic' colour-coat, with barbotine ivy leaf decoration to the body between an upper and lower band of rouletting. A typical mid-third to early-fourth century vessel copying the earlier Rhenish ware beakers. At Verulamium II (No. 1807) similar vessels start to appear in contexts dated c. A.D. 250–280 and continues into the early-fourth century. At Dover they appear in late-third century contexts.

PERIOD VIII, Hypocaust fill (DV–9711).

No. 240 Cooking-pot with an outcurved and slightly rolled rim of sandy ware. Grey-brown fabric and dark grey surface with traces of burnishing to rim. Similar to No. 183, dated from the mid-second and third centuries A.D.

PERIOD VIII, Dumped deposits, (Figs. 36 and 37 Nos. 241–275). Painted House 1971, (DV–2371). Painted House 1975, (DV–9619). Bingo Hall 1976, (DV–3069, 3070, 3071, 3072, 3074, 3075, 3076).

No. 241 Dish with a bead rim and chamfered base of sandy ware. Dark grey fabric and surface. Black burnished all over and decorated with diagonal line pattern. Similar to No. 137 above, dated c. A.D. 130–210.

No. 242 Dish with a bead rim of sandy ware. Black fabric and grey-black surface. Burnished all over and decorated with a diagonal line pattern. Similar to No. 175 above, dated A.D. 140–180.

No. 243 Dish with a bead rim of sandy ware. Grey fabric and surface. Burnished all over and decorated with lattice pattern. B.B.2. Similar to No. 99, dated A.D. 130–140+.

No. 244 Dish with a bead rim of sandy ware. Brown fabric and grey-brown surface, burnished all over and decorated with acute lattice pattern. B.B.2. Similar to No. 188 dated c. A.D. 150–250.

No. 245 Dish with a bead rim of sandy ware. Grey-brown fabric and dark grey surface. Burnished interior. Similar to No. 98 dated from the late-second century to c. A.D. 250.

No. 246 Deep dish with a heavy bead rim of sandy ware. Grey fabric and dark grey surface, black burnished all over. B.B.2. Similar to No. 98 dated late-second century to c. A.D. 250.

No. 247 Deep dish with a large bead rim of sandy ware. Grey fabric and surface, burnished black all over. B.B.2. Similar to No. 98 above, dated from the late-second century to *c.* A.D. 250.

No. 248 Dish with a flanged rim of sandy ware. Grey fabric and a grey-brown surface. Burnished all over and decorated with intersecting arc pattern. Similar to No. 95 above dated *c.* A.D. 240–270.

No. 249 Dish with an upright grooved rim of sandy ware. Grey fabric and surface, burnished dark grey all over. Similar to No. 94, dated *c.* A.D. 120–250.

No. 250 Dish with an upright grooved rim of sandy ware. Grey fabric and grey-brown surface with traces of black burnishing all over. A larger version of No. 94 dated *c.* A.D. 120–250.

No. 251 Straight sided dish with a plain upright rim and a chamfered base of sandy ware. Grey fabric and dark grey surface, burnished all over. Similar to No. 178, dated *c.* A.D. 190–208.

No. 252 Dish with a plain rim of sandy ware with occasional grog inclusions. Grey fabric and surface, burnished all over. Similar to No. 215, dated A.D. 210–270.

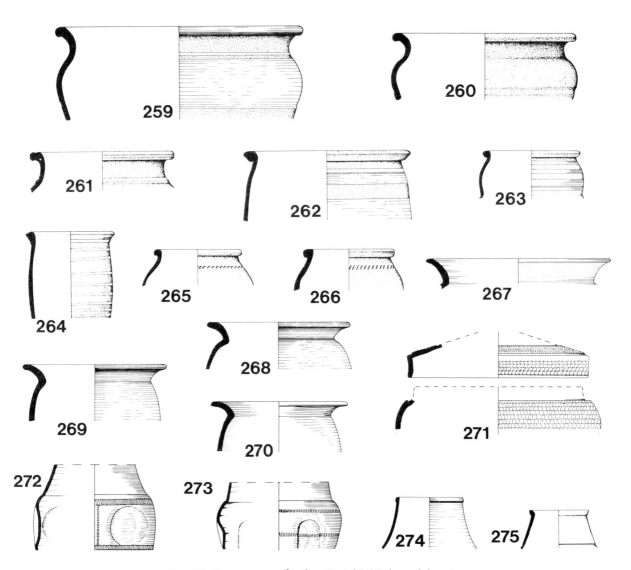

Fig. 37. *Coarse pottery (¼), from Period VIII dumped deposits.*

No. 253 Dish with a plain upright rim of sandy ware. Grey fabric and surface, burnished all over. Similar to No. 215 dated A.D. 210–270.

No. 254 Hand-made dish with a plain upright rim of sand, grog and quartz grit-tempered ware. Dark grey fabric heavily tempered with grog, mudstone and grit inclusions, with a brown surface that is burnished all over. Similar to No. 216 but without the intersecting arc decoration, dated here to c. A.D. 250–270.

No. 255 Dish with a plain upright rim of grog, grit and sand-tempered ware. Dark grey fabric, heavily tempered with grog and grit inclusions and a grey-brown surface. Burnished all over. A smaller version of No. 254 dated here to c. A.D. 250–270.

No. 256 Dish with a plain upright rim of grog, grit and sand-tempered ware. Dark grey fabric, heavily tempered with grog and grit inclusions. Grey-brown surface and black burnished interior. Exterior, brown burnished and decorated with a zig-zag scribble outside. Similar to Portchester (Type 107) where they are dated A.D. 280–345. At Dover from contexts dated c. A.D. 270.

No. 257 Single-handled flagon with an outcurved rim of sandy ware. Orange fabric and surface with traces of a handle at the neck, not shown on drawing.

No. 258 Amphora (rim missing) of fine hard sandy ware. Cream fabric and surface. It has a single two-ribbed handle.

No. 259 Bowl with an outcurved rolled rim of sandy ware. Dark grey fabric and surface. Decorated with burnishing to rim, band on neck and a wide zone on body. Similar vessels from Richborough IV (Pit 184, No. 425) and Dover (No. 408) date from the late-first to mid-second centuries A.D.

No. 260 Cooking-pot with an outcurved rim of sandy ware. Grey-brown fabric and grey surface. Burnishing to rim and shoulder with two horizontal lines at waist and a faint groove on the shoulder. Similar to No. 232, dated c. A.D. 150–350 overall, but here in late-third century contexts.

No. 261 Cooking-pot with an outcurved grooved rim of sandy ware. Grey fabric and dark grey surface with a cordon at base of neck.

No. 262 Wide-mouthed bowl with an angular rim of North Gaulish ware. Sandy grey fabric and dark grey surface with burnished bands on the body. Imported ware. Similar vessels from London, New Fresh Wharf, (Fig. 1, Nos. 1–3) are dated from the mid-second to early-third centuries A.D.

No. 263 Biconical sided jar with a small rolled rim of North Gaulish ware. Sandy grey fabric and surface, decorated with bands of burnishing to the body. Imported ware. Similar vessels from London, New Fresh Wharf, (Fig. 1, Nos. 6 and 9) are dated from the mid-second to early-third centuries A.D.

No. 264 Cylindrical jar with an outcurved angular rim of North Gaulish ware. Sandy grey fabric and surface with burnishing to rim and bands on the body. Similar vessels from London, New Fresh Wharf (No. 6) and from Dover (No. 669), are dated from the late-second to the early-third centuries A.D.

No. 265 Jar with a slightly rolled rim of hard sandy ware. Grey fabric and surface. Decorated with one band of stick-stabbing on the shoulder. Not common, imported. Similar vessels from Dover (Nos. 636 and 699) are dated from c. A.D. 150–210.

No. 266 Jar with a slightly rolled rim of hard sandy ware. Grey fabric and surface, with two bands of stick-stabbing on the shoulder. Similar to No. 265, dated c. A.D. 150–210.

No. 267 Cooking-pot with a cavetto rim of sandy ware. Dark grey-black fabric and surface with black burnishing to body and inside rim. B.B.1. A variant of No. 208 above dated A.D. 210–270.

No. 268 Cooking-pot with a cavetto rim of sandy ware. Dark grey fabric and surface with burnished exterior and inside rim. B.B.1. A variant of No. 208 dated A.D. 210–270.

No. 269 Cooking-pot with a cavetto rim of grog, grit and sand-tempered ware. Dark grey fabric heavily tempered with grog and quartz grit inclusions. Black surface with burnishing to rim and exterior. This ware is indigenous to late-third and fourth century sites in eastern

Kent, East Sussex and Wessex. Several production centres are suggested. As well as cavetto rim cooking-pots, dog dishes as No. 254 and flanged dishes as No. 230 are represented. This particular vessel is a variant of No. 208 and probably shares a similar date here of *c.* A.D. 210–270.

No. 270 Cooking-pot with a cavetto rim of gritted sandy ware. Buff-brown fabric and grey-brown surface. Burnishing to exterior and inside rim. B.B.1. A variant of No. 208, dated here *c.* A.D. 210–270.

No. 271 Lid and bowl with a plain upright rim of colour-coated ware. Orange-buff fabric. The surface is covered with an orange-brown colour-slip and decorated with bands of rouletting. This vessel is commonly known as a Castor Ware box and lid. As Gillam (Type 341 and 342) but of a different fabric. At Verulamium I (No. 119) a similar lid of what appears to be the same fabric type can be compared. Date-wise these vessels seem to range between the late-second to fourth centuries A.D. At Dover it is from a late-third century context.

No. 272 Beaker with indented sides (rim missing) of colour-coated ware. Fine creamy-buff fabric with a dark grey 'metallic' colour-slip to the exterior. The body of the vessel is decorated with circular indentations between an upper and lower band of rouletting. This is a typical mid-third to early-fourth century vessel, of a form common on many sites and is a probable product of the Nene Valley kilns. Vessels of similar form start appearing at Verulamium I (No. 1060) in contexts dated A.D. 230–275, becoming more common in the later-third and early-fourth centuries; at Fishbourne (Type 367) they first appear *c.* A.D. 250–275 and at Colchester (Form 407A) similar vessels from Kiln 32 were produced *c.* A.D. 250–300. This date-range is consistent with the appearance of these colour-coated wares at Dover *c.* A.D. 250–270.

No. 273 Beaker with indented sides (rim missing) of colour-coated ware. Fine grey-white sandy fabric, exterior surface covered with a dark grey-black 'metallic' colour-slip. Body of vessel is decorated with indentations and bands of rouletting. Similar vessels from Verulamium I (Nos. 1105, 1106 and 1132) are dated from the mid-third to early-fourth centuries A.D. This is consistent with the first appearance of these colour-coated wares at Dover *c.* A.D. 250–270.

No. 274 Narrow-mouthed beaker with a slightly beaded rim of fine sandy colour-coated ware. Buff fabric and coated with an orange-brown colour slip. Possibly a product of the Oxfordshire Kilns, see Oxfordshire Type C.22.1, broadly dated to A.D. 240–400+. At Dover these vessels occur in late-third century contexts.

No. 275 Beaker with a small rectangular rim of Oxfordshire Ware. Orange-buff fabric and surface. Coated with a red-brown colour-slip and a groove on shoulder. Oxfordshire type C.23.1, broadly dated A.D. 270–400+. At Dover these vessels occur in late-third century contexts.

G. THE BOX-FLUE TILES (Figs. 38 and 39, Nos. 276 to 283)

by John Willson, M.I.F.A.

During the excavation of the Painted House site many pieces of box-flue tiles were recovered, but as most were of a very fragmentary nature no attempt has been made to carry out an exhaustive study. However, at least eight are substantial enough to comment on and illustrate. These box-flue tiles fall into three basic types and two distinct fabrics, as follows:

1. Type 1:   Box voussoir-tile decorated on broad face. (No. 276) Fabric A.
2. Type 2:   Long rectangular box-flue tiles, with a pair of rectangular lateral vents on each of the narrow sides, broad faces decorated. (Nos. 277 and 278) Fabric A.
3. Type 3:   Medium length, rectangular box-flue tiles, with a single lateral rectangular vent on each of the narrow sides, broad faces decorated and some are stamped 'CLBR', the insignia of the *Classis Britannica*. (Nos. 279 to 283) Fabric B.

Both Types 1 and 2 were recovered from the rubble filling of the hypocaust channels of the Tufa Block Building Period IV (Nos. 276 to 278). Type 3 was found exclusively in the Painted House. Of the latter four (Nos. 279 to 282) were found *in situ* in Room 1 and thus belong to Period VI and one (No. 283) was recovered from the demolition rubble in Room 2, Period VIII, but probably relates to the heating arrangements in that room. Many more of Type 3 tiles remain *in situ* in the preserved extant Painted House building, but are largely obscured by wall-rendering. However, where seen their size and shape all conform with the published examples.

The fabrics are as follows:

Fabric A: A brownish-red, coarse sandy fabric, with occasional small irregular shaped red, black and white inclusions. Source unknown. Tile Types 1 and 2 (Nos. 276 to 278).

Fabric B: A reddish-pink coloured, smooth clay fabric, relieved by streaks, lenses and swirls of creamy-white clay. Source, either Sussex Weald or on Romney Marsh, *Classis Britannica* Fabric 2 (Ref. 59). Tile Type 3 (Nos. 279 to 283).

(a) VOUSSOIR TILE Period IV. – From rubble in the hypocaust channel of the Tufa Block Building (DV–9866).

Tile – Type 1.

No. 276 Hollow Voussoir box tile, incomplete, of type 'A' fabric. Wedge shaped, it measures a minimum of 23.5 cm. in length (probably 30 cm. actual) by 25 cm. tapering to 23 cm. in width, a minimum of 2.3 cm. deep (probably about 16 cm. when complete) and 1.7 cm. thick. Only a broken face fragment survives, this being decorated from corner to corner with a combed cross and a horizontal combed band across its centre and enclosed by a combed frame around its edges. This combing provided a key on the surface for the subsequent mortar application.

Only one voussoir tile was recovered from this site. Usually such tiles are used in the construction of vaulted roofs, most often in bath-houses. Being hollow they reduced the weight of the roof by forming hollow ribs linked to vertical wall vents. In this way they also allowed the hot air from the underfloor hypocaust-system, passing up through the vertical wall vents to circulate inside the actual roof structure. This also increased the insulation and reduced internal condensation.

Voussoir tiles are known from a number of British sites and similar decorated examples can be paralleled at Fishbourne (Fig. 24, No. 20) (Ref. 60) in contexts dated *c.* A.D. 100–280 and at Reculver (Ref. 61) from the third century bath-house.

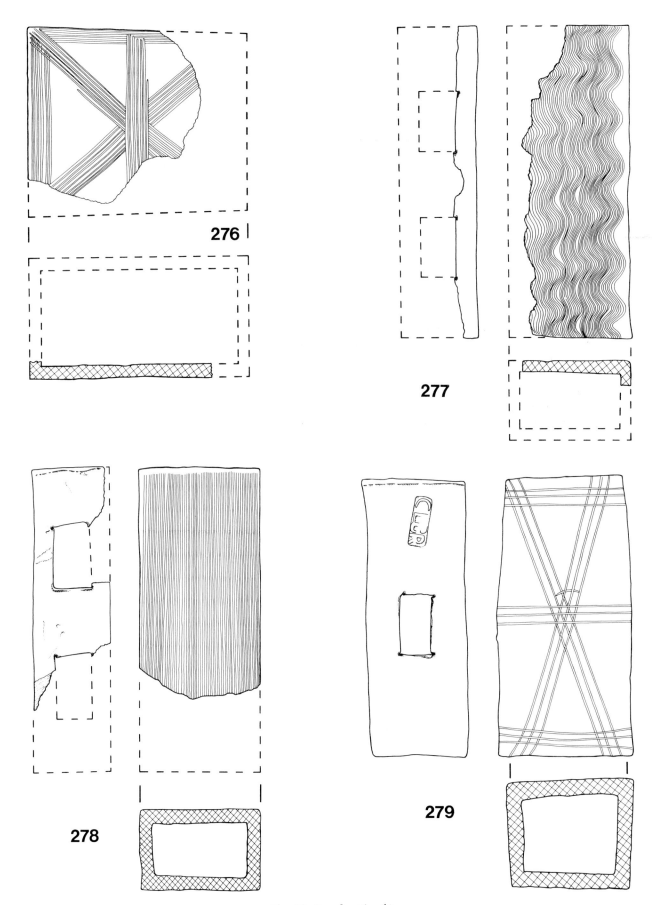

Fig. 38. *Box-flue tiles* ($\frac{1}{5}$).

(b) BOX-FLUE TILES

Rectangular box-flue tiles, or '*tubuli*', were used to construct vertical ducts to carry hot air from the ends of horizontal hypocaust systems up through the walls to the roof and thus outside. Sometimes they led to vaulted roofs constructed with voussoir tiles. Mostly they were set singly, or in batteries along vertical wall faces where heat could travel laterally as well as vertically.

The box-flue tiles under discussion here formed a series of single vertical chimney-flues set in the corners and centres of the walls in each room. This is clearly the case for in the Painted House building many are still *in situ* (Ref. 62). A similar arrangement may have existed for the Tufa Block Building, but as this was demolished to below floor-level no exact evidence survives. Two basic types of rectangular box-flue tiles have been identified on this site, Tile Types 2 and 3.

Tile Type 2. From the Period IV Tufa Block Building (Nos. 277 and 278). DV–9866

Only two tiles of this type were recovered, both being generally longer and not as deep as the Type 3 tiles. They appear to average 40–41 cm. in length; 16.5 cm. in width; 10.5 cm. in depth and between 1.5 and 1.7 cm. in thickness. Each tile has a pair of rectangular vents in each of its narrow sides, set vertically above each other and generally about 8 cm. by 5 cm. in size. The vents have signs of knife marks and finger impressions where the vents have been cut out. Both of the tiles recovered have combed decoration on their broad faces to form a key for mortar or plaster rendering. Two designs are evident, one of densely combed vertical lines and the other with a densely combed, vertical wavy line pattern.

Tile Type 3. From the Period VI Painted House Building (Nos. 279–283). DV–3064

Of some 25 box-flue tiles seen, 20 are still *in situ* and are largely obscured by rendering, but the dimensions of most were obtainable. Their sizes vary slightly as does their decoration and all are shorter than the Type 2 tiles. They appear to range between 34.5 cm. and 37 cm. in length; 16 cm. to 18 cm. in width; 10 cm. to 14.5 cm. in depth and are generally 2 cm. to 2.5 cm. in thickness. Each tile has a single rectangular vent set upright in each of its narrow sides and these are generally between 6 cm. and 9.5 cm. by 3.5 cm. to 5.5 cm. in size. Many of the vents have signs of knife marks and finger impressions where the vents have been cut out. At least three of the visible tiles carried a tile-stamp (CLBR) on one of the narrow sides above the vent.

All of the tiles illustrated and several ones still *in situ* have combed decoration to the broad faces of the tile to form a key. The decoration is largely in the form of multiple grooved crosses, diamond cross-hatch, vertical wavy lines, vertical lines or intersecting vertical curves.

These Type 3 box-flue tiles from Dover seem very similar indeed to the Type 'A' box-flue tiles (also stamped CLBR) from the bath-house at Beauport Park (Ref. 63) where they have been given a date range of early-second century to mid-third century A.D. Hence the date of *c.* A.D. 200 for the Painted House construction fits comfortably within these dates and also its links with the *Classis Britannica*.

PERIOD IV. From the Tufa block building (DV–9866).

No. 277 Box-flue tile, incomplete, of Type 2, Fabric A. Rectangular, 41 cm. in length, a minimum of 14.7 cm. in width (probably 16.5 cm. actual), a minimum of 3 cm. in depth (probably 10.5 cm. actual) and 1.5 cm. in thickness. It has a pair of rectangular vents, set upright in each of the two narrow sides, measuring 8 cm. by 5 cm. (min.). The two wide faced surfaces are decorated with a dense wavy line combed pattern to serve as a key for mortar.

No. 278 Box-flue tile, incomplete, of Type 2, Fabric A. Rectangular, a minimum of 31.5 cm. in length (probably about 40 cm. actual) by 16.5 cm. in width, 10.5 cm. in depth and 1.7 cm. in thickness. It has a pair of rectangular vents, set upright in each of the two narrow sides, measuring 8.5 cm. by 5 cm. The two wide faced surfaces are decorated with dense, narrow spaced vertical combing.

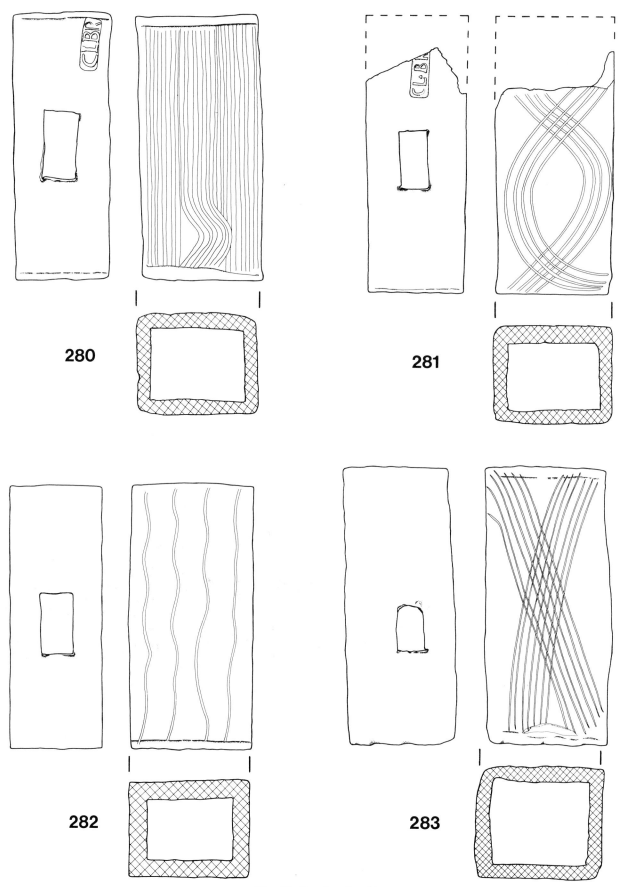

280

281

282

283

Fig. 39. *Box-flue tiles* ($\frac{1}{5}$).

PERIOD VI. Painted House building – from Room 1 (DV–3064).

No. 279 Box-flue tile of Type 3, Fabric B. Rectangular, measuring 36.5 cm. in length, 16.5 cm. in width, 14.5 cm. in depth and 2 cm. in thickness. It has a single rectangular vent set upright in each of the two narrow sides, measuring 8.2 cm. by 4.2 cm. The two wide faced surfaces are decorated from corner to corner with a three grooved combed cross, with three horizontal bands of three grooved combing, positioned at the top, middle and bottom of the face respectively. One of the narrow sides is stamped CLBR with the mark *Classis Britannica* (Type M5/K1: No. 26, of report on tile-stamps).

No. 280 Box-flue tile of Type 3, Fabric B. Rectangular, measuring 35 cm. in length, 16.5 cm. in width, 13.5 cm. in depth and 2 cm. in thickness. It has a single rectangular vent set upright in each of the two narrow sides, measuring 9 cm. by 4.5 cm. The two wide faced surfaces are decorated with vertical combing and one of the narrow sides is stamped CLBR (Type K1: No. 27, see report on tile-stamps).

No. 281 Box-flue tile, incomplete, of Type 3, Fabric B. Rectangular, measuring a minimum of 32 cm. in length (probably 36.5 cm.), 16 cm. in width, 13.5 cm. in depth and 2 cm. in thickness. It has a single rectangular vent set upright in each of the two marrow sides, measuring 7.5 cm. by 3.7 cm. The two wide faced surfaces are decorated with two intersecting, four grooved combed arcs. One of the narrow sides is stamped CLBR (Type K7: no. 33, of report on tile-stamps).

No. 282 Box-flue tile, of Type 3, Fabric B. Rectangular, measuring 34.5 cm. in length, 16.5 cm. in width, 12.5 cm. in depth and 2.3 cm. in thickness. It has a single rectangular vent set upright in each of the two narrow sides, measuring 8 cm. by 4.5 cm. The only wide faced surface visible is decorated with four, widely spaced, combed grooves in a wavy line pattern. The tile is still *in situ* so it was not possible to check to see if it was stamped as the sides are built into the wall of the structure.

PERIOD VIII. Demolition deposits over floor of Room 2 – Painted House (DV–2306).

No. 283 Box-flue tile, incomplete, of Type 3, Fabric B. Rectangular, measuring 36.5 cm. in length, 16.5 cm. in width, 14.5 cm. in depth and 2 cm. in thickness. It has a single sub-rectangular vent measuring 6 cm. by 3.5 cm. set upright in each of the two narrow sides. The two wide faced surfaces are decorated from corner to corner with a seven grooved combed cross giving a lattice effect in the central area. No stamp seen on surviving pieces.

CHAPTER IV

THE PAINTED WALL AND CEILING PLASTER (Figs. 40–101).

The very large quantity of painted plaster from the Painted House and Bingo Hall sites was found either:-

a. *In situ* on the walls of six rooms and the North Passage inside the Roman Painted House (page 105).
b. In the demolition layers within the Painted House, or incorporated in the rampart above it (page 139).
c. In the demolition debris of the Clay Walled Building added to the north side of the Painted House, or incorporated in the rampart above it (page 224).

Each of these groups is dealt with separately below.

Of the *in situ* material about 30 sq. mts. survives in Room 2; about 6 sq. mts. in room 3; about 4 sq. mts. in Room 4 and some 21 sq. mts. in the North Passage, thus totalling some 61 sq. mts. in all.

In addition, a total of 22,508 fragments of fallen, or dumped, plaster was found in association with the Roman House and another 6,430 fragments came from the Bingo Hall site. These probably represent together another 40 sq. mts. of plaster. Hence, collectively, about 100 sq. mts. of Roman plaster were located and this seems to represent the largest and most complete collection of Roman plaster so far found anywhere north of the Alps.

A. THE *IN SITU* PAINTED PLASTER IN THE PAINTED HOUSE

By Brian Philp

The *in situ* painted plaster mostly remains to surviving wall-top level in Rooms 2, 3 and 4 and also on one side of the North Passage (Figs. 41 and 42). Following substantial demolition all this section of the Roman House had been buried by the soil rampart constructed behind the fort wall about A.D. 270. In Rooms 5 and 6 only slight traces of painted plaster, close to floor-level, have survived owing to the almost total destruction of the rooms lying in front of the fort wall. Similarly, only very slight traces of the dado survive in Room 1, for this room lay beyond the rampart and clearly suffered many years of subsequent use and decay. Externally, only two small areas of painted plaster have survived *in situ* on the south side of the building.

It seems clear from a study of the mortar (page 226) and the painted designs (page 114), that all six rooms were painted at one time and this to a largely uniform design. There can be little doubt that this was carried out just after the construction of the building in about A.D. 200. Although the internal mortar rendering (Fabric A) of each wall is identical, it contrasts sharply with the much thinner plaster (Fabric B) thought to have fallen from ceilings inside the Painted House and with the much poorer quality external plaster (Fabric C) found on the outer walls and in the North Passage.

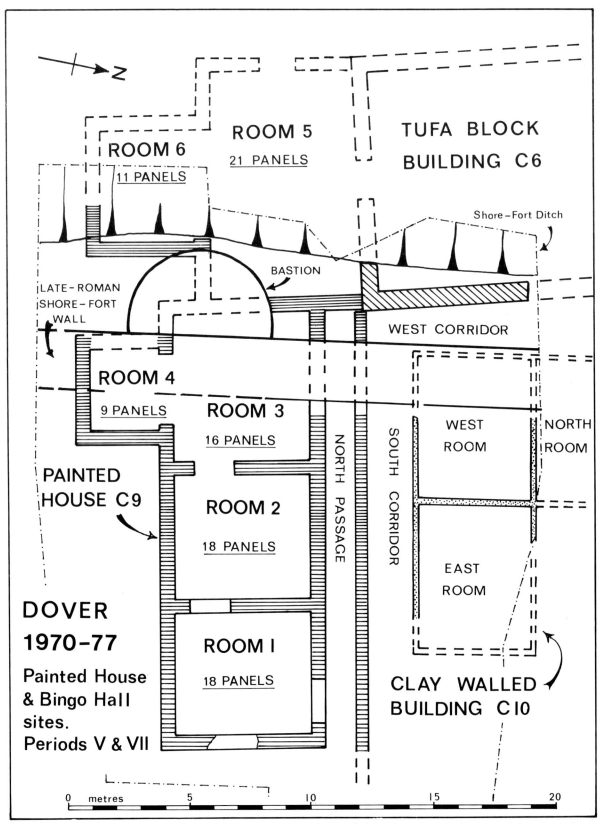

Fig. 40. *Plan showing the rooms in the Painted House C9 and the Clay Walled Building C10, which contained the painted plaster, both in situ and fallen.*

In the following text the surviving painted plaster in each room is briefly described first (page 108). This is followed by a more detailed description of the designs and motifs (page 114) and ultimately by a discussion (page 132) of all the plaster from the Painted House. Measurements are given in metres, centimetres and millimetres.

From the combined evidence of the *in situ* plaster and the reconstructed subjects (see page 145), it is clear that the design and layout were massive in scale, cleverly conceived, finely detailed and brilliant in colour. The vertical wall planes had been divided into three main horizontal elements, commonly the basis of many wall-plaster designs throughout much of the Roman world. A low-level dado and a high-level frieze both framed the central, major component of the scheme. In the Painted House this central division contained a dominant architectural design, laid out symmetrically, painted in perspective and adorned with bright colours and carefully chosen motifs (Fig. 44).

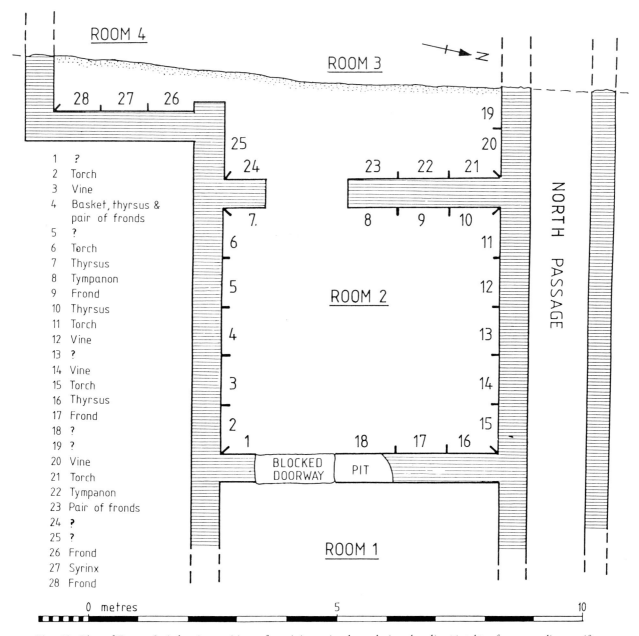

Fig. 43. *Plan of Rooms 2–4 showing positions of surviving painted panels (numbered) with table of corresponding motifs.*

1). Outline Description of the surviving plaster in each of the Rooms. (Figs. 41–43).

Room 1.

This room matches Room 2 in size and form and it is likely that it served a similar function. It is also very likely that the same decorative scheme had been applied. Unlike Rooms 2–4 in the house, however, it had not been buried beneath the shore-fort's rampart at the end of the third century, but had clearly remained in use for several more decades. This is shown by the extremely worn state of the floor, contrasting sharply with the almost perfect condition of the floors buried beneath the rampart. In addition, virtually all of the plaster had fallen from the walls and only very small areas of a mottled red dado survive on the west and north walls near floor-level. This matches the dados in Rooms 3 and 5. It seems likely that Room 1 had also contained 18 panels (see below). No trace of fallen plaster was found on the floor and it seems clear that this was removed, probably by periodic cleaning.

Room 2 (Panels 1–18).

The painted plaster survives remarkably intact on all four walls of this room and represents the most complete painted design ever found within a Romano-British structure (Plates XXIII–XXV). The mottled green dado is delimited by a maroon band and survives, with some considerable pitting on the south and north sides, substantially intact. A patch of orange colouring at the east end of the north wall may represent a burnt surface. Twelve pairs of vertical lines on the dado mark the positions of the twelve column bases, of which parts of at least ten survive. The pairs of vertical lines vary in width, with the majority about 19–22 cm. apart, but several are between 26–31 cm. apart. The two door-openings are lined in red, the east lining being 3.5 cm. wide and the west lining up to 10 cm.

The open field, or stage, above the dado continues round all the walls as does the podium which surmounts it, originally with twelve large projecting bases. The combined horizontal and vertical planes of the podium are mostly 9–10 cm. wide. Substantial parts of eight of the podium bases and six of the columns survive, the latter varying in height from 28–67 cm. though none is complete. This room originally had 18 large white panels, of which some 15 partially survive (Fig. 43).

Panel 1   This panel occupies the extreme right-hand side of the east wall, just to the right of the blocked doorway and it originally had a yellow border. No trace of the actual panel survives, but a broad vertical dark red band borders both the panel and the door-opening. No trace of a motif survives.

Panel 2   The left-hand panel on the south wall has a bright yellow border, mostly 9–11 cm. wide which is separated from the actual corner by a dark red band about 13 cm. wide (Plate XXIII). The yellow border is lined internally with a thin maroon line about 2–3 mm. wide, which is itself some 14–18 mm. inside a green-black inner frame 2–4 mm. wide. The white panel so lined is about 51 cm. wide and survives to a minimum height of about 46 cm. Running diagonally across the lower right-hand side of the panel is a yellow-brown 'torch' motif (Motif A), whose broad end rests on the stage. The upper, or handle, end seems to originate within the yellow border on the right and thus the 'torch' had an overall length of about 90 cm. Its shadow falls to the left.

Panel 3   This panel is the second from the left along the south wall and it has a dark red border, mostly 10–13 cm wide on at least three sides (Plate XXIV). It is flanked on both sides by fine fluted columns, whilst its inner edge is lined in maroon. A 12 mm. space separates a 5–7 mm. green-black lining, thus leaving an open white panel about 55 cm. wide and at least 44 cm. high. The centre of the panel is occupied by the vine motif (Motif B), in green, which originates from the stage. Its shadow falls to the left, as do the shadows on the two podium bases which flank it. This panel and the plaster beneath it are pick-marked and stained where a cess-pit has been dug down the face of the wall in Victorian times.

Panel 4   This panel is in the centre of the south wall and it has a salmon pink border, mostly 9–12 cm. wide, again lined internally with a maroon line and also enclosing a green-black line as an inner frame (Plate XXV). The main white area is at least 56 cm. wide and at least 16 cm. high. The central motif is the stem of a probable thyrsus rising from what appears to be a shallow basket, in brown, containing foliage and fruit (Motifs C and D). A pair of matching green fronds have been painted facing each other across the open field and the podium, one on each side of the basket. Their shadows fall left and right, respectively, as do those of the flanking podium bases. This shows that the panel was intended to be the central view-point.

Panel 5   This panel is the inner right-hand panel on the south wall, but is has been largely destroyed. Its flanking podium bases partially survive. Both bases throw shadows to the right and indeed the shadow of the missing motif can also be seen falling to the right. By analogy with the north wall of this room this panel should have contained a matching vine motif, within a dark red border, slight traces of which survive. A large section of the upper part of this panel, displaying a dark red border and a green garland, was found in the adjacent demolition rubble and has been reconstructed (Subject 1).

Panel 6   This extreme right-hand panel on the south wall has also largely been destroyed but slight evidence of a yellow border and the lower end of another yellow-brown 'torch' motif survives, the latter casting a clear shadow to the right. Traces of dark red suggest an upright band lining the precise corner, largely matching that in the left-hand corner of the same wall.

Panel 7   This is the first left-hand panel on the west wall. Most is destroyed, but a long thin shadow on the stage, falling to the left, survives and there is trace of a possible thyrsus. A broad vertical red band frames the door-opening.

Panel 8   This is the centre panel on the west wall being separated from Panel 7 by a wide door-opening, here again framed by a broad vertical red band. It has a salmon pink border of unknown width. The faint outline of a tympanon (Motif G) rests on the stage casting its shadow downwards.

Panel 9   This is the next panel to the right and it has a dark red unlined border, with a green-black line forming an inner frame (Plates XXVI–XXVII). The white panel so outlined is about 59 cm. wide and at least 12 cm. high. The motif here is a large, single frond (Motif F), placed diagonally from the right, extending from the bottom border down to the stage with its shadow falling to the right. This panel is flanked by parts of two of the best columns in the room, sitting on sharply defined rectangular podium bases which both cast their shadows to the right.

Panel 10 The right-hand corner panel on the west wall has a yellow border of varying width (Plate XXVIII). Its left side is 11.5 cm., its right side is 12.5 cm., but its bottom border is only 11 cm. wide. The panel is lined with a maroon line and has an inner frame of green-black, leaving the white panel about 53 cm. wide and surviving to a maximum height of 57 cm. The right-hand corner of the room has been cracked by the heat from the vertical flues set in the wall behind it. The motif associated with this panel is a fine thyrsus (Motif E), which springs from the right of the panel and ends on the stage where it casts a shadow to the right. The thyrsus has a large fillet tied near its centre. The extreme right-handed corner of the room here is painted with a dark red vertical band about 10 cm. wide edged in pale green. Again, on the west wall, the shadows all show that the centre panel was intended to be the main view-point.

Panel 11 The north wall clearly had five panels, of which parts of four survive. Again the extreme left-hand corner is lined with a dark red band, about 9 cm. wide, edged in pale green. The left hand corner panel (Panel 11) has a yellow border, mostly 8–11 cm. wide, which is edged with a maroon line and framed internally by a green-black line

3–5 cm. wide, tinted with orange (Plate XXIX). The panel area is 47 cm. wide and at least 19 cm. high. The motif in this corner is again the 'torch', originating from the top right to cross the yellow bottom border and ending on the stage with its shadow to the left.

Panel 12   This is the next panel along the north wall and it is separated from Panel 11 by a fine column, on its podium base, at least 27 cm. high. Very little survives of the panel, but it is bordered in dark red and the base of the familiar vine survives on the stage, again with its shadow to the left.

Panel 13   The centre panel on the north wall has been almost totally destroyed, with the possible exception of a shadow to the right, probably from one of a pair of fronds matching those on the south wall.

Panel 14   The adjacent right panel is also substantially destroyed, but the base of a vine on the stage is quite clear. This has a shadow on its right side.

Panel 15   A podium base marks the division between Panel 14 and the right-hand corner Panel 15. This, too, has been largely destroyed, but sufficient survives to show that it has a yellow border. The head of an inverted yellow-brown 'torch' survives on the stage showing that it had been painted diagonally left across the panel and throwing its shadow to the right. Again, the shadows, falling to the left and right, strongly suggest that the middle panel (missing Panel 13) was intended to be the main view-point on the north wall.

Panel 16   The east wall must originally have had four panels and a wide door-opening making up its length. The extreme left-hand panel (Panel 16) has been partially cut away by a large medieval pit. What survives shows that it has a yellow border some 10–11 cm. wide. This was lined internally by a faint red line and had an inner frame of green-black. Part of a curved thyrsus survives, springing from the left side of the panel with its base resting on the stage near the podium base. Traces of its shadow fall to the left. A large settlement crack through the wall runs diagonally downwards to the right, almost to floor-level (Plate XXX).

Panel 17   The next panel to the right, separated by part of a fine column and its base, has a dark red border at least 12 cm. wide. The actual panel has been destroyed, but a large downturned frond motif rests diagonally right on the stage, casting its shadow to the left.

Panel 18   This would have been the centre panel on the east wall, but it has been totally removed by a medieval pit. To the right of this is the original door-opening into Room 1, later blocked.

Room 3 (Panels 19–25).

The painted plaster survives on the extant sections of the north and south walls and also along the entire east wall, except for its door-opening (Plate XXXI). The mottled red dado largely survives on all these sections, though it is badly pitted and mortar-splashed on the north side. A neat hole has been smashed through it into the vertical wall-flue at the south-east corner. Its top is delimited by a maroon band. The dado on the east and north walls is about 73 cm. high above floor-level, but that on the south wall is about 81 cm.! A pair of vertical lines on the north dado marks a podium base, whilst two more pairs mark two more bases on the east wall. The spacing between these vertical lines in each pair varies from about 18–25 cm.

The open field, or stage, above the dado largely survives on the north and east sides, again beneath the familiar podium. On the east wall, however, the two planes of the podium are squeezed into about 7 cm. for most of the length, but expand to about 12 cm. at the extreme north end. The dark red line bordering the upper part of the podium here seems to have been accidentally painted about 5 cm. too high. Similarly, there are variations on the short length of the podium on the north wall. Although the pair of vertical lines on the dado here suggests a podium base, the dark red line which normally outlines such a base continues straight to the corner of the room. This is then 7 cm. lower than the corresponding line on the east wall and the difference has been reconciled with a shaky, near-vertical line.

Panel 19 This is missing though the dado survives in part beneath it.

Panel 20 This is the only panel surviving on the north wall and it seems to have a dark red border. The projecting podium forms a broad step below the panel and the base of another vine rises from the stage with its shadow falling to the right.

Four panels and a door-opening fill the whole of the east wall, as in Room 2. The only two columns thus required on this wall, to the left of the door-opening, survive and both bases cast their shadow to the left.

Panel 21 The left-hand corner panel of the east wall is framed in dark red, in contrast to the corner panels in Room 2 which are all yellow. Part of the familiar yellow-brown 'torch' motif, again placed diagonally downwards to the left, survives with a faint shadow falling to the left.

Panel 22 The next panel to the right has an unusually wide yellow border, at least 18 cm. to the broken edge (Plate XXXII). The panel, too, must therefore have been very narrow, perhaps in the region of about only 32–40 cm. In view of this it is possible that the panel was not white, but solid yellow and thus in sharp contrast to those in Room 2. It is fronted by a tympanon in red and pale green, resting on the stage and casting its shadow to the left.

Panel 23 The centre panel seems to have a salmon pink border and is fronted by a pair of opposed fronds in green, each casting its shadow outwards.

Panels 24 and 25. A wide door-opening divides Panels 23 and 24, but the latter and Panel 25 have been destroyed.

It seems clear from the surviving shadows on the east wall, that the view-point was intended to be the centre panel as in the other rooms and regardless of the doorway. The exact north-east corner of the room is lined with vertical dark red bands, each about 10 cm. wide, both edged in very pale green. The door-opening appears to have been lined in red to a maximum width of 8 cm., perhaps in two applications.

Whilst the evidence for the painted designs in Room 3 is less abundant than in Room 2, there is clearly a broad similarity. However, whilst coloured borders survive *in situ* no trace of a white panel remains. Many fragments of plaster with clear traces of white panel were found on the floor of Room 3 and it must have included at least several white panels. In addition, several fragments of a solid red panel with a human figure overpainted on it were also found. So, too, there is a possibility that Panel 22 could have had a solid yellow panel for the yellow found was much wider than a normal border. There is thus some evidence to suggest that Room 3 had both white and coloured panels.

Room 4 (Panels 26–28).

The painted plaster only survives on the complete east wall, on the stub of the south wall and also on the east respond flanking the wide opening with Room 3 (Plate XXXIII). The mottled green dado survives on all three sections though it is badly damaged at the south-east corner, where acidic soils filling a medieval pit have made deep marks. The top of the dado is delimited by a maroon band. Three vertical lines on the dado reflect the positions of two podium bases and clearly a fourth line has been accidentally missed. The dado is 75 cm. high above floor-level.

The open-field, or stage, survives in part as do sections of the podium, but only on the east wall. Here only one of the two podium bases survives in good detail. One faces left and the other right, showing the centre panel to be the intended focal point of this wall. The shadows again confirm a central view-point, whilst the column-spacing suggests that the centre panel was the largest of the three.

Panel 26   The left-hand panel is largely missing, but below it is a single large frond casting its shadow to the left. The panel border seems to be yellow.

Panel 27   The centre panel has a salmon pink border and beneath it is a large syrinx (Motif H), casting its shadow downwards.

Panel 28   Very little of the right-hand panel survives, though it seems to have a yellow border and another large frond seems to be indicated beneath the panel.

Room 5.

This lay on the outer side of the shore-fort wall in the area of the intended berm and thus its walls had been reduced to almost floor-level. In addition more than half the room had been destroyed by the excavation of the great defensive ditch, whilst the south-east segment was later buried beneath the added bastion. Only a very small strip of *in situ* plaster survived and this lay along the north wall, just above floor-level. This revealed traces of a dark red marbled dado similar to that used in Rooms 1 and 3.

Room 5 seems to have been considerably larger than Rooms 1, 2 and 3 (see p. 108) and it seems likely that with panels averaging about 95 cm. each, the original number would have been 21. No trace of any of these was found either *in situ* or fallen.

Room 6.

This room also lay outside the shore-fort wall and it had also been substantially removed by the shore-fort ditch. However, parts of the east and south walls survived and both displayed patches of a mottled green dado, similar to that in Rooms 2 and 4. It seems probable that Room 6 was an extension of Room 5 and that together they created a double-room, in much the same way as did Rooms 3 and 4. As Room 6 was larger than the corresponding Room 4 (see above page 111), it is probable that it had originally been provided with eleven panels. No trace of these survived, either *in situ* or fallen.

NORTH PASSAGE (Fig. 42)

The painted design in the North Passage flanking Rooms 1, 2 and 3 was plain and simple compared with those in the main rooms. It was found only on the south wall of the passage, but with the poor condition of the north wall it is not known if it had been plastered or painted at any time.

A total length of 7.63 m. of painted plaster was found *in situ*, surviving in height from 30 to 122 cm. Parts of eight large plain white panels still survive, each panel being separated from the next by a group comprising one band and two lines, all vertical. The white panels vary in width from 85 cm. (one panel), 88 cm. (one panel), 89 cm. (three panels) and 90 cm. (one panel) and sit on a single black horizontal line some 15 cm. wide, which in turn forms the top of a white dado. The dado only survives in places to a maximum height of 10 cm. below the dado band, whereas its original height was probably about 25 cm. taken from the estimated floor-level.

The central vertical band in each group is painted black and 4–6 cm. wide. Its base joins the thinner black line at right-angles above the dado. On each side of the vertical black band is a thin red line, 7–14 mm. wide, spaced 3–5 cm. from it. Hence the centre-line of one black band to the next is 1.03–1.04 m. and this really represents the intended overall divisions. It also demonstrates the accuracy of the original marking-out and provides a contrast to the finished painted version with its frequent, though minor, variations. Furthermore, from this it seems likely that in the total length of the passage, allowing for only one door into Room 1, twelve panels had originally existed.

In terms of the design it seems highly probable that, as elsewhere in Roman Dover, the broad vertical black band rose to join a corresponding horizontal band, perhaps about 1.5 m. above floor-level. Certainly the panels were not square, for what survives already shows that they were

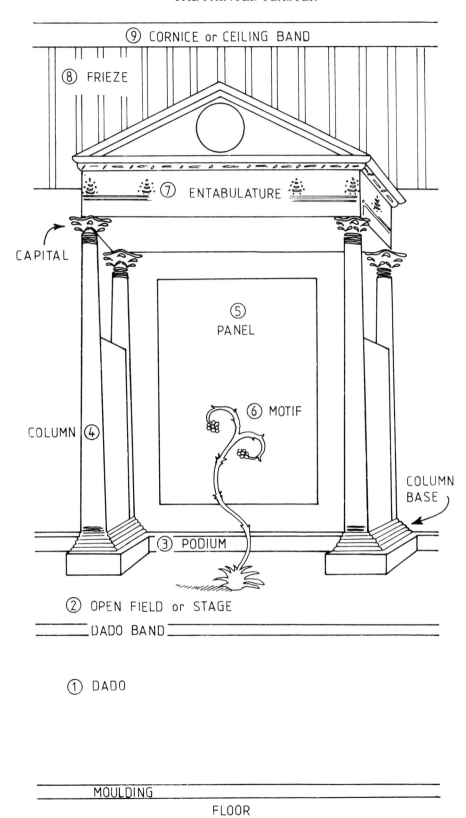

Fig. 44. *Outline drawing showing the main decorative elements and vertical dimensions in the Painted House design.*

taller than they were wide. A height/width ratio of 1½:1 or 2:1 seems likely. The inner red lines would almost certainly have risen to within 3–5 cm. of the full height of the conjectured horizontal black band and then turned inwards to line each panel. This arrangement of a broad overall framework, divided into panels lined with a secondary colour, is largely typical of the adjacent Clay Walled Building (page 227) and elsewhere in Roman Dover. Of the 278 fallen fragments of plaster recovered from the North Passage, very few reflect the *in situ* design. It is thus unclear what design or colour scheme bordered the tops of the panels, or whether the wall was painted white to ceiling-level.

2). Description of the Painted Schemes used in the Painted House

In outline (Fig. 44) each room had a marbled dado (1), below an open field, or stage (2), the latter in turn surmounted by a continuous rectilinear podium (3) set with massive projecting bases. On the latter sat an equally massive colonnaded structure, consisting of short transverse screen walls, fronted by fine fluted columns (4), on large moulded bases. The columns framed large, upright rectangular panels (5) themselves outlined with borders in three main colours. A series of highly significant motifs (6), painted in forward perspective, preceded each panel, or adorned it in some way. It is clear that the flanking columns supported capitals which, in turn, supported a horizontal entablature (7). On the complete walls this incorporated pairs of aediculae (with added pediments at least in Room 3) and certainly there was a background frieze (8) above and a painted cornice band (9) at ceiling-level.

The *in situ* and the fragmentary plaster together provide some precise height dimensions for most of the elements described, but the remaining ones are estimated. Together these suggest an estimated original wall height of 2.80–3.00 m. Each element is described below (Nos. 1–9).

(1) THE DADO (Fig. 44 and Plate XXIII).

The lower zone of decoration nearest to the floor (the dado) was a very common element in Roman wall-painting. It was generally of little interest to either the artist or the house-owner, for it lay well below eye-level and would have been partly obscured by furniture. In each of the rooms of the Painted House the dado is painted in a single main colour and flecked to imitate marble veneer. In Rooms 2, 4 and 6 the dado is mottled dark green and mid-green, flecked all over with small pale green spots. In Rooms 1, 3 and 5 the dado is a mottled dark red, flecked over with small pale red spots. The dado in Room 2 is 52–63 cm. high above the floor moulding; in Room 3 it is some 66–74 cm. high and in Room 4 about 69 cm. high. In each case the dado is delimited by a thin maroon line and a scored line along its base, but with a maroon band, mostly 4–5 cm. wide, along its top. The maroon band is delimited on its lower side by a thin white line, mostly 5–8 mm. wide.

At regular intervals along all the dados are pairs of nearly vertical stripes, each pair carefully arranged to fit symmetrically beneath the base of a column. Each stripe consists of a central white line, mostly 2–8 mm. wide, defined unevenly on each side by a maroon line. The inner maroon line of each pair is generally only 5–10 mm. wide, whereas the outer maroon line of each pair is generally 10–17 mm. wide. Each pair of stripes has a slight upward taper and this leads the viewers eye upwards to the main design above. All the lines noticeably lean to the right, though this seems to add nothing to the design and may simply have been an error due to quickness or parallax. The internal space between the stripes of each pair varies from 19–31 cms. and their presence helps to fix the exact position of several missing columns. One bad error occurs in Room 4, where the left-hand column (between Panels 26 and 27) only has a single stripe beneath it!

(2) THE OPEN-FIELD, OR STAGE (Fig. 44 and Plates XXIV–XXV).

Immediately above the maroon band framing the top of the dado is a continuous open-field, largely free of detail. This forms a surface upon which the bottom of the podium, column bases and motifs rest. If this is regarded as a horizontal surface it creates a receding 'stage' starting at the dado-band and setting-off the whole scene above.

This zone is mostly 23–33 cm. wide and appears in three bright colours, all toning to blend with each other. In general the lower part is either pink-red or dark yellow, the centre a pale yellow and the top a pink-cream. These colours have been quickly applied by means of long, horizontal brush-strokes. The pink-red seems initially to have covered most of the zone, with a pale yellow added over it and the pink-cream applied last.

(3) THE PODIUM (Fig. 44 and Plate XXVII).

Bordering the top of the open-field, or stage, is a neat rectangular podium that is about 9.5 cm. high and continues around each room at between 95–105 cm. above the floor. Projecting from this horizontal podium are large rectangular bases which are angled forward and downwards into the open-field. Both the podium and the bases are shown three-dimensionally. The bases divide each wall into roughly regular units and as there are no bases at the corners of the rooms the design was for each complete wall to have four bases, framed by five panels.

The podium and the attached bases are painted pink, with a slightly darker pink being used for the vertical faces and a pale pink mostly being used for the horizontal faces. The vertical faces of both the podium and the bases have faint traces of diagonal lines, in creamy-pink, painted on them. The bottom lines of both the podium and the bases have been sharply outlined in dark red, almost certainly ruler drawn, to help enhance the three-dimensional effect.

What is of special interest is that on each complete wall with four bases, the two bases on the left of the centre are angled to the left, whilst the two bases to the right of the centre are angled to the right. This clearly indicates a central viewpoint and as the shadows of the bases also fall left and right, respectively, a central light-source is also indicated. The shadows of the individual motifs (see below) also fall to left and right, respectively, in an identical manner and thus maintain the overall perspective. Where walls are not continuous, for instance where they are broken by a door opening, they simply have a pair of columns on the complete side. The east wall of the much smaller Room 4 has two bases, framed by three panels, again angled left and right, respectively, to maintain the central viewing-point. Similarly, the surviving shadows follow the same overall scheme and this again demonstrates a central light-source.

(4) THE FLUTED COLUMNS (Includes Column Bases and Capitals). (Figs. 44 and 45 and Plate XXVIII).

Each rectangular base along the podium supported a short transverse wall finished with a fine fluted column at its outer end. The implication is that each column must have been three-quarter attached to the transverse wall. This is supported by a series of six painted horizontal white lines, clearly representing mouldings, which vary in length and suggest a base in Doric style. Some five or six more white lines appear to return along the transverse wall, again suggesting a base with distinctive mouldings. At the internal junction of the transverse wall with the back wall are at least five more white lines which suggest the base-mouldings of another quarter-column fitting

116

DETAIL of COLUMN BASE

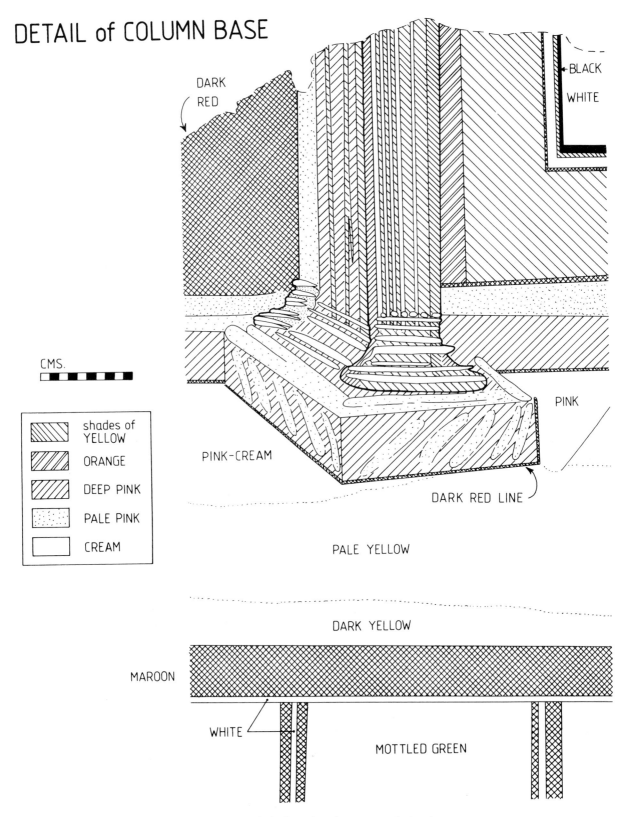

DARK RED

BLACK

WHITE

CMS.

shades of YELLOW

ORANGE

DEEP PINK

PALE PINK

CREAM

PINK

PINK-CREAM

DARK RED LINE

PALE YELLOW

DARK YELLOW

MAROON

WHITE

MOTTLED GREEN

Fig. 45. *Detail of column base between panels 9 and 10.*

snugly in the corner. The application of the rear most white lines greatly enhances the three-dimensional effect of the scheme. In addition the horizontal white lines are separated from each other by yellow-brown lines, the latter returning up each side of the fluted column and also along the bottom of the transverse wall. It seems clear that these brown lines are intended to represent shadows, cast by the adjacent mouldings, highlighted in white. Again this adds to the overall three-dimensional effect.

In detail, the columns are created by a series of finely painted yellow-cream vertical lines, over a yellow-brown band giving the illusion of shadows and highlights on what is meant to be a fluted marble column. At least six vertical lines seem to be present in most cases, each one reflecting the central light source striking the ridge of the fluting.

The columns probably had a height of at least 1.00 m., in suitable proportions to the panel heights (see below) and it must be that they were finished with capitals. None survives *in situ*. Architecturally, the scheme requires Doric-style capitals but none was found amongst the 25,000 fragments from inside the building! The only evidence of capitals are fragments of some seven individual examples. One rather uncertain fragment forms part of Panel 5 in Room 2. The other six, however, all came from Room 3 and are somewhat free-style in character, but very much Corinthian in form. These share some common colour and design elements with the vertical *in situ* columns and it must be that they formed a part of the same basic scheme (see below, No. 6 and discussion). From this it seems likely that in part artistic considerations superceded strictly orthodox architectural conventions and indeed this is supported by other evidence from the painted scheme. The columns were mostly 70–75 cm. in width and survive to a maximum height of about 60 cm. above the bases.

(5) THE PANELS (Figs. 43 and 44 and Plate XXIII).

Another important element in the design of each room was a series of large upright white panels, placed roughly at eye-level and each bordered by a broad band of a single colour. Clear evidence of 22 such panels survives *in situ*, whilst 6 more are implied by related detail. The estimated total of original panels for all six rooms is 93 (see below). In the three rooms where panels survive the borders are predominantly red, yellow or pink.

Room 2 (green dado) : 18 panels				
Panel	Wall	Border	Motif	Shadow
1	East	Yellow	–	–
2	South	Yellow	Torch	Left
3	South	Red	Vine	Left
4	South	Pink	2 fronds/thyrsus in basket	Left and Right
5	South	Red	?	Right
6	South	Yellow	Torch	Right
7	West	–	Thyrsus	Left
8	West	Pink	Tympanon	Beneath
9	West	Red	Large frond	Right
10	West	Yellow	Thyrsus	Right
11	North	Yellow	Torch	Left
12	North	Red	Vine	Left
13	North	–	?	–
14	North	–	Vine	Right
15	North	Yellow	Torch	Right
16	East	Yellow	Thyrsus	Left
17	East	Red	Large frond	Left
18	East	–	?	–

Room 3 (red dado) : 16 panels				
19	North	–	–	–
20	North	Red	Vine	Right
21	East	Red	Torch	Left
22	East	Yellow	Tympanon	Left
23	East	Pink	2 fronds	Left and right
24–25	–	Destroyed	?	–
35–43	–	Destroyed	?	–
Room 4 (green dado) : 9 panels				
26	East	Yellow	Large frond	Left
27	East	Pink	Syrinx	Beneath
28	East	Yellow?	Large frond	?
29–34	–	Destroyed	?	–
Room 1 (red dado) : 18 panels – destroyed				
Room 5 (red dado) : 21 panels – destroyed				
Room 6 (green dado) : 11 panels – destroyed				

Table listing painted panels in the Roman House

The panels in each room mostly alternated with fluted columns so that in Rooms 1 and 2, for instance, each extant wall was planned to have four columns and five panels. This arrangement was broken by the door-openings, which were rather wider than a single panel and its flanking columns, which reduced these walls to only four panels each. The total number of panels in Room 2 was therefore 18 and of these clear evidence survives of 14. Room 1 appears to have been almost identical in size to Room 2 and allowing for west and north doorways, it too must have been provided with 18 panels. No trace of these has survived.

It is, however, possible to estimate the number of panels in Room 3 and elsewhere within the house on the basis of the substantially complete panels and their components. On the south wall of Room 2 five panel elements, on a wall 4.84 m. in length, have an average width of 97 cm. The 3 panel elements on the east wall of Room 4 have an average width of 93 cm. Whilst panels clearly varied slightly in width there was almost certainly a need to provide odd numbers of panels to maintain the balanced architectural scheme based on a centre-point panel on each wall.

On this basis Room 3 certainly had 4 panels and also a door-opening on its east wall and a single panel on each side of the wide opening with Room 4 on its south wall. Its longer, main north wall probably had only 5 panels and its west wall also 5 panels, hence some 16 panels in all.

Only parts of three panels survive on the east wall of Room 4, but with an average panel width of about 93 cm. each, the three walls there should thus have had three panels each, thus producing a total of nine panels in all.

The reconstruction of Room 5 (p. 28) suggests that this room was the largest in the building. Only a small section of dado survived *in situ*. Again, by using the same criteria, it seems likely that the north wall would have had eight panels and a single doorway; the west wall four panels and a doorway; the east wall five panels and the south wall two panels on each side of the wide opening with Room 6, hence 21 panels in all.

Only the east wall of Room 6 had survived intact, but little of its plaster remains *in situ*. Based on the reconstruction of this room and also the average panel spacing it seems likely that the south wall may have contained five rather smaller panel elements and its east and west walls three rather larger panels each, hence a total of eleven panels in all. This produces a grand total of 93 panels in all, of which clear evidence for 22 survived *in situ*.

In detail, although only five complete white-ground panels survive in Room 2, it seems clear that these varied in width from 47–54 cm. The narrower ones were at the sides and the wider ones inside them whilst the central panels (all missing) are estimated to have been about 64 cm. wide. With the panels diminishing in width away from the central viewing point the general perspective was enhanced. Where the panels have not survived the same diminishing progression can be calculated from the surviving column bases. Paradoxically, however, Panel 22 on the east wall of Room 3 appears unusually narrow, whilst the panels on the short door responds must have been restricted to about 43–56 cm.

Nowhere does a white-ground panel survive to its full height. The most complete is Panel 2 where the total height surviving is about 48 cm., including the internal lining. The adjacent Panel 3 survives to a total height of about 46 cm. and this contains the greater part of a vine motif. Clearly another 10 cm. or more has to be allowed to complete the motif and this then produces a minimum height of about 56 cm. Now Panel 3 almost certainly matched Panel 5 (see above) and as the top of Panel 5 survives as a very large articulated fragment it seems clear that both had hanging garlands across their tops. The surviving garland takes up about 30 cm. of the centre of the top of the panel which, allowing for the full height of the vine, produces a minimum height of 86 cm. Presumably there was at least a modest space between the garland and the vine and if so then a vertical panel height of about 90 cm. may be indicated.

There is some modest circumstantial evidence to suggest such a panel height. Almost invariably elsewhere panels have heights which exceed their widths. This is both artistically more acceptable and it also produces a better balance. A good ratio seems to be about 2:3, for a panel ratio of (say) 2:4 appears to be rather too high for a good balance, or for the architectural design in terms of the column-height and column-base ratio. The minimum height of Panel 2 is 48 cm., and its width 56 cm., whilst the large centre panel is about 70 cm. Clearly, the panel heights had to be constant all round and thus with varying widths the exact ratio would also vary. The suggested height of 90 cm. produces a sound 2:3 ratio for Panels 2 and 3 and rather less for Panel 4 (about $2\frac{1}{3}$:3). A much greater height would certainly heavily overbalance the narrower panels, particularly those flanking door-openings. For these reasons a panel height of about 90 cm. has been assumed for the panels in all the rooms. This dimension also helps create a height of about 1.80 m. for the central zone of the scheme, which is itself within acceptable limits (see above).

It seems clear from the surviving plaster in Room 2 that a set colour-scheme was adopted for the panels borders. The most complete south wall had bold yellow bordered panels at the corners, dark red panels inside these, whilst the centre panel was salmon pink. Enough survives of the other three walls to show that the same colour sequence was followed in each case. In Room 3, however, the surviving east wall has a dark red bordered panel in the north-east corner, a bright yellow one next to it and a salmon pink panel at its centre. No details are known of the other panels, but it is clear that at least a marginally different colour-scheme was used in Room 3. The middle panel on the east wall of Room 4 had a salmon pink border and traces of a yellow border can just be seen to the left of it.

A possible variation to the overall panel pattern may be indicated by a panel (No. 22) on the east wall of Room 3. Here the yellow border is unusually wide (at least 18 cm. to the broken edge) whilst the total panel border space is itself narrow (about 68 cm.). It is possible that the yellow does not represent a border, but a solid yellow panel instead. This suggestion is partly supported by plaster fragments found nearby which show a male figure (Subject 9) painted on a red ground which almost certainly formed part of a solid red panel on the north wall. This evidence could suggest that Room 3 had some coloured panels.

(6) THE MOTIFS (Figs. 46–49).

It is clear from what both survives *in situ* and from the many fallen fragments that few of the large white panels, enclosed within their coloured borders, had been provided with a centrally placed design, or motif. It is, however, certain that each panel was at least partially superimposed by one or more highly interesting motifs, some unique and some often repeated. At least eight motifs (Motifs A–H) can be identified and parts of several others can be identified from fallen fragments (see below page 145). Those motifs that are repeated generally have the same coloured frame around the white panel.

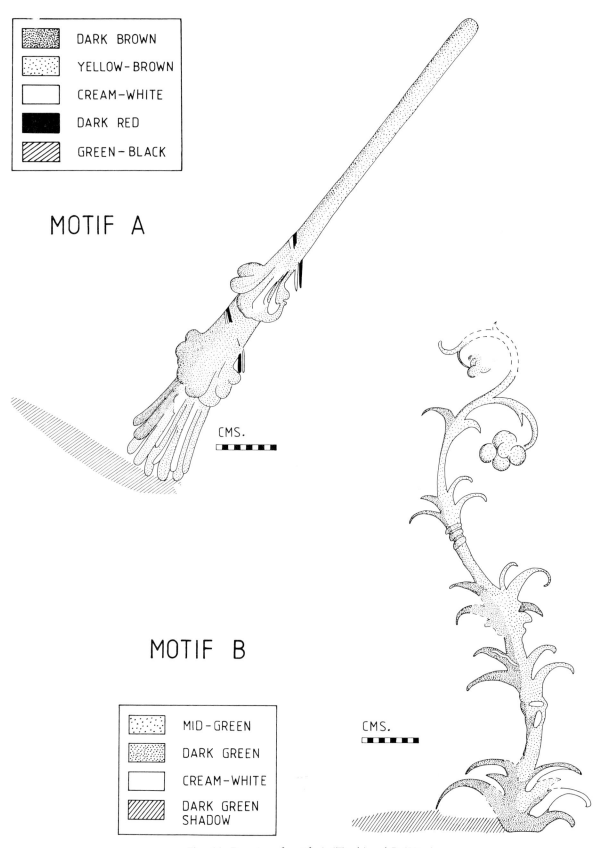

	DARK BROWN
	YELLOW-BROWN
	CREAM-WHITE
	DARK RED
	GREEN-BLACK

MOTIF A

CMS.

MOTIF B

	MID-GREEN
	DARK GREEN
	CREAM-WHITE
	DARK GREEN SHADOW

CMS.

Fig. 46. *Drawing of motifs A (Torch) and B (Vine).*

Room 2, which contained the most intact painted plaster, accordingly has the most *in situ* motifs. The south wall (with four partially intact panels) has a large yellow-brown torch (Motif A) in its corner panels, a green tree-like vine (Motif B) on the inside panels and a pair of downturned fronds (Motif C) with a shallow bowl or basket (Motif D) under the central panel. The opposing north wall seems to have supported the same motifs in identical positions.

The west wall of Room 2 has a different sequence of motifs. The north-west corner panel supports a green-black thyrsus (Motif E) and this seems to have been repeated at the south-west corner. Certainly the inside panel at the north-west is underlaid by a large single frond (Motif F) and the central panel appears to have been underlaid by a tympanon (Motif G). It seems probable that the east wall matched the west wall, in the same way that the north and south walls did.

In Room 3 the three surviving panels on the east wall display again the torch, the tympanon and the pair of fronds, whilst the single panel surviving on the north wall displays another vine. The three panels on the east wall of Room 4 repeat the large single frond on each side of a syrinx (Motif H), the well-known pipes of Pan. The choice of these rather unusual motifs, taken collectively, is highly significant. The following detailed study of the motifs by Wendy Williams has shown convincingly that, in association, they represent much of the paraphenalia associated with the cult of Bacchus (see discussion on p. 137).

Motif A. Torch, Panels 2, 6, 11, 15 and 21. (Fig. 46 and Plate XXIX).

This appears at least five times, always associated with a corner panel. There are four in Room 2 (Panels 2, 6, 11 and 15) in yellow-bordered panels and one in Room 3 (Panel 21) in a red-bordered panel. The best example is in Panel 11. A comparative study of the five individual paintings shows an overall pictorial similarity although there are slight variations in width, length and angle of placement. The object is linear, slightly tapered at its upper end and gradually fanning out at its lower end. It is thickened in two places and displays two pairs of ribbon-like attachments (fillets) above each thickened region. The object has been identified as an inverted, unlit torch which is propped on the stage at an angle of about 45° and leaning against the panel border. All the torches lean away from the corners of the rooms.

A three-dimensional effect has been created by the application of a darker pigment along one side of the motif, combined with pale highlights along the other, suggesting a light-source from somewhere near the centre of both rooms. The illusion is further enhanced by the addition of a shadow cast on the stage which extends sideways and slightly upwards from the base of each torch. The torches are painted in shades of brown, the main colour being a middle-tone yellow/brown, perhaps intended to represent wood. Shading is done in a darker brown while the highlights are picked out in cream/white. The shadows are all dark green/black in Room 2, while in Room 3 the shadow is brown.

The overall length of the most complete torch (Panel 2) is about 90 cm. The handle is about 55 cm. long and broadens from about 3 cm. wide at its rounded tip to about 3–4 cm. wide where it meets the head of the torch. Here the design splays outwards to form a half-circle cluster of five petal-shaped lobes about 10 cm. wide by 8–9 cm. long. The centre of this is about 36 cm. above the lower limit of the motif. A further two, or so, lobes overlie the centre of the cluster and are picked out in cream-white highlight.

A further extension of the torch-head emerges from this cluster with a width of about 5–6 cm. and this broadens gradually for about 7 cm. until it is about 7 cm. wide. It then splays outwards into another, larger half-circle of about eight petal-shaped lobes, the centre of the cluster being about 19–20 cm. above the lower limit of the motif. This second cluster is about 11–12 cm. wide and 9 cm. long.

A group of about 11 blunt, stick-like objects protrude downwards and fan slightly outwards until they are about 12 cm. wide near the rounded lower end of the torch. The shortened 'sticks' at the sides and the three or so in cream-white highlight, overlying the group, suggests a bundle of twigs or sticks with the longest ones being in the centre of the bundle.

The two pairs of narrow fillets tied loosely around the torch are best seen in Panel 11. One pair is around the handle and the other is between the two lobed clusters. Both pairs are draped diagonally across the torch with the loose ends hanging vertically and finishing at about the same level. Each pair of fillets is composed of a dark red strand and a cream-white one. The fillets vary from 3–7 mm. in width. The centre of the upper pair of fillets is about 43 cm. above the inverted end of the torch and the lower pair is about 26 cm. above the same point. In the topmost pair the dark red fillet and the cream-white fillet lie together with the red fillet uppermost. The lower pair begins with the red fillet above, which then crosses over so that the cream fillet hangs uppermost. The loose ends are about 3–4 cm. long. The tapered shadow cast by the torches is about 31 cm. long and 5 cm. wide. On Panel 6 the lower edge of the shadow is lined with about 1 cm. of dark green-black.

Amongst the fallen fragments of plaster in Room 2 are several displaying part of a large green garland over a yellow bordered panel top (see text on Plaster Fragments, Subject No. 1). It seems highly likely that the garlands were shown draped across the upper zones of the panels containing the torches, but were linked with the adjacent red-bordered panels (see reconstruction).

Motif B. Vine, Panels 3, 12, 14 and 20. (Fig. 46 and Plate XXIV).

This certainly occurs four times, three times in Room 2 and once in Room 3, in each case with a red-bordered panel. The most complete example is Panel 3. Another red-bordered panel (Panel 5) in Room 2 displays part of a green shadow on the stage and a vine here would mirror the plant in the opposing Panel 12 on the north wall. A study of the four individual paintings shows a basic similarity. A winding stem rises from a small clump of foliage on the stage to branch and terminate in at least two bunches of small, rounded green 'fruits', possibly grapes. This plant may, therefore, be intended to represent a stylised grape-vine.

Again a three-dimensional effect has been achieved with the use of shading, highlights and a shadow. The plant is mid-green with darker green shading and cream/white highlights. The shadow cast on the stage is also green.

A stem, which is between 2.6–4.2 cm. thick rises in a shallow S-shape from a clump of five to seven pointed, out-curved volutes. These basal clumps are 11–12 cm. in height and 25–27 cm. in width. The sides of the stem are partly corrugated (clearest in Panels 12 and 20) with bulges about 2 cm. long which seem to represent a twisting growth. At intervals along the stem there are further clusters of outcurved, pointed volutes which reduce in size towards the top of the plant. At a point which is 73 cm. above the base the stem divides into two branches, each about 1 cm. thick. One curves upwards and the other downwards which together form an estimated span of 21.5 cm. They terminate in rounded clusters (7–8 cm. across) of globular green fruits which are between 2 and 3 cm. wide. About 50 cm. above the lower limit of the motif there are three horizontal 'tendril bindings' about 1 cm. deep, 3 cm. wide and about 0.5 cm. apart. There may be another such feature about 21 cm. above the lower limit.

The green shadows cast on the stage are about 31 cm. long and about 4 cm. wide, and taper in a largely horizontal plane away from the base of the plant.

According to the most complete example in Panel 3 the top of the S-shape bends towards the centre panel and this feature is likely to have been common to all the other vine motifs. A very large fallen section of plaster found below Panel 5, again with a broad red panel border, displays a large green garland motif (see Fallen Plaster Fragments, Subject 1). It seems likely that other garlands once existed above the other vine motif, at least in Room 2.

Motif C. Downturned pair of fronds, Panels 4 and 23. (Fig. 47 and Plate XXV).

This design occurs twice, once each in Rooms 2 (Panel 4) and 3 (Panel 23), in pink bordered central panels. The best example is in Panel 4. A study shows that each frond rests on the stage and is shown foliage downwards. Each leans at an angle of 55°–60° and is propped against the 'plinth', or on the panel border. The pair of fronds in Room 2 oppose each other and lean away from the centre of the panel whereas those in Room 3 lean towards both each other and the panel centre. In Room 2 the fronds are associated with a bowl containing a thyrsus (?) and perhaps also foliage and fruit (Motif D), centrally placed between them. There is no evidence of these in Room 3, although the painted plaster here is worn and damaged. The bowl and frond motifs in Room 2 were likely to have been mirrored on the opposing north wall, the relevant section of which largely does not survive.

As with the single frond motif (Motif F) which is similar, although larger, a three-dimensional effect is achieved by use of highlights, shading and a shadow. The intended light source falls centrally between each pair of fronds thus creating opposing shadows. As with the single frond motif, the individual element of each pair displays a ribbon tied in the shape of a knot, or bow, with hanging ends.

A study shows slight variations in size and general outline, although each frond is pictorially similar. The right-hand frond of the pair in Room 3 shows the greatest variation and the leaves appear to have been painted in a more vigorous way. This frond also partly overlaps the vertical dark red band which frames the doorway into Room 2. The colours used are dark green, mid-green and cream-white highlighting. The shadows cast on the stage are brown in Room 2 and mid-green in Room 3. The remaining trace of a shadow in Panel 13, Room 2 is dark green-black, which may be a variant if this mirrored the pair of fronds on the opposing wall.

In detail each frond shows as a long-handled, splayed object with an overall length of about 37 cm. The upper part of the object is stick-like, varying in width from 1.5 cm. at the upper end to about 2 cm. towards the centre of the motif. The upper end of this narrow section displays a flange which projects downwards, away from the main axis, for about 5 cm. and outwards for about 2 cm. The lower 12–16 cm. of the object splays outwards and downwards, separating into a cluster of about 14 irregular lobes. Some 5–6 of these which are shorter and overlie the centre of the cluster are highlighted in mid-green and cream. The lobes vary from about 1–3 cm. wide while the whole cluster is 11–14 cm. wide. The fronds represent leafy branches torn from a tree with the heel intact.

The position of the bow is approximately central and is between 23–26 cm. from the lower limit of the motif. A rounded knot, or bow, projects from the upper side of the branch with two 'tassels' hanging from it. The bow is between 3–3.5 cm. wide and projects for 1.8–2.5 cm. The tassels, always one shorter than the other with the shorter one being 4–8 cm. long from the centre of the bow, and the longer one 8–11 cm. long from the same point. They vary in individual width from 1–2.5 cm. The longer end hangs to a point while the shorter end is cut off straight.

The ovoid shadows are about 32 cm. long by 6 cm. wide in Room 2 and 21 cm. long by 4 cm. wide in Room 3. They angle slightly upwards away from the base of each frond, except in the case of the right-hand frond in Room 3 which overlaps the painted door frame and may, therefore, have had no shadow. The shadows in Room 2 are outlined with a dark brown ring about 1 cm. wide.

Motif D. Basket with thyrsus, Panel 4. (Fig. 47 and Plate XXV).

The lower part of this design occurs only once on the *in situ* plaster in Room 2 (Panel 4) and the upper part in adjacent fallen fragments. In Room 2 it occurs in the centre of the pink bordered central panel (south wall) in direct association with the pair or downturned fronds (Motif C) and

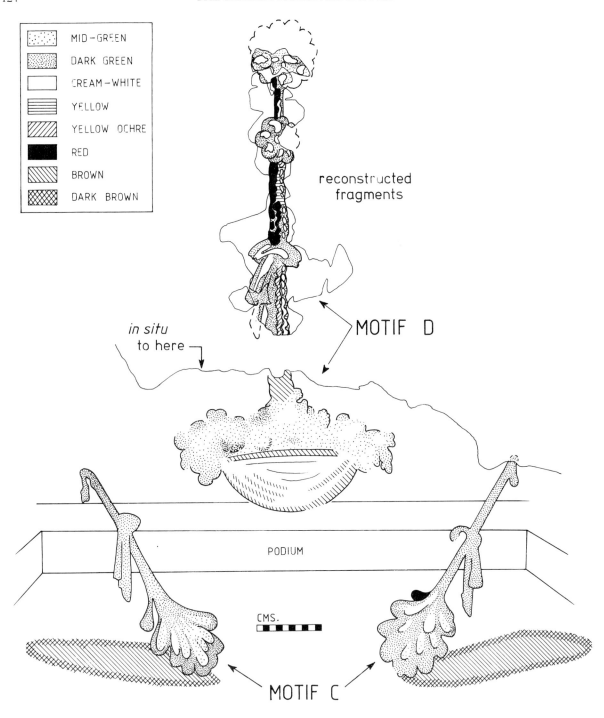

Fig. 47. *Drawing of motifs C (Pair of Fronds) and D (Basket and Thyrsus).*

it seems highly probable that another was mirrored in the opposite Panel 13. Unlike all the other motifs which appear to rest on the stage, this one sits on the horizontal plinth. The motif appears to be a semi-circular basket, or bowl, containing foliage and perhaps fruit with a single thick stem rising out of the centre of it.

Reconstructed fallen fragments from this panel suggest that the stem was the lower part of an elaborate thyrsus decorated with a bow and two bunches of grapes.

A three-dimensional effect is again achieved by the use of shading and highlight, suggesting that the light-source is directly in front of the motif, with outline shading on both sides. There is no visible shadow. The colours used are brown with cream-white highlights for the bowl and mid-green to green-brown tones for the foliage. This foliage spills out of the bowl with highlights picked out in cream-white. What appears to be a thick, central stem, is brown.

A study shows that the lower part of the motif (the bowl/basket) is a half-circle shape 9 cm. deep and an estimated 21.7 cm. wide, with the curved lower edge resting on the plinth. The entire semi-circular shape is outlined in brown, the straight upper edge of which may be intended to represent a rim 0.6–1.1 cm. deep. The central region of this bowl is painted in cream and brown bands which reflect the curved outline and become darker towards the base. This creates a ridged appearance which, together with the colour, resembles a basket. Above and partially obscuring the upper corners of the basket is an irregular mass of what appears to be fruit or foliage which rises above the bowl for 6.5–7 cm. and has an overall width of 34 cm. The left hand side as viewed has a globular outline which is mid-green and may represent grapes. The right-hand side is a more green-brown tone with cream highlights and a rather more irregular outline. Out of the centre of this mass rises a brown stem which is 3.7 cm. wide and a minimum of 4 cm. high to the point where it is broken away.

A group of 26 largely articulated fragments, found on the floor close to the position of Panel 4, display a linear motif on a white ground (motif D, upper). The object appears to be a staff, or branch, adorned with two bunches of grapes and a broad ribbon tied in a bow. This has been identified as the upper part of a be-ribboned thyrsus, more elaborate in form than those surviving *in situ* (motif E).

A three-dimensional effect has been achieved by the use of shading and highlights suggesting a light-source from the right. The shaft of the thyrsus is painted dark green or red along the shadowed left side, with yellow or yellow ochre, highlighted with cream-white, on the right side. The bow is dark green with cream-white highlights on the knot and on the hanging ends. The grape clusters are mid and dark green, again with cream-white highlights.

The overall surviving length of the thyrsus is 42.5 cm. The shaft is 3.6 cm. wide at its broken lower limit, narrowing to 1.2 cm. wide where it apparently terminates in a bunch of grapes. The sides of the shaft are largely corrugated with bulges which are between 1.5–2.5 cm. in length. The centre of the drooping bow is about 12 cm. above the broken lower limit and is 8 cm. wide and about 3.5 cm. deep. Two tassels hang from the bow down the left side of the shaft and are about 8.5 cm. and a minimum of 10.5 cm. long from the central point, respectively. The shorter one, which appears to be cut straight, is about 2 cm. wide and slightly overlaps the longer tassel which is largely missing.

There is a circular cluster of at least 7 globular 'fruits' overlying the shaft with a central point about 29 cm. above the broken lower limit of the motif. This has been identified as a cluster of green grapes with a diameter of about 7 cm. Each grape is highlighted in cream-white and is about 2.5 cm. in diameter. Above the first cluster and 4.2 cm. away from it there may be a second similar cluster, little of which survives. It appears to be larger than the first with an estimated diameter of about 10.5 cm. From the topmost grape cluster, down to the top of the bow, the left side of the staff has been covered in rivulets of red paint. The left side of the shaft below the bow is dark green.

The overall estimated length of the thyrsus from the broken lower limit to the estimated top of the presumed terminal grape cluster is about 47 cm. If these fallen fragments are reconstructed onto the *in situ* motif in Panel 4 then the overall minimum height of the thyrsus from the point

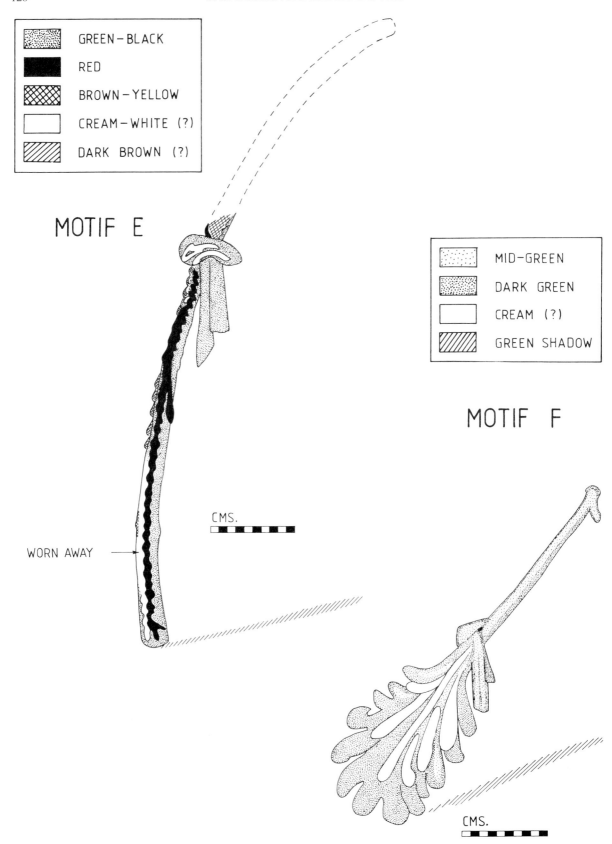

GREEN–BLACK
RED
BROWN–YELLOW
CREAM–WHITE (?)
DARK BROWN (?)

MOTIF E

CMS.

WORN AWAY

MID–GREEN
DARK GREEN
CREAM (?)
GREEN SHADOW

MOTIF F

CMS.

Fig. 48. *Drawing of motifs E (Thyrsus) and F (Large Frond).*

where it emerges from the foliage in the basket is about 53 cm. The overall estimated height of the entire basket/thyrsus motif is therefore 69–70 cm.

It should be noted that although the thyrsus appears to stand vertically in the basket, there may be a slight lean towards the left as suggested by both the hanging ends of the bow and the remaining *in situ* portion of the staff.

Motif E. Thyrsus, Panels 7, 10, 16 and possibly 19. (Fig. 48 and Plate XXVIII).

This motif certainly occurs three times in Room 2 and perhaps once in Room 3. It is associated with yellow bordered panels in Room 2 and also possibly in Room 3. A study shows a slender, slightly curving rod-like object with what appears to be a fillet tied around it in a knot, or bow, with hanging ends. This has been identified as a thyrsus, the 'magic wand' associated with the God Bacchus.

The best surviving examples are Panels 10 and 16, (Room 2) whilst the two badly worn and fragmentary examples are Panel 7, (Room 2) and Panel 19, (Room 3). It is assumed that there must have been a similar motif in Panel 1, (Room 2) to mirror Panel 7, although a careful search revealed nothing on the limited surviving surface.

The motif stands on the stage in each case and casts a narrow ribbon of shadow from its base. The thyrsi in Room 2 all arch towards the corners of the room, but the example in Room 3 may arch away from the corner. The latter is suggested by the close proximity of its base to the plinth at the corner. The base of the thyrsi otherwise start near to a column plinth which is away from the direction in which they arch.

Only one *in situ* thyrsus is sufficiently complete to display the large bow which is tied around it (Panel 10, Room 2). There are, however, fallen fragments of plaster showing at least one more bow. Again a three-dimensional effect has been created using shading, highlighting and a shadow.

The two best examples show that the main colour used was a very dark green/black with a strip of shadow, which is perhaps dark brown. An unpainted area on the knot of the bow suggests a highlight of unknown colour.

A comparative study shows a long, slender, arching rod-like object with a known length of 49.3 cm. and a reconstructed length of 75–100 cm. The base is slightly rounded and is about 3 cm. wide. The shaft narrows gradually until it is 2.3 cm. wide at its upper limit on Panel 10. The Panel 10 thyrsus displays what appear to be 'rivulets' of red and brown-yellow paint applied to the left side of the shaft as viewed, some of which run right down to its base producing a corrugated effect. A small amount of red along the Panel 16 thyrsus suggests that this feature also existed here.

A large dark green bow is tied around the thyrsus with its centre being 45.6 cm. above the base. The knot of the bow is 7.7 cm. wide by 2.30–3.50 cm. deep. The thickest portion of the knot is on the left as viewed. A pair of unpainted swirls across the knot may represent the 'negative image' of light cream-white highlight, now worn away. Two large loose ends hang from the knot, the longest being about 12 cm. long and 2 cm. wide, the shorter being about 8.50 cm. by 2.2 cm. The shorter ribbon is cut straight and slightly overlies the longer ribbon which tapers to a point on the left as viewed. The narrow pencil of brown shadow, which is 21 cm. long (Panel 10) and only about 0.8 cm. wide is cast sideways and slightly upwards to the right from the base of the thyrsus, showing a pictorial light source from the left as viewed.

Motif F. Downturned single frond, Panels 9, 17, 26 and 28. (Fig. 48 and Plate XXVII).

This motif occurs four times, twice in Room 2 with red-bordered panels 9 and 17 and twice in Room 4 with yellow-bordered panels 26 and 28. It has been identified as a leafy frond, the best example of which is in Panel 9. In Room 2 they occur opposite each other between the corner and centre panels on the east and west walls. In Room 4 they occur in the panels which frame the centre panel on the east wall.

Each frond rests, foliage downwards, on the stage and appears to be propped against the plinth at a 45°–60° angle. A three-dimensional effect is achieved by the use of shading and highlights as well as a shadow cast on the stage. The two fronds mirroring each other in Panels 9 and 17 display bows. A study of the individual fronds shows that they have been painted freehand and display slight variations in proportion, while maintaining pictorial similarity. The main colour is mid-green with darker green shading and cream highlights. The shadows are also green. The two most complete examples which are in Room 2, both display a ribbon tied around the frond in a bow.

A comparative study shows a long-handled, splayed object with an overall length of 46–49 cm. The upper part of the object is narrow and stick-like varying in width from 1.2 cm. at the upper end to about 2 cm. towards the centre of the object. The upper end of this narrow section displays a flange which projects downwards, away from the main axis, for about 4 cm. and projects for about 1.50 cm. The lower half of the object splays outwards and downwards, separating into a cluster of about 12 irregular lobes. A further six or so shorter lobes are depicted against the centre of this cluster and may have been highlighted in cream although only the 'negative impression' now remains. The individual lobes vary from about 1– 3 cm. in width and the whole cluster is between 20–21 cm. long and 14–16 cm. wide. The motif appears to be a branch, torn from a tree with the heel intact, with a cluster of blunt, narrow leaves at the end.

The centre of the bow is about 24–28 cm. above the lower end of the frond. The knot is between about 3–4.50 cm. long and projects from the branch for between 1.7–2.0 cm. There are two tassels, the longer being 8–10.5 cm. in length from the centre of the bow and 1.8 cm. in width. The shorter one is 5.5–8 cm. in length and 1–1.5 cm. in width. Both ends are cut straight and in each case (Panels 9 and 17, Room 2) the shorter tassel slightly overlaps the longer one.

A clear shadow underlies each frond and all are angled diagonally upwards from the lower end. They are about 20–25 cm. in length and 1.5–4 cm. in width. The fronds in Room 4 are similar to the ones in Room 2 but are slightly more upright because the panels are narrower.

Motif G. The Tympanon, Panels 8 and 22. (Fig. 49 and Plate XXXII).

This motif occurs twice, once in Room 2 with a pink bordered panel and once in Room 3 in a yellow bordered panel. By far the best example is Panel 22. The object appears as an ovoid, inclined to the left and it has at least three small downward curling tendril-like projections along one side. The object has been identified as a tympanon seen in three-quarter view. The tympanon, or hand drum, was similar to a modern tambourine.

Both tympania rest on the stage and appear to be propped against the plinth and panel borders at an angle of about 55° (Room 3) and 75° (Room 2), respectively. The tympanon in Room 3 is between the left corner and centre panel and leans to the left as viewed. The Room 2 example is in the centre panel and leans slightly to the left. Shading and shadow all help to create a three-dimensional effect consistent with a pictorial light-source from near the centre of the room in each case.

A detailed comparison shows that they are pictorially similar. The greater part of the motif is pale green with a darker green shading along the edge furthest from the intended light-source.

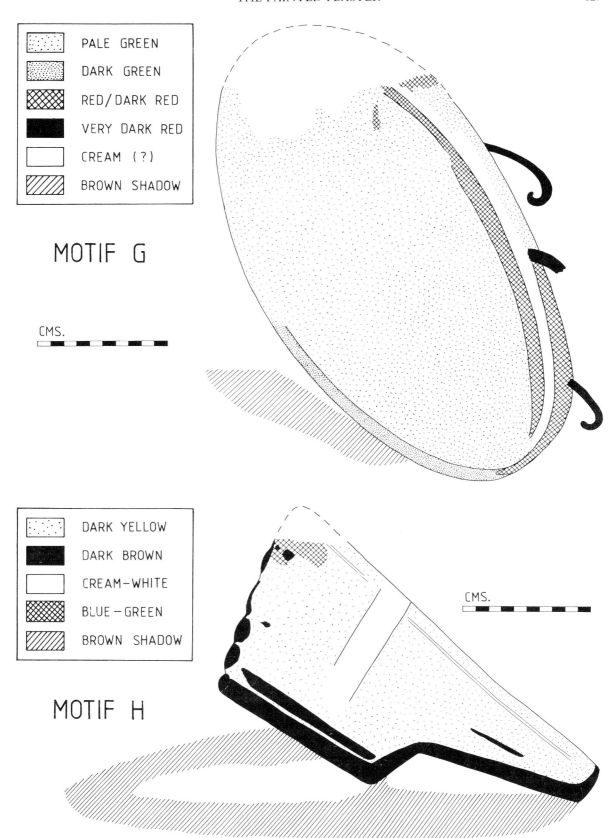

MOTIF G

PALE GREEN
DARK GREEN
RED/DARK RED
VERY DARK RED
CREAM (?)
BROWN SHADOW

CMS.

MOTIF H

DARK YELLOW
DARK BROWN
CREAM-WHITE
BLUE-GREEN
BROWN SHADOW

CMS.

Fig. 49. *Drawing of motifs G (Tympanon) and H (Syrinx).*

The example in Room 3 clearly shows that the edge which is pictorially nearest the viewer is vertically banded with red, cream and pale green. The three tendril-like projections are very dark red. The shadow is brown in Room 3 and green in Room 2. The example in Room 3 has a surviving length of about 34 cm. and has an estimated overall length of about 38 cm. The maximum width is 21 cm. in Room 3 and 19 cm. in Room 2. Apart from general shape the details in Room 2 are obscure. In Room 3 the tri-coloured band is 2–3.3 cm. in width. The innermost colour is red to dark red and varies from 0.6–1.4 cm. in width; the central zone seems to be cream although the pigment is very indistinct and is 0.8–1.1 cm. in width. The outer colour is red towards the lower end and becomes pale green at a point where the centre tendril-like projection emerges from the band. The width varies from 0.7–1.5 cm. and near the top end the pale green is about 2 cm. in width.

Projecting from this band are three very dark red, downward curling tendrils. The two most complete project from 2.8 cm (lower) and 3 cm. (upper) respectively. The width of the tendrils varies from 0.5–0.8 cm. and these features may have been intended to represent decorative ribbons. A small, poorly defined area of red paint across the upper limit of the band (where it is broken away) together with an adjacent red spot may represent another 'ribbon'.

The shadow in Room 3 is brown and extends diagonally upwards at an angle of 30° from the left side of the bottom, as viewed. It is 2.5–3.5 cm. in width and at least 16 cm. in length. The shadow in Room 2 is green-black and extends for at least 2.5 cm. below the tympanon. This is perhaps the shadow cast by the backward tilt of the object revealing the lower edge, which is depicted in dark green shading 2 cm. wide, extending all around the base and partly up the sides.

Motif H. Syrinx, Panel 27. (Fig. 49 and Plate XXIII).

This motif occurs only once in Room 4 where it is associated with a pink-bordered panel in the centre of the east wall. It appears as a sub-rectangular object, placed diagonally with a long straight side being uppermost and it can be readily identified as a syrinx, or Pan-pipes. It rests on the stage at an angle of about 45° and appears to be propped against the 'plinth'. The light source is from the right with a horizontal shadow being cast to the left. Again a three-dimensional effect has been achieved with dark shading along the underside of the motif, while traces of pale highlight are still just visible along the top. The main colour is dark yellow (yellow ochre) with dark brown shading and cream-white highlight. There are faint traces of blue-green pigment in the upper corner of the motif, part of which is broken away.

The overall estimated length is 31 cm. The rounded lower end is 3 cm. wide and this broadens gradually along the lower left side for about 13 cm. until the object is 8 cm. wide. At this point the lower side suddenly broadens to about 12 cm. and then continues to broaden gradually until it is an estimated 15 cm. wide.

The left-hand side has five corrugated ridges varying from about 1–3 cm. in length, each of which contains an oval of dark brown shading. These represent the open ends of the syrinx reeds across which the musician would blow. They are represented here in three-quarter view and are up to 1 cm. wide. A dark brown shadow has been painted along the lower side of the syrinx and is generally about 1 cm. wide. A cream-white band about 2–3 cm. wide crosses the syrinx near its centre and seems to represent some form of binding which holds the reeds together. The faint trace of blue-green pigment in the upper left corner may represent additional highlighting.

The tapering, brown, horizontal shadow on the stage below the syrinx is about 40 cm. in length and about 8 cm. in width. The centre of this shadow appears to have been unpainted thus leaving a brown outer band 2–4 cm. wide. This brown band touches both of the lower points of the syrinx showing that they rested on the stage.

(7) THE ENTABLATURE (Fig. 50) AND THE EVIDENCE FOR AEDICULAE. (Figs. 50– 51).

It seems clear from the architectural viewpoint, at least, that the short transverse walls with their fine columns and capitals, must have supported some sort of substantial architrave or entablature. Nothing of this level survives *in situ* and indeed its greater part must have been removed during the demolition processes for little of it survived amongst the 25,000 fragments lifted in Rooms 2, 3 and 4.

In Room 2 a single, though large, articulated mass of plaster, about 87 by 74 cm. had clearly formed the top of Panel 5 on its south wall (Subject 1, see detailed description on p. 145). It was found, face down, immediately adjacent to this panel and its dark red border matched that of Panel 5 still *in situ*. This shows a large hanging green garland, but also the upper part of the left-hand column, a small section of a capital and evidence of a simple horizontal architrave. The latter appears to create a canopy above the panel, where three horizontal lines in orange may represent shadows. These are beneath a frieze with vertical cream bands, similar to that found in Room 3. This suggests that the columns support a continuous projecting entablature around the room, but Dr. Tom Blagg has remarked (in a brief report) that the absence of supporting columns in the corners of the rooms demonstrated that this cannot be the case. Instead this suggests that the entablature must have been missing from above the two corner panels on each wall and suggests its maximum width as that of the three centre panels. Even this produces a somewhat overbearing and massive entablature which tends to reduce the three-dimensional effect of the column bases, the podium and also the motifs with their deliberate shadows. The sensible solution to this unsatisfactory composition is for the centre panel to have been left open (thus matching the corner panels) with the entablature being thus confined to the panel on each side of the centre. This creates a substantial projecting aedicula on each side of the centre panel and these are shown in the reconstruction (Fig. 50 and Plate XXXV).

Indeed, in Room 3, a group of 200 fragments from this high level had fallen onto the floor by the north wall. This has been shown by Peter Keller in his reconstruction (Subject 2, detailed description on p. 149) that the design included a pair of projecting aediculae, one on each side of a large yellow-bordered panel. Here Corinthian capitals support a massive horizontal architrave, the latter displaying a pair of mouldings, some small decorative devices placed centrally and surmounted by bold cornice mouldings. Above the latter was a large yellow area, of uncertain form, but tentatively shown as a pediment, itself decorated with a green motif, probably circular. The recess between the aediculae was provided with horizontal bands, surmounted by a thin dark red rail, which in turn, partly overlaps the vertical cream bands of the frieze. The reconstructed design (Fig. 51 and Plate XXXVI) also shows that the transverse screen walls of the aedicula were open at the top and that there were additional pairs of columns with capitals at the back. The lower part of the transverse wall appears solid to match the known arrangement of which so much remains *in situ* in Room 2.

From these two reconstructions it seems clear that such projecting aediculae were a major component of the design on the main walls of Rooms 1 to 3 and probably Rooms 5 and 6, but it is difficult to see how this could have been adapted for the smallest Room 4. The complete scheme on the north wall of Room 3 is rather more elaborate in detail than that in Room 2 and this is probably because Room 3 was a principal double-room. Indeed, its north wall appears to have been its main wall as it faced the wide extension (Room 4) on the south side.

Room 2 was not a double-room and its slightly less lavish treatment at entablature level may reflect its lesser importance. Even so, it seems highly probable that it provides a model for most of the other rooms in the house. Only in Room 5, which like Room 3 was a double-room, can it be suggested that the rather more lavish entablature would have been provided, again on the north wall! Whilst the general scheme was for a pair of matching aediculae on each long wall, the presence of door-openings would have reduced several walls to a single effective aedicula.

(8) THE FRIEZE (Figs. 44, 50 and 51).

An important element in many painted decorative schemes in the houses of Roman Britain, or indeed far beyond, was a high-level frieze forming the upper zone close to the ceiling and above the central design. Nothing survives at this level in the Roman House and again comparatively few fragments from the frieze were found in the demolition rubble.

A detailed study of the large articulated mass (Subject 1) has shown that in Room 2 the frieze surmounted the two aediculae and the open panels on each wall and was outlined along its base with a maroon stripe. At intervals along this there were small maroon projections, perhaps torus bases, from which rose vertical cream bands over a white field. The upper edge of the frieze was bordered by a wide maroon band from which was suspended at least one ornamental shield (Subject 4). The vertical bands are again present at this higher level and they seem to have been a major element in the frieze design. The surviving fragments show that the frieze had a minimum width of 21 cm. It would anyway need to be in proportion with the dado and central zone, the other two major components of the design, and a width of between 21–40 cm. seems to maintain a reasonable balance.

In Room 3, similar vertical bands, also cream, are also present and they certainly occupied the frieze zone between the two aediculae. It seems likely that they also filled the space behind the suggested pediment and helped create a frieze of much the same depth as in Room 2.

(9) THE CEILING CORNICE BAND. (Figs. 44, 50 and 51)

At a height estimated at about 2.80–3.00 m. above the floor, the vertical wall-face must have joined a horizontal ceiling in the normal way. Indeed, six fragments of plaster seem to represent the junction between these two planes. These fragments, found scattered in Rooms 2, 3 and 4, are mostly thick, coarse pieces poorly painted wih a maroon band, flanked by blue and white (see Subject 24). This band seems to have acted as the cornice.

All six pieces exhibit slight evidence of two surfaces joining at about 90°. The main surface represented, mostly 30–40 mm. thick, always seems to represent the vertical wall-face. In at least three cases this shows as two distinct layers, the lower one being a thick rendering which clearly curves outwards to meet an adjacent surface. The upper layer is a slightly finer mortar laid to infill the curved corner left by the lower layer and to create a right-angled corner. Slight traces of paint on part of the surface of the lower plaster could indicate that these layers were not laid at the same time.

In all six cases the exact corner appears as a tiny external lip marking the broken joint between the two planes. In at least three cases traces of distinctive plaster, taken to represent the ceiling plaster of Room 2, at least, can be seen attached to these fragments. This provides additional evidence that these fragments represent the high-level cornice of the rooms. The poor, uneven quality of the rendering and painting at this level could be explained by the obvious difficulty of reaching up to this very high point. The relationship of the ceiling band with the reconstructed complex ceiling designs is discussed below (page 221).

3) Discussion of the Painted Plaster from the Roman House.

Whilst most of the information on the painted plaster from the Roman House, found both *in situ* and fallen, is presented here for the first time, it is clear that continuing work may add new details on the individual designs and perhaps refine the overall decorative scheme represented. In the meantime, various aspects of the painted plaster and its application are discussed here.

(A). THE CRAFTSMEN.

It is at once clear from the large areas of painted walls and ceilings with their intricate and brilliant designs, that the skills of specialised craftsmen were required inside the Painted House. Indeed Vitruvius records (Ref. 64) how this specialised work was carried out. In modern building terms this 'finishing' work would be left to the very end of the building programme, when a small specialised team of decorators would move into a largely completed building. At Dover, although the floors, walls, door-linings and ceilings must have been completed before the painting began, the quarter-round floor mouldings were inserted *after* the dados, at least, had been painted.

The task of decorating the Painted House was a fairly major undertaking in itself. The six rooms, clearly forming a compact group, contained a total linear length of almost exactly 100 m. of vertical walling, even excluding the presumed door-openings. These walls seem to have been about 3 m. high and thus the area to be covered must have been about 300 sq. mts. There is some evidence to suggest that an upper storey existed and if it did, then the total area would have been as much as 600 sq. mts. Nor is this all. Very recent excavations have shown that at least four more rooms, of matching construction, were built at the same time as the Painted House, but to the east. If these represent a balancing range, as they probably do, then the total area that required painting could have been as much as 1200 sq. mts. Even this excludes the North Passage and all the exterior wall surfaces! The ceilings in six rooms which seem to have been painted on substantially different plaster, would add about another 170 sq. mts., or on two floors about 340 sq. mts. and in the two wings of the range, another 680 sq. mts. This produces a grand total of 1880 sq. mts. of internal surfaces to be painted. By modern domestic standards this would be a substantial contract, that would require a large volume of paint, a team of two or three men working for several weeks and it might cost many thousands of pounds and then working in only single colours. The Roman contractor at Dover was clearly working in at least eight different colours (see below page 268) and had to provide the materials. His pigments were mainly derived from local minerals, but the vermillion (cinnabar), at least, had to be imported from Spain!

Whatever the precise quantities and time required for completing the Painted House, it must be that the Roman contractor had to be highly organised, skilled and needed to spread his work over several weeks. His team would need at least one or two highly skilled artists for the large amount of detailed painting and these would need to be supported by semi-skilled workers for the simple areas, such as the dados and main borders. Unskilled workers could have carried out the labouring jobs such as moving the trestles, equipment and paint. In view of the size and complexity of the contract, a team of 4–6 men might have produced the most effective operation.

Just who these specialist craftsmen were is difficult to gauge. It seems clear that they must have been fairly mobile or even itinerant, for only in very large towns is it likely that there would have been enough regular work to support a permanent team. Similarly, the provision of floor mosaics, again a specialised skilled craft, required mobile craftsmen though it has been suggested that this was done on a regional basis (Ref. 65). Whilst, mosaicists and interior wall decorators must initially have been imported into Roman Britain it seems likely that Romano-British crafts had developed by the second century and remained until the fourth. The Dover painting (of about A.D. 200) could thus have been the work of a developed British craftsman, though the sophisticated designs at Dover were not inspired by Romano-British traditions but rather reflect the very centre of metropolitan Roman life itself. Clearly, the artists were working from pattern-books imported from the Mediterranean, though the possibility of personal contact, either by means of early training or of entrepreneurial enterprise into the province, should not be ruled out. Nor should the possibility that the *Classis Britannica* imported specialist craftsmen from Boulogne, or its Gaulish hinterland for the great naval base there was only 26 miles (40 km.) from Dover and thus much nearer than London and most other British towns. So, too, is it possible that marines of the British fleet were seconded to assist the painting operations, probably for the labouring work and just possibly for some of the semi-skilled operations.

(B). THE APPLICATION AND DESIGN.

Whatever his origins, the contractor was faced with blank walls and ceilings of varying lengths, punctuated by wide door-openings and presumed high-level window-openings. Into this rigid framework he had to fit his designs. Had he opted for an open, free-style decorative scheme this would not have mattered, but the chosen design was a rectilinear architectural scheme, in three-dimensions! This was based on a series of upright panel-elements, of largely standard size, for which the very wide door-openings and short responds caused significant variations.

Each wall surface had to be divided up into panel-elements, some having three (as surviving in Room 4), some five (as surviving in Rooms 2 and 3) and even nine (estimated for the north wall of Room 5). With a centre-panel view-point each wall had to have an odd number of panel-elements. Indeed this, with door-openings included, seems to have been the case though clearly the panel widths had to vary to fit in with the varying widths of the wall. Hence the average panel width on the south wall of Room 2 was 97 cm. and on the east wall of Room 4 it was 93 cm. An odd number of panels was also required for all the larger walls in the building for each had at least one pair of matching aediculae (as certainly in Rooms 2 and 3), or even two pairs (as conjectured for the north wall of Room 5). Even so, the wide door-openings clearly damaged the total effect, though it is not yet known how the contractor treated these to lessen their impact on his overall decorative scheme. So, too, the varying sizes of the ceilings would have demanded variations in any overall ceiling design and all these dimensional problems would have had to have been resolved in advance of the actual work.

It seems probable, on grounds of modern practice at least, that the ceilings were completed before the walls. Either way, the contractor had to apply the final coat of very fine lime plaster (*intonacco*) over the rendered surfaces of the walls. Whilst this was still wet he had to apply the colours to obtain the true 'fresco' technique. Clearly the painting had to be done with some speed and it seems likely that each wall would have been completed as part of a single operation, sensibly lasting one whole day. A much longer time may have seen the plaster-coating too dry for fresco-work, or else other techniques may have been introduced to effect the same result. An analysis by Peter Morgan has shown that some of the painted surfaces were burnished (see below, page 270).

In spite of the speed needed to complete each wall, no trace of marking-out lines has been found *in situ* at Dover, as occasionally elsewhere, though clearly some form of instant demarcation must have been employed. The final result looks fairly accurate, but a check shows several minor errors. The centre-point of the central panel of the south wall of Room 2 (the most complete surviving) is about 6 cm. nearer the west wall than it is the east. On a wall 4.84 m. in length this represents an error of just over 1%! The effect of this error was to make Panel 6 somewhat smaller than its matching Panel 2. In addition, the podium bases project forward at angles varying from 135–142°. In particular the two on the right side of the south wall of Room 2 appear parallel whilst the corresponding two on the west wall are substantially different. So, too, in Room 2 the top of the dado band on the south wall is 69 cm. above floor-level, only 58 cm. on the north wall with the east and west walls producing diminishing intermediate measurements to allow the band to be continuous. In addition a vertical line on the dado in Room 4, clearly intended to be one of a pair, has been missed altogether. This again may have been due to the hurried nature of the work. It is also clear that with walls some 3 m. high it was essential for the contractor to use scaffolding. Boards on trestles would be the most readily portable, but it is clear that even with these it was difficult for the painter to reach the highest part of the wall, for the ceiling band was poorly finished. Flecks of red paint from this high-level operation had splashed onto the main zone and the dado in places in Room 2. An excellent illustration of the combined plastering, painting and mixing processes is shown on a tombstone from Sens, France (Ref. 66).

As regards design it is clear that considerable thought went into the whole scheme. The wall height was divided into three basic units, the low dado, the central main zone and the high-level frieze, in a ratio of 24 : 59 : 17, respectively. The marbled dados were arranged alternatively in red (Rooms 1, 3 and 5) and green (Rooms 2, 4 and 6). The main zone was laid out in each room with a deliberate perspective to create a 'trompe-l'oeil' effect. A central viewing-point and light-source was selected for each wall with the central panel of each complete wall being the largest and the two panels on each side diminishing progressively towards the corners. Of the four columns on each complete wall, the two on the left, face the centre and throw their shadows to the left. Similarly, the two on the right, face the centre and throw their shadows to the right. So, too, do all the motifs throw shadows in an identical manner. The three-dimensional effect was further enhanced by corresponding shadows on the projecting podium bases, whilst the podium was out-lined in red on its horizontal and leading edges. The three-dimensional effect of each individual wall was good, but the overall concept tended to fail at the corners where adjacent columns appear to be opposed.

The general architectural scheme seems to have varied in detail, certainly between Rooms 2 and 3, with pairs of plain aediculae in Room 2 and more pretentious aediculae in Room 3. These variations probably reflect the importance of the respective rooms and there is a good prospect that the larger Room 3, with its south annexe (Room 4) may have been one of the principal rooms of the complex. In addition the motifs in Rooms 2, 3 and 4, whilst following the same Bacchic theme, were carefully varied. It seems certain that the south and north walls of Room 2 mirrored each other as did its east and west walls. However, the same order was not followed in Rooms 3 or 4. The former certainly repeated the vine, the torch, the tympanon and the pairs of fronds, whilst although the latter repeated the large frond it included the syrinx. Even so it seems probable that the motifs on the east walls of Rooms 3 and 4 were repeated on the corresponding west walls of these rooms. Exactly how the contractor went about painting the many ceilings with the intricate coloured design suggested (page 220), is perhaps beyond the scope of this Report!

(C). THE ARTISTIC MERIT.

Considering the apparent lack of marking-out and the speed with which the work had to be done, the result was remarkably good. Clearly, the artist was highly organised, efficient and very skilled. This was commercial art at its best and it could compare with any in Roman Britain, though perhaps it was not quite so finely executed as the very best of the wall-paintings in Italy.

The numerous straight lines, both on the panels and the podium, must indicate that a straight-edge was used and this probably not less than a metre in length. A straight-edge may also have been used for the column shafts. Here the tonal variation through a range of browns and whites is highly skilled and very effective. These colour variations create the highlights and shadows of a fluted marble column. The same technique, again in white and yellow-brown, is used to show the horizontal mouldings on the column-bases and on the transverse walls.

The motifs, of which parts of 22 survive, were clearly hand-painted, probably by the same person. Wendy Williams has shown that these were not produced by means of a template for repeated motifs all vary in some small way. Nonetheless, whoever painted them knew exactly what he wanted to produce and this suggests a high degree of familiarity. So, too, with the human figures, the artist clearly understood human proportions and what flourishes were required.

The overall colour scheme was both good and indifferent, in places. The panel borders, clearly the greatest obvious area of colour, were either mostly red or yellow, with the central panel-borders in pink. This red-yellow emphasis, enclosing white fields, seems to have been fashionable in the second half of the second century (Ref. 67). These wide borders were plain and unimaginative, though perhaps provided as a deliberate contrast with the fluted columns. The plain borders were balanced by vertical bands in the corners of the rooms and as borders of the dado, the ceiling and the door and the window-openings, always in maroon, or dark red. The dados were broad, largely plain areas of colour, stippled or flecked over to imitate marble, in an almost universal way.

Further skill in the use of colour, apart from the fluted columns and the base mouldings, is shown in the open-field, or stage, where a combination of three colours was applied in the sequence pink-red, pale yellow and pink-cream. This clever blend of colour in undefined zones created an illusion of 'space' in front of the grand architectural scheme. There was also the clever use of tones of pink, used to show the horizontal and vertical planes of the podium and also the main outline of the corresponding entablature above.

(D). PARALLELS.

In Roman Britain painted wall-decoration was widely used in towns, villas and even forts. Over 100 Roman sites, spread across much of the country (though mostly in the civil, lowland zone) have produced evidence of plaster though the extremes of climate, robbing and early excavations have left much of this very fragmented. The original number of Romano-British sites where painted plaster was an important element within a structure was perhaps 10 or 20 times the number so far known! Seldom has much survived *in situ*. At Combe End in Gloucestershire (Ref. 68) a length of some 6 m. and mostly about one metre high was found in a villa in about 1794. An early painting shows the dado and the very bottom of the main frieze with human feet and column bases. In 1897 a villa, at Iwerne Minster, Dorset (Ref. 69) revealed at least two walls with plaster surviving in total for at least 3 m. to a maximum height of about one m. It showed a white marbled dado with pink spots beneath a series of lined rectangular panels (as in the South Corridor of the Clay Walled Building at Dover). Apart from these and small amounts of low-level plaster at a few other sites, the Painted House at Dover is by far the best surviving plaster from Roman Britain. Rooms 2, 3 and 4 contained about 26 m. of linear *in situ* plaster, which survives to an average height of about 1.00 m. and thus produces a total area of about 27 sq. mts. When the North Passage is added this total increases to nearly 32 sq. mts.

The majority of British examples were perhaps simple rectilinear schemes of decoration, mostly consisting of repetitive lined panels in a limited range of colours. These seem mostly to have decorated minor buildings or the less important walls of major buildings. Indeed in Dover itself they occur in the narrow North Passage of the Painted House, in the adjacent Clay Walled Building and in at least two other buildings outside the naval fort. The more elaborate painted schemes in Britain occurred in the more important buildings, often in the principal rooms. Clearly this was the case at Dover for the Painted House range with its spectacular designs can (tentatively) be identified as part of the *mansio* of the port-of-entry for Roman Britain.

Although significant parts of some 30–40 fairly elaborate designs are known in Britain, many display a two-dimensional provincialism, in sharp contrast to a few much more finely executed designs. The general fine quality of the Painted House painting, in concept, detail, balance and perspective is at once clear and it thus belongs to a small group which includes fine painted wall-designs at Leicester (Ref. 70), Southwark (Ref. 71) and York (Ref. 72).

In detail, the alternating panel-column framework is repeated at Lullingstone (Ref. 73) and Verulamium (Ref. 74), but both are of inferior quality and later in date. The three-dimensional architectural arrangement at Dover is partly matched at Caerwent (Ref. 75), Rudston (Ref. 76), Southwark and Winchester (Ref. 77) and doubtfully, also, at Sparsholt, Hants (Ref. 78), though again most are artistically inferior. Significantly, perhaps, two small fragments from a villa at Wigginton, Oxfordshire (Ref. 79), seem to match some of the architectural aspects of the Dover arrangement and hint at a similar, if smaller, overall scheme. The Dover motifs are mostly unmatched in Britain, though broadly similar garlands occur at Southwark. Human figures occur, occasionally, at Dorchester (Ref. 80), Kingscote, Gloucester (Ref. 81), Lullingstone, Southwell (Ref. 82) and Winterton (Ref. 83), though these are mostly of different scale and form from those in the Painted House. That the motifs are unmatched elsewhere in Britain may, however, reflect the comparatively small quantities of plaster recovered, or studied, rather than an original lack of parallels.

It was, however, predictable that the best parallels for the Dover paintings would come from the Mediterranean area, or indeed from Italy itself. This proves to be the case. Even in 1971 Professor J. Toynbee (Ref. 84) had offered the Pompeian Second Style as the inspiration for the Dover paintings. However, as that town was obliterated by Vesuvius in A.D. 79, all the paintings there would have been at least 120 years earlier than those in the Painted House. Even so, allowing for changing fashions and ideas in that time, some of the paintings in the Villa of

Mysteries, the House of Vettii, the House of Pinarius Cerialis and the House of Siricus (Ref. 85) broadly reflect the panels and architectural elements of Dover. Whilst nothing at Pompeii provides a direct parallel for the whole Dover scheme, certain elements of the Dover composition seems to reflect these earlier paintings.

The better parallels come from Rome and Ostia (Ref. 86), where second and third century paintings have survived and some, at least, must be contemporary with those in the Painted House. The basic concept of a three-dimensional architectural scheme with columns and panels, finds its origins more easily there about the middle decades of the second century, or a little later. The House of Muses, in particular Room V, incorporates two white perspective columns on each wall, though the three panels so created are in solid colours with red and yellow predominating. Similarly, the Villa Negroni has perspective columns separating upright panels, with the columns sitting on neat bases.

Rather nearer the Dover concept still are walls from the *Via Merulana* in Rome where columns seem to frame red-brown panels, with animals, birds and fruit decorating the podia. Similarly, walls of a house excavated near S. Crisogona in Trastevere and in the House beneath the Baths of Caracalla, show perspective double columns on large bases with fine capitals, framing white-field panels containing floating figures and with a variety of animals and objects on the podia. Most of these elements strongly reflect corresponding elements at Dover, though inevitably the detail is different. Even closer to Room 3 at Dover, is Room VI of the House of Muses where a central aedicula is formed by two pairs of columns. Room X has a similar aedicula, but framing a yellow panel and it, too, has smaller flanking panels! So, too, with Room A of the Villa Grande double columns support aediculae, with a dominant central panel and some panels, at least, with white fields. Most of the latter examples date from the mid-second century to the mid-third century.

Whilst the overall architectural framework of the Dover scheme clearly matches those of several of the broadly contemporary grand houses of Rome and Ostia, the individual decorative elements occur widely, though predictably not in the same precise association. Hanging garlands are common. So, too, are human figures floating on white or coloured grounds. Bowls and canthari were popular devices and the thyrsus certainly occurs in a corridor of the Villa beneath the Lateran apse, also dated to the Severan period. The specific Bacchic theme at Dover is in part reminiscent of the Dionysic theme of a room in the House of the Painted Ceiling in Ostia. There, dancing figures are associated with musical instruments, including the tympanon and again hanging garlands. Bacchic cult objects were anyway common and reflect the cheerful image associated with his cult. Inevitably, comparison has to be made with the much earlier Villa of Mysteries, outside Pompeii, though the framework and figures there are substantially different from those at Dover.

(E). THE SIGNIFICANCE OF THE PAINTINGS.

Whilst the excellent quality of the design and painting was in good accord with the importance and scale of the building, it is clear that the total scheme was intended to represent a very specific theme. The broad architectural framework was anyway a popular design in metropolitan Italy (see above), often with panels and columns and three-dimensional *trompe l'oeil* effect. It is, however, the stage, the individual motifs and the human figures that provide the significant detail. From these there can be little doubt that the specific theme chosen related to the cult of Bacchus.

A detailed study of the *in situ* motifs (page 121), by Wendy Williams has shown that the association of these objects together, is in itself highly significant. Four of the motifs, the two different thyrsi (D and E), the tympanon (G) and the syrinx (H), may all readily be associated with a Bacchic scene. In addition four more, the torch (A), the vine (B) and the small and large fronds (C and F), are clearly complementary. Thus all eight fit comfortably within the general paraphernalia of known Bacchic rites, scenes or representations.

Similarly, Peter Keller has studied the additional motifs and human figures found on the fallen fragments from Rooms 2–4 and identified clear Bacchic associations. In particular he has shown that the three canthari (Subjects 21–23) are mostly regarded as *bona fide* Bacchic devices, whilst the garlands (Subject 1), candelabrum (Subject 6) and the bowls of fruit (Subject 5) may again all be regarded as complementary subjects. In addition both he and Wendy Williams have shown that the eight human figures (within Subjects 9–20) form an evenly balanced group. Their clear association within a building including many specific, or complementary, Bacchic motifs almost certainly shows that they too were part of Bacchic symbolism. This association suggests that the three female dancing figures were in fact maenads. For the same reason a fourth figure (Subject 9), a standing male holding a staff of uncertain form, could in fact represent Bacchus himself. Similarly, the seated and draped female figure could represent Venus, or more likely Ariadne, both frequently found in association with Bacchus.

On this evidence it seems clear that the Bacchic theme certainly prevailed in Rooms 2–4, as mostly shown by the *in situ* plaster. Additionally, the fallen plaster fragments, some very probably from upper rooms, also suggest that the Bacchic theme was used throughout all or most of the Painted House range. Indeed it is even possible to suggest that the figure of the presumed Bacchus on a red ground, mostly found on the north side of Room 3, came from a large centre panel on the north wall. It was anyway the main wall of this major double-room (with Room 4) and a central position here would be entirely appropriate for such a candidate within the overall Bacchic scheme. This suggestion requires the centre-panel to have a red ground and whereas this cannot have been the case in Room 2, there is some evidence to suggest coloured panels in Room 3 (page 110). The reconstructed plaster (Subject 2) suggests that the centre panel had a yellow border and thus both this and the red-ground Bacchic figure are shown in the ultimate reconstruction (Fig. 51).

Similarly, if the seated female figure, found mostly in Room 2, was Ariadne, then she too was probably the principal figure in the room, possibly seated at frieze level. Whilst artistically this appears an unlikely location, it must be said that clear traces of the frieze-type 'torus bases' survive behind her. The other female standing figures, floating on white grounds, do not easily fit in Rooms 2 and 3 and it seems more likely that they came from upper rooms, either within lightly framed panels, or even in continuous sequence without division!

In detail, the thyrsus can be recognised as a principal Bacchus device, the staff so often carried by the God himself. So, too, the tympanon, a form of small hand-drum, occurs frequently in Bacchic scenes. Similarly, the syrinx, or pipes of Pan, show the known association of Bacchus with Pan. Indeed, on the well-known Mildenhall dish and platters (Ref. 87), Bacchus, Pan, maenads, the syrinx, the tympanon and the thyrsus are all shown as part of a certain Bacchic theme. The vine, so frequent in the Painted House, strongly highlights the abundant wine of Bacchic festivals, whilst the canthari clearly held the wine at these events. The torch is also known in Bacchic rituals, amongst others, perhaps lighting the victory of life over death. The draped garlands and fronds are also appropriate symbols of the Bacchic ritual. Similarly, the dancing female figures are an almost essential element of Bacchic festivals, with or without the flowing garments. The garlands in their hair are another festive flourish, much like the ribbons (or fillets) on the thyrsi, the torches, the tympanon and the fronds. The fillets on the tympanon are, incidentally, reproduced on the tambourines on the 4th century Mildenhall platters.

Bacchic connections at Dover were originally identified by Professor Toynbee in 1971 followed by Peter Keller in his detailed conservation work on the plaster in 1978–85 and Wendy Williams in 1986. The same view was published by Ling in 1985 (Ref. 88) and readily accepted by Valerie Hutchinson in her detailed study of Bacchus in Roman Britain, published in 1986 (Ref. 89). Martin Henig, a constant advisor on mythological figures and paraphernalia, also readily accepted most of the motif identifications as Bacchic, or Bacchic-related, and that the standing male figure could be Bacchus himself. He also accepts the suggestion that the seated female figure could, in this context, be Ariadne. In addition, the Bacchic concept was one favoured by military personnel, to judge by military gemstones, which, with the marines of the *Classis Britannica* immediately south of the Painted House (and probably involved in its actual construction), is entirely appropriate. Finally, the role of Bacchus as patron of the theatre, seems to find expression in the balancing of the many motifs on the open-stage, in front of rather grand architectural scenery!

Whilst the Bacchic theme of all the rooms seems quite clear, what is less certain is its significance to Dover and the occupants of the Roman house. There can be no suggestion that the Painted House was intended to serve as a temple, for the heated rooms were clearly domestic in character. Indeed, there is a strong likelihood that the Roman house range formed part of a massive *mansio* (see discussion on page 281). In such a building, the function of the painted designs generally was to provide a decorative background and certainly this must have been true of linear and simple decorative schemes. Even so, the very strong Bacchic theme would have been recognised and appreciated by both occupants and visitors and this must have been a deliberate conception agreed and planned in advance.

Bacchus was anyway a god with a fairly universal appeal. Originally (through Dionysus) he was a patron of wine, viticulture and the theatre. Latterly, he evolved into a god of personal salvation, with some military exploits and strong ties with Ariadne and Pan. Satyrs, fauns and maenads also frequently accompanied him. The popular conception of Bacchus is his association with prolonged celebrations, with abundant consumption of wine and a variety of revelries involving satyrs, fauns and maenads. These themes, instantly popular to most, might very well suit important Roman travellers staying in the Painted House *mansio*. Here, might they celebrate their pending departure from isolated Britain, or else their safe arrival following a Channel crossing.

(B) THE PAINTED PLASTER FRAGMENTS FROM THE PAINTED HOUSE SITE.

by Peter Keller, A.I.F.A.

1). INTRODUCTION

The large collection of painted plaster considered here all came from excavations on the Painted House site in either 1970, 1971 or 1975. In all, some 22,508 fragments were recoverd and these probably represent the largest collection of such material ever recovered from a Roman building in Britain. In this report the plaster has been quantified according to stratigraphic context, location and fabric type (Table 1).

Fabrics / Groups	A (As in situ designs)	A (New Designs)	B	C	D	E	F	G	H	I	J	K	Total
Related demolition contexts	13,695	3,495	1,812	203	99	25	13	10	–	3	–	6	19,361 (86%)
Derived and intrusive contexts	1,591	223	49	30	47	14	11	38	–	–	1	4	2,008 (9%)
Unstratified contexts	764	158	98	9	96	1	3	–	1	–	1	8	1,139 (5%)
Totals	16,050 (71%)	3,876 (17%)	1,959 (9%)	242 (1%)	242 (1%)	40 –	27 –	48 –	1 –	3 –	2 –	18 –	22,508 (100%)

TABLE 1 – Distribution of plaster fragments found on the Painted House site, arranged in broad context groups and classified by fabric.

Of the whole assemblage, predictably, a large majority (some 16,050 fragments, representing about 71%) directly match, both in fabric and design, the plaster remaining *in situ* in the Painted House. These fragments do not add significantly to the surviving designs and although catalogued they are not described in this report. The remaining fragments (some 6,458, representing 29%) mostly represent plaster similar to that *in situ*, but with different designs; or else fabrics and designs not matched in the main Painted House. It is these categories that are discussed in this report where 36 new Painted House designs are also illustrated.

The plaster has been studied under three broad context-groups, as follows:-

a. Related Demolition Contexts (86% – 19,361 fragments). These are those deposits directly relating to the Roman House, either found in Rooms 1–6, or in adjacent demolition contexts.
b. Derived and Intrusive Contexts (9% – 2,008 fragments). These are the deposits either dumped to form part of the rampart-bank for the shore-fort wall; or in the foundation-trench for the fort wall; or in the later pits or robber-trenches.
c. Unstratified Contexts (5% – 1,139 fragments).

A preliminary analysis of the plaster fabrics (Table 2) shows that the plaster can be divided into at least eleven basic fabric-types (Types A-K). Of these, three types (Types A, B and C), almost certainly came from the Painted House itself, whilst the remaining eight fabrics (Types D-K) mostly seem to have been introduced on to the site from elsewhere in Dover (see below, page 143).

Location Fabrics	A (As *in situ* designs)	A (New designs)	B	C	D	E	F	G	H	I	J	K	Total
ROOM 1	307	174						8				6	495(2%)
ROOM 2	7,665	1,812	1,533	128	28		12			2			11,180(58%)
ROOM 3	3,795	1,241	179	8	20		1			1			5,245(27%)
ROOM 4	738	224	93					2					1,057(6%)
ROOM 5	73	13	2										88(1%)
ROOM 6	37					25							62(1%)
General demolition other areas	1,080	31	5	67	51								1,234(6%)
Total	13,695	3,495	1,812	203	99	25	13	10		3		6	19,361(100%)

TABLE 2 – Detailed distribution of plaster fragments found in the Demolition Contexts on the Painted House sites arranged by fabric.

The Lifting, Treatment and Study of the Plaster Fragments

The three rooms (Rooms 2–4) containing the great bulk of the fallen plaster were excavated in 1971 under considerable pressure from very urgent rescue-work on adjacent sites about to be destroyed. Two major soil baulks then had to be maintained across the main Rooms 2 and 3, but it was largely possible to excavate the other rooms on an open-plan basis. To meet these circumstances a simple grid of rectangles, mostly about 1 m. by 1½ m. (Fig. 52), was devised across Rooms 2, 3 and 4. These rectangles were identified by letter (A-W), firstly in the order of excavation (A-P) and ultimately during removal of the cross-baulks (Q-W), with the areas destroyed by later pits being uncoded.

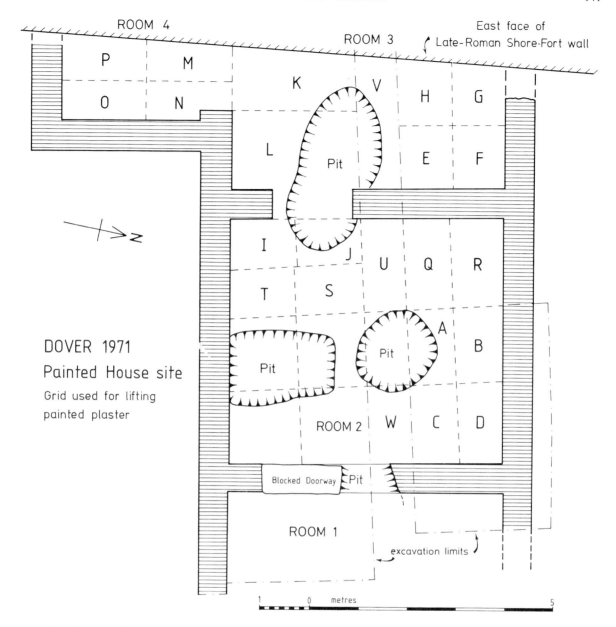

Fig. 52. *Plan of Rooms 1–4 of the Painted House C9, showing lettered grid used for lifting the Roman plaster.*

The plaster in each lettered rectangle was lifted in layers, each layer receiving its standard context number, its grid letter and a special number to show its vertical position (hence DV–2307, B, L. 2). All the fragments were then carefully placed in wooden trays though several larger articulated masses were first cleaned, treated with P.V.A. and reinforced prior to lifting. Problems of transportation, storage and study then followed, all severely hampered, initially, by no funding and subsequently by serious under-funding.

The plaster was carefully moved from the site to a disused room in the Keep Yard at Dover Castle, kindly provided by the Dept. of the Environment, but where there was no scope for work. A year later it again had to be moved to a large store-room in a disused building near Cannon's Gate, where the initial sorting was carried out. This work was badly interrupted by yet another move in 1974, this time across the road to re-conditioned premises where there was at last both heat and light. Unhappily, in January 1980, these premises were flooded due to unlagged water-pipes in the roof and damage was then done to some records and materials.

Several of the boxes containing plaster lost their original labels and this has caused some difficulty with the reconstructions. During the recovery work all the plaster was transferred to special sorting-trays so study could continue.

The initial work on the enormous task of sorting, coding, identifying, matching and joining of the many fragments for reconstruction was started in 1972 under the supervision of Miss Frances Brennan (now Mrs. F. Kneller) and continued in 1973 under the supervision of Mrs. C. Robertson, but then had to stop. Mr. Ralph Mills continued the work in the winter months of 1975–1976, when in just seven weeks, he devised an effective retrieval system which laid the basis for subsequent work. The writer first undertook work on this project for 18 weeks in 1977 and then fully restored Subject 1 for display purposes (discussed below). During this time it became apparent that some of the plaster was either similar in fabric to that *in situ*, but with different designs, or else of different fabrics and designs not matched in the Painted House. Further work was undertaken by the writer, assisted by Mrs. G. Bowers and Mr. P. Mungovan, during 1982 and 1985, totalling just 16 weeks, to quantify this plaster and to reconstruct as many of the designs as possible. This work showed that some 6,458 fragments (29% of the total assemblage), were represented by eleven plaster fabric-types, and had been decorated with a large variety of motifs and geometric patterns not represented on the surviving walls of the Painted House structure. Some 6,077 fragments of these (representing 94.1%) are of Fabrics A–C and almost certainly derive from the Painted House. It has been possible to combine 2,670 of these fragments to reconstruct 36 designs (Subjects 1–36). These are considered to be of special interest and are fully described in the following catalogue. The remaining 381 fragments (representing 5.9%) of this plaster, are of Fabrics D–K and seem to have been introduced onto the site from elsewhere in Dover. The latter will form part of a separate study of plaster from all the other Dover sites to be published in the future. For this reason the fabric descriptions and the reconstructed designs decorating their surfaces have not been included here.

Excavations north of the Painted House in 1976 on the Bingo Hall site recovered an additional 90 fragments from derived and unstratified contexts (see below). These have been included in Subjects 5, 9, 31, 32 and 36. In addition some 56 fragments from the Cause is Altered site, excavated in 1971, share similar characteristics in fabric and design to plaster forming Subject 32 and these have also been included.

All the motifs and geometric patterns have been reconstructed and studied as individual Subjects, based on key fragments selected from the total number sharing similar characteristics, whilst the remaining fragments generally confirm the picture which emerges. Additional reconstruction has been offered, in a limited number of cases, to combine Subjects to form larger designs. Future work will continue this process in the hope that it will allow larger designs and, perhaps, whole schemes to be reconstructed.

Owing to limited time and resources the present study is somewhat preliminary in nature and forms part of a much broader and more detailed study of all the plaster from Dover sites. However, a full catalogue of all plaster fragments recovered during the 'Painted House' excavations, a catalogue of the plaster fabric-types and a detailed account of the methods of conservation, reconstruction and restoration are held in the site-archive.

For the purpose of this Report the fabric-types are discussed first and this is followed by a detailed catalogue of the Reconstructed Subjects (Nos. 1–36), also arranged in fabric-type order. The catalogue records, under each subject, the deposit codes, room or area location and grid rectangles, as lifted. This is followed by a description of the key plaster groups and also of the colour scheme. Collectively, the key fragments then form the basis of a larger Reconstructed Design, which is then discussed in terms of both its implications and location within the Painted House. All measurements in this section of the report are expressed in millimetres for reasons of precision.

Most of the key plaster groups or fragments are illustrated and usually followed by an illustrated reconstructed design based on all the available fragments for that subject, though only positions for the key fragments are shown. A precise position for every fragment within the overall reconstruction is difficult and for this reason the remaining fragments are not shown.

Some identifications may be open to other possible interpretations, but the descriptions and drawings are as objective as possible.

(2) PLASTER FABRIC-TYPES.

An examination of the 22,508 fragments of plaster from the Painted House site revealed that eleven basic fabric-types (Types A-K) could be identified (Tables 1 and 2). These show that Fabrics A-C represent 98% of the total plaster and all of this appears to have come from the Painted House itself. The remaining fabrics (D-K) are likely to have been introduced onto the site and are not described in this Report.

The mortar fabrics have been differentiated by eye with the aid of an optical glass with a magnification of 1:3. The colours were compared with a Munsell colour chart and, where applicable, given its code, though this is only given as a guide since the colour is never totally homogenous. Some hues and tones, not present on the chart, have been described independently. In describing the fabric, the quantity of grits in the mortar has been standardised as follows:

occasional	=	less than 10%
moderately frequent	=	10–50%
frequent	=	50–80%
very frequent	=	over 80%.

In describing the grits:

small	=	2 mm. or less
medium	=	2–6 mm.
large	=	6–10 mm.

Plaster Fabric A

Some 19,926 fragments, or 89% of the wall plaster recovered from the site, consist of a distinctive fabric, almost identical to that *in situ* in the Painted House. Of these 17,190 fragments were recovered from demolition deposits relating to the Painted House structure. The remaining 2,736 fragments were retrieved from either derived, intrusive or unstratified contexts. The plaster is composed of at least three layers collectively measuring a minimum of 65 mm. in thickness and comprising in order of application:

(i)   a hard, coarse creamy-white (Munsell 10 YR 8/2) plaster, a minimum of 50 mm. thick, with frequent medium and small white, light-brown and blue-grey flint grits with traces of chopped straw or chaff.
(ii) a hard, slightly gritty, cream-white plaster, up to 14 mm. thick, with moderately frequent small brown and blue-grey flint grits with occasional chalk grits.
(iii) a fine white mortar (intonacco) up to 1 mm. thick to which the paint was applied.

Of the total fragments in this group, some 3,876 display motifs and patterns not represented by surviving *in situ* wall-paintings in the Painted House. Of these 3,495 fragments were recovered from related demolition deposits. Just 1,112 fragments have been combined to form Subjects 1–26. A further six fragments were recovered from the Bingo Hall site and can be matched with fragments forming Subjects 5 and 9 and have been combined with them. The remaining 2,764 fragments await further study.

Plaster Fabric B

Some 1,959 fragments, 8% of the plaster recovered from the site, consist of a fabric sharply contrasting with Fabric A. Of these 1,812 fragments were recovered from related demolition contexts, the remainder were from either derived, intrusive or unstratified contexts. The plaster is composed of at least three layers collectively measuring up to 40 mm. in thickness and comprising in order of application:

(i) a moderately hard, very pale brown (Munsell 10 YR 7/4) plaster, up to 30mm. thick, with frequent small black, reddish-brown and white flint grits with traces of chopped straw or chaff.

(ii) a fine cream-white plaster, 9–12 mm. thick, with occasional small black, reddish-brown and white flint grits.

(iii) a fine white plaster (intonacco) up to 1 mm. thick to which the paint was applied.

Some 1,462 fragments have been combined to form Subjects 27–34. A further 69 fragments were recovered in demolition deposits during the 1976 Bingo Hall excavations. These match fragments forming Subjects 31 and 32 and have thus been combined with them. An additional 56 fragments were recovered during the excavation in 1971 on the Cause is Altered site and these share similar decorative characteristics with plaster forming Subject 32 and have thus been combined with it.

Subjects 27–29, although of plaster B fabric, are listed collectively under the heading 'Floral and Foliate Motifs', within the Fabric A group.

This fabric is of a finer quality and much thinner than other fabric types. Many fragments show the backing plaster to be flat suggesting that it had separated quite freely from the surfaces to which it had been applied. Several fragments show faint narrow ridges of plaster alternating with flat areas on the backing and it seems likely that they represent impressions left by small flat timbers. In view of this, the fineness of the plaster and the fact that much of this plaster was found directly on the floors of Room 2, it seems highly likely that this was ceiling plaster applied onto narrow wooden battens. Clearly very little has survived!

Plaster Fabric C

Only some 242 fragments, 1% of the plaster recovered from the site, consist of a similar distinctive fabric, substantially different from Fabrics A and B. Of these, 203 fragments were located in related demolition contexts whilst the remainder came from derived, intrusive or unstratified contexts. The plaster is composed of at least three layers collectively measuring up to 27 mm. in thickness and comprising in order of application:

(i) soft, slightly sandy, pale brown (Munsell 10 YR 8/3) clay-like plaster, up to 20 mm. thick, with frequent small and medium chalk grits and traces of chopped straw or chaff.

(ii) a hard, fine light grey (Munsell 5Y 7/1) plaster, 4–6 mm. thick, with moderately frequent small chalk grits and snail shell.

(iii) a fine white plaster, intonacco, up to 1 mm. thick, to which the paint was applied.

This fabric compares closely with plaster surviving *in situ* on the external south wall of the 'Painted House' structure and in the North Passage and it seems clear that this plaster also derived from an external wall of this building.

Some 94 fragments have been combined to form Subject 34. In addition, a further 17 fragments were recovered from derived contexts on the Bingo Hall site in 1976 and these have been included in Subject 36.

3). CATALOGUE OF DESIGNS RECONSTRUCTED FROM THE FRAGMENTS OF PLASTER FOUND ON THE PAINTED HOUSE SITE.

This catalogue describes some 36 painted designs on the fragmentary Roman plaster found in direct association with the Painted House, but *not* represented by the *in situ* designs (which are discussed above). The great majority of these new designs (Subjects 1–26) are on Fabric Type A plaster and almost certainly came from the internal walls of the Painted House; several more (Subjects 27–35) are on Fabric Type B plaster and appear to derive from the ceilings of the Painted House, whilst one design (Subject 36) is on Fabric Type C which certainly came from the external walls of the House.

The title of each subject contains a broad description and this is followed by details of the location of the corresponding fragments within the Roman House. Selected key fragments of each subject are then described and illustrated and from these a larger design is reconstructed. A discussion on the position of these designs within the House is then provided at the end.

SUBJECT 1 – Hanging green garland, over a maroon framed white panel with flanking column, beneath an architectural frieze (top of Panel 5). (Fig. 53)

A key group of articulated plaster (Fabric A); measuring 870 x 760 mm., was found lying face down in the south-west corner of Room 2 within the demolition layer (DV–2308, areas I and J). It was carefully lifted using plaster of Paris. The surface, although badly fractured, revealed the uppermost portion of a maroon-bordered white panel adjacent to a column up to frieze level. It has now been fully conserved and restored and is on display in the Painted House cover-building. From its position in the room, this key group almost certainly derived from the south wall and probably formed the upper part of Panel 5.

The lifted portion consisted of 153 (conjoining) key fragments. The impact of the fall badly fractured the surface causing further damage to the broken edges resulting in some loss of precise joins at surface level, but the body of the plaster beneath the surface still formed 'true' joins with neighbouring fragments.

The restored portion shows an internal 90° corner of a dark red-bordered, white panel. The white field (min. 480 mm. x 470 mm.) is framed by a dark red band (between 120–125 mm. in width) and lined with a white interval (up to 10 mm.); a pale green stripe (up to 7 mm.) and a maroon stripe (4–6 mm.).

A foliate motif, painted in two shades of green and probably representing a garland of leaves, decorates the panel. This measures between 30 and 70 mm. in width and is suspended from the top of the maroon border, 280 mm. from the top left external corner, to curve down to the right, probably through the border.

To the left of the panel and adjacent to the dark red border is a series of vertical bands representing a column. This consists of a light yellow-brown band (60 mm. wide) treated with at least seven parallel yellow-cream stripes (up to 4 mm. wide) that represent fluting on the front of the column. These are capped by two horizontal convex stripes of cream 5 mm. wide and 5 mm. apart. To the left of the column is a dark green band (30 mm. wide) followed by a band of pale pink treated with cream-white vertical stripes, (up to 3 mm. wide) that may also represent fluting. This sequence projects above the panel top by some 35 mm. where the green band terminates almost level with the convex cream stripes and is angled 110° up to the left. This may represent the beginning of a splayed capital which projects upwards a minimum distance of 40 mm.

To the left of the junction and the presumed capital is a small area of pink (min. 5 mm.) that

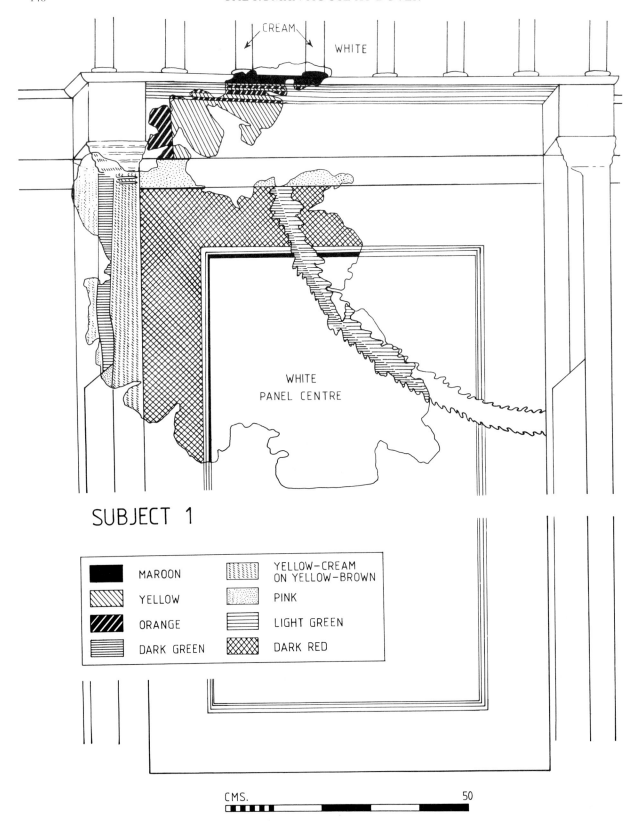

SUBJECT 1

	MAROON		YELLOW-CREAM ON YELLOW-BROWN
	YELLOW		PINK
	ORANGE		LIGHT GREEN
	DARK GREEN		DARK RED

CMS.   50

Fig. 53. *Drawing of plaster fragments and reconstructed design, Subject 1.*

almost certainly represents the pink border of the adjacent centre panel. Above the dark red panel border is a horizontal pink band (60 mm. wide), edged at the top and bottom with a dark maroon line (up to 1 mm.). Above this is a broad zone of yellow ochre (155 mm. wide) capped by another maroon band (20 mm. wide). Immediately below this band, lying over the yellow ochre, are three parallel orange stripes arranged in the following sequence (from top as viewed):- space (5 mm.); orange stripe (6 mm.); space (5 mm.); orange stripe (10 mm.); space (10 mm.) and orange stripe (4 mm.). To the left of, and laterally framing, the orange zone, an orange band (50 mm. wide) projects upwards from the pink for a minimum of 110 mm.

Above the uppermost maroon band is a zone of white (min. 50 mm. wide) over which has been painted at least one vertical cream band (40 mm. wide) projecting upwards from a strip of maroon (50 mm. in length and 10 mm. wide) resting on the maroon band. A second maroon strip is just visible 100 mm. to the left.

This reconstructed design represents the top left-hand corner of a rectangular white panel framed on at least two sides by a dark red border, itself internally lined with a series of stripes in pale green and maroon. The panel is further embellished with a hanging garland. Adjacent to the left side of the panel border is part of a column facing to the right and very similar to those *in situ* on the internal walls of the Painted House. The column terminates just above the panel tops. The surfaces of the plaster fragments at this point are badly abraded and show little or no detail. For this reason it has not been possible to positively reconstruct the capital. The painted detail that survives on adjacent fragments may, however, confirm the presence of a capital or capitals in this position. The green band is similar to detail on fragments incorporated into Subject 2 and may represent background between two columns at this level. The lower portions of the columns may be joined by the transverse screen-wall as suggested for Subject 2, Room 3. The upper limit of such a screen-wall is suggested by a change of colour from green to pink at a point some 370 mm. from the lowest point of the capital. The pink meets the green diagonally at about 50°, suggesting that the upper limit of the screen-wall was above eye-level.

The panel is surmounted by a broad zone of yellow. Above this is a horizontal maroon band supporting a series of vertical cream bands (30–40 mm. wide) painted on white. Each band rests on a horizontal maroon strip and they are spaced a minimum of 120 mm. apart. They may represent minor architectural elements which appear elsewhere (Subjects 2, 3 and 4), where they are spaced at 150 mm. and are a minimum of 208 mm. high. The capital almost certainly extended up to the horizontal maroon band evidenced by the vertical orange band over the yellow zone that may suggest shadow cast by its abacus. This arrangement may be confined over pairs of columns (here the right pair) forming a structure or aedicula as shown in Subject 2. The three parallel orange stripes over the broad yellow zone seem to represent the underside of the 'canopy' of such a structure. The dark red-bordered panel and adjacent column shown here match the decoration surviving *in situ* in Room 2 of the Painted House.

The new decorative elements revealed on this articulated group of fragments clearly continue the general illusionistic-architectural scheme. The treatment of the upper portion of the bordered panels, here enlivened with a garland of leaves, to the tops of the columns and to the frieze zone above the panel tops is now clear.

An additional 80 fragments of plaster in Fabric A show portions of at least three more curving garlands (not illustrated), similar to the one depicted here. Some 60 of these fragments were recovered from the north-west corner of Room 2 in a general demolition context (DV–2306). These show at least two separate garlands hanging from top left and curving to the right over yellow-bordered panels. The garlands are painted in shades of light green above with the underside painted dark green representing shadow to emphasise the curved shape. Each garland has a minimum length of 600 mm. From their location in the room it is likely that the motifs came from the west and north walls and almost certainly decorated yellow-bordered panels, perhaps either Panel 10 or 11. The precise arrangement can clearly be seen in the upper portion of Panel 5 (as discussed above). The remaining 20 fragments, 13 of which are articulated, were recovered from the north-east corner of Room 3 in a general demolition context (DV–2307). These show a garland hanging from top right and curving to bottom left over a yellow-framed

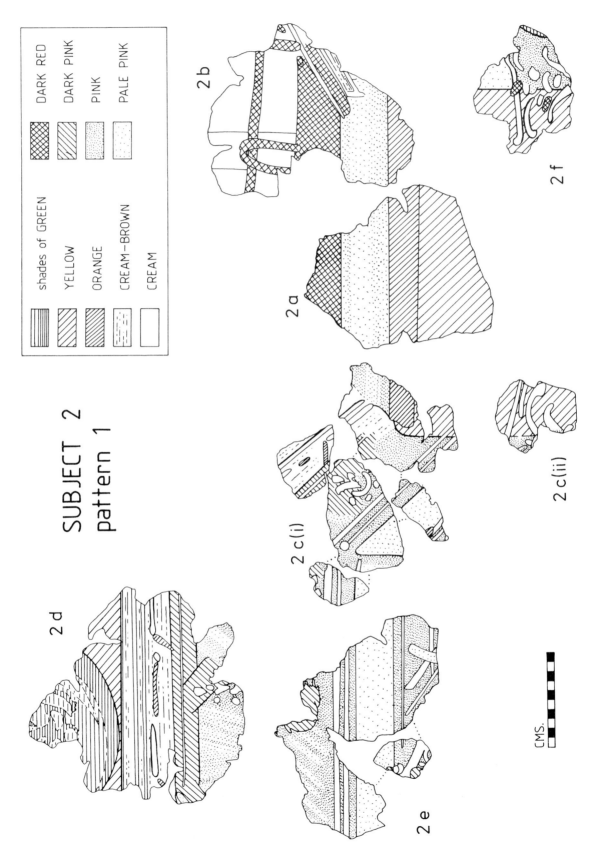

Fig. 54. Drawing of plaster fragments, Subject 2, pattern 1.

panel and these are also painted in light green, shaded along the underside in dark green. The garland extends for a minimum length of 500 mm. From its location in the room the motif seems likely to have come from either the east wall or the north wall and decorated one of the yellow-framed panels that survive *in situ* (either Panel 19 or 22). It is highly probable that the garland adorned the upper portion of the panel as depicted on Panel 5. The evidence shows that the upper portions of at least four framed panels (Panels 5, 10 and 11 within Room 2 and either Panel 19 or 22 within Room 3) were ornamented with a curving garland motif.

SUBJECT 2 – Multi-coloured architectural aedicula and recess. (Figs. 54– 56).

Some 192 fragments of plaster (Fabric A) seem to have formed part of an elaborate architectural aedicula and recess, painted in perspective. These were recovered from the following deposits:-

Room No.	No. of Fragments	Deposit No.	Area Code
2	3	DV–2306	Not certain
3	216	DV–2307	E, F, G, H.
3	4	DV–1162	General layer
5	4	DV–4381	Hypocaust Channel
Shore-fort Wall	6	DV–4076	Robber-trench
Unstratified	1	DV–1166	General layer
TOTAL	234		

Of these, only 49 key fragments have been used in the reconstructions. All the fragments relate to a broadly similar scheme, but two distinct patterns emerge (2A–2F and 2G–2H) and these are discussed separately.

PATTERN 1 – (2A–2F). (Fig. 54).

(2A)   Four conjoining fragments show a broad zone of yellow (min. 82 mm. wide) surmounted by an orange band 33 mm. wide edged with yellow up to 6 mm. wide. This merges into a broad band (46 mm. wide) painted in shades of pink which is in turn surmounted by a zone of deep red (min. 40 mm. wide).

(2B)   11 conjoining fragments show a similar arrangement to that depicted on 2A. A portion of the orange band is shown (min. 29 mm. wide) edged with yellow (up to 8 mm.) that similarly merges into a pink band here 40 mm. wide. Surmounting this pink is a broad, deep red band (45 mm. wide), the top of which is slightly concave. A pale cream-white band (40 mm. wide), shaded down the left side (as viewed) with light grey, projects vertically upwards from this red band and is painted over a white ground (min. 97 mm. wide). Similar devices are depicted on Subjects 1, 3 and 4 where they occupy a position at frieze level. Superimposed over this vertical band is a strip of deep red (8 mm. wide) that projects upwards from the horizontal red band some 60 mm. and arches over to form a U-shaped loop (20 mm. wide). A portion of a second loop can be seen 100 mm. to its right (as viewed). A slightly wavy horizontal deep red stripe (8 mm. wide), applied in wash and parallel to the red band (at a distance of between 34– 45 mm. from it) passes behind these 'loops' (10 mm. from their tops) and in front of the vertical cream band. This effectively connects the 'loops' creating a continuous rail-like device. Additional detail has been added to the right (as viewed) and shows a series of parallel stripes and bands projecting upwards at an angle of 148° (for a min. distance of 115 mm.) from the horizontal pink band. The arrangement is as follows: (from top to bottom as viewed) cream stripe (3 mm. wide); red band (10 mm. wide) and yellowish-cream band (min. 15 mm. wide).

(2C(i)) Eight conjoining fragments show part of a similar sequence, yellow zone (here min. of only 60 mm.) surmounted by a band of orange, (28 mm. wide) above which is a zone painted in shades of pink. A band of cream-brown (min. of 45 mm.) and highlighted with parallel cream stripes, up to 5 mm. wide and 4 mm. apart, projects upwards approximately 130° to the left (as viewed) from the pink band. Painted over this, and placed at random are two orange dashes up to 5 mm. wide and 20 mm. in length. Immediately below and parallel to this cream-brown band is a strip of pink-red (32 mm. wide) not quite meeting the orange band and including a V-shaped zone of similar pink-red (min. 35 mm. wide and 30 mm. in length). Below this is a zone of brighter pink (30 mm. wide) turning through 130° to frame the yellow zone and orange band. Applied to this and partly over the pink-red band is a palm-like motif painted in cream-yellow consisting of a crescent (up to 6 mm. wide) edged below with at least three cream spots (up to 6 mm. in diameter). This is surmounted by a splayed V-shaped element which is in turn capped by a blob of cream-yellow. The motif is approximately 50 mm. in length. Below the brighter pink zone and parallel to it, also at 130° is a darker pink band (25 mm. wide). Painted over this and lining the bright pink are two parallel cream-yellow stripes (up to 5 mm. wide and 5 mm. apart). The lower stripe terminates in a roughly circular spot (9 mm. in diameter), also painted cream-yellow. At this point the stripes realign through approximately 135°, leaving a gap of at least 15 mm., for a minimum distance of 40 mm. The dark pink at this point turns through 40° lying at right angles to the realigned cream-yellow stripes and parallel to the yellow zone at an angle of approximately 130°. The space between has been painted in a very pale pink.

(2C(ii)) Two conjoining fragments show a pink band (here viewed left), (min. 20 mm. wide), from which project, to the right a series of curving and straight cream-pink stripes (up to 7 mm. wide), painted over a yellow field. These stripes almost certainly represent part of a Corinthian capital. The angle of the top straight line suggests that the column is shown in three quarter view and is facing to the left. The vertical pink band adjacent to the yellow field is opposite to the sequence shown on 2F and quite clearly represents a separate capital. The pink and yellow sequence shown on 2C(i) suggests that these fragments are closely related and therefore have been illustrated together. These would then show a right hand capital adjacent to a yellow field corresponding to the left hand capital shown in 2F.

(2D) Twelve conjoining fragments show a zone painted in shades of dark pink, a minimum of 50 mm. wide, over which at least two slightly lighter pink stripes have been painted diagonally (14 mm. apart, measuring up to 5 mm. wide). Painted above this is a parallel pink-red band (25 mm. wide) from which two diagonal 'spurs' (30 mm. wide) project downwards approximately 40 mm. in opposite directions on to the pink ground. A palm-like ornament decorates this zone. A narrow creamy-pink stripe (up to 3 mm.) is painted over and along the pink-red band slightly off-centre. Adjacent to this pink-red band is another painted in pale cream-brown (up to 56 mm. wide). Two continuous cream stripes (up to 4 mm. wide and 6 mm. apart) lie along this pale cream-brown band and parallel to the pink-red band at a distance of 30 mm. A third orange and cream stripe (up to 4 mm. wide) is discontinuous and lies 22 mm. from and parallel to the pink-red band. This stripe is further punctuated by two oblique orange dashes similar to the fragments on 2C (1). A cream line (up to 2 mm. wide) separates the cream-brown band from a broad zone of yellow (min. 100 mm.). Over this yellow is painted a roundel in shades of green (min. 97 mm. in diameter).

(2E)   Seven conjoining fragments show from bottom to top, a band of pink, (min. 50 mm. wide), over which has been painted two parallel cream-pink stripes (up to 5 mm. wide and 28 mm. apart). Two similar parallel stripes have been painted diagonally across this band (10 mm. apart) and project over the outer stripe. Suggestion of further decoration over this band is seen in the nature of a cream stud (up to 10 mm. in diameter) adjacent to maroon dashes of uncertain character. Immediately above this band is a band of pale pink (39 mm. wide) followed by a broad zone of dark pink (62 mm. wide). Two parallel cream-yellow stripes (up to 8 mm. wide and 5 mm. apart) lie adjacent to the pale pink band at a distance of 7 mm. from it. The dark pink band has been further enlivened with a pink-red motif of uncertain character and a series of diagonal, slightly lighter pink stripes (up to 8 mm. wide and up to 8 mm. apart), of which at least seven can be seen. Five more adjoining fragments (not illustrated) show that a similar palm-like ornament like 2C and 2D decorated this zone. The band is edged with pink-red (min. 2 mm. wide).

(2F)   A further seven conjoining fragments show from left to right a zone of yellow, (min. 68 mm. wide), beside a zone of dark pink. These have been further treated with cream-pink dashes and stripes (up to 8 mm. wide) with an occasional maroon dash (up to 7 mm. wide) which may represent a stylised Corinthian capital. A dash of green over the dark pink may suggest that a foliate motif occupied a position here.

The design emerging certainly appears to form a bold architectural scheme, incorporating two opposing aediculae with a recess between. This seems to be a more elaborate version than Subject 1.

The back wall of the recess (Subjects 2A and 2B) is rendered partly or wholly in yellow, surmounted by an orange band (30–35 mm. wide). This band may represent the shadow cast by a slightly projecting architrave above represented by a band in shades of pink, perhaps to imitate fluted stonework. Above this is a third band supporting a 'looped rail' in deep red fronting a series of vertical cream bands and representing the lower frieze. A pair of columnar structures may be seen projecting from the back wall, thus creating the recess. The left structure, viewed in perspective from the right, may be seen to consist of a pair of projecting columns (approximately 95 mm. wide) with Corinthian capitals represented by creamy-pink dashes over yellow and dark pink, (Subject 2F). The columns appear to support a monumental entablature (Subjects 2D-F), (approximately 210 mm. deep), the architrave of which is approximately 40 mm. deep and painted in pale pink. The frieze above this (90 mm. deep) is painted in a darker pink and is further embellished with diagonal cream stripes and decorative motifs. Two parallel cream stripes at the junction of architrave and frieze may be intended to represent decorative moulding (20 mm. deep). A cornice (60 mm. deep) above the frieze and painted in a mottled, pale cream-brown, perhaps to imitate stone, possibly supports a triangular pediment of uncertain height painted in yellow. This would almost certainly be enclosed in a border imitating stone thus matching the cornice. A roundel painted in shades of green may have been centrally placed within the pediment. Subject 2B suggests a similar columnar structure projecting from the back wall to the right and viewed in perspective from the left.

Owing to the fragmentary nature of the plaster precise proportions of the scheme cannot be determined. The perspective treatment shares many similarities with the *in situ* design decorating the walls of the Painted House in Rooms 2–4 and probably formed a major element of the general scheme. The suggested pair of aediculae clearly flanked each side of a panel, probably the central panel on a major wall. Each aedicula also enclosed its own panel and it is likely that another panel existed beyond each aedicula, thus giving a total of five panels in all. The centre panel, at least bordered with yellow, would now be seen as the central focal point within the scheme. A corresponding pair of columns may have supported the rear of the canopy. The vertical cream bands over white, above the recessed centre panel may represent the similarly decorated frieze zone to that depicted in Subject 1. Here, however, further embellishment has been added in the form of a 'looped rail' above the central recess.

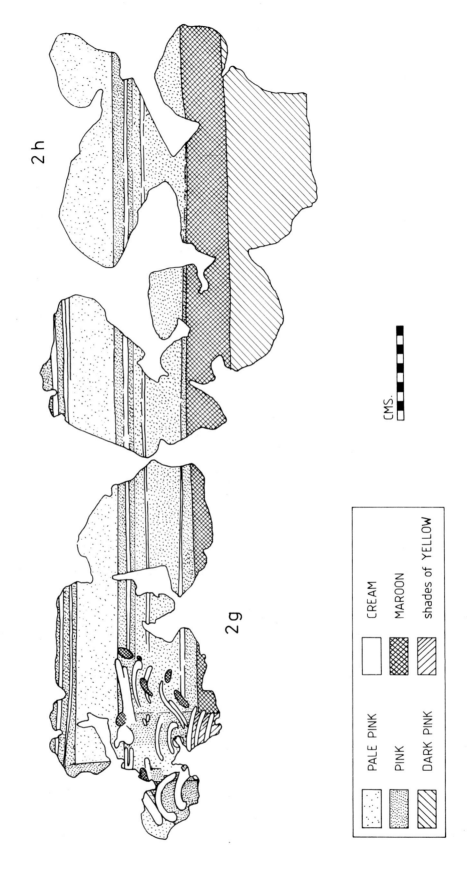

Fig. 55. *Drawing of plaster fragments, Subject 2, pattern 2.*

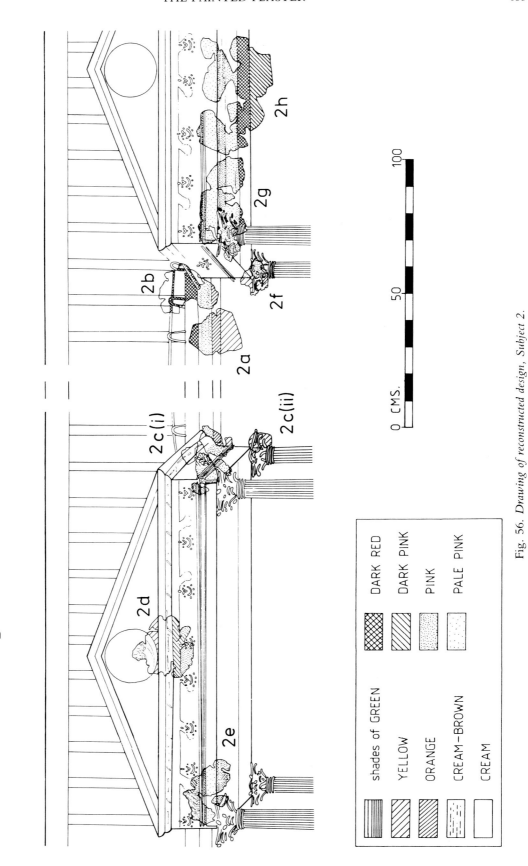

Fig. 56. *Drawing of reconstructed design, Subject 2.*

Almost all the fragments constituting Subject 2 came from the north-east corner of Room 3, or very close by, strongly suggesting that this design formed part of the north wall of this room. This was the main wall facing the wide opening into Room 4 and thus the focal point of this 'double' room. The elaborate scheme suggests that Subject 2 was the principal design, perhaps even within one of the principal rooms. The interpretation of the design offered here was generally confirmed by Dr. T.F.C. Blagg who kindly made useful comments based on his own examination of the fragments.

PATTERN 2 (2G–2H). (Fig. 55).

This pattern includes two articulated groups of plaster, totalling 42 fragments, which seem to relate to a specific scheme, somewhat different in detail to Pattern 1. These were recovered from the north-east corner of Room 3 (DV–2307) and are included in the location table.
(2G–2H) The first group consists of 24 conjoining fragments (2G) and the second group (2H) consists of 18 conjoining fragments.

Group 2H shows a broad zone of dark pink (min. 90 mm. wide) surmounted by a maroon band (between 30–45 mm. wide). This supports a broader band of pink (80–85 mm. wide), above which is painted a pale cream-pink band (45 mm. wide). Above this is painted a pink band (min. 30 mm. wide) which has been further decorated with at least two parallel, horizontal cream stripes (up to 4 mm. wide and 7 mm. apart). This scheme is reflected on Group 2G where further detail, to the left (as viewed), seems to represent the top of a column with a stylised Corinthian capital. The column drum (min. 40 mm. wide) lies adjacent to the maroon band and is painted in yellow shaded down the right side to emphasise roundness. Three parallel, slightly convex, cream stripes (4 mm. wide and up to 6 mm. apart) over the drum seem to represent the basal mouldings of the capital which then rises upwards to support the pale cream-pink band above. The main body of the capital may be represented by a zone (60 mm. wide) painted in shades of pink, rising above the drum. Over this has been painted a series of cream-pink curved stripes (up to 9 mm. wide) that may be intended to represent acanthus leaves. These are similar to those in 2F. The width of the capital is 170 mm. Further embellishment has been added in the form of reddish-brown 'blobs' of paint. Above the capital a vertical band of darker pink, to the left of the horizontal pale cream-pink band, suggests that the design changes to the left of the column. Oblique brush-strokes to the lower left of the capital, over pink, may indicate that perspective treatment has been employed here to show the column and its adjacent sequence, projecting forward of any scheme to the left.

The emerging picture seems to represent a section of an aedicula seen in perspective from the left. Part of what may be regarded as an entablature and part of the underside of the canopy of this structure are depicted here. The front left (as viewed) corner of the entablature is supported by a column, shown almost in three-quarter view, with a Corinthian capital. This columnar structure projects forwards of the flanking backwall, possibly adjacent to the central recess, similar to the main design in Room 2. The pink zone to the right of the column and thus below the aedicula may represent a panel-border. The illustrated Groups 2G and 2H share very similar decorative elements to those of 2A-2F and it is almost certain that they formed part of the same scheme but perhaps decorating another wall.

SUBJECT 3 – Foliate Motif in green and maroon, over a yellow field and beneath horizontal stripes. (Fig. 57).

Some 117 fragments of plaster (Fabric A) appear to be part of a yellow ochre field embellished by green and maroon curving foliate motifs. The yellow field is bordered above by a horizontal

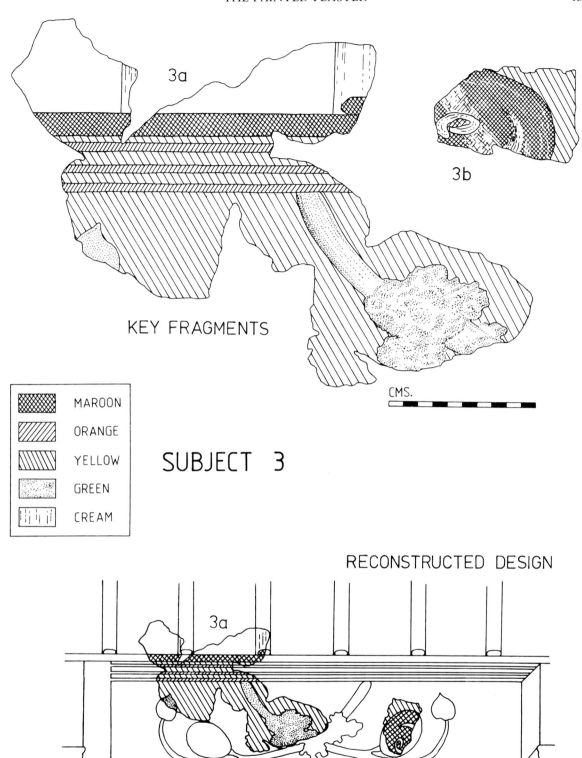

KEY FRAGMENTS

MAROON

ORANGE

YELLOW

GREEN

CREAM

SUBJECT 3

CMS.

RECONSTRUCTED DESIGN

CMS.

Fig. 57. *Drawing of plaster fragments and reconstructed design, Subject 3.*

maroon band and overlaid by three horizontal orange bands. Surmounting this border and at 90°
to it are a series of vertical cream bands over a white field. The location of the fragments is as
follows:-

Room No.	No. of Fragments	Deposit No.	Area Code
2	27	DV–2306	Q, R and U
2	56	DV–2308	I, J and T
3	29	DV–2307	G
3	2	DV–1162	G
3	2	DV–2341	G
North Passage	1	DV–1145	General Layer
TOTAL	117		

The reconstructed design is based on ten key fragments, which form three key groups (Nos.
3a–c).

3a.   Eight conjoining fragments show a deep yellow ochre field (min. 160 mm. wide)
bordered on one side (here shown top) by a horizontal maroon band (15 mm. wide),
adjacent to a white field. Projecting from the border over the white field are two
cream-white bands (about 115 mm. apart). As viewed, the left band measures a
minimum of 10 mm. and the right a minimum of 26 mm. in width, respectively. One
fragment (not illustrated) shows the full width of a cream band as 30 mm. Elsewhere a
width of between 40 mm. (Subject 4) and 50 mm. (Subject 1) is recorded and it may
therefore be assumed that these bands also measure between 30–50 mm. The right band
has been treated with a maroon strip (11 mm. wide) at its junction with the maroon
band.

    Immediately below the maroon band and over the yellow field, are three parallel
orange stripes arranged as follows (from top as viewed): space (4–5 mm.); orange stripe
(3–5 mm.); space (8 mm.); orange stripe (5 mm.); space (7 mm.) and an orange stripe (4
mm.). The yellow zone is embellished by a curving foliate motif in shades of green,
perhaps a garland which curves steeply down to the right. The main stem (15–18 mm.
wide) projects down from the lower orange stripe opening up into a spray (70 mm.
wide and a min. 70 mm. in length) at approximately 85 mm. below the orange stripe.

    A pale green heart-shaped leaf, 130 mm. to the left of the garland and 20 mm. below
the lower orange stripe, suggests another plant motif. Several fragments (not illustrated)
show similar stems and leaves suggesting that the yellow zone may have been treated
with a continuous foliate pattern.

3b.   One fragment (a min. of 85 mm. x 52 mm.) is partly painted in maroon over a yellow
ground and is highlighted with cream streaks. From such a small fragment it is difficult
to determine its precise representation, but it may depict either fruit or a stylised head,
perhaps that of an animal.

3c.   (Not illustrated). A single fragment shows the same arrangement of parallel orange
stripes over a yellow zone. A black band replaces the maroon above the area of yellow.
The stripes appear to meet a broad vertical band of orange (min. 15 mm. wide) at 90°
which borders both the yellow and the white zone above. An area of ill-defined
secondary detail is painted over this junction and thus obscures it. This may represent an
area of shadow adjacent to a column capital, perhaps represented by the secondary
detail, as shown on Subject 1, or it may show the junction with another wall at 90°.

These key fragments collectively may represent a broad yellow ochre zone enlivened by curving garlands and foliate sprays that form a scroll-like pattern. Further embellishment may have been added in the form of an ovoid pattern in maroon which may represent either fruit or the stylised head of an animal, the cream streaks serving as facial markings. A narrow horizontal band of maroon, surmounting the yellow zone, supports a series of vertical cream bands (approximately 110 mm. apart and 30–50 mm. wide) over a white ground. These divide the white field into narrow strips framed by the maroon band below and perhaps by a corresponding band above. A similar arrangement existed above Panel 5 (Subject 1) in Room 2, which was partially lifted intact and is now restored in the Painted House cover-building. Subject 3 almost certainly formed part of the frieze within Room 2, as partly shown in Subject 1. This seems to have included part of an entablature, with the vertical bands and the horizontal maroon band lying forward of the yellow zone. The three horizontal orange stripes appear to represent mouldings or shadows beneath the projecting entablature above. These particular fragments probably came from an aedicula (see below, page 218). The broad yellow zone, which was above the panels, seems to have been richly embellished with foliate motifs, perhaps arranged in a continuous scroll pattern and further enlivened with possible fruit or zoomorphic heads or masks. This arrangement superficially resembles the elaborate design known as the 'Peopled Scroll' found during excavations at Verulamium in 1956 (Ref. 90) which is now in the British Museum. Here the design, similarly painted over a bright yellow ground, also incorporates a foliate scroll, the spirals of which encompass feline masks and pheasants. It is believed to have derived from the frieze of the north-west wall of the courtyard of building 2, Insula XXI and dated to c. A.D. 180.

SUBJECT 4. Semi-circular Ornament hanging from ceiling band. (Fig. 58).

Some 28 fragments of plaster (Fabric A) show a broadly semi-circular ornament suspended from the ceiling band and partly superimposed over vertical bands. The location of these fragments is shown in the following table:-

Room No.	No. of Fragments	Deposit No.	Area Code
2 (north-west corner)	19	DV–2306	Q, R, U
3 (south-west corner)	9	DV–2308	L
TOTAL	28		

The reconstructed design is based on only 19 conjoining key fragments and shows a broad maroon band (min. 87 mm.) bordering a white zone (min. 206 mm.). Projecting from the maroon band and overlying the white field is a parallel series of pale cream bands, irregularly spaced. From left to right (with the maroon band at the top) the design consists of white (70 mm. min.); cream band (41 mm.); white (163–168 mm.); cream band (40 mm.); white (48 mm. min.); cream band (40 mm.) and white (65 mm. min.). The cream bands may been have positioned asymmetrically, but it could be that a band was omitted in the wide space to allow room for the overlying motif. This basic arrangement is similar to that in Subjects 1 and 3, but varies in detail.

The main motif appears to be a semi-circular ornament in shades of olive-yellow, decorated

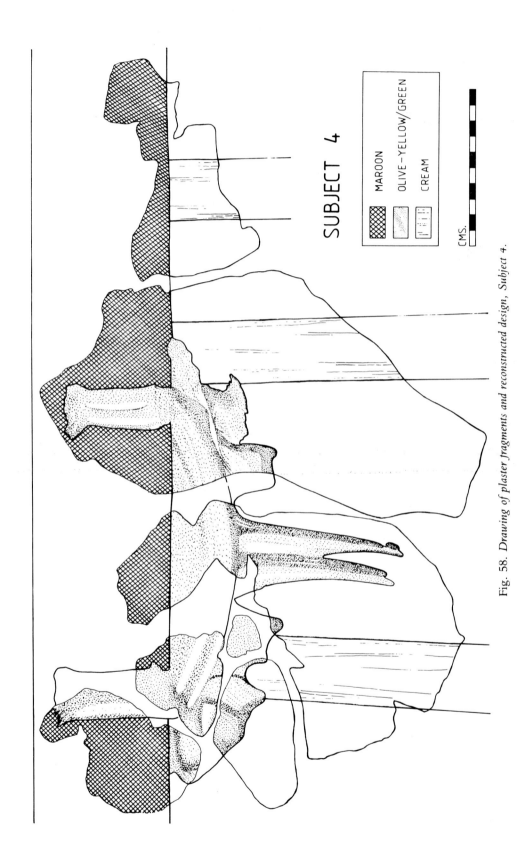

Fig. 58. Drawing of plaster fragments and reconstructed design, Subject 4.

with a ribbon, and is placed between and slightly overlapping the second and third vertical bands.

The ornament projects down from the maroon band (45 mm.) and is approximately 220 mm. in length. At either end of this motif are two blunt strips painted in olive-yellow, (152 mm. apart) projecting 90° upwards over the maroon band. These may represent brackets securing the device to the maroon band. The right bracket measures 24–28 mm. in width and 70 mm. in length whilst the left one measures 30 mm. by 75 mm. Streaks of cream and dark olive-green applied vertically over these brackets may represent fluting. What may represent the tassels of a bow (45 mm. wide and 110 mm. in length) are painted in shades of olive-yellow and highlighted with cream streaks and hang centrally from the 'ornament'. The ends of the bow, or knot, painted in shades of olive-green adorn either end of the ornament.

The precise reconstruction and proportions have not yet been determined, but the vertical cream bands are similar to the frieze zone above Panel 5 (Room 2, Subject 1 and Subject 3). It seems highly probable that this subject also occupied a position at frieze level, within Room 2.

The motif appears to represent an ornament decorated with ribbons suspended from the maroon band, the latter probably being the ceiling band. Superficially this device resembles an ornament suspended from a portal and projecting into a white field containing architectural fantasies from a painted wall in the House of the Vettii at Pompeii (Ref. 91). The latter appears to be attached to the outside of the portal which is out of view to the onlooker.

Two similar devices, seen in full frontal view decorate a columnar structure in a wall painting from Herculaneum. There they have been interpreted as 'golden shields' and are decorated with ribbons and wreaths (Ref. 92). The Dover ornament may have been intended to represent such a device, seen from the rear and suspended between the vertical cream bands and the maroon ceiling band. The olive-yellow colour chosen for the Dover ornament could be intended to represent gold.

SUBJECT 5 – Blue and green bowls with fruits in red and brown. (Fig. 59).

Some 31 fragments of plaster (Fabric A), share the same basic characteristics and seem to represent two bowls, one containing fruit. The location of these fragments is shown in the following tables:-

Room No.	No. of Fragments	Deposit No.	Area
2	22	Group 23 (as lifted)	Floor
2	8	Group 31 (as lifted)	Floor
Shore-fort Robber-trench	1	DV–4185	General Layer
Bingo Hall Site	1	DV–3030	General Layer
Bingo Hall Site	2	DV–3031	General Layer
Bingo Hall Site	1	DV–9890	General Layer
TOTAL	35		

The reconstructed designs are based on nine key fragments and show the following:

5a.   A single fragment shows a broad field of bright blue (min. 38 mm.) painted over a white

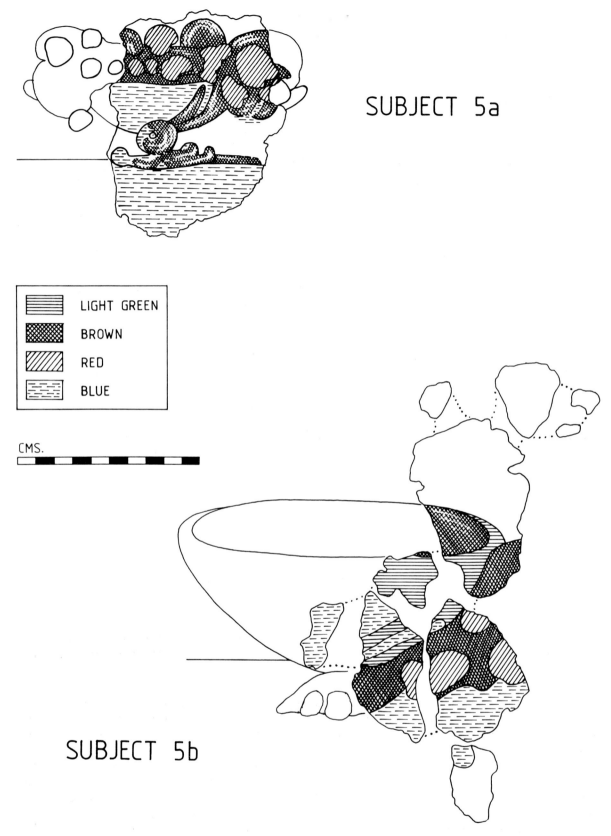

SUBJECT 5a

LIGHT GREEN
BROWN
RED
BLUE

CMS.

SUBJECT 5b

Fig. 59. *Drawing of plaster fragments, Subjects 5a and 5b.*

ground (min. 80 mm. wide). Surmounting this blue zone is a stemmed, hemispherical bowl of bright blue applied almost in wash. Supporting the bowl is a globular stem (approximately 20 mm. in diameter), over a foot-ring (50 mm. wide). A spot of white (unpainted plaster) in the centre of the stem emphasises its roundness. The colour and thin application of the paint may suggest that the artist intended the bowl to represent a metallic or glass vessel. The bowl contains what appears to be fruit, irregularly spaced and up to 20 mm. in diameter, painted in shades of pink-red over a dark brown base. The fruit seems to overspill from the right lip (as viewed) of the bowl which casts a dark brown shadow down the side to the base (4–12 mm. wide). The bowl is up to 26 mm. deep and stands 45 mm. high from foot-ring to rim.

5b.   Some eight conjoining fragments show a zone of bright blue (between 30 mm. and 45 mm.) painted over white. Surmounting this are three circular 'spots' of deep red, over brown, probably representing fruit, similar to those in key fragment 5a. Above and to the left of this in light green is what appears to be a bowl. The use of brown indicates its interior, possibly empty (unless full of liquid). The brown shown to the right of the bowl may represent loosely draped fabric. Precise details are difficult to distinguish as the surface is badly fractured and the pigments have partly flaked off. The body of the bowl seems to be highlighted with streaks of blue, apparently reflected from the blue zone that it stands upon, thus emphasising its roundness. The height of the bowl is approximately 65 mm.

These fragments seem to depict part of a still-life scene comprising of at least two bowls, one of which is overspilling with fruit. They are both painted over a white ground and standing upon a blue zone. It is not clear whether the blue represents a border, separating areas of white or whether it is intended to represent a table. If the latter then it may well have served to decorate the centre of a white panel, one perhaps within the general 'Painted House' scheme from Rooms 1–4. Alternatively, it may have decorated the wall of a room as yet unlocated.

SUBJECT 6 – Part of possible candelabrum motif (Fig. 60).

Two conjoining fragments in Fabric A form part of what may represent a candelabrum motif. These were found in the north-west corner of Room 2 in general demolition context DV–2306.

The motif is painted over a white ground and is here viewed suspended from a horizontal cream band (22 mm. wide) lined along the top with light grey, (min. 12 mm. wide). The device consists of an umbrella-like cover (min. 34 mm. in diameter) viewed from beneath so that only the underside, painted in light pink and part of the rim, painted in dark pink, is visible. From the top of this cover, as if fixed, projects what may represent a stem (measuring 38 mm. in length and up to 06 mm. wide). This has been painted in light pink and shaded down the right side (as viewed) with dark pink that represents shadow and emphasises its roundness. The stem, further decorated midway along the shaft with probable ribbon work, is suspended from the cream band above. Painted decoration projecting from the underside of the cover may represent a second stem extending below the cover perhaps to repeat the design further down.

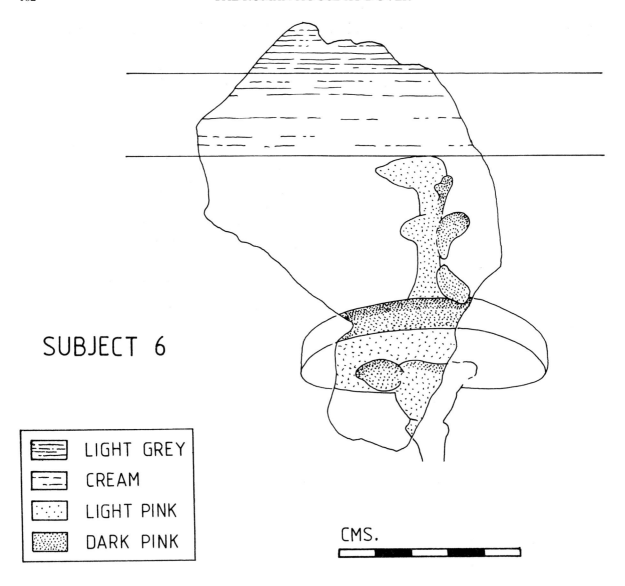

SUBJECT 6

| LIGHT GREY |
| CREAM |
| LIGHT PINK |
| DARK PINK |

CMS.

Fig. 60. Drawing of plaster fragment, Subject 6.

The painted decoration on these fragments may represent part of a candelabrum motif of the so called 'umbrella-type' that is well represented at Cologne associated with Bacchic imagery (Ref. 93). The Dover example appears to be suspended from a cream border that frames on at least one side the field of white which accommodates the candelabrum. The perspective in which the device is painted suggests that this portion at least was incorporated into a scheme above eye level, perhaps at lower frieze level. The precise arrangement incorporating this motif is difficult to determine. Such devices were often employed to lavishly ornament wide panel interspaces in the panel-system as at Cologne (Ref. 94) or otherwise employed as framing devices on larger fields as at Leicester (Ref. 95).

The position the fragments occupied is also difficult to determine. They do not fit easily into the main scheme decorating the walls of Rooms 2–4 and may, therefore, have decorated walls of other rooms. They may have been incorporated into a more delicate scheme that also included the human figures.

SUBJECT 7 – Rectangular White Panel with Green Frame (Fig. 61).

Some 77 fragments of plaster, (Fabric A), appear to form part of a rectangular white panel framed by a green border and outlined with a maroon stripe. Their locations are shown as follows:-

Room No.	Fragments	Deposit No.	Area
2	6	DV–2306	general layer
2	8	DV–2302/3	general layer
2	46	DV–2308	I, J, T.
3	17	DV–2307	E, F, G.
TOTAL	77		

Only 16 of the fragments need to be used in the reconstructed design and these form four key groups (Nos. 7a–7d).

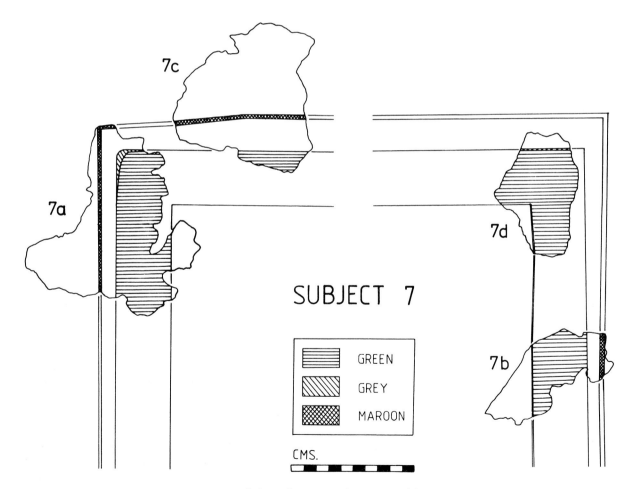

Fig. 61. *Drawing of plaster fragments and reconstructed design, Subject 7.*

7a.   Ten joining fragments show an external corner with a broad mottled green band (35 mm. wide) enclosed by a thin maroon stripe (3 mm. wide), all painted over a white field. The green corner is edged by a light grey stripe (up to 2 mm. wide). The white zone between the green band and the maroon stripe is 12 mm. wide on one side (here left), and 18 mm. wide on the other (here top).

7b.   Four joining fragments show a similar green band (44 mm. wide), again with a maroon stripe (4 mm. wide), spaced some 12 mm. away on its presumed outer side. The small variations in the border widths may indicate that the group is part of another side of the panel (here shown right).

7c.   A single fragment of the same green border, again with the outer maroon stripe (4 mm. wide), but this time misaligned and 26 mm. apart. This seems to be the continuation of the 18 mm. spacing of key group 7a and as such it has been shown as the top of the frame.

7d.   Another fragment shows an internal corner of the same green band (43 mm. wide), again partially edged in light grey and over a white ground. It is shown here as the top right corner of the frame.

The design which emerges is that of a rectangular white panel framed by a green border, partially edged with a light grey stripe and enclosed by a thin maroon stripe. The panel width is undetermined and it is not known whether the panel contained a motif. The precise arrangement and derivation of this panel is not known but it seems likely that it was an upright panel, perhaps one of a series with simple coloured frames and borders over a white ground. Such designs were common in Roman Dover, being the predominant scheme in both the adjacent Clay Walled Building and the long North Passage in the Painted House itself. In all these cases the panels surmounted coloured dados and it seems highly likely that this panel did too.

SUBJECT 8 – Angled Green Frame over White Field (Fig. 62).

A total of 63 fragments of plaster (Fabric A), seem to show part of an angled green frame, lined on both sides with a light grey stripe over a white field. It may have formed part of a 'frame in perspective'. The fragments were located as follows:-

Room No.	No. of Fragments	Deposit No.	Area Code
2	15	DV–2306	D, R
2	34	DV–2308	I, J
2	3	DV–2303	Floor
3	11	DV–1162	General Layer
TOTAL	63		

Only 16 key fragments have been used and these show a green angled frame (37 mm. wide) over a white field with part of a maroon band (min. 20 mm. wide), parallel to one arm of the frame (here shown left), probably representing a border.

The vertical left arm (as viewed here) of the green frame, 90 mm. from the maroon band, bends downwards to the right to form a 60° angle. The green frame continues for a distance of 400 mm. (externally) and then turns down again forming an angle of 120° to be parallel with the left arm. Both sides of the frame are lined with a light grey stripe (up to 4 mm. wide).

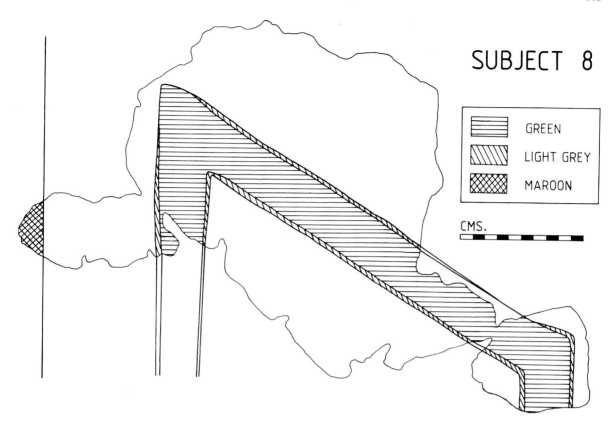

SUBJECT 8

	GREEN
	LIGHT GREY
	MAROON

CMS.

Fig. 62. *Drawing of plaster fragments, Subject 8.*

Several fragments (not illustrated) show slight foliate details painted in shades of green over white, one of which depicts a heart-shaped leaf adjacent to a green band. It is possible that these motifs decorated the white inner area (300 mm. by min. 82 mm.) created by the frame.

The precise arrangements, proportions and the plane in which the subject was intended to be viewed are difficult to determine. The design may have required that large areas of white be divided into square or rectangular panels demarcated by coloured borders including maroon (here shown left). The panels may have been further decorated by an oblique frame marked out by a continuous green band, the angles of which are set at 60° and 120°, enclosing an area of white on at least three sides. The frame, (measuring 400 mm. by min. of 140 mm.) may have returned through 120° to enclose a fourth side, thus forming a complete parallelogram. If so, the frame may have been intended to represent a perspective frame, adjacent to a maroon border within an architecturally illusionistic scheme. The enclosed space may have contained foliate or floral detail. Alternatively, the fourth side may have remained open, with the green band perhaps turning through 60° to repeat the general pattern, in reverse, thus forming a continuous design within a larger white zone framed by maroon. The design doesn't easily fit into the scheme surviving from the excavated Rooms 2–4, unless it was incorporated into the architectural illusionistic scheme shown in Subject 2 thought to derive from the north wall of Room 3. Here the device may have decorated the centre of one, or a pair of aediculae, perhaps representing a door shown in perspective to be partly open. There may have been more than one such feature employed in the scheme. A similar device is seen on plaster recently recovered from Southwark also depicting a grand architectural scheme (Ref. 96).

SUBJECTS 9–20 – Human Figures (Figs. 63–71)

Some 227 fragments of plaster show elements which clearly appear to form parts of various human figures. Twelve subjects are illustrated and these must represent an absolute minimum of eight human figures. The location of the fragments is shown in the following table:-

Room No.	No. of Fragments	Deposit No.	Area
2	6	DV–2301	On floor
2	115	DV–2306	B, D, Q, R, U
2/3	20	DV–2307/8	E, I, J
2	7	DV–1167	General Layer
3	38	DV–2307	E, F, G
4	20	DV–2309	N, O
Passage	1	DV–1145	General Layer
Shore-fort Robber-trench	1	DV–4185	General Layer
Shore-fort Robber-trench	5	DV–4076	General Layer
Shore-fort Robber-trench	3	DV–4158	General Layer
Stoke-hole	3	DV–1188	South Side
Unstratified	6	DV–1100	
Bingo Hall Site	2	DV–3070	North Passage
TOTAL	227		

Only one subject (No. 9) is painted over a red ground, whilst all the rest (Nos. 10–20) are over white. The reconstructions are based on only 100 key fragments, but the remainder either form part of the figures identified or may represent others.

Six of the figures appear to represent females (Subjects 10, 11, 12, 13, 16 and 20) whilst three are almost certainly male (Subjects 9, 17 and 19). At least three figures are robed (Subjects 10, 11 and 18) and at least five are depicted either partly, or wholly, nude (Subjects 9, 12, 16, 17 and 19). At least seven of the figures are depicted in a standing posture (Subjects 9, 10, 12, 16, 17, 18 and 19), of which at least three appear to be engaged in movement (Subjects 10, 12 and 16) that may be intended to represent dancing. One figure is seated (Subject 11) and appears to recline upon what may represent an entablature. The female head in Subject 14 has been used in the reconstruction of Subject 11.

The positions occupied by the figures in the overall design cannot be determined at present. Subject 11 may have occupied a space within the frieze zone in Rooms 1–6 whilst the remainder may either have occupied a similar position, or were centrally placed within white panels framed by coloured borders (apart from Subject 9 which was painted over red) within the same or other rooms. Most of the figures, however, appear to be of similar proportions (about ¼ life-size) which may indicate that they occupied similar positions in the decorative scheme, perhaps forming a whole or a series of scenes. That the majority of figures are either nude or partly so, that some are engaged in movement, perhaps dance, whilst others are seated may indicate that they form a scene or scenes of ritual representation, depicting both participants and spectators (see page 137). In describing the figures, 'left' and 'right' apply to the subject's left and right, not as viewed, unless otherwise stated.

SUBJECT 9 – Male Human Standing-figure, Holding Staff, on Red Field (Fig. 63).

The location of these seven fragments (Fabric A) is shown as follows:-

Room No.	No. of Fragments	Deposit No.	Area
2 3 Bingo Hall Site	5 2	DV–2306 DV–2307 DV–3070	General Layer General Layer General Layer
TOTAL	7	–	–

The five fragments recovered from Rooms 2 and 3 show part of a human figure holding a staff or rod, on a deep red ground. A further two fragments recovered during excavations in 1976, on the Bingo Hall site to the north of the Painted House show part of a human torso over deep red, that almost certainly belong to the same figure. The reconstructed design is based on seven key fragments which form three key groups (9a–9c).

(9a)   Four fragments show part of the face and right arm, including the shoulder, painted in various shades of pink and light brown over a deep red ground. Details of the face, of which only part of the right side survives, are not clear. However, it does appear to be facing slightly to the right. Dashes of cream-buff over light brown adjacent to the forehead may represent hair perhaps adorned with a garland. The bared right arm is extended out from the shoulder and bent at the elbow upwards at 90° to the upper arm. The arm has a rather muscular appearance emphasised by darker shades of brown outlining the biceps, underlining the upper arm and lining the forearm. A narrow band (7 mm. wide), painted in maroon (4 mm.) on the right and cream-buff (3 mm.) on the left, lies parallel to the forearm and crosses the upper arm.

(9b)   A single fragment shows a narrow cream stripe (4 mm.), protruding from an area of pink and light brown (up to 25 mm. wide), which may be seen to represent a hand holding a staff or rod.

(9c)   The remaining two fragments show part of a naked torso and part of the underside of the left upper arm, in shades of pink over a deep red ground.

The fragments appear to represent a figure, probably standing, partly if not wholly nude, with its head, possibly garlanded, looking slightly to the right. The right arm holds a staff or rod. Key group 9c shows that the left arm is raised at or above chest level. The arm and torso have a well rounded, bulky or muscular appearance which may imply that the figure is male. An imaginary light-source falls on the figure from the left (as viewed). Part of a figure in a similar pose, painted over black, was found at Otford, Kent, and thought to be from the villa there (Ref. 97). The attitude differs slightly in that the right arm holding a spear is held higher as though in the act of lunging, whereas the Dover example suggests that the staff or rod is planted firmly on the ground. It seems likely that this was a major figure in the decorative scheme for Room 3, perhaps even a representation of Bacchus (see discussion p. 219 and 137).

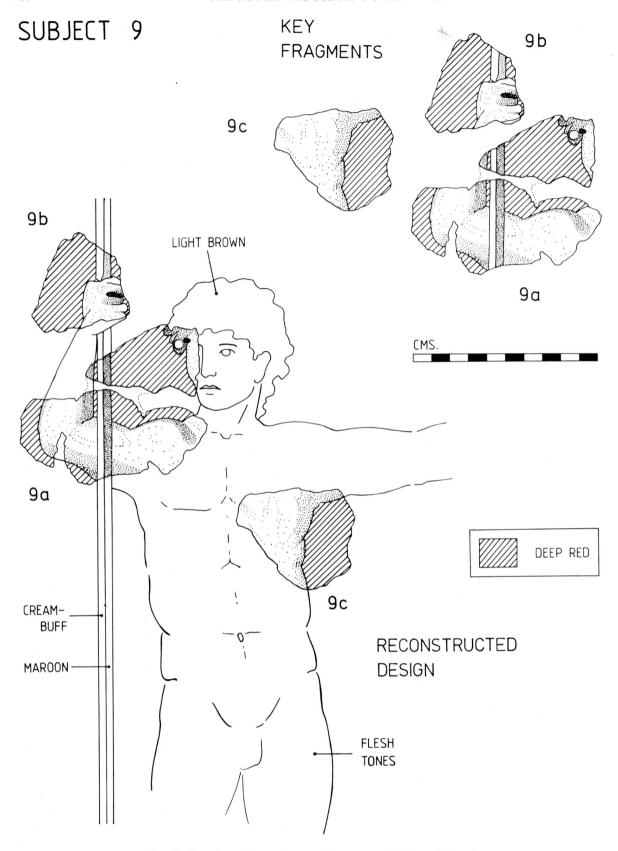

SUBJECT 9

KEY FRAGMENTS

9b

9c

9b

LIGHT BROWN

9a

9a

9c

CMS.

DEEP RED

CREAM-BUFF

MAROON

RECONSTRUCTED DESIGN

FLESH TONES

Fig. 63. *Drawing of plaster fragments in reconstructed design, Subject 9.*

SUBJECT 10 – Female Human, Robed Standing-figure, on White Ground (Fig. 64).

Some 24 fragments (Fabric A) of plaster seem to depict a standing female figure, robed, shown in three-quarters view facing to her right and painted over a white ground. The location of these fragments is shown in the following table:

Room No.	No. of Fragments	Deposit No.	Area
2	24	DV–2306	B and R (North Side)

The painted elements depicted on these fragments almost certainly derive from the same figures. Two key groups, one containing two fragments and one of twenty key fragments, conjoin.

(10a)   This larger group shows almost the complete lower part of the body (from the waist down, min. 262 mm.) which is seen in three-quarters view facing right. The body is covered by at least two garments. A long outer robe, painted in shades of deep pink and highlighted with maroon streaks, is open at the front mostly exposing the inner garment and reaches down to just above the ankles. The garment is likely to have been worn loosely hung from one or both shoulders. A patch of pink paint adjacent to the right shin may represent the bottom edge of the garment raised and ruffled as though disturbed by movement. Alternatively, this may represent the lower part of a veil billowing across the legs. The inner garment is painted in yellow ochre highlighted with pink and cream streaks over a pale pink ground. This garment may have been lightweight and worn next to the skin, perhaps extending to the neckline and hung from one or both shoulders. It extends to finish slightly short of the outer robe. The lower legs and feet are bared and painted in shades of pink highlighted with cream-white streaks. The left foot is shown in three-quarters view facing left with the heel slightly raised and the ball of the foot supporting the bodyweight. The right foot, shown in profile facing right, also with the heel slightly raised, appears to be pointing the toe in the act of stepping forward. The right foot appears closer to the viewer than the left, but the attitude of the figure is such that the left side is slightly turned. Perhaps the figure is completing a full or part pivot. The disturbance of the outer garment or veil is characteristically that which results from someone turning or pivoting sharply and may confirm the position suggested. An area of white extends below the feet a minimum of 150 mm. The left hand is almost wholly visible positioned adjacent to the left thigh. The thumb and index finger are extended and held slightly apart whilst the remaining fingers are slightly flexed into the palm.

(10b)   A single fragment shows the deep pink outer garment and part of the left upper arm which is bared and held at a slight distance from the body.

(10c)   Two conjoining fragments show parts of the right arm, shoulder, neck and chin. The arm, painted in shades of pink, is raised up with the forearm at 90° to the shoulder. Pale cream-pink streaks highlight the forearm whilst the darker pink lining the arm emphasises roundness. The arm and shoulder are bared suggesting that the garments (described above) were worn draped from only one shoulder (in this instance the left). Little can be distinguished from the small portion of neck and chin visible, but light yellowish-pink and the dashes of deep pink or light maroon may represent hair, a garland, drop earring or even a ribbon.

SUBJECT 10

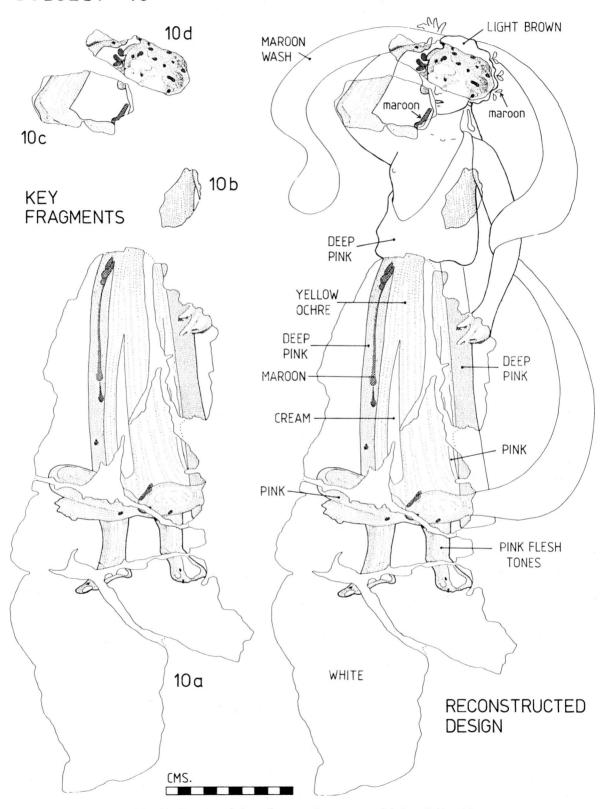

10 d

10 c

KEY
FRAGMENTS

10 b

10 a

MAROON
WASH

LIGHT BROWN

maroon

maroon

DEEP
PINK

YELLOW
OCHRE

DEEP
PINK

MAROON

DEEP
PINK

CREAM

PINK

PINK

PINK FLESH
TONES

WHITE

RECONSTRUCTED
DESIGN

CMS.

Fig. 64. *Drawing of plaster fragments in reconstructed design, Subject 10.*

(10d)   The final fragment shows part of the face and head and part of the right hand. Although the details of the face are not clear it can be seen to be facing slightly to the right shown in three-quarters view. It is painted in shades of pink over a pale yellow ochre ground. Hair is shown in shades of light brown and highlighted with streaks of pink. The fragment is too small to determine the style in which the hair is arranged although it does appear to have been kept away from the forehead. Dashes and spots of maroon painted over the hair may represent a garland. Part of the wrist and thumb, of the right hand, painted in shades of pink, can be clearly seen almost touching the head. The attitude adopted by the thumb suggests that the hand is either held open with fingers outstretched and palm visible, as though in the act of waving; or slightly bent back, palm uppermost, as though supporting an object from beneath. It is possible that the figure is holding a veil, suggested by a streak of maroon wash across the wrist. It swirls over her head, cascading down her left side, and billows in front of her legs above the ankles.

          This is clearly a female figure, attired in a two-piece garment and engaged in movement. She is shown in three-quarters view and looks to her centre-right. The attitude of her feet perhaps suggests a pivoting movement. Such a movement might be caused either by offering a greeting or taking part in a dance. The original height of the figure was about 420 mm. which is about $\frac{1}{4}$ life-size.

SUBJECT 11 – Reclining Female Human Figure, in Green and Yellow Robes (Fig. 65).

Some 44 fragments of plaster (Fabric A) appear to show a seated female figure. These fragments were recovered from Room 2 (DV–2306, area 'U'). Only twelve key fragments have been used in the reconstruction.

Two key groups, one of eight fragments (11a) and one of four fragments (11b) conjoin and show a robed figure on a white ground reclining on a horizontal maroon band in three-quarters view with the body facing to the left.

(11a)   This group shows part of the torso and right arm in a slightly reclined position. The arm, bared and painted in shades of pink highlighted with dashes of white, supports the body at a slight incline with the hand firmly placed palm down, on a maroon band (25 mm. wide), surmounting a deep red (here a minimum of 5 mm.). Behind the hand is part of a maroon strip (min. 40 mm. long by 10 mm. wide), with a further dash of maroon decorating its top. The upper part of the body is robed in a pale green garment highlighted with dashes of white and streaks of red-brown and appears to be gathered at the waist. The lower part of the body is covered in a garment, painted in shades of yellow and pink, which covers the legs and may have been worn beneath the green garment.

(11b)   This group depicts the lower garment covering the left knee and it again shows a short strip of maroon (45 mm. long by 10 mm. wide) surmounting the maroon band, with a further dash of maroon decorating its top.

The position occupied by the maroon band and projecting strips in Subject 1 is above the panel tops as part of the lower frieze zone supported by the main columns. These projecting strips, or 'plinths', shown to be fairly evenly spaced, support vertical cream-white bands, perhaps representing small columns and as discussed in Subjects 1 and 3, may be seen to form an entablature above the panel tops in Room 2 and possibly Rooms 3 and 4. If the strips of maroon

SUBJECT 11

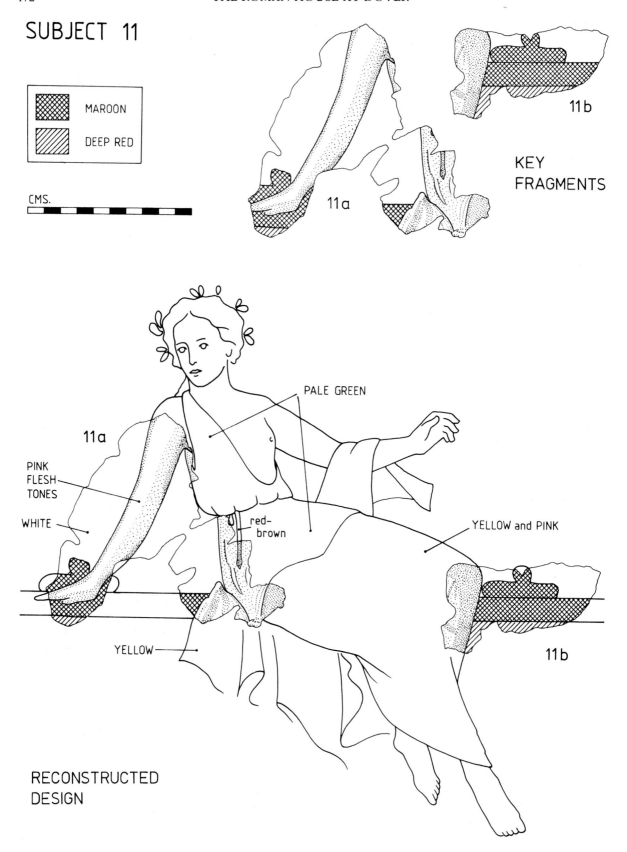

KEY
FRAGMENTS

Fig. 65. *Drawing of plaster fragments in reconstructed design, Subject 11.*

in Subject 11 represent such a 'plinth' then the robed figure, most likely female, would be seated at frieze level. This seems an unlikely arrangement within the overall Painted House scheme, nor is it supported by any other evidence (see discussion).

The female head depicted on Subject 14 has been included here in the reconstruction to form a single figure. It is difficult to assess the full height of the figure, but it is probably about $\frac{1}{4}$ life-size.

SUBJECT 12 – Female Human, Robed Standing-Figure, on White Ground (Fig. 66).

Three conjoining key fragments (Fabric A) from the north-west corner of Room 2 (DV–2306, area 'R') depict part of the torso (min. 130 mm. in length) and left arm of a semi-naked female figure in three-quarters view, facing to her left. The body is painted in shades of pink over a pale yellow ground and outlined with yellowish-brown. The arm, similarly painted, is bent slightly at the elbow and outstretched so that the inner forearm is uppermost. The small, almost imperceptible, breast outlined with pale maroon and the roundness of the lower abdomen suggests that the figure is female, perhaps a youthful maiden. What appears to be a veil, painted in a maroon wash, is draped over the elbow and passes behind the body. This garment is likely to have been worn loosely draped over both arms thus exposing the front of the body. Another garment, painted in maroon and highlighted with pink is worn low on the hips and presumably covered the legs to the ankles. A billowing veil may be represented by the dash of maroon wash across the wrist. The stance is consistent with the figure being engaged in motion, perhaps in a dance of ritual nature. The veil she holds in her outstretched hand may be billowing out, above her head, to emphasise her movement. The original height of the figure was about 430 mm. which, again, is about $\frac{1}{4}$ life-size.

SUBJECT 13 – Female Human Head (to right), over White Ground (Fig. 67).

Two conjoining key fragments (Fabric A) recovered from within the north-west corner of Room 2 (DV–2306, area 'Q'), show a garlanded female head, in almost three-quarter view looking to her right. The face, of which the features are almost indistinguishable, has been painted in shades of pink over a pale green wash. The hair, falling to her left over the nape of her neck, has been treated in a pale red-brown with maroon garland painted in wash. The head measures 60 mm. from the tip of the chin to the crown and is a minimum of 45 mm. across at its widest point.

SUBJECT 14 – Garlanded Human Head, over White Ground (Fig. 67).

Three key fragments (Fabric A) recovered from within the north-west corner of Room 2 (DV–2306, area 'Q'), show either (i) the upper part of a female head, garlanded, or (ii) part of the side of the face and forehead of a male figure. The hair is painted in shades of red-brown, highlighted with dashes of pale pink. The garland is treated with a similar maroon wash to that of Subject 13. Option (i) could form part of Subject 11.

SUBJECT 12

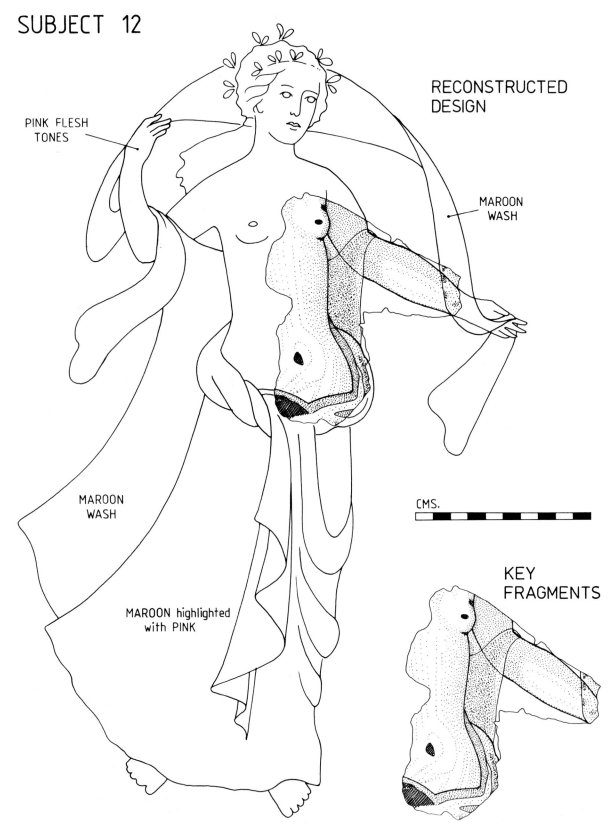

RECONSTRUCTED
DESIGN

PINK FLESH
TONES

MAROON
WASH

MAROON
WASH

MAROON highlighted
with PINK

CMS.

KEY
FRAGMENTS

Fig. 66. *Drawing of plaster fragment in reconstructed design, Subject 12.*

SUBJECT 13

KEY FRAGMENTS

PALE RED-BROWN

MAROON

RECONSTRUCTED DESIGN

SUBJECT 14

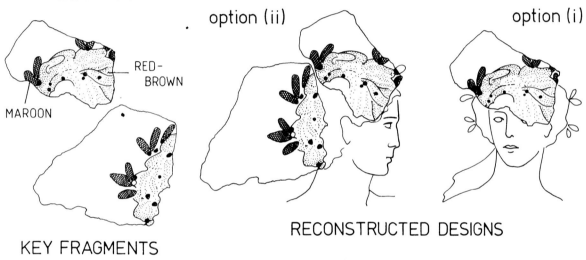

option (ii)

option (i)

RED-BROWN

MAROON

KEY FRAGMENTS

RECONSTRUCTED DESIGNS

SUBJECT 15

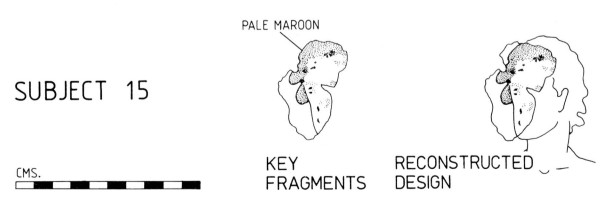

PALE MAROON

KEY FRAGMENTS

RECONSTRUCTED DESIGN

CMS.

Fig. 67. *Drawing of plaster fragments in reconstructed designs, Subjects 13, 14 and 15.*

SUBJECT 15 – Human Head (to right) over White Ground (Fig. 67).

Two conjoining key fragments (Fabric A) from Room 3 (DV–2307) show part of a head in three-quarters view looking right. The face has been painted in shades of pink, the surface of which has all but flaked off, over a primary coat of pale yellow. None of the features of the face can be distinguished. The hair has been painted in a pale maroon, almost in wash.

SUBJECT 16 – Female Human Lower Body Standing Front, over White Ground (Fig. 68).

Two conjoining key fragments (Fabric A) from Room 4 (DV–2309, area 'N'), depict what probably represents the lower torso of a naked or partly naked figure painted in shades of pink over a pale yellow-cream base. This probably shows the stomach and the right thigh and the top of the left thigh shown in three-quarter view facing left. The figure can be identified as female. It is just possible that the arm in Subject 20 could relate to this subject. The figure is painted about $\frac{1}{4}$ life-size.

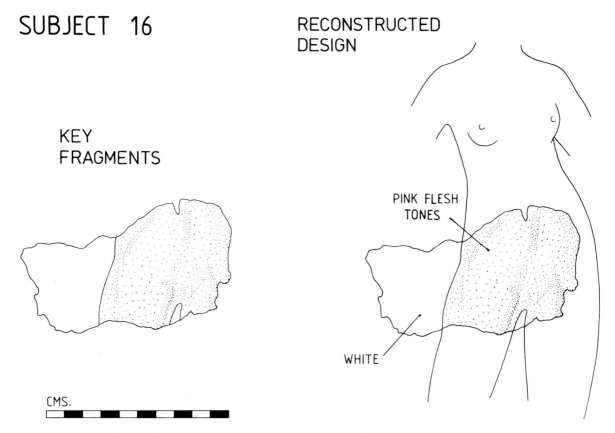

Fig. 68. *Drawing of plaster fragments in reconstructed design, Subject 16.*

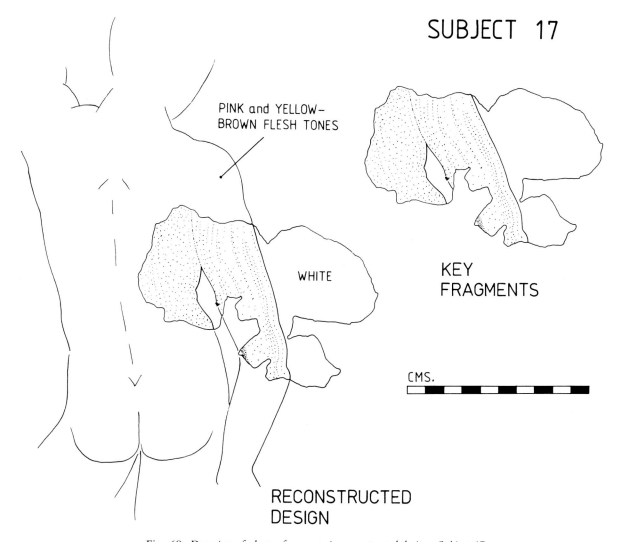

Fig. 69. *Drawing of plaster fragments in reconstructed design, Subject 17.*

SUBJECT 17 – Male Human Arm, over White Ground (Fig. 69).

Five conjoining key fragments (Fabric A) from Room 4 (DV–2309, area 'N') show what appears to be the upper part of the right arm, trunk and hip of a partly, or wholly, naked figure viewed from behind. The arm, painted in shades of pink and yellow-brown, has a muscular appearance and suggests a male figure. The torso is painted in shades of pink. The arm is painted about ¼ life-size.

SUBJECT 18 – Human Foot (right), over White Ground (Fig. 70)

A single key fragment (Fabric A) from Room 3 (DV–2307/8) depicts a foot painted in shades of pink over a yellow-brown wash and outlined in yellow-brown. It projects from beneath a garment of dark pink, lightly overpainted with a cream-white wash and edged with a dark pink strip 4 mm. wide. The foot points to the figure's right and it seems likely that this is the right foot. The heel and toes are missing. Light appears to be striking the front of the lower shin casting a heavy shadow to the rear. The foot may be painted about ¼ life-size.

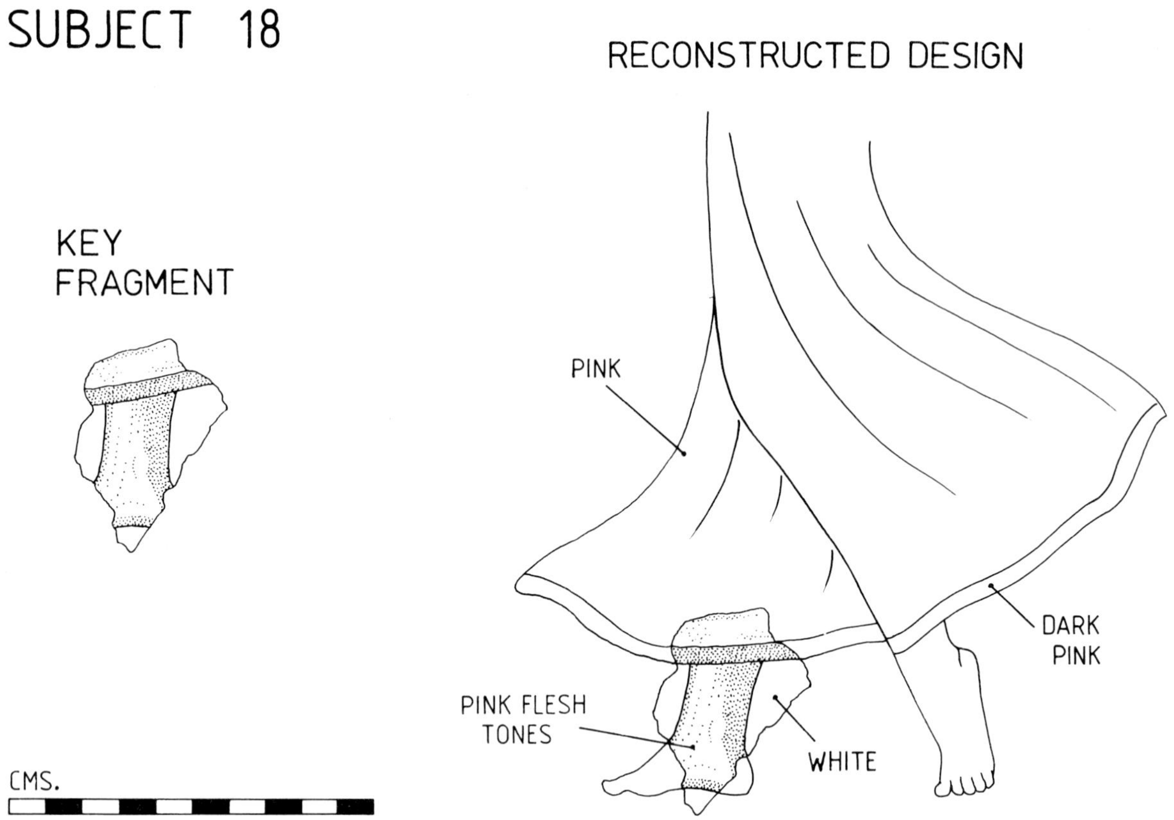

SUBJECT 18

RECONSTRUCTED DESIGN

KEY
FRAGMENT

PINK

DARK
PINK

PINK FLESH
TONES

WHITE

CMS.

Fig. 70. *Drawing of a plaster fragment in reconstructed design, Subject 18.*

SUBJECT 19 – Male Human Leg, over White Ground (Fig. 71).

Six conjoining key fragments (Fabric A) recovered from the west side of Room 2 (DV–2306, area 'U') show part of the right leg of a partly or wholly naked figure. The leg, painted in shades of pink, is depicted in three-quarter view facing right, slightly outstretched and bent at the knee as though in the act of vigorous movement, perhaps striding. Dashes of white highlight the inside of the thigh and calf whilst dark pink outlining the top of the leg in shadow emphasises roundness. The muscular appearance suggests that the leg is part of a male figure. The original height of the figure may have been about 260 mm. which is about $\frac{1}{8}$ life-size.

SUBJECT 20 – Female Human Arm, over White Ground (Fig. 71)

A single key fragment (Fabric A) from the west side of Room 2 (DV–2306, area 'U'), shows part of the forearm bared and painted in shades of pink. Pale pink highlights the outer arm whilst darker pink on the inside emphasises the roundness. The delicate appearance suggests that it is part of a female figure. The arm could either represent the left arm in which case it would be positioned at the side of the body, or the right arm where it could be outstretched at shoulder level or, more likely, flexed upwards from the elbow with the upper arm perhaps held away from the body. It is just possible that this arm could fit Subject 16.

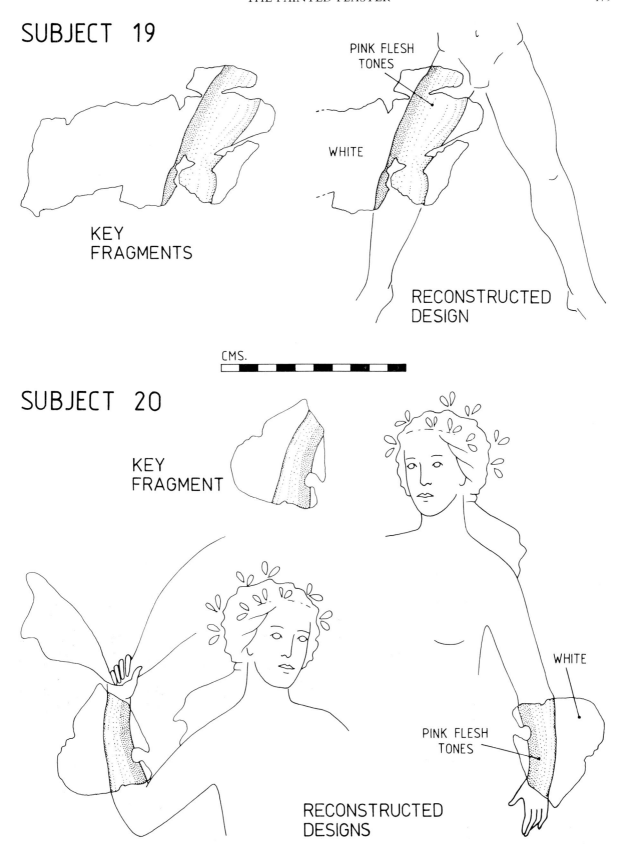

SUBJECT 19

KEY
FRAGMENTS

PINK FLESH
TONES

WHITE

RECONSTRUCTED
DESIGN

CMS.

SUBJECT 20

KEY
FRAGMENT

WHITE

PINK FLESH
TONES

RECONSTRUCTED
DESIGNS

Fig. 71. *Drawing of plaster fragments in reconstructed designs, Subjects 19 and 20.*

SUBJECTS 21–23 – Ornamental Vessels (Fig. 72).

Some nine fragments of plaster (Fabric A), show what may represent ornamental vessels or cups. They form three key groups (Subjects 21–23). The fragments were recovered from the following deposits:-

Subject	Room	No. of Fragments	Deposit No.	Area
21	3	2	DV–2307	E, F, G.
22	2	2	DV–2306	Q, R, U
23	2	5	DV–2306	R
TOTAL		9		

SUBJECT 21

Two conjoining key fragments show part of a cylindrical motif (measuring 56 mm. in width and a minimum of 70 mm. high) painted in shades of light-brown to orange-brown, highlighted with blue streaks over a white field. The motif may represent a vessel but there is no indication on the fragments that handles, such as those depicted on Subject 22, were present. Flora or decorative ribbons project from each side of the rim and are painted in a similar orange-brown with blue streaks and 'splashes'. A probable leaf, painted in green, is positioned 14 mm. above the vessel. This undoubtedly forms part of a separate foliate motif further enlivening the white zone. A small 'dash' of grey (54 mm. to the left, as viewed) may represent a vertical band that frames the decorated white field on at least one side.

SUBJECT 22

Two conjoining key fragments show part of a cylindrical motif (measuring 57 mm. in width and a minimum of 72 mm. high) but unlike Subject 21, this has been painted in shades of olive green over a white field. At either side of the motif (42 mm. below the presumed top), is a single upright crescent painted in olive-green, the ends of which spring from the body of the design. The motif may be seen to represent a two-handled vessel, or cup. Flora or decorative ribbons project from each side of the rim and are also painted in olive-green. Some 54 mm. to the right (as viewed) of the vessel is a grey band (a minimum of 7 mm. in width and 25 mm. in length). This may represent a vertical band framing the decorated white zone similar to Subject 21. This band may have been treated with further decoration suggested by grey paint projecting 6 mm. from the band into the white field.

SUBJECT 23

Five conjoining key fragments show part of a cylindrical motif measuring a minimum of 45 mm. wide and a minumum. of 87 mm. high. It has been painted in shades of light brown highlighted with blue and cream streaks over a white field. The motif may represent a cup or ornamental vessel. No handles are indicated on the surviving fragments. Flora or decorative

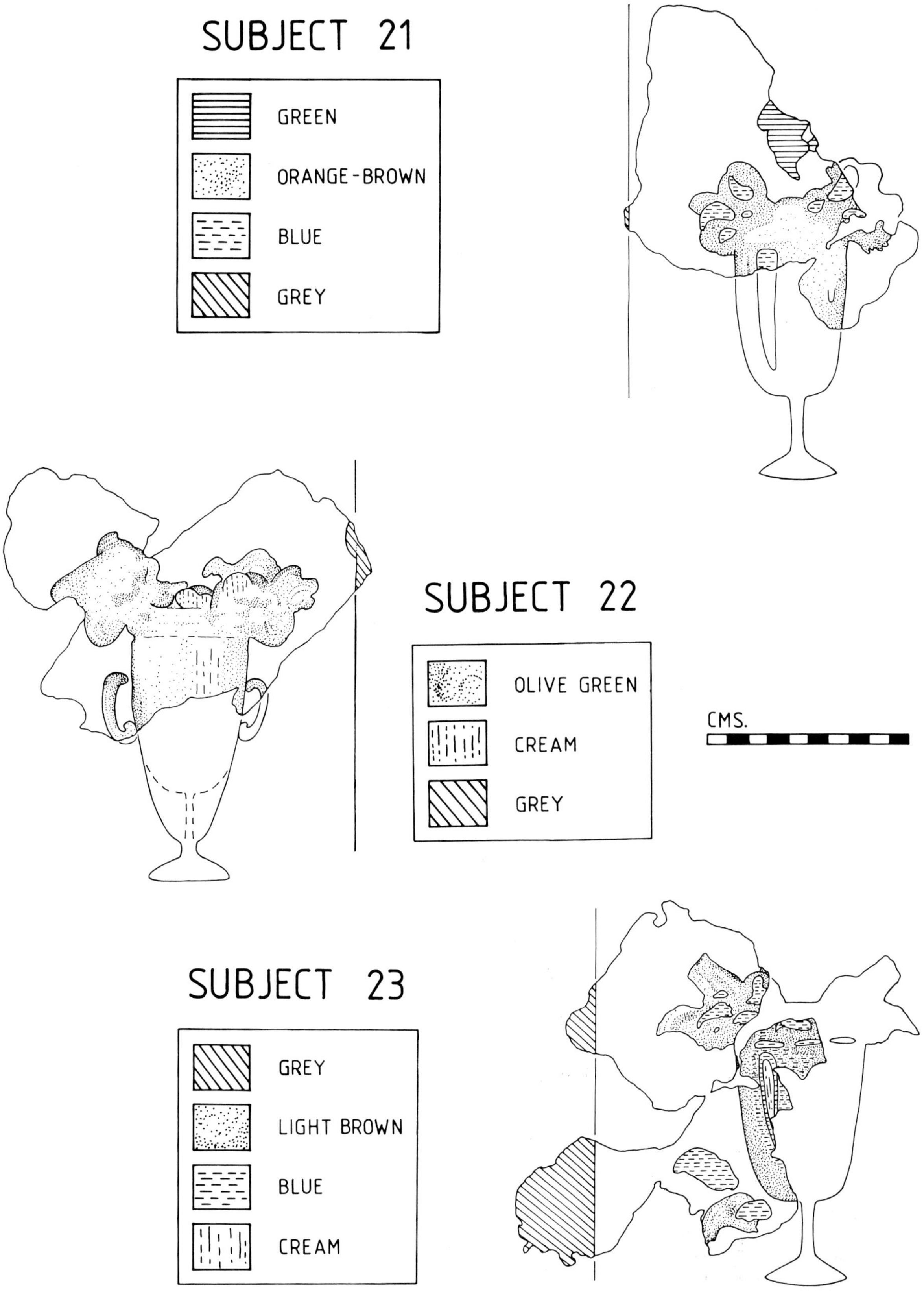

SUBJECT 21

GREEN	
ORANGE-BROWN	
BLUE	
GREY	

SUBJECT 22

OLIVE GREEN	
CREAM	
GREY	

CMS.

SUBJECT 23

GREY	
LIGHT BROWN	
BLUE	
CREAM	

Fig. 72. *Drawing of plaster fragments in reconstructed designs, Subjects 21, 22 and 23.*

ribbons painted in light-brown, highlighted with blue, project from the presumed left rim of the vessel (as viewed). Similar decoration may be seen adjacent to and below the bowl of the vessel. These embellishments may also have been present on the missing right side. It is possible that the motif is meant to be viewed with both decorations seen here uppermost, thus representing the rim of a vessel (compare Subjects 21 and 22). A broad band of light green over light grey (min. 40 mm. wide) frames the white field (71 mm.) and is here positioned vertically to the left of the vase.

All three motifs (Subjects 21–23) share many similarities. All are painted over a white ground and are framed by a grey or grey-green band, to the left of the vessel in Subjects 21 and 23, and to the right in Subject 22. All have flora or decorative ribbons projecting from them. Subjects 21 and 22 are the same size and are the same distance from the grey border. Subject 23 may also be of similar size but is a little further away from the border. The motifs all appear to be representations of ornamental vessels, at least one of which is two-handled (Subject 22). It is possible that they are intended to represent 'canthari' and may therefore be of ritual significance within a scheme employing framed, decorated white panels covering one or more walls.

The combination of decorated white field framed by a grey border does not fit easily into the schemes employed in Rooms 1–6, unless these designs relate in some way to a larger scheme that employs Subject 2 from the north wall of Room 3.

SUBJECT 24 – Geometric Frames in Blue and White under a Maroon Ceiling-band.

Some 347 fragments of plaster (Fabric A) share similar decorative characteristics and appear to relate to the frieze zone above the main design. These were recovered from the following deposits:-

Deposit No.	Room	Area	Fabric A	Fabric B	No. of Fragments
DV–2302	2	S. Wall	.	6	6
DV–2306	2	Q, R, U	27	10	37
DV–2308	2	I, J	41	13	54
DV–2366	2	Floor	23		23
DV–1167	2	General Layer	1		1
DV–2307	3	E, F, G	36	9	45
DV–2309	4	General Layer		52	52
DV–1182	Shore-fort Foundation-Trench	General Layer	29		29
DV–2350	Shore-fort Foundation-Trench	General Layer	31		31
DV–1163	Unstrat.		65		65
DV–1170	Unstrat.		4		4
TOTAL			257	90	347

An initial study of these fragments suggests two probable patterns and these are based on 47 key fragments (24A-K). It is, however, difficult to define a comprehensive design as there is a variety of combinations. Nor is it easy to determine the precise number of fragments belonging to each of the patterns owing to the close similarity of the decorative elements. The main common element seems to be geometric designs in blue and white, mostly associated with the upper frieze or the ceiling band. Significantly, the colour blue is totally absent from the low-level *in situ* designs.

PATTERN 1 – (A–G) (Fig. 73).

A minimum of 36 fragments of plaster seem to have formed part of this design. Twelve fragments are illustrated (Nos. 24A-G) and show the following sequence:-

(24A)   This single fragment shows a broad maroon band (40 mm. wide) lined along one edge with a lime-green stripe (7–8 mm. wide). Adjacent to this is a blue band (40–45 mm. wide) over which, and at 90° to the lime-green stripe is a painted white stripe (12 mm. wide), that divides the blue band into at least two probably rectangular zones (a minimum of 50 mm. in length).
This band is in turn edged with a cream stripe (10 mm. wide) that in turn lines a zone of white (a minimum of 4 mm.).

(24B)   A group of three conjoining fragments show a similar maroon band (up to 60 mm. wide) and edged with a cream stripe (up to 10 mm.). Adjacent to this is a zone of white (40 mm. wide) bordered by a blue band (min. 15 mm.) and edged with cream (8 mm. wide) that forms a corner with the maroon band.

Closer examination of the illustrated fragments shows that the decoration described above is painted over a secondary rendered surface. The original rendering, also in Fabric A, forms a curving angle of approximately 45°. The original surface appears to have been treated with at least one maroon stripe of up to 2 mm. wide painted over white (not illustrated). Subsequently, this surface had been re-plastered filling in the curve of the original rendering. It seems likely that this curvature formed the junction of two separate surfaces, almost certainly the wall and ceiling. Thus the maroon border has here been positioned horizontally at the top of the design as a ceiling band (40–60 mm. wide), surmounting a zone divided into small blue and white rectangular panels.

(24C)   A single fragment shows a zone of blue divided into three rectangular panels (the most complete of which is 66 mm. by a minimum of 90 mm.) by white stripes (7–12 mm. wide). This arrangement is painted over a white field.

(24D)   A further fragment shows a blue zone (min. 66 mm. wide), edged with a creamy-white stripe (10 mm. wide). This borders a white zone (min. 7 mm.) on two sides. The white forms a 120° corner that encloses the blue. The blue has been further decorated with two white stripes (10 mm. wide, and at least 50 mm. apart), that project from the edge of the blue and meet at a point about 75 mm. away thus forming a V-shape (here shown inverted).

(24E)   A minimum of four fragments of which two conjoin, show the following sequence. The two conjoining fragments show from right to left (as viewed here) a broad zone of blue (min. 66 mm. wide). This appears to have been painted over a light-grey undercoat. Next to this is a zone of yellow ochre (min. 45 mm. wide) over which has been painted a vertical cream stripe (15 mm. wide) at a distance of 11 mm. away from and parallel to the junction with blue. Traces of paint indicate that the blue and yellow zones were flanked by a cream stripe (up to 9 mm. wide) here shown at top.

(24F)   A single fragment shows a similar sequence to 24E from right to left as viewed. The same broad blue zone (min. 56 mm. wide) can be seen here to surmount a zone of white (unpainted plaster) (min. 14 mm.) lined at its junction with the blue by a cream stripe (11 mm. wide). Both the blue and white zones are bordered by the same yellow ochre zone (here min. 48 mm. wide), to that seen on key fragments 24E. A cream stripe (here 12 mm. wide) has also been painted over this yellow zone at a distance of 11 mm. parallel to the blue/white zones. The paint has been applied more thickly to the left side

SUBJECT 24   pattern 1

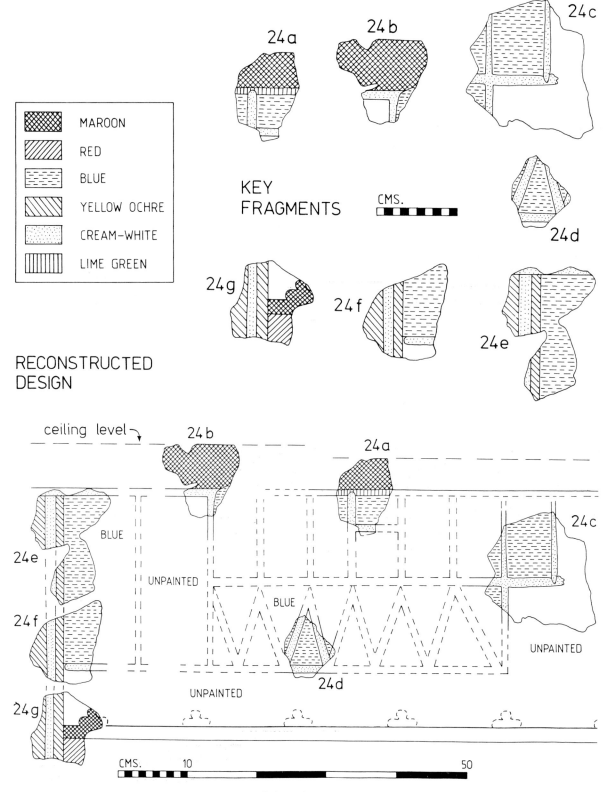

Fig. 73. *Drawing of plaster fragments, Subject 24, pattern 1.*

of this stripe (as shown) and may be a result of uneven loading of the brush during application.

(24G) The remaining fragment shows the same yellow ochre zone (min. 45 mm. wide, here shown left) with the familiar cream stripe (12 mm. wide) at a distance of 11 mm. parallel to the right edge of the yellow. This yellow zone can be seen here to border a zone of red (min. 35 mm. wide) capped by a horizontal maroon stripe (17 mm. wide). Surmounting this stripe some 22 mm. to the right from the yellow band, is a vertical projection. The upper part (12 mm. in length) is offset 12 mm. from the left edge of the lower part (min. 35 mm. in length). These elements project onto a field of white (here shown at top, min. 47 mm. wide). The short maroon projections surmounting a maroon stripe are also on Subjects 1, 3 and 11 where, painted over white, they support narrow vertical cream bands which occupied frieze level. It is likely, therefore, that this design also derives from the frieze and the red band is here shown at the bottom of the design. The white field above the red band and maroon projection, at present of unknown depth, is surmounted by a broad blue zone perhaps divided up into smaller rectangular panels and itself capped by a cream or lime green stripe above which is a maroon band. The yellow band is now seen to the left as viewed, vertically framing the zones of red, white and blue.

At present it is difficult to determine the precise arrangement that these fragments occupied within the overall design, but the similarity with subjects 1, 3 and 11 may indicate a position at frieze-level, perhaps from a room as yet unlocated. The yellow band to the left may represent a framing element. A corresponding band would have been employed to the right, used in order to highlight the enclosed design.

PATTERN 2 – (H–K). (Fig. 74).

Eleven fragments have been used for this pattern, seven of which are illustrated (24H-K).

(24H) This single fragment shows a maroon band (min. 23 mm. wide). This has been shown here at the top of the design as two fragments (not illustrated) show the rendering forming an angled curve that represents its junction with a new surface, perhaps ceiling/wall. Below the maroon band is a lime green stripe (12 mm. wide) followed by a broad light fawn zone (min. 65 mm. wide). The fawn has been further enlivened by three oblique brown-yellow stripes, the most complete of these being 18 mm. wide and 62 mm. in length. They are suspended from the lime green at an angle of approximately 30° to the right as viewed. A 'blob' of cream-white paint decorated the lower ends. The stripes are 28 mm. (approximately) and 56 mm. apart from left to right, respectively.

(24I) Another fragment also shows this lime green stripe (here a min. of 5 mm.) over the fawn. Below the fawn band (48 mm. wide) is a light grey horizontal stripe (min. of 3 mm.). Parts of two similar brown-yellow oblique stripes, as seen on key fragment 24H, enliven the fawn, the ends of which are also decorated with 'blobs' of cream-white paint.

(24J) Three conjoining fragments show the same fawn (here a min. of 26 mm.) and shown uppermost, embellished with two 'blobs' of cream-white paint almost certainly at the ends of oblique strips as shown in key fragments 24H and 24I. Below this is a light green-grey band (45 mm. wide) incorporating at least three narrow horizontal parallel cream lines, irregularly spaced within the band. Below this is a zone of blue (min. 70 mm. wide) painted over a light grey undercoat that is exposed in places, especially at the edges of the fragments, where the blue pigment has worn off. The blue is lined, shown here at the bottom, with a white stripe (8 mm. wide) which in turn separates a zone of white (unpainted plaster) (a minimum of 5 mm.) from the blue zone above. An almost vertical white stripe (10 mm. wide) is painted over the blue dividing it into at least two rectangular zones (min. 115 x 70 mm.).

SUBJECT 24   pattern 2

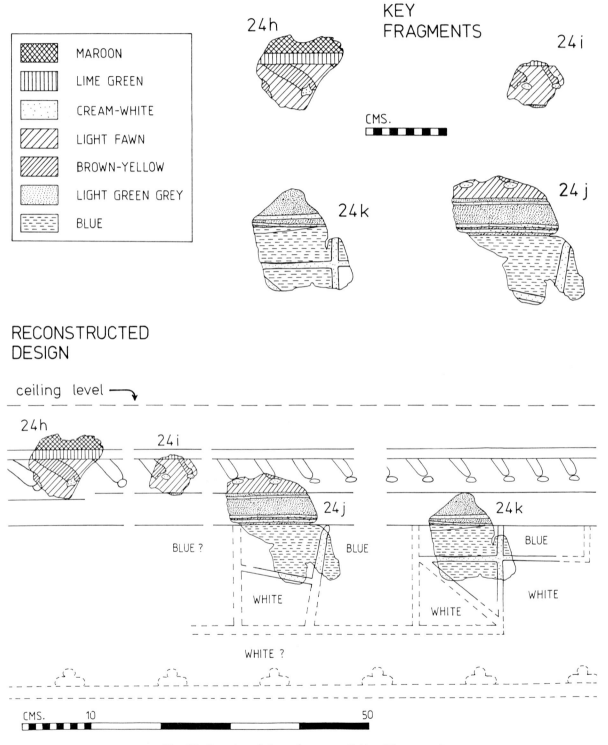

Fig. 74. *Drawing of plaster fragments, Subject 24, pattern 2.*

(24K) Two adjoining fragments show a similar arrangement of blue adjacent to light green-grey. The blue zone (a min. of 70 mm. wide), frames on two sides an area of white (20 x 25 mm.). This forms a corner, here shown right, creating a rectangular panel lined with a cream-white stripe (7 mm. wide). A second enclosed white zone, here shown left (unmeasurable) is indicated by a cream stripe (a min. of 5 mm. wide) lining the blue at approximately 40–45° to the first enclosed white zone. Two white stripes (7 mm. wide) are painted over the blue both projecting from the corner of the first enclosed white zone, here shown top left. One stripe extends upwards to the grey band above the blue, whilst the other extends to the left, parallel and at a distance of 40 mm. to the grey band. These stripes effectively divide the blue zone into at least three smaller rectangular zones, of which one is a minimum of 40–95 mm. The emerging pattern shows a maroon ceiling-band above a broad zone of fawn, decorated with oblique brown-yellow stripes and 'blobs' of cream-white paint. These occur at regular intervals and may represent a receding plane. Below this is a horizontal band of light-grey lined with irregularly spaced, horizontal cream stripes. This is followed by a broad zone of blue that has been divided up into small geometric panels by horizontal, vertical and oblique white stripes. This blue zone, edged with cream, is painted over a white field which either frames or is framed by the blue. This appears to create rectangular and triangular zones of white edged with cream-white stripes. The precise shapes and arrangements are difficult to determine from so few disarticulated fragments. There are several combinations in which the decorative elements could be arranged, only one of which is shown. Future work may produce more conclusive results.

SUBJECTS 25–29 Floral and Foliate Motifs (Figs. 75–78).

Some 523 fragments of plaster appear to represent parts of either floral or foliate motifs. The location of these fragments is given in the following table:-

Room No.	No. of Fragments	Deposit No.	Area
1	10	DV–9674	General Layer
2	4	DV–2302	Floor
2	324	DV–2306	B, D, Q, R, U
2	3	DV–2308	I, J
2	5	DV–1168	General Layer
2	6	DV–1167	General Layer
Floor of Room 2	19	DV–2302	Groups 1 and 5 as lifted
3	38	DV–2307	E, F, G, H
3	2	DV–1162	General Layer
3	1	DV–1195	General Layer
4	64	DV–2309	N, O
5	2	DV–3056	Floor (Subject 29)
Passage	1	DV–1145	General Layer
Passage	2	DV–2351	General Layer
Shore-fort Rampart	8	DV–1153	General Layer
Shore-fort Rampart	3	DV–2333	General Layer
Shore-fort Rampart	3	DV–9618	General Layer

Room No.	No. of Fragments	Deposit No.	Area
Shore-fort Robber-trench	18	DV–4076	General Layer
Unstratified	10	DV–2342	
TOTAL	523		

Of this number, only 177, seem to depict five recognisable plants and flowers (Subjects 25–29). Although the remaining 346 fragments do show a wide variety of leaves, stems and petals, it is not possible to confidently reconstruct additional flora owing to the fragmentary nature of the plaster. All are painted on a white ground and decorate two distinct plaster fabrics. Subjects 25 and 26 are painted over Fabric A, whilst Subjects 27–29 are painted over Fabric B. The latter may have derived from the ceiling either decorating areas of white, or used as framing, or filling elements within the general pattern and may combine with Subjects 30–33. Subjects 25 and 26 may have served a similar function within a pattern decorating a wall surface, but not obviously from Rooms 2–4 of the Painted House.

SUBJECT 25 – Plant with Green Leaves, Maroon Bloom, beside Decorative Border (Fig. 75).

Some 22 fragments of plaster (Fabric A) seem to show part of a flowering plant motif, on a white field, beside maroon 'quaver' motifs. These were recovered from layer DV–2306 within Room 2 and lifted as Group 12, from Area 'D'.

The reconstructed design is based on eight conjoining key fragments and shows a broad green-brown stem (between 16–20 mm. wide) supporting small green heart-shaped leaves and maroon flowers. The leaves are positioned on either side of the stem and are seen in full view. Five are spaced up to 20 mm. apart to the left (as viewed) of the stem and four are spaced up to 30 mm. apart to the right. A single leaf is painted over the stem 148 mm. distant from a similarly positioned bloom. The bloom is roughly oval (50 mm. x 40 mm.) and is painted in shades of maroon enclosed by a cream edging. Two centrally placed cream 'dashes' may represent the stamen. To the left, and adjacent to the plant are two maroon 'quaver' motifs (85 mm. apart, each 30 mm. in length and a minimum of 15 mm. wide). Both are probably painted with a single brush-stroke (here up to 10 mm. wide). Centrally placed between these two motifs is a probable inverted-V painted in maroon. Only the 'point' survives and this is level with the ends of the two flanking 'quavers'. These motifs are identical to those decorating the maroon borders in Subjects 30 and 31 and may be closely related.

These fragments seem to have formed a flowering plant of unknown proportions with maroon flowers and green leaves sprouting from a green-brown stem. This subject almost certainly occupied a position within a plain white panel framed by a coloured border (here shown left) further treated with 'quaver' motifs (compare Subject 31). The plant may have been confined to the edge of the panel and aligned parallel with the border, whilst the panel centre remained either bare or contained other decoration.

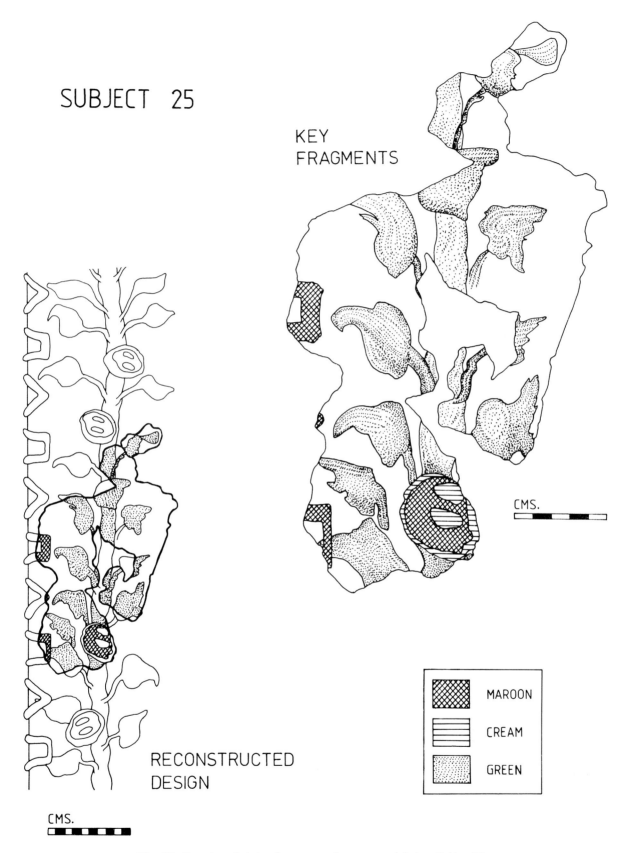

SUBJECT 25

KEY
FRAGMENTS

CMS.

RECONSTRUCTED
DESIGN

MAROON

CREAM

GREEN

CMS.

Fig. 75. *Drawing of plaster fragments and reconstructed design, Subject 25.*

SUBJECT 26 – Band with Linked Green Foliage, over a White Field (Fig. 76).

Some 25 fragments of plaster (Fabric A), seem to show part of a cream band supporting a green and brown foliate motif on a white field. Their location was as follows:-

Room No.	No. of Fragments	Deposit No.	Area Code
1 4	10 15	DV–9674 DV–2309	General Layer N, O
TOTAL	25		

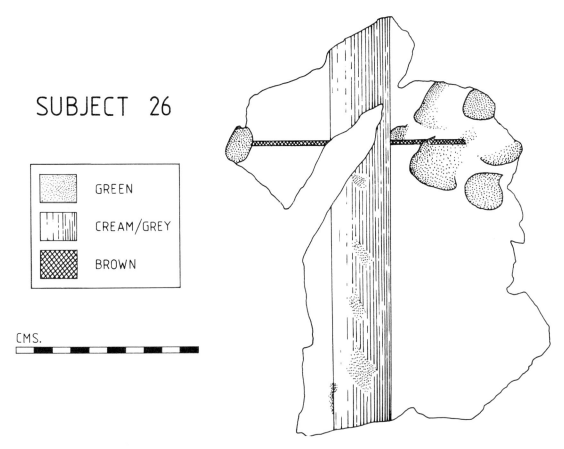

SUBJECT 26

GREEN

CREAM/GREY

BROWN

CMS.

Fig. 76. *Drawing of plaster fragments in reconstructed design, Subject 26.*

Only five key fragments are used in the reconstructed design and these show a cream band (32 mm. wide) shaded along one side (here shown right) with grey (up to 21 mm. wide). This is painted over a white ground. The cream band (shown vertically) intersects a narrow horizontal brown stem (up to 2 mm. wide) at 90°, from which sprout at least five green leaves, unevenly spaced with four on one side of the cream band and one on the other. The leaves are of irregular shape and measure approximately 24 mm. x 21 mm. Traces of green over the cream band may suggest further leaves which appear to be coiled around the band.

Although this is a very difficult subject to interpret the design may represent a cream frame enhanced by shading along one edge, supporting a sinuous creeping plant with green leaves, resembling ivy. This frame may divide areas of white into square or rectangular panels, either plain or decorated. A more delicate arrangement might be achieved if the bands were to frame areas of white on only two sides with the remaining two sides demarcated by the plant crossing the frame at 90°. The frame could thus represent a 'trellis'. The shading along the edge of the cream band may be an attempt to emphasise roundness.

SUBJECT 27 – Plant with Green Leaves and Blue and Maroon Flowers (Fig. 77).

Some 64 fragments of plaster (Fabric B) appear to show a green foliate motif with blue and maroon petalled flowers. Their location is shown in the following table:-

Room No.	No. of Fragments	Deposit No.	Area Code
2	56	DV–2306	B, D, Q, R, U (Groups 15, 31, 37)
Shore-Fort Robber-Trench	8	DV–4076	General Layer
TOTAL	64		

Only 14 key fragments are used in the reconstructed design and these form two key groups (Nos. 27A and B).

27a   Nine conjoining fragments show a brown stem (up to 4 mm. wide) supporting fully opened flowers. Two are seen here about 140 mm. apart, centre to centre. The innermost part of the flower has been painted in two tones using maroon and vermilion, over which has been applied a dash of cream paint which may represent the stamen. This arrangement is encircled by bright blue paint (up to 13 mm. wide, thus a minimum of 40 mm. in diameter overall) representing petals. A minimum of four leaves, painted in pale and dark green, are shown in full view extending from the main stem.

27b   Five conjoining fragments show a similar flower fully opened and roughly oval in shape (about 65 mm. x 55 mm.). The suggestion of a second flower is adjacent to the first at a distance of 3 mm. At least three leaves are shown in full view.

The design seems to depict a flowering plant of unknown proportions with blue/maroon flowers and green leaves sprouting from a brown stem. Although it is not clear what species the flower represents it may be a rose.

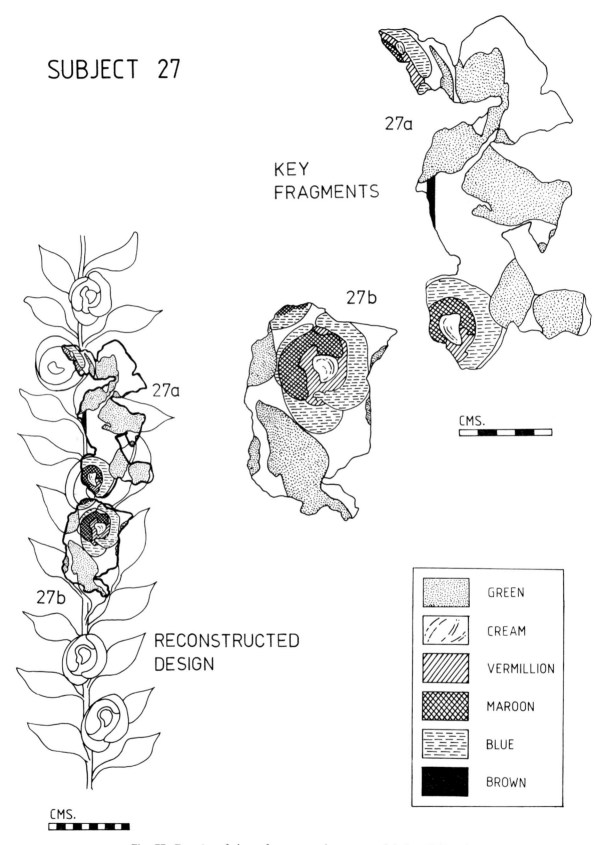

SUBJECT 27

KEY
FRAGMENTS

27a

27b

27a

27b

RECONSTRUCTED
DESIGN

CMS.

CMS.

GREEN

CREAM

VERMILLION

MAROON

BLUE

BROWN

Fig. 77. *Drawing of plaster fragments and reconstructed design, Subject 27.*

SUBJECT 28 – Plant with Green Leaves and Yellow Flowers (Fig. 78).

Some 25 fragments of plaster (Fabric B) recovered from layer DV–2306 within Room 2, and lifted as Group 21, appear to show a flowering plant with yellow flowers and green leaves sprouting from a brown stem. The reconstructed design is based on four key fragments which form two key groups (Subjects 28a and b).

Three conjoining fragments (28a) show a broad green leaf (30 mm. wide and min. 40 mm. long), in full view over a brown stem (up to 4 mm. thick). Immediately adjacent to the leaf are two flowering buds of irregular shape (up to 27 mm. x 23 mm.), painted in bright yellow, one of which is also over the stem. A single fragment (28b) shows two green leaf stems (up to 3 mm. wide), supporting at least one leaf immediately adjacent to and partly over a main stem painted in brown and up to 4 mm. wide.

The design seems to represent a flowering plant of unknown proportions. It is not clear what species is represented, but its appearance suggests a creeper of some sort.

SUBJECT 29 – Plant with Green Leaves and Red Flowers (Fig. 78).

Some 41 fragments of plaster (Fabric B) appear to show red flowers and green leaves sprouting from a brown stem. These were recovered from layer DV–2306 within Room 2 and mostly lifted as Group 29. Two more similar fragments were found on the floor of Room 5.

The reconstructed design uses seven key fragments which form two key groups (Nos. 29a and b). The first group (29a), consisting of three fragments, shows a bright red flowering bud (about 28 mm. x 26 mm.). A second flower is just below the first and visible beside a pale green leaf. The second group (29b), consisting of four fragments, shows a brown stem (up to 7 mm. thick), supporting a bright red flower and green leaf. The design seems to represent a flowering plant, of unknown proportions, with red flowers and green leaves sprouting from a brown stem.

SUBJECT 30 – Maroon Tendrilled Plant, over a Yellow Field with Decorated Green and Maroon Border (Figs. 79 and 80).

Some 204 fragments of plaster (Fabric B) appear to form part of a rectangular yellow panel framed on at least two sides by a foliated green border which is lined internally with cream and black stripes. A maroon band may form the lower edge of the panel. The panel is decorated with a maroon tendrilled plant. The fragments were located as follows:-

Room No.	No. of Fragments	Deposit No.	Area Code
2	142	DV–2306	B, C, D, Q, R, U
3	62	DV–2307	E
TOTAL	204		

Only 42 of the fragments are used in the reconstructed design and these form five key groups (Nos. 30 a – e).

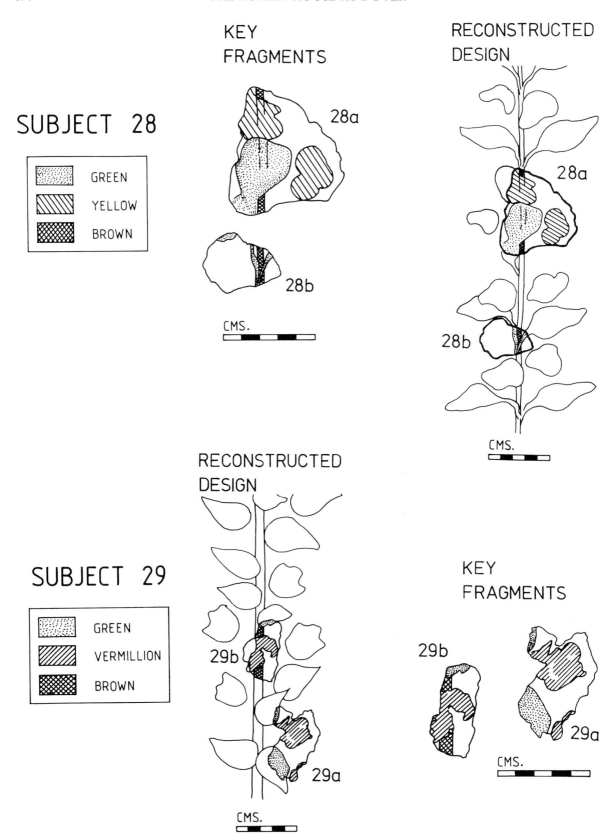

Fig. 78. *Drawing of plaster fragments and reconstructed designs, Subjects 28 and 29.*

30a   Three conjoining fragments show an internal corner (90°) enclosing a yellow field (a minimum of 34 mm. x 39 mm.), which is framed by black (5 mm.) and cream (5–8 mm.) stripes and part of an outer light green border, here shown left.

30b   Fifteen conjoining fragments show a series of stripes or bands which seem to form part of the same scheme. From left to right these show a light grey stripe (1–4 mm.); a light green band (40–45 mm.); a cream stripe (5–8 mm.) and a black stripe (5 mm.) followed by part of a yellow field (at least 30 mm. wide).

30c   Thirteen fragments, three of which join, and are illustrated here, show a maroon tendrilled plant over a yellow field. At least four tendrils (up to 6 mm. wide) sprout from a main stem (3–6 mm. wide). Brush strokes indicate that the tendrils curved upwards from the stem.

30d   Five fragments, three of which join and are illustrated show green foliage sprouting from a grey stripe and light green band. These appear to be the same as the grey stripe and green band described in 30b. The green leaves are shown to project between 10 and 20 mm. into an adjacent white field (here shown left) (a minimum of 30 mm. wide). Another fragment (not illustrated) shows further leaves projecting up to 25 mm. into a white field.

30e   Six fragments, four of which are illustrated, show a small section of a maroon band (min. 15 mm. wide) bordering a yellow field. Assuming that the yellow field is part of the same panel described above, the maroon border has been reconstructed as its base. Surmounting the maroon band and projecting into the yellow are a series of small maroon 'quaver' motifs (min. 24 mm. high and 30 mm. wide). Their distance apart cannot be determined but similar motifs decorating Subject 25 are shown approximately 85 mm. apart and this has been used as a guide.

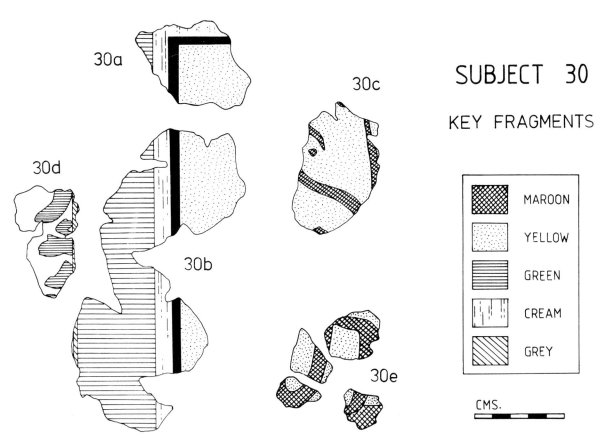

Fig. 79. *Drawing of plaster fragments, Subject 30.*

SUBJECT 30   RECONSTRUCTED DESIGN   (COLOUR CODE – SEE KEY FRAGMENTS)

Fig. 80. *Drawing of plaster fragments in reconstructed design, Subject 30.*

The picture which emerges from these five groups, is that of a rectangular yellow panel of unknown overall dimensions, framed by a foliated green border on at least two sides and lined internally with cream and black stripes. A maroon band seems to form the base of the panel. Although the precise arrangement cannot be determined it seems most likely that the maroon band decorated with 'quaver' motifs served as a primary border from which this framed panel projected. The tendrilled plant decorating the yellow zone may have been centrally placed (as shown) sprouting upwards from the maroon border. The white zone of unpainted plaster adjacent to the green border (shown left) and enlivened at the edge with a foliate pattern may have served as either a plain area in between brightly painted panels, or as a white panel centre.

The exact position of this design within the overall scheme of the Painted House has not yet been confidently determined, but the comparatively finer quality of plaster here may suggest it derived from the ceiling level where a lighter plaster would have been required. The painted decoration may combine with Subjects 27–29, 31–34 to form part of the same scheme employed on the ceiling of Room 2.

SUBJECT 31 – White Panel with Maroon Frame, Decorated with 'Studs' and 'Quavers' (Fig. 81).

Some 50 fragments of plaster (Fabric B) appear to form part of a white rectangular panel, framed by a maroon border. The border is decorated with cream-white and buff studs, the cream-white in groups of five forming a cross pattern linked by a row of buff. The border is further enlivened with a series of 'quaver' motifs overlapping the inner white field. Their location is as follows:-

Room No.	No. of Fragments	Deposit No.	Area Code
2	6	DV–2301	Floor
2	36	DV–2306	B, Q, R, U
2	5	DV–2346	General Layer
4	2	DV–2309	N
Bingo Hall Site	1	DV–3071	General Layer
TOTAL	50		

The reconstructed design is based on eight key fragments forming three key groups (Nos. 31a–c).

31a.   Six conjoining fragments show a broad maroon band (at least 153 mm. wide) here shown horizontally bordering a white field below (min. 96 mm.). The maroon band is decorated with seven roughly circular studs (between 6–12 mm. in diameter), five cream-white and two buff. The cream-white are arranged to form a cross pattern, with a central stud being surrounded by the other four. The horizontal arm of the cross is then continued by the two buff studs to form a line of studs 70 mm. from and parallel to the edge of the border. It is not known if the 'cross' pattern is repeated, although it seems likely considering its occurrence in Subject 32. The edge of the maroon band is decorated with a maroon 'quaver' motif (27 mm. square) projecting onto the white field. This is flanked on either side by diagonal maroon stripes (up to 15 mm. wide and 10 mm. apart) on each side of the squares.

SUBJECT 31

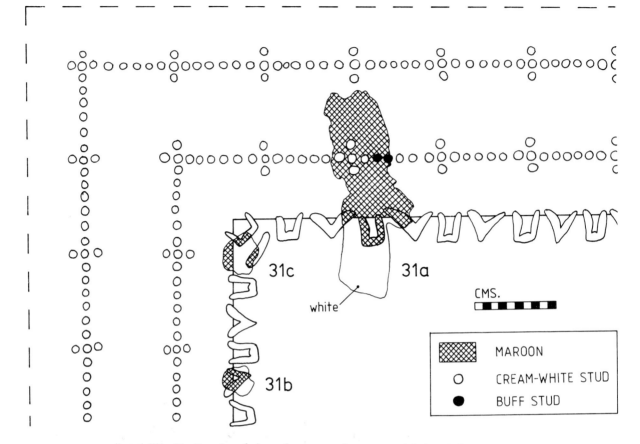

Fig. 81. *Drawing of plaster fragments and reconstructed design, Subject 31.*

31b.   This single fragment shows a 'V' motif (up to 20 mm. in length and 30–60 mm. in width at the base) projecting from a similar maroon border and clearly representing the diagonal motif either side of the 'quaver', as depicted on 31a.

31c.   A single fragment shows a 'quaver' striking a maroon band at an angle of 45°. This must represent a corner (here shown top left in the reconstructed design) which has been further decorated by the addition of a parallel maroon stripe 15 mm. above the 'quaver'. It seems likely that the maroon band formed a border (here shown top) framing a white field lined with a pattern of alternating 'quavers' and 'V-motifs'. This treatment is reminiscent of the ovolo arrangement employed in the suggested decoration of the coffer-painted ceiling from the frigidarium of the Fortress Baths at Caerleon (Ref. 98). The row of studs is not centrally placed within the border which may indicate that there were originally two parallel rows equidistant from the panel edge. If so, the border would have been at least 250 mm. wide.

The precise arrangement and proportions cannot yet be determined, but the decorative border may represent either a primary border from which a series of panels projected, or more simply it may have served as a complete frame for the white zone, two sides of which are suggested by key fragment 31c. Subject 25 also displays identical 'quaver' motifs projecting onto a white field which is further decorated with a floral motif. Although composed of a different plaster fabric, this could suggest the work of the same artist and a similar floral design may have adorned the white panel here. The position of Subject 31 in the general scheme is not known, but the finer quality of the plaster suggests that this derived from a ceiling. The painted decoration may combine with Subjects 27, 30, 32 and 34 to form part of the same scheme decorating the ceiling in Room 2.

SUBJECT 32 – White Panel with Wide Blue and Vermilion Frame Decorated with Studs. (Fig. 82).

Some 602 fragments of plaster (Fabric B) appear to form part of a rectangular white panel, framed by a broad vermilion border decorated with cream and buff studs and lined internally with a blue-grey band. Their location was as follows:-

Room No.	No. of Fragments	Deposit No.	Area Code
2	18	DV–2304	General Layer
2	481	DV–2306	D, Q, U, R
2	8	Group 16 (as lifted)	Floor
3	43	DV–2307	E, F, G, H
3	16	DV–2308	L, K
4	24	DV–2309	N
5	2	DV–4381	Hypocaust Channel
Shore-fort Rampart Dump	10	DV–1172	General Layer
TOTAL	602		

A further 68 fragments of similar fabric and decoration were recovered during the excavation of the adjacent Bingo Hall Site. These were found in deposits representing demolition debris of which 34 fragments came from the East Room and 16 came from the floor in Room 5. Interestingly, some 56 fragments of similar fabric and decoration were also recovered from the Cause is Altered Site excavated in 1971 where they may have been dumped.

Only some 60 key fragments are used in the reconstructed design and these form six key groups (32a-f).

(32a)   A group of 42 articulated fragments show a 90° corner of a white panel with its adjacent border. This shows, from left to right as drawn, a white field (min. 7 mm.); a maroon line (2 mm. wide); a white space (10 mm. wide); a maroon stripe (10 mm. wide) and a band of vermilion (95–98 mm. wide) enlivened by a row of at least five cream-buff studs (7 mm. apart and 9 mm. in diameter), almost centrally placed. Edging the vermilion is a thin stripe of unpainted plaster (up to 4 mm. wide) over which is painted a cream-buff stripe (up to 10 mm. wide) which overlaps the vermilion (by 4 mm.). A deep groove beneath the cream-buff stripe at the junction of vermilion and white may indicate the use of marking-out lines. A similar groove can be seen between two of the cream-buff studs. Adjacent to the vermilion and sharing the cream-buff edging strips is a band of pale blue-grey (46–50 mm. wide). This turns through 90° to form a corner (here shown top left) enclosing an area of white (min. 105 mm. wide). Lining the blue-grey band at a distance of between 23–27 mm., is a thin maroon stripe up to 4 mm. wide.

(32b)   Two adjoining fragments show part of the same vermilion border and maroon stripe (as in 32a), adjacent to a field of white (here shown left at least 32 mm. wide). The white is overlaid by a maroon line (2 mm.) running parallel to and at a distance of 10 mm. from the border.

SUBJECT 32

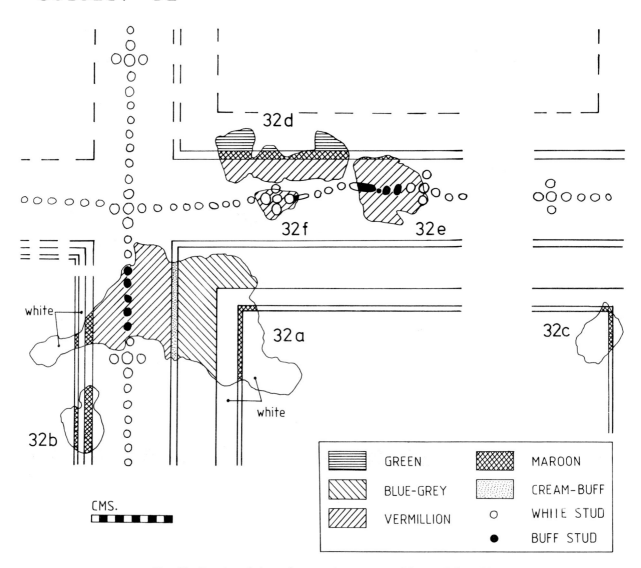

Fig. 82. *Drawing of plaster fragments in reconstructed design, Subject 32.*

(32c)   A single fragment shows a narrow maroon stripe (5 mm. wide) painted over white and turning through 90° to form an internal corner. This is shown as a second corner of the stripe which lines the white panel.

(32d)   Four adjoining fragments show the vermilion border edged with a maroon band (11 mm. wide), this time adjacent to a green band (min. 27 mm. but elsewhere seen to be at least 45 mm. wide). In places the green and maroon are separated by a strip of white unpainted plaster (up to 4 mm. wide). Edging the green band are traces of a thin grey stripe (up to 2 mm. wide). Clearly, the green band depicted on this group forms a different adjacent field to that shown in 32a and 32b and is thus shown here at the bottom of the panel.

(32e)   Nine adjoining fragments show the vermilion border decorated with five studs (three white and two buff) and a buff dash. Four of the studs, two white (10 mm. diameter) and two buff (10 x 7 mm.) are arranged in a single row 7 mm. apart and 27–30 mm.

from and parallel to the maroon edging strip. This row degenerates into a single buff dash (7 mm. wide and at least 18 mm. long). The top white stud has a second white stud to its right, presumably forming part of a cross pattern as in 32f. These studs are almost certainly a continuation of those shown in 32a.

(32f) Two adjoining fragments again show an arrangement of white studs decorating the vermilion border as in 32e. In a group of five, three continue the line formed by the buff studs, whilst two, placed either side of the central stud, form the cross-bar. A similar arrangement of studs can be seen on Subject 31 painted over a maroon border.

The various elements seem to show a white panel of unknown proportions elaborately framed by a combination of vermilion and blue-grey border on at least two and probably four sides. The white panel is lined with an inner narrow maroon frame. It is not known if the panel contained any motif(s). The vermilion border is ornamented with a pattern of white and cream-buff studs and is edged, externally, by a narrow maroon band. This arrangement is further outlined by a narrow maroon line over a white field which is probably continued both beside and above the multi-coloured frame. A green band of uncertain proportions seems to underlie the lower edge of the panel. It is likely that the vermilion border, richly ornamented with a row of cream and white 'studs', served as a primary framework enclosing a series of white panels lined with blue-grey and green bands and outlined with maroon stripes. These may have been arranged either (i) in an alternating pattern or (ii) with blue-grey framed panels arranged around a centrally placed green framed compartment, thus forming a 'cross' pattern. The latter arrangement may have formed the main centre pattern of an elaborate scheme incorporating Subjects 27–31, 33 and 34, that decorated the ceiling above the excavated room/or rooms of the Painted House from where it is thought that this finer quality plaster fabric derives (see discussion below).

SUBJECT 33 – White Panel with Green and Vermilion Frame (Fig. 83).

Some 221 fragments of plaster (Fabric B), appear to form part of a white panel bordered on at least two and probably three sides by a green band and on the fourth side by a vermilion band. Their location was as follows:-

Room No.	No. of Fragments	Deposit No.	Area Code
2	2	DV–2302/3	Floor
2	21	DV–2302	Floor
2	17	DV–2306	B
2	159	DV–1167	General Layer
3	22	DV–2307	E, F, G
TOTAL	221		

The reconstructed design is based on two key groups of plaster found lying face down (Subjects 33a and b) and measuring 244 x 205 mm. and 195 x 105 mm. respectively. Although the surface was badly fractured the fragments, when lifted in a bed of plaster, remained in their relative positions and are drawn as found.

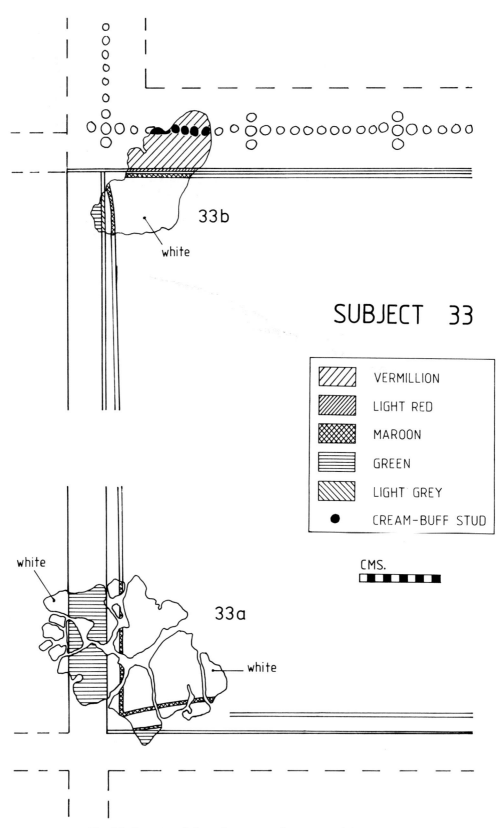

Fig. 83. *Drawing of plaster fragments and reconstructed design, Subject 33.*

(33a)   A group of 50 conjoining fragments shows a broad green band (45 mm. wide) partly edged internally with a light grey stripe (up to 2 mm.) painted over white. The band turns through 90°, thus forming an internal corner and each of its sides is lined on its inside (at a distance of 14 mm.) by a maroon stripe (4 mm. wide) now meeting at about 80°. One stripe is slightly convex and probably represents an attempt at re-alignment.

(33b)   Three conjoining fragments show a broad band of vermilion (min. 69 mm. wide) edged with a light red stripe (up to 2 mm.), adjacent to an area of white (min. 75 mm. wide). Decorating the vermilion is a row of cream-buff, roughly circular studs (up to 10 mm. in diameter), up to 6 mm. apart and 40 mm. parallel to and from the edge. A deep groove along one side of these studs may indicate the use of a marking-out line. At 90° to this band and thus forming a corner (here shown top) is part of a green band (min. 13 mm.) edged with light grey (up to 4 mm. wide), clearly the same as on 33a. The junction of vermilion and green is missing and the precise relationship is not known. The maroon stripe (3–5 mm.) lies parallel to both bands at a distance of between 3–8 mm., slightly convex where it flanks the green. This almost certainly represents the same maroon stripe depicted on 33a.

It is clear from these two key groups that two different corners are represented. The fact that the light grey stripe lining the green on 33a is absent along one edge may indicate that this corner was positioned opposite 33b.

The combined elements may show a white panel of unknown proportions framed on at least three sides by a green border. This green border is edged with light grey on at least two sides and lined internally by a thin maroon stripe. A fourth side (here shown top) is framed by a vermilion border, itself edged in light red and with an internal maroon stripe, and ornamented with a row of cream-buff studs. It seems more likely that the pattern formed part of the same design incorporating Subjects 27–32. The green bands may have served as framework that projected from a central vermilion-bordered pattern forming a series of white panels alternately lined with maroon and containing foliate decoration (see discussion, page 221).

Some fragments show the back of the plaster to be extremely flat, which suggests that it had separated freely from that over which it had been rendered. As this plaster is unlikely to have separated so cleanly from an underlying surface into which it would have been keyed (e.g. stonework), it seems reasonable to assume that it had been rendered over a timber surface perhaps constructed using joists and employed at ceiling level above the excavated rooms (Rooms 1–6). It seems likely therefore that this design formed part of the ceiling decoration above these rooms.

SUBJECT 34 – Yellow Border Lined with Blue, Framing Maroon Band, over Vermilion and Green Borders (Fig. 84).

A total of 14 fragments of plaster (Fabric B) seem to show a broad maroon band decorated with V-shaped motifs enclosed by a yellow frame lined with blue. This arrangement appears to be superimposed over a vermilion and green frame. These fragments were recovered from a general demolition layer (DV–2306) confined to Room 2. Only six key fragments are used in the reconstructed design and these form two groups (Nos. 34a and 34b) each of three conjoining fragments.

(34a)   The first group shows a broad maroon zone (min. 51 mm. wide) beside a white field (min. 23 mm. wide). The edge of the maroon band is decorated with a maroon V-shaped motif, the point of which projects a minimum of 19 mm. into the white zone. The widest part of the 'V' measures a minimum of 30 mm. A similar arrangement can be seen decorating Subject 31 where the 'V' motif is flanked by maroon 'quaver' motifs.

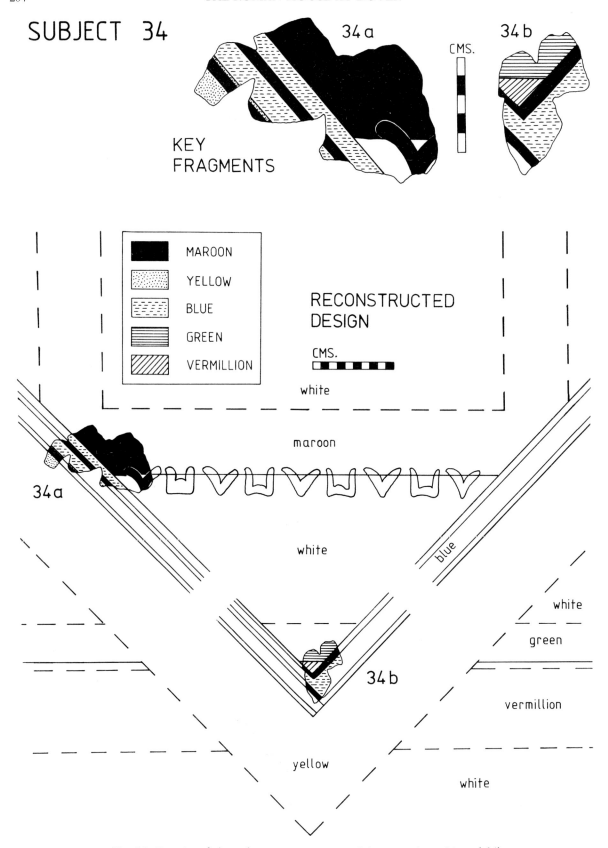

Fig. 84. *Drawing of plaster fragments in reconstructed designs, Subjects 34a and 34b.*

The maroon border joins a light blue band (29 mm. wide) at 45°, thus framing the white field. The blue band is further decorated with a strip of maroon, parallel to and at a distance of 10 mm. from the junction of the maroon border. Below this blue band a zone of yellow-ochre (min. 20 mm. wide) has been painted and is lined at its junction with the blue with another maroon strip of 6 mm. wide.

(34b)   The second group shows a blue band (min. 22 mm. wide) forming a 45° corner, the inner edge of which is lined with a maroon stripe (3–6 mm. wide). The outer edge of the blue has also been decorated with a maroon stripe (up to 4 mm. wide) along one side, thus making one arm of the blue only 9 mm. wide. A small triangular area within the angle formed by the blue-bordered corner has been treated with vermilion. Immediately adjacent to this and framed by the maroon-bordered blue on two sides is a zone of green (min. 22 mm. x 40 mm.).

The two groups were almost certainly incorporated into the same design, but it is difficult to establish the precise arrangement. It seems more likely that the yellow band lined with blue forms a frame enclosing an area of white on at least two, and probably four, sides and is superimposed at 45° onto a vermilion border lined with green. The centre of the square, or rectangular, framed panel thus created contains a maroon frame projecting 45° from the border and is likely to have formed a smaller framed panel from within the yellow frame.

The position occupied by this subject in the decorative scheme employed in the Painted House is not known. The plaster fabric, however, as noted elsewhere, may have been used to render the ceilings above the excavated rooms. If so, this subject may have formed part of an elaborate decoration perhaps incorporating Subjects 27–33 that decorated the ceiling above Room 2. The interlaced frames suggested here may have been employed at the centre of the scheme. (See discussion below, page 221).

SUBJECT 35 – White Panel with Maroon and Grey Frame (Fig. 85).

Some 152 fragments of plaster (Fabric B) appear to form part of a white zone, bordered by a maroon band and divided into panels by light grey stripes, all lined internally by a narrow maroon stripe. The fragments were recovered from deposits confined to Room 2 (DV–2302, 2306 and 1167). The reconstructed design uses only ten key fragments, forming four key groups (Subjects 35a-d).

(35a)   Four conjoining fragments show a broad band of maroon, (80 mm. wide), over white. Parallel to it and at a distance of 15 mm. is a narrow maroon stripe (4 mm. wide).

(35b)   One small area of plaster (200 x 190 mm.) was found lying face down and although the surface was badly fractured the fragments, when lifted, remained in their relative positions. This key group shows the same maroon band (min. 26 mm. wide) and also the parallel maroon stripe (4 mm. wide) at a distance of between 15–18 mm. The latter flanks an area of white (min. 172 mm. wide). These decorative elements are clearly a continuation of 35a. At a distance of 160 mm. from the narrow maroon stripe are small traces of bright red.

(35c)   A single fragment shows the same combination of maroon band and adjacent maroon stripe over white, but here the stripe turns through 90° thus forming a corner, here positioned bottom left. A band of light grey (min. 21 mm. wide) lies parallel, at a distance of 20 mm. to the re-aligned maroon stripe and at 90° to the maroon band. The two bands do not quite meet.

(35d)   A further four fragments show part of the same maroon band (min. 25 mm. wide) adjacent to the same light grey band (up to 45 mm. wide) and at 90°. This is shown bottom right.

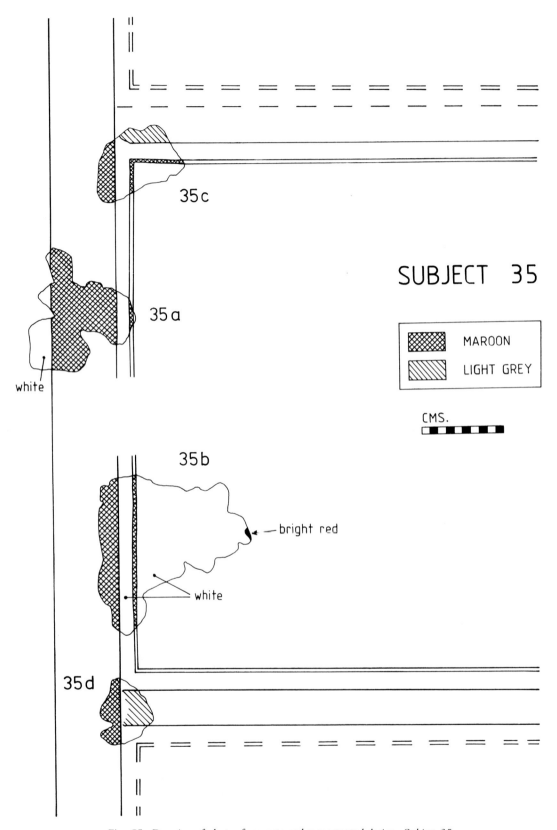

35c

35a

white

SUBJECT 35

MAROON
LIGHT GREY

CMS.

35b

bright red

white

white

35d

Fig. 85. *Drawing of plaster fragments and reconstructed design, Subject 35.*

These fragments show that an area of white is enclosed on at least two sides by a maroon and light grey border, joining at right-angles and lined internally with a continuous narrow maroon stripe. The corner element, 35d, cannot form part of the same corner shown in 35c and must therefore represent a separate, but closely related junction, with similar characteristics.

Although the total individual scheme here cannot be worked out with certainty, several basic facts emerge. The grey bands are narrower than the maroon bands and are therefore likely to be secondary. In addition, the grey bands butt-up to the maroon bands in at least two places and this also suggests that the maroon bands are the major components represented here. This in turn suggests a main framework of maroon, with smaller sub-divisions in grey, together framing white panels lined with thin maroon stripes. It seems likely that this scheme formed part of the ceiling decoration inside the Painted House (see discussion on page 221). It does not, however, easily fit into the reconstructed scheme tentatively offered incorporating Subjects 27–34 which probably derive from the ceiling above Room 2.

SUBJECT 36 – White Panel with Maroon Frame Above Possible Yellow Dado. (Fig. 86)

Some 111 fragments of plaster (Fabric C) appear to represent a white panel, within a three-sided maroon frame, lined in yellow, over a broad green band surmounting a possible yellow dado. The location of these fragments was as follows:-

Room No.	No. of Fragments	Deposit No.	Area Code
2	38	DV–2306	Uncertain
2	2	DV–2373	General Layer
2	2	DV–1167	General Layer
2	47	Groups 1 and 4 as lifted	Floor
3	1	DV–2307	F, G.
3	4	DV–1162	General Layer
Bingo Hall Site	2	DV–3019	General Layer
Bingo Hall Site	1	DV–9815	General Layer
Bingo Hall Site	14	DV–9878	General Layer
TOTAL	111		

Only eight fragments were used in the reconstructed design and these form five key groups (Nos. 36a–e).

(36a)   Two fragments are still attached to an original wall fragment constructed of roughly coursed flint nodules, set in a coarse cream-white mortar with small blue-grey, brown and white flint grit inclusions. The painted plaster covers an area of 175 x 141 mm. and shows a series of parallel stripes and bands painted over white.
From left to right (as illustrated) these are; white (min. 97 mm.); a mustard-yellow stripe (3 mm. wide); white (21 mm.); maroon band (15 mm.); white (28 mm.);

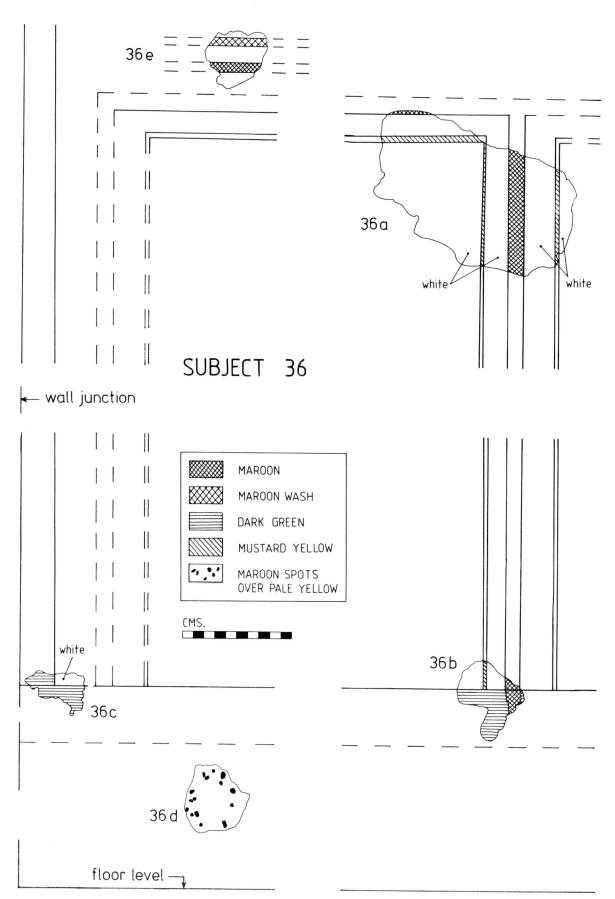

Fig. 86. *Drawing of plaster fragments and reconstructed design, Subject 36.*

mustard-yellow stripe (4 mm.) and white (min. 16 mm.). The top of the left-hand yellow band turns a 90° internal corner to continue (6 mm. wide) towards the left. The main maroon band almost certainly turned above it in a similar manner, though the actual corner is missing, but a small portion of it (min. 4 mm. wide) survives 35 mm. above the horizontal mustard-yellow stripe.

(36b) Two conjoining fragments show a broad dark green band (min. 45 mm. wide) surmounted at right-angles by a narrow mustard-yellow stripe (3 mm. wide), parallel to and 16 mm. from a maroon band (min. 14 mm. wide). The maroon projects over the green by a minimum of 23 mm.

(36c) A single fragment shows the dark green band (min. 25 mm.) turning through 90° enclosing an area of white.

(36d) One fragment shows irregular maroon spots, up to 5 mm. in diameter, flecked at random, over a pale yellow ground, almost certainly a dado.

(36e) Two conjoining fragments show a narrow stripe in maroon wash (7 mm. wide), parallel to and 15 mm. from a dark maroon stripe (up to 8 mm.) over white.

The design emerging from these key fragments seems to include a dado, painted pale yellow and flecked with maroon to imitate marble veneer, which is capped by a dark green horizontal dado band. The plain white area above this is divided into rectangular panels of unknown proportions by vertical maroon bands, which rise to join a continuous horizontal maroon band which forms the panel tops. An internal stripe of mustard-yellow enlivens the panels on three sides. The two parallel stripes of light and dark maroon do not fit easily into this scheme, but they may form a pattern above the panel tops. Such treatment above a simple panel is known elsewhere in Dover, from the Market Hall Site, 1982 and Gaol Lane Site, 1984 (Ref. 99). The precise arrangement and proportions have not been determined, but the simplicity of the design shares similarities with the decorated plaster, much of it *in situ*, in the North Passage of the 'Painted House' (discussed above) and also in the Clay Walled Building (see below).

The plaster fabric carrying this design matches that still lining some external wall faces of the 'Painted House' and that used in the North Passage. It is highly likely, therefore, that this plaster lined a similar wall face of this structure, perhaps the outer wall of the North Passage.

ANGLED AND MOULDED FRAGMENTS (Figs. 87–89, Nos. 1–9).

Some 92 fragments of fallen plaster (all Fabric A) were angled or moulded and these can be classified into five main groups. Four of these (A, B, D and E) can be sub-divided further by shape and decoration. All the fragments are painted with either broad or narrow maroon or pink bands, whilst B2 has an adjacent black stripe.

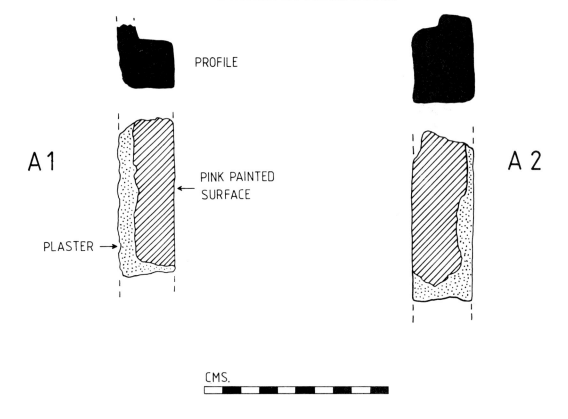

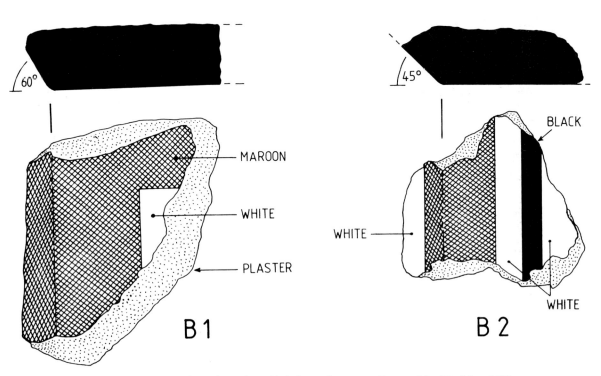

Fig. 87. *Drawing of angular and moulded plaster fragments, Groups A1, A2, B1 and B2.*

The location of these fragments is shown below:-

Context	Room No.	Shaped Groups	No. of Fragments	Deposit No.	Area Code
Demolition	2	B7	3	DV–2327	General Layer
Layers	2	B6	8	DV–2306	General Layer
"	2	D2	1	DV–2306	General Layer
"	2	E2	2	DV–2306	General Layer
"	2	A2	1	DV–2308	J
"	2	B5	24	DV–2308	I, J.
"	2	D1	6	DV–1167	General Layer
"	3	A1	11	DV–2307	E, F.
"	3	B4	3	DV–1162	General Layer
"	3	B3	2	DV–1193	General Layer
"	4	B7	9	DV–2309	N, O.
"	4	C	10	DV–2309	N, O.
Furnace Area to the South of Structure		B2	1	DV–1189	South Side
Saxon Pit		B1	1	DV–9712	
Unstratified Context		B3	3	DV–1100	
"		B7	1	DV–1100	
"		E1	1	DV–1100	
"		B7	5	DV–1170	
TOTAL			92		

GROUP A (A1 and A2).

Twelve fragments seem to be from a narrow fillet of two varying types.

A1 (Fig. 87). Eleven fragments of narrow fillets of plaster, are rectangular in section and measure 21 mm. by up to 30 mm. Three surfaces are flat, one of which is painted pink and one which incorporates a slight lip (up to 6 x 10 mm.) suggesting that it was moulded around either tile or timber. The fourth side is slightly convex, with an uneven finish.

A2 (Fig. 87). The remaining fragment is a wider fillet, rectangular in section and measuring 46 mm. by up to 30 mm. The surfaces are similar to those in A1. The pink surface appears to be the only one intended to be seen, although it was not smoothed before paint was applied.

GROUP B (B1–B7).

A total of 60 fragments show two painted surfaces forming a splayed angle. It has been necessary to sub-divide these into seven broad groups because of variations in both the angle of splay and surface pattern.

B1 (Fig. 87). One fragment is splayed approximately 60° for a minimum distance of 30 mm. The joint is slightly rounded. Decorating the flat surface is a broad maroon band (50 mm. wide) which turns 90° to form a corner, enclosing an area of white (up to 20 mm. wide). The splay is also painted maroon.

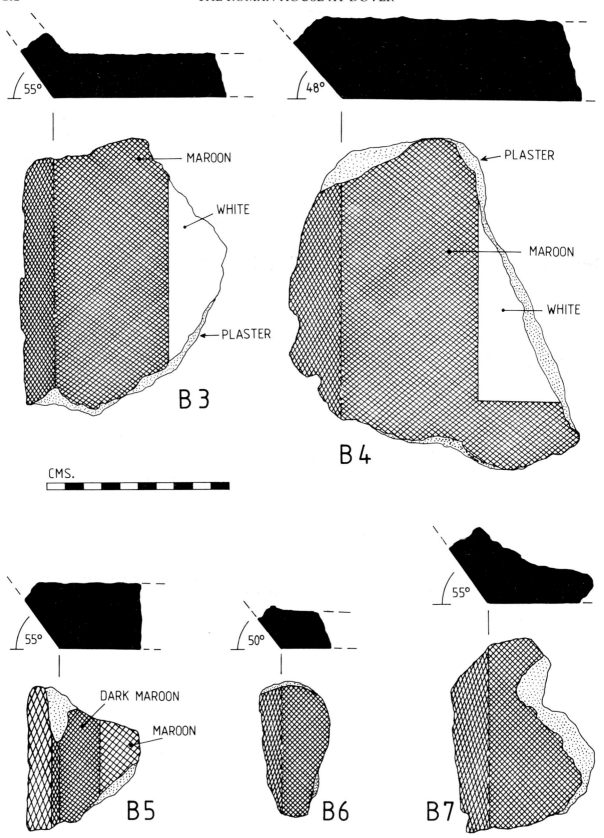

Fig. 88. *Drawing of angular and moulded plaster fragments, Groups B3–B7.*

B2 (Fig. 87). One fragment is splayed at approximately 45° for a minimum distance of 30 mm. The main surface (min. 70 mm.) is decorated with a black stripe (11 mm. wide). This is painted over white and lies parallel (at a distance of 13 mm.) to a maroon band that measures 29 mm. to the joint and a further 13 mm. into the splay, totalling 42 mm.

B3 (Fig. 88). Five fragments are splayed at approximately 55° for a minimum distance of 30 mm. One fragment shows that the main surface (min. 95 mm. wide) is decorated by a maroon band that measures 63 mm. to the joint, where it then turns into the splay completely covering its surface.

B4 (Fig. 88). Three fragments are splayed at approximately 48° for a minimum distance of 40 mm. One fragment shows that the main surface (min. 130 mm. wide) is decorated by a broad maroon band that measures 75 mm. up to the joint where it then turns into, and completely covers the splay. The band on the surface turns through 90° to form a corner to enclose an area of white (min. 42 mm. wide).

B5 (Fig. 88). 24 fragments are splayed at appoximately 55° for a minimum distance of 32 mm. The main surface (min. 65 mm. wide) is painted maroon and carries over the splay. A darker maroon band (totalling 28 mm. wide) decorates the joint with 22 mm. of it projecting on to the main surface and 6 mm. into the splay.

B6 (Fig. 88). Eight fragments are splayed approximately 50° for a minimum distance of 20 mm. The main surface (min. 30 mm.) and splay are very slightly convex and painted deep maroon.

B7 (Fig. 88). 18 fragments are splayed at appoximately 55° for a minimum distance of 35 mm. The main surface (min. 50 mm.) and slightly convex splay are painted deep maroon.

GROUP C (Fig. 89).

Ten fragments show two painted surfaces at a splayed angle of 85° for a minimum distance of 17 mm. The main surface (min. 76 mm.) and splay are painted deep maroon.

GROUP D (D1 and D2).

Seven fragments show a flat surface to which paint has been applied, whilst one edge of the plaster backing has been chamfered. These can be sub-divided as follows:-

D1 (Fig. 89). Six fragments show that the main surface has been treated with a broad maroon band (52–55 mm. wide) adjacent to a white ground (min. 60 mm. wide). The backing plaster is chamfered at approximately 119°, up to 45 mm., corresponding to one edge of the maroon band.

D2 (Fig. 89). One fragment has been similarly chamfered (125°), however, the main surface, (min. 55 mm.) painted deep maroon, is slightly convex.

GROUP E (E1 and E2).

Three fragments have two splayed surfaces and can be sub-divided, as follows:-

E1 (Fig. 89). One fragment shows two splayed surfaces, one at approximately 40° the second at

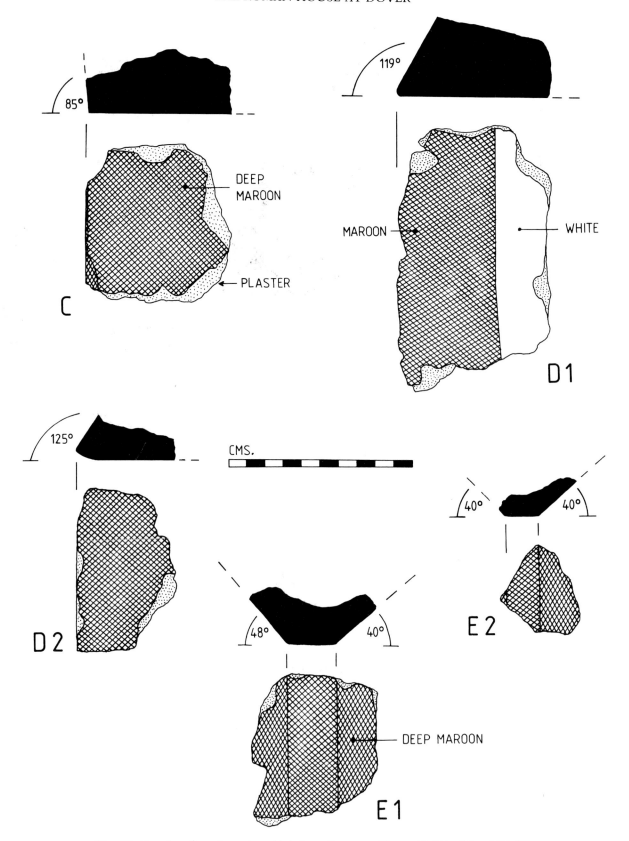

Fig. 89. *Drawing of angular and moulded plaster fragments, Groups C, D1, D2 and E1–E2.*

approximately 48°, for a minimum distance of 30 mm., either side of a flat surface (28 mm. wide). All three surfaces are painted deep maroon.

E2 (Fig. 89). Two fragments show two splayed surfaces each at approximately 40°, for a minimum of 28 mm., either side of a flat surface (18 mm. wide). These surfaces are also painted deep maroon.

The precise position and function of these shaped fragments is uncertain. It seems most likely that Group A served as a fillet perhaps at floor level or edging around doors or under openings. Perhaps Group B served to render splayed openings such as windows or doors. The decoration of the main wall surface is carried into the opening from which the plaster may have been further angled from the splay, so that it aligned 90° to the main surface (perhaps represented by Group E). Group C may have served a similar purpose, perhaps over a door jamb. The angle and flatness of the backing to Group D suggests that it formed a mitred corner with another building medium such as timber or tile, either at ceiling level or perhaps incorporated into an architectural feature within the main fabric of the wall. These fragments indicate the likely presence of openings or windows within the fabric of the Painted House structure, and they may serve to illustrate the method in which such openings were treated. Some of these fragments (Group C and possibly D) are likely to have derived from the door-openings located within the Painted House structure.

PLANT IMPRESSIONS LEFT ON THE PLASTER SURFACE

The surfaces of some 254 fragments of plaster from the site bear impressions of the stalks and leaves of a climbing plant, almost certainly identified as ivy. The table below shows the location of the fragments across the site. This shows that 234 fragments were found in related demolition contexts within the excavated Rooms 1–3 and the North Passage. A further 17 fragments came from the Bingo Hall Site, to the north of the Painted House structure, whilst three fragments were unstratified. The impressions are over two plaster fabrics; Type A (143 fragments) and Type C (111 fragments) and over some Subjects (7, 8 and 36) and moulded fragments Groups B7, D1 and 2, B3 and 4.

The presence of such plant impressions on the fallen plaster has significant implications. The 111 fragments of Fabric Type C mortar are known to be from the external walls of the Painted House, which could indicate that these plants were allowed to grow freely. However, it seems certain that the 143 fragments of Fabric A plaster, including parts of several reconstructed subjects, came from internal walls. Whilst it is just possible that some of this came from walls left exposed after the major demolition took place (as with Room 1), the majority was found in Rooms 2 and 3. This suggests that parts of these rooms, or even those rooms above them, may have been in a ruinous state, or at least partially exposed, for plants to grow inside the buildings. If so, then the Painted House had already been abandoned some years before the shore-fort was built.

Subject/ Description	Deposit	Room	Grid	Area	Plaster Fabric	No. of Frags.	Total
Subject 7	2302/3	2	General Layer	S. Wall	A	3	
" 7	2306	2	B C D	N. Wall	A	4	
" 7	2308	2	I T	SW Corner	A	6	
" 7	2307	3	E	NE Corner	A	2	
" 7	2307/8	2/3	I J L	S. Wall	A	10	25
" 8	2306	2	Q U R	NW Corner	A	10	
" 8	2308	2	–	SW Corner	A	32	42

Subject/ Description	Deposit	Room	Grid	Area	Plaster Fabric	No. of Frags.	Total
" 36	2306	2	–	N. Wall	C	38	
" 36	2373	2	General Layer		C	2	
" 36	1167	2	General Layer		C	2	
" 36	Groups 1 + 4 as lifted	2		Floor	C	47	
" 36	2307	3	F G	NW Corner	C	1	
" 36	1162	3	General Layer		C	4	
							94
" 36	3019	Bingo Hall Site 1976	General Layer		C	2	
" 36	9815	"	General Layer		C	1	
" 36	9878	"	General Layer		C	14	
							17
Shaped B7 and Moulded D2 Fragments D1 B4 B3	2327	1	General Layer		A	2	
	2306	2	R	NW Corner	A	1	
	1167	2	–		A	6	
	1162	3	General Layer		A	3	
	1100	Unstratified			A	3	
							15
Miscellaneous	2302/3	2	General Layer	S. Wall	A	7	
Non-Subjects	2306	2	General Layer	N. Wall	A	6	
	2308	2	I T	SW Corner	A	5	
	1167	2	General Layer		A	14	
	2307	3	General Layer	NW Corner	A	11	
	1162	3	General Layer		A	2	
	1145	North Passage	General Layer		A	4	
	2352	Unstratified			A	3	
	2350	S-F Foundation Trench	General Layer		A	8	
	1182	"			A	1	
							61
TOTAL							254

Table showing context and location of plaster fragments with plant impressions arranged in Subject order.

4). THE POSITIONING OF THE RECONSTRUCTED SUBJECTS.

A full discussion on the large plaster assemblage from the Painted House site must await completion of a final study of the many fragments. This study will also include the plaster from all the other Roman sites excavated in Dover since 1970. It is, however, possible to offer general comments on the positioning of the reconstructed subjects (Nos. 1–36).

Of the total plaster recovered from the Painted House site, 98% seems most likely to have derived from the Painted House, built about A.D. 200. Some 90% of this plaster (Fabric A) almost certainly derived either from the excavated rooms, or from adjoining rooms (as yet unlocated) and served to decorate the internal walls. Of this material 19% revealed geometric patterns and motifs not represented on the surviving walls of the building. Most of these have been reconstructed and described (Subjects 1–26). Another 9% of the plaster derived from the site (Fabric B), seems likely to have served as ceiling rendering, probably from the excavated rooms or from those above. Again, new designs are represented and have been reconstructed (Subjects 27–35). The remaining 1% of the plaster (Fabric C – Subject 36) matches the plaster in the North Passage and also the small area of external plaster on the south wall.

The remainder of the total plaster from the site (2%) seems to have been introduced from elsewhere, perhaps brought into the partly demolished building as debris. Eight different plaster fabrics are represented (D-K) and these would have lined the walls and ceilings of one, or more, nearby structures that were perhaps demolished at the same time as the Painted House, towards the end of the 3rd century A.D. The simplicity of the designs seen on this plaster share many similarities with the decorated plaster found on the Bingo Hall site in 1976. It is likely, therefore, that these fabrics derived from a building, or buildings, to the north of the present structure that have yet to be located.

THE PLASTER FRAGMENTS FROM THE INTERNAL WALLS (Fabric A).

A total of 19,926 fragments of plaster from the site almost certainly derived from the internal walls of the Roman structure. Some 3,876 fragments are decorated with motifs and geometric patterns not easily matched *in situ* and of these 1,112 fragments have been combined to form new designs (Subjects 1–26). These are discussed here under four broad groups (Groups 1–4).

GROUP 1 – Architectural Subjects (Subjects 1, 2, 3 and 4).

This group relates directly to the *in situ* schemes in Rooms 2–4. Subjects 1, 3 and 4 were almost certainly included in the same scheme in Room 2 and have thus been combined.

Subject 1 was found almost complete and lying face down within the south-west corner of Room 2 and represents a key group for reconstructing the decorative scheme here to frieze level. This shows part of the arrangement above the panel tops which, from the position found within the room, almost certainly derived from the south wall and probably formed the upper portion of Panel 5. This restored portion (Subject 1) shows the top left hand corner of a dark red framed white panel (a minimum of 615 mm. high to the top of the border) decorated with a hanging garland motif. Portions of at least three other garlands are known, painted over a yellow border (none is illustrated). This ornament may have been repeated over adjoining panels, thus creating a looped-foliate decoration. This device appears to have been popular on painted classical architectural scenes. Similar hanging garlands are a prominent decorative feature on recently discovered wall plaster from Southwark (Ref. 100), also depicting flanking architectural structures reminiscent of those at Dover. A similar garland painted in blue and white and shaded with dark green over a red ground decorating wall plaster was recovered during excavations at Dyer Court, Cirencester, 1957 (Ref. 101). To the left (as viewed) of the framed-panel in Subject 1, a column projects forward to the right. Above the panel top is a band of pink (60 mm. wide) followed by a zone of yellow ochre (up to 155 mm. wide) that may represent an architrave. Above the architrave is a horizontal maroon band (20 mm. wide) supporting a series of vertical cream bands over short maroon strips, the latter representing uncertain architectural detail. These are painted over a white ground and are also on Subjects 3, 4 and 11. This frieze zone above Panel 5 (Subject 1) seems to represent a monumental entablature, or just possibly a high-level balcony that projects forwards of the panel scheme below and is supported by the main columns. The superstructure carried above the columns may have been interrupted, forming separate architectural elements. From this articulated group of plaster, now fully restored and displayed within the 'Painted House' cover-building, it is possible to offer a tentative reconstruction of the wall decoration from floor to upper frieze level in Room 2 (Fig. 50).

The highly elaborate perspective treatment of Subject 2 seems to have derived from Room 3 and probably decorated at least the north wall. The design depicts parts of two columnar structures that almost certainly represent aediculae. These project forwards of the main wall divided either into solid coloured panels, or white panels with coloured borders or a mixture of the two alternating along the length of the wall. The canopy and entablature of the two projecting aediculae are supported by the main columns shown *in situ*. Each of these may be joined by a screen wall (*in situ* detail), but separated higher up to represent two columns one behind the other, thus supporting the front and rear corners of each side of the aediculae respectively. The Corinthian capitals appear to support an elaborate entablature painted to look like a stone on top of which may have arisen a classical pediment, possibly triangular, perhaps decorated with an orb device or medallion. Hanging garlands may have been an added further decoration. It is possible that the angled frame in Subject 8 may have been incorporated into the back wall behind an aedicula and represents a perspectival portal. A scheme similar to that depicted on these walls can be seen in Rome in the *Domus Aurea* (Ref. 102) decorating a wall in Room 33. Although a much more elaborate scheme several of the basic principles and devices used are comparable to Dover.

The painted architectural detail in Room 3 shares many similarities with the decoration of the walls of Room 2 (Subject 1). This more elaborate scheme may have formed the focal point on the north wall of the major 'double' Room 3 and 4 and which faces the wide opening into Room 4.

The scroll-like foliate motif over yellow (Subject 3) almost certainly derived from the frieze level above the panel tops in Room 2. Identical detail, of parallel orange stripes over a broad yellow zone beneath maroon band and vertical cream 'straps', is clearly seen on Subject 1 above Panel 5. It is thus almost certain that a painted foliate scroll pattern, further enlivened with fruit or zoomorphic heads or masks, occupied this position either as a continuous or a centralised design. Likewise the semi-circular ornament (Subject 4) was almost certainly derived from the frieze-level above the panels within the Room 2 scheme. The painted detail here, of vertical cream 'straps' over white, can be matched with the detail shown on Subject 1. Here the 'straps' join a wide maroon band that most probably represents the ceiling band. The ornament, decorated with ribbons, is suspended from the band and may either have appeared in total view, or partial view, to the onlooker.

GROUP 2 – Miscellaneous Subjects (Subjects 5–8, 21–23 and 24).

These subjects do not easily fit into the general scheme decorating the existing walls of Rooms 2–4. They may derive from another part of the same structure decorating walls of rooms as yet unlocated. The fragments forming these subjects were all found amongst the demolition rubble within Rooms 1–3. These may have been derived either from a possible upper storey, or were introduced into the rooms as debris from nearby demolished rooms. Subjects 7 and 8 show simple treatment of the plaster surface. Here narrow bands of colour divide areas of white into panels or zones. These may form repetitive patterns covering large areas of wall surface as part of the main scheme or be confined to smaller areas framed by more elaborate decoration. Subject 8 appears to be the more ambitious of the two, representing a frame shown in perspective. This could have occupied a central position behind one of the aediculae in Room 3 (Subject 2), such as appears on recently discovered plaster from Southwark (Ref. 103). The still-life scenes (Subjects 5, 21–23) almost certainly occupied a position within white framed panels, possibly even those represented by Subjects 7 or 8. These elements may also have formed a scheme that incorporated the human figures (Subjects 9–20) and the floral motifs (Subjects 25 and 26). The bowl of fruit (Subject 5), superficially similar to one decorating a wall in the Villa at Boscoreale (Ref. 104), may have rested on painted secondary architectural detail. The two-handled cups, (Subjects 21–23) could have a ritual significance and indeed canthari were often associated with Bacchic imagery (Ref. 105). Viewed in this light these elements would complement each other in a single scheme. The candelabrum (Subject 6) almost certainly would have served as ornament separating areas of white in a more delicate panel scheme.

The complex geometric patterns emerging within Subject 24, clearly seems to serve as decoration near the junction of wall and ceiling, deriving either from the excavated rooms, or rooms not yet seen. The patterns could have been incorporated into the general scheme of either Rooms 2 or 3 at frieze level. The patterns forming on these fragments may have been intended to represent stylized windows in this position, perhaps even balancing the scheme with real window openings. Work continues on these complicated patterns.

The variety of shaped and moulded fragments may give some idea as to the architectural treatment of windows and doorways. The many fragments recovered from Rooms 2 and 3 suggest that window-openings were included within the main fabric of the structures. These were probably located at the proposed frieze-level on the south wall.

Future work on the remaining plaster within this category may produce fresh designs that may combine with those discussed above to reveal whole schemes. From this it may be possible to show how other rooms were decorated.

GROUP 3 – Human Figures (Subjects 9–20).

This group of human figures is not represented at all on the *in situ* plaster. As a group they share many characteristics and may represent either a single group occupying a space in a single scene, or a series of scenes in just one room. The classical postures, attire and general attitude of the figures strongly suggests that they form part of a cult group. All are of similar proportions representing just under a quarter actual life-size. The majority is depicted wholly, or partly nude (Subjects 9, 12, 16, 17 and 19) whilst others are robed (Subjects 10, 11 and 18). Some are engaged in movement that may be considered dance (Subjects 10, 12 and 16) and one is seated (Subject 11). This careful, almost identical, yet individual detail chosen for this group of figures almost certainly indicates that they formed part of the same scene, or scenes, of ritual representation depicting both participants and spectators. Viewed in the light of recent research and the identification of many of the painted motifs used in Rooms 2–4, as representing Bacchic imagery (for discussion see above), these figures may convincingly be seen as portraying Bacchantes, followers of the cult of Bacchus. The female figures (Subjects 10–13, 16 and 20) bear striking resemblance to the many representations of maenads found in mainstream Roman art. The standing male figure over a red ground (Subject 9) may possibly represent a youthful Bacchus, such as identified on a seascape painting from a house in Rome at the time of Hadrian (A.D. 117–138) (Ref. 106). If this figure does represent Bacchus then the reclining female figure (Subject 11) could represent his consort; either Venus as depicted in the same painting (op. cit.) or, more likely, Ariadne. The latter appeared frequently with Bacchus in processional and ritual scenes (Ref. 107).

The precise position these figures occupied in the general decorative scheme employed in the Roman House is not yet known, but, there are several options:-

(i)   Centrally placed within the white panels, framed by coloured borders, from the excavated rooms.

(ii)   Centrally placed within white panels, framed by coloured borders, from a similar scheme employed upstairs, or from a room as yet unlocated.

(iii) Decorating extensive fields of white as part of a substantially different delicate design (perhaps even incorporating Subjects 5, 6 and 26) from upstairs, or from rooms not yet found.

All except one figure (Subject 9) are painted over a white field and any of these could be included in any of the three options. Subject 9, however, is over a deep red field and cannot therefore have occupied a position in Room 2 where only framed white panels exist. It is likely that some solid coloured panels may have been a feature of Room 3. If not, such panels may have been employed in rooms not yet seen, perhaps alternating with white panels and further enlivened with symbolic human imagery. Work continues on these figures.

GROUP 4 – Foliate (Subjects 25 and 26).

These two subjects depict foliate motifs not represented *in situ* within Rooms 2–4. The plant with green leaves and bearing a maroon bloom (Subject 25) may have served either as a filling, or framing, element within a white panel from the excavated rooms, or from others not yet located. The remaining subject (Subject 26) is of a more modest design, probably representing a 'trellis' supporting a green plant of the creeper type. Such a design may have covered part of, or the entire, wall surface from a room yet to be located. It is possible that this subject could have combined with Subjects 5–7, 9–23 and 25 to form a scheme incorporating plain and coloured panels delicately framed by candelabra devices (Subject 6) and foliate 'trellis' work (Subject 26), enlivened with human figures (Subjects 9–20), still-life (Subjects 5, 21–23) and floral scenes (Subject 25).

PLASTER FRAGMENTS FROM THE CEILING OF THE EXCA-VATED ROOMS (Fabric B)

Some 1,812 fragments of broken plaster recovered from the Roman structure are very likely to have derived from the ceilings of the excavated rooms. This is suggested by the comparative fineness of the plaster fabric and its difference in composition to the plaster found on the internal walls (Fabric A). It is also thinner and the back much flatter. That this plaster too was mostly found on the floor in Room 2 may also indicate that it derived from the ceiling there. Some 1,587 fragments of this plaster have been combined to form Subjects 27–35. This includes 69 fragments recovered from the Bingo Hall site, to the north of the Roman Painted House (incorporated into Subjects 31 and 32) and 56 fragments recovered from the Cause is Altered site (also combined in Subject 32).

(A) FOLIATE DECORATION (Subjects 27–29).

Three subjects (Nos. 27–29) show floral motifs that almost certainly served as filling elements within geometric framed panels or broader zones of colour. Subject 27 shows a flowering plant with blue/red flowers and green leaves sprouting from a brown stem. This may represent a rose and is painted over a white ground. Subject 28 shows a flowering plant with yellow flowers and green leaves sprouting from a brown stem also painted over a white ground. This may represent a creeper. The third subject (Subject 29) depicts a plant with green leaves and red flowers sprouting from a brown stem and this may also represent a rose.

These may combine with Subjects 30–34 to form an elaborate scheme decorating the ceiling above Room 2 (see below).

(B) GEOMETRIC PATTERNS

Six subjects (Subjects 30–35) show a series of brightly painted borders of either vermilion and blue/grey or green (Subjects 32 and 33); maroon and light-grey or green (Subjects 30 and 35) or maroon (Subject 31) that frame square or rectangular (or very possibly triangular) panels of white (Subjects 31–35) or yellow ochre (Subject 30). The narrow width of the panel borders shown in Subjects 30 and 33 (up to 45 mm.) may indicate that the panel areas were of fairly modest proportions. The panel areas of Subjects 31, 32 and 35 may have been greater, perhaps suggested by the wider borders, here 80–153 mm. (Subjects 31 and 35 respectively). The border edges to Subjects 30 and 31 have been further treated with 'quaver' and 'inverted-V' decoration projecting into the panel. An identical motif, also decorating the border edge at similar intervals, is employed in Subject 25 (Fabric A). Further decoration has also been added to the borders of Subjects 31 and 32. This takes the form of a series of cream and white 'studs' arranged in a single row. Subject 31 may have contained two parallel rows, equidistant from the border edges, whilst Subject 32 contains a single row centrally placed. A plant tendril, painted in maroon, occupies a position within the yellow panel depicted in Subject 30. Subjects 30–34 share similar decorative elements and may indicate that these were closely related, perhaps in one scheme (see below), also incorporating Subjects 27–29.

(C) TENTATIVE RECONSTRUCTION OF CEILING IN ROOM 2.

Some 1,345 fragments of plaster have been combined to form eight subjects (Subjects 27–34). A tentative attempt to reconcile these subjects and designs has been made and is illustrated (Fig. 90). The plaster found represents less than 5% of the total area of the ceiling. On this slender evidence several combinations and variations are possible for the various elements in Subjects 27–34. Of the two most likely arrangements that emerge, one scheme only is discussed as this best fits all the available evidence. This reconstruction is identified as the ceiling of Room 2 from where it is assumed, from the high percentage (84%) of this plaster group found on its floor, that Subjects 27–34 derive. As the total area of this room is known a complete model can be attempted.

The room is rectangular (not square) measuring 5.54 m. x 4.85 m. with its long axis aligned north-south. The total area is thus 26.87 sq. m. It is reasonable to propose that a simple scheme

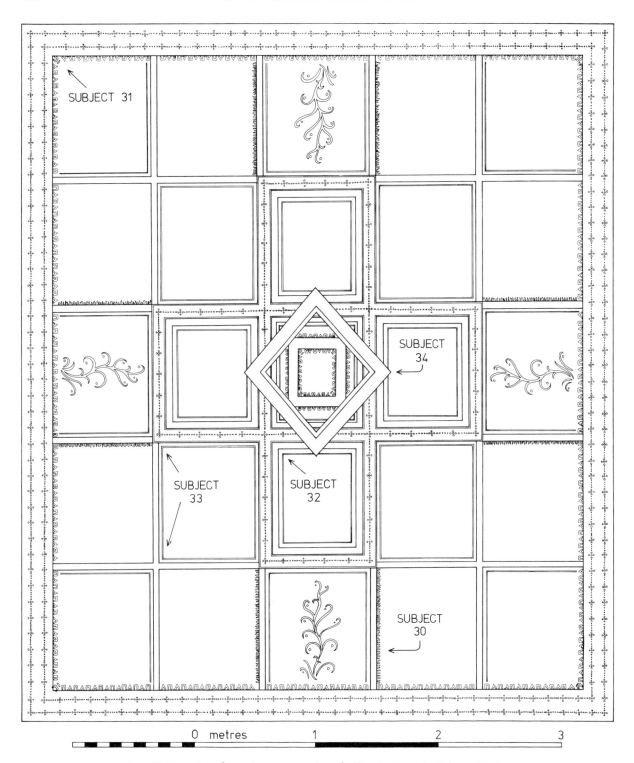

Fig. 90. *Drawing of tentative reconstruction of ceiling in Room 2, Subjects 30–34.*

based on a rectangular panel arrangement, repeated at regular intervals and perhaps arranged around a central design, may have been adopted. A recent study indicates that such decorative schemes were fairly typical of ceilings in Italy during the 2nd and 3rd centuries A.D. (Ref. 108). Such an arrangement on the ceiling above Room 2 would certainly compliment the wall decorations where a panel-system is also used. The wall and ceiling may thus have formed a unified decorative ensemble.

The ceiling, where it meets the wall, may have been lined with a maroon band (*c.* 250 mm. wide) decorated with white and cream studs and 'quaver' and 'inverted-V' devices (Subject 31). This band may represent a continuation of the maroon ceiling-band which lined the tops of the walls (Subject 4), so that the decoration of the wall and ceiling would appear to be continuous.

The framed area remaining, measuring 5.06 m. north-south by 4.35 m. east-west (22 sq. m.) would have needed to have been marked off diagonally and laterally, providing guide-lines from which to mark out the main geometric design. This area can be sub-divided into 25 rectangular compartments, each measuring 1.00 m. by 0.87 m. This creates five rows of five compartments on either axis. This arrangement then reflects the five panel designs on each of the walls within the room!

A vermilion frame (Subject 32) ornamented with white and cream studs may have been confined to the centre five compartments (as shown), thus forming a 'cross' pattern of framed white panels (each 780 x 650 mm.). The radial arms of the cross are lined with blue (50 mm. wide – Subject 32) which frame the white panels that have been outlined with thin maroon stripes. The centre compartment is lined with green (40 mm. wide – Subject 34) which also frames the white panels similarly outlined with a thin maroon stripe. A maroon frame (80 mm. wide), decorated with 'quaver' and inverted 'V' motifs (Subject 34), occupies the centre of this panel enclosing white. A yellow diamond frame (100 mm. wide) lined with a blue band (30 mm.) is superimposed upon and at 40° to the centre green-framed panel and measures 980 x 850 mm. (Subject 34). The 'points' of the diamond then project into each of the 'radial' panels whilst the middle of each side touches internally the four external corners of the inner maroon frame. The outer vermilion frame of the 'cross' and the inner green frame of the centre panel are highlighted with a maroon edging strip (Subject 32). This arrangement of superimposed, possibly interlaced, geometric frames is the most likely central decorative element of the scheme around which all other elements are arranged. Superimposed and interlacing frames are a fairly common device in geometric mosaic patterns (Ref. 109) and such a device could have been used on a ceiling.

The remaining 20 compartments would thus form rectangular panels (*c.* 960 x 810 mm.), largely framed by green bands (50 mm. wide). This network of bands would link the centre vermilion cross arrangement (Subject 33) to the maroon border at the edge of the ceiling (Subject 30e), thus completing the demarcation of ceiling space. Four of these framed panels were probably painted yellow (as Subject 30) and contain a maroon inner frame and maroon, tendril-like foliate motifs. The remaining panels are shown largely white, but these may also have contained floral decoration (perhaps as Subjects 27–29). The position occupied by the yellow panels should logically be the centre panel on each side. If they were set in the corners then the foliate device would almost certainly be painted diagonally to keep the symmetry. Brush marks, however, clearly indicate that this device was painted either along the panel, or across it, but not diagonally, so it seems they were positioned away from the corner. By positioning the yellow panels in the centre of each side, in plan the paramount central cross arrangement would continue to the edges.

Subjects 30 and 33 imply that alternate green-framed panels were lined with a thin maroon stripe. This arrangement seems most likely to have commenced from the outer corner panels. Alternate panels in the lateral rows and each panel in the diagonal rows would, therefore, be lined. Finally, if the Fabric B plaster did not line a ceiling then it may have rendered a surface where a finer plaster was required, e.g. partition-walling either related to the 'Painted House', perhaps from an upper storey, or to a nearby demolished structure as yet unlocated. Subjects 27–34 might then be seen to represent framed and decorated panels enlivening one or more vertical surfaces.

PLASTER FRAGMENTS FROM THE EXTERNAL WALLS (FABRIC C).

These fragments match the plaster fabric that survives on the external faces of the walls of the 'Painted House' structure (Fabric C), though this precise design does not survive *in situ*. One group (Subject 36a) is still attached to an original wall fragment, which is of similar fabric to the walls of the excavated building. Tables 1 and 2 (pages 139 and 140) show that this fabric represents just 4% of the total fallen plaster assemblage. Some 203 of these fragments (84%) were recovered from demolition deposits relating to the building, over half of which (63%) came from Room 2. A further 17 fragments, including the portion still attached to its wall, were found during the Bingo Hall excavations to the north where they were found in derived or intrusive contexts. The fragments show that the decorative treatment of the plaster surfaces was of a fairly modest design. This consisted of a coloured dado with crude imitation marbling; a broad dado band and a main zone above divided into upright panels by means of straight lines of various colours. Some 111 fragments, including 17 pieces recovered from the Bingo Hall site, have been combined to form Subject 36 which shows such a scheme. This is a fairly common general scheme used in Roman Dover, both in the Clay Walled Building (see below) and on the Gaol Lane site (Ref. 110). Similar treatment of wall surfaces is seen elsewhere in the Western Empire, notably at Druten in the Netherlands (Ref. 111).

═══════════════════════

C). THE PAINTED PLASTER FROM THE BINGO HALL SITE

by Wendy Williams

1) INTRODUCTION

Excavation of the Bingo Hall site in 1975–6 produced a total of 6,430 fragments of Roman painted plaster from a variety of contexts across the site. This number includes both large and small fragments as well as about 20 large articulated sections, each of which has been counted as a single piece. The total area which these surviving fragments could have covered has been very roughly estimated as about 50 sq. m. Apart from these fallen fragments several large areas of *in situ* plaster were also studied.

The subject of this report is the painted plaster relating to the Clay Walled Building (Period VII, Building C10) where several areas of plaster were found *in situ*. Of the 3,919 fallen fragments associated with the demolition of this structure, only 2,091 of them relate to the *in situ* plaster and are discussed here. The remainder probably derive from structures beyond the limits of the Bingo Hall excavation. Some 107 fragments have been incorporated into the subjects reconstructed by Peter Keller (see above). The collection has been examined and catalogued and various other interesting groups are still being studied.

HOW THE PLASTER WAS LIFTED

The deep (6 m.) and complex Bingo Hall site lay in a restricted area and had to be excavated under bad conditions through the winter months. Although it was always likely that more plaster would be discovered, it was not possible to carry out an open-plan excavation since major soil-baulks had to be retained for recording, access and safety purposes. This prevented the simultaneous exposure of all the plaster from the Clay Walled Building and other structures.

The lifting of the plaster was ultimately carried out by four different excavators. In general, scattered fragments of plaster were lifted by context, but the fallen articulated plaster (mostly lying face-down) was first covered by a grid and each group coded by letter. Much of this was then backed with reinforced plaster of Paris and lifted in convenient sizes. All the plaster was boxed, labelled and taken to the Unit's Headquarters at Dover Castle.

THE TREATMENT AND STUDY OF THE PLASTER

A brief study was initially made of the plaster as it was removed from the site when sketches and preliminary reconstructions were made. These supplemented the photographic records, vertical soil sections and plans which collectively showed the relationship of the plaster to the structures.

The lifted plaster was carefully cleaned and left to dry. The most important fragments were then immersed in a 1:6 solution of Unibond and water to consolidate the surface and backing. All the plaster was then bagged and stored until 1984 when the post-excavation work was scheduled to begin.

The detailed study of the fragments was carried out from December, 1984 to March, 1985. Initially all the plaster was counted and sorted into site contexts. In this way it soon became apparent that about two thirds of the plaster derived from contexts which related to the Clay Walled Building. Two other groups related to the Painted House North Passage and the Tufa Block Building, respectively.

All the most informative of the decorated fragments have been drawn actual size and these are held with the site archive. This archive includes 72 boxes or trays of plaster (codes DV–3000's and DV–9000's). All the boxes are numbered and the contents listed in one of the three post-excavation folders relating to the painted plaster from this site. For the present study only key fragments of painted designs on which reconstructions are based are illustrated here. Many hundreds of fragments have been left out of the final reconstructions as they would confuse the drawings. The plaster fabric-types have been identified by Peter Keller.

Context	No. of Fragments
Clay Walled Building	3,919
Tufa Block Building	160
Painted House Passage	278
Mainly Shore-fort rampart dumps and disturbed contexts	2,073
Total fragments from Bingo Hall site	6,430

TABLE A. Painted Plaster Fragments from the Bingo Hall Site.

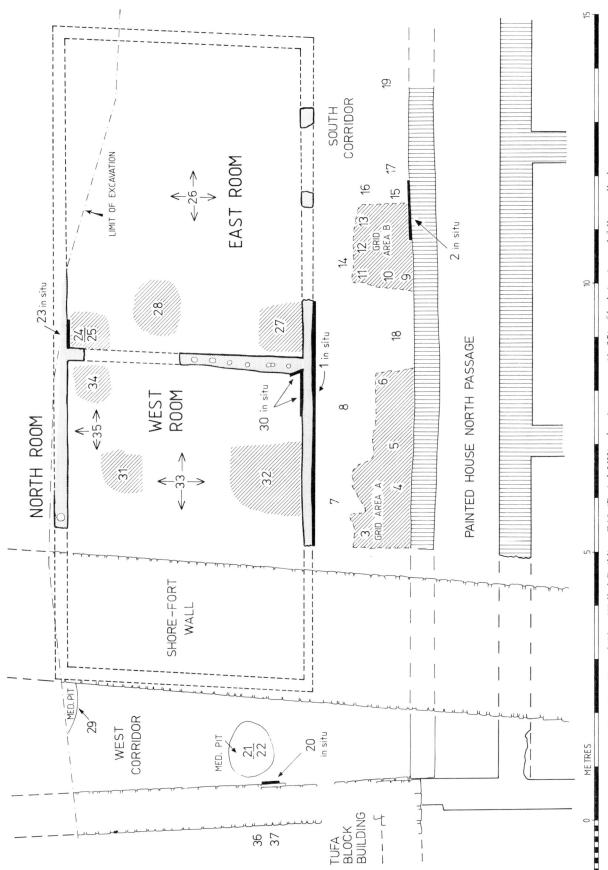

NORTH ROOM

LIMIT OF EXCAVATION

23 in situ

24/25

34

35 →
←

WEST
ROOM

31

33 →
←

32

30 in situ

28

26 →
←

EAST ROOM

27

1 in situ

SOUTH
CORRIDOR

19

16

15

17

2 in situ

14

12 13

11

GRID
AREA B

10

9

18

8

6

5

7

4

3 GRID AREA A

PAINTED HOUSE NORTH PASSAGE

SHORE-FORT
WALL

MED. PIT

29

WEST
CORRIDOR

MED. PIT

21/22

20
in situ

36

37

TUFA
BLOCK
BUILDING

METRES

0   5   10   15

Fig. 91. Plan of Clay Walled Building C10 (Period VII), showing groups (1–35) of both in situ and fallen wall-plaster.

2) THE IN SITU AND FALLEN PLASTER RELATING TO THE CLAY WALLED BUILDING (C7) (Fig. 91).

The Clay Walled Building, consisting of at least two rooms (East and West) and parts of two corridors (South and West), was built in the angle formed by the Tufa Block Building to the west and the Painted House to the south. It appears to have been an extension, or annexe, of these earlier buildings and was certainly not so grand in construction. The walls and floors were mainly of clay and there was no underfloor heating system.

The walls had, however, been decorated with painted plaster and some still remained *in situ*. Careful on-site recording of the related fallen fragments was invaluable in providing information for reconstructions. At least 2,091 (53%) of the 3,919 fallen fragments found in the demolition of the structure belonged to the *in situ* decorative schemes. The remainder were either plain white, small unidentified fragments or fragments which may have been dumped here from elsewhere. A further 70 fragments relating to the *in situ* plaster were recovered from other contexts.

As regards dating it is clear that the Clay Walled Building was later than the Period I–VI structures on the site and that it was constructed about A.D. 200–230 (see above). Two phases of rebuilding work were carried out before the structure was demolished for the construction of the late-Roman shore-fort about A.D. 270. The reconstructed designs relate to the latest period of rebuilding (Phase III).

Description	South Corridor	West Corridor	East Room	West Room	Total
Found in Clay Walled Building and forming part of *in situ* decorative schemes	1,656	41	129	265	2,091
Found in Clay Walled Building but uncharacteristic of *in situ* decorative schemes	697	193	418	520	1,828
Totals found in context	2,353	234	547	785	3,919
Forming part of *in situ* decorative schemes, but from other contexts	46	14	6	4	70

TABLE B. Painted plaster fragments found in or near the Clay Walled Building

(A) THE SOUTH CORRIDOR OF THE CLAY WALLED BUILDING (Fig. 91).

The South Corridor lay along the southern side of the East and West rooms of the Clay Walled Building and was contemporary with them. The north wall of the corridor was built of clay and the south wall of masonry. This masonry south wall also functioned as the north wall of the Painted House Passage (Period VI) which ran parallel to the South Corridor. The subsequent construction of the Roman shore-fort wall had caused considerable damage to the west end of the South Corridor, whilst at the eastern end the related deposits and the (clay) north wall had been removed leaving only part of the (masonry) south wall surviving. At its west end the South Corridor appears to have made a right-angled turn towards the north thus forming the West Corridor.

Large areas of *in situ* painted plaster were found on both walls of the South Corridor. In addition the area produced the largest amount of fallen painted plaster relating to the Clay Walled Building, with a total of 2,353 fragments and articulated groups being recovered from ten stratified deposits representing the upper (or final) demolition together with Phase III demolition, occupation and floor.

Of these 2,353 fragments found in the South Corridor, only 1,638 appear to have formed part of the decorative scheme as represented by the *in situ* plaster. Another 18 of the fragments belong to other parts of the Clay Walled Building, whilst the remaining 697 fragments are either uncharacteristic of the *in situ* plaster or unidentifiable.

A further 84 fragments of South Corridor type plaster were found elsewhere. These include 38 fragments from other parts of the Clay Walled Building and 46 fragments from miscellaneous contexts across the site (including five fragments of dado belonging to the masonry side of the South Corridor which were found in an unstratified context on the south side of the Painted House in the 1975 excavation there).

Table C gives the overall totals of the painted plaster fragments relating to the South Corridor while Tables D and E explain the provenance of the fragments in more detail.

Where groups of deposit numbers have been bracketed together in Table C it means that the feature referred to was allocated more than one deposit number during the excavation.

Group numbers 1–18 refer to two areas of *in situ* plaster and 16 assemblages of key fragments or graffiti, many of which are illustrated.

All fragments of white plaster found in Grid Areas A and B were considered to form part of the South Corridor decorative scheme. White plaster from other deposits is generally classed as unidentifiable.

Provenance	No. of Fragments
Total fragments found in the South Corridor	2,353
South Corridor-type fragments found elsewhere within the context of the Clay Walled Building	38
From contexts other than the Clay Walled Building	46
Total fragments relating to the South Corridor	2,437

Table C. Derivation of all painted plaster fragments relating to the study of the decorative scheme in the South Corridor

Provenance	Deposit Number	Belonging to South Corridor decorative scheme	Belonging to other parts of the Clay Walled Building	Uncharacteristic or unidentifiable fragments	Total	Group No.
North Wall *in situ* + related frags. (Area IX)	DV–3049	134		–	*in situ* + 134	1
South Wall *in situ* + related frags. (Area XIV)	DV–9940	28		–	*in situ* + 28	2
Upper Demolition	DV–3030 DV–9825 DV–9971	3	2 East Room	118	123	–
	DV–9836	1		23	24	–
Phase III Demo. (Area VI) + associated fragments	DV–3031	588		13	601	Grid A 4–9
Phase III Demo. (Area I) + associated fragments	DV–9841	298		–	298	Grid B 10–18
Phase III Demo.	DV–9847	–	2 East Room	40	42	–
Phase III Demo. (Area II)	DV–9867	28	14 West Room	49	91	3
Phase III Demo. (Area III)	DV–9868	–		26	26	–
Phase III Occupation	DV–3032 DV–9894	3		24	27	–
Phase III Floor	DV–9869 DV–9895 DV–3033 DV–9978	555		404	959	–
Total nos. of plaster fragments found in the South Corridor		1,638	18	697	2,353	

Table D. Analysis of painted plaster fragments found in the South Corridor of the Clay Walled Building.

Provenance	Deposit	No. of Fragments	Total
East Room	DV–9824	9	
	DV–9819	4	
	DV–9841	5	
West Room	DV–9837	19	
West Corridor	DV–9850	1	
Total fragments found elsewhere within the Clay Walled Building		38	38
Painted House Corridor	DV–3070	1	
	DV–3073	1	
	DV–3074	1	
	DV–3075	3	
Shore-fort rampart dump	DV–9811	1	
	DV–9812	8	
	DV–9815	2	
	DV–9835	1	
Shore-fort footing trench	DV–3029	2	
Period VI dump in South Corridor	DV–3038	1	
Medieval pit	DV–9840	1	
Later demolition	DV–9886	1	
Unstratified	DV–9800	18	
Painted House 1975 excavation, south side	DV–9601	5	
Total fragments from contexts other than the Clay Walled Building		46	46
Total fragments found beyond the limits of the South Corridor			84

Table E. Fragments of painted plaster belonging to the South Corridor decorative scheme which were found beyond the limits of the South Corridor.

South Corridor Plaster Fabric Type
South wall (masonry) = similar to Type A
North wall (clay)   = similar to Type C

THE *IN SITU* PLASTER

Group 1, North Wall (not illustrated). (DV–3409).

A large area of painted plaster was found *in situ* on the (clay) north wall. Its unbroken length was 4.49 m. from the west end, which had been cut by the shore-fort wall, to its east end which had been damaged by later levelling. The maximum surviving height from floor-level was 22 cm. The plaster was 1–4 cm. thick.

The design represented a marbled dado decorated with vertical red stripes. The marbling was achieved by a random flecking of red paint onto a pale brownish-yellow background. The

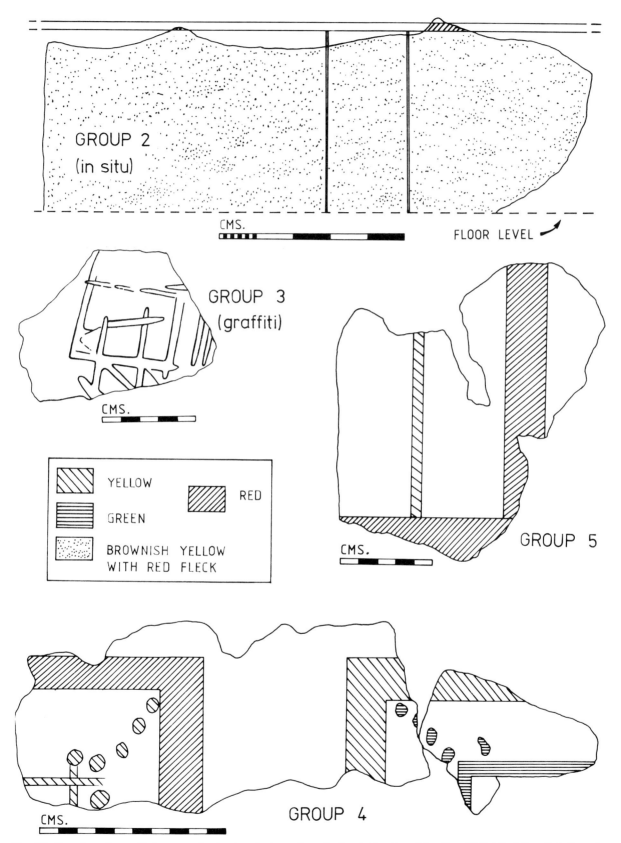

Fig. 92. *Drawing of assembled groups of painted wall-plaster from the South Corridor of the Clay Walled Building C10 (Period VII), Groups 2–5.*

vertical red stripes were 6 mm. wide and were grouped in pairs, three of which survived. Each pair of stripes tapered together slightly towards the floor and were 27, 30 and 29 cm. apart, respectively. The spaces between one pair of stripes and the next varied from 89, 80 and 87 cm. respectively. Two sections of this clay wall and 134 fragments of dado were retained for study.

Group 2, South Wall (Figs. 91, 92 and 95) (DV–9940).

Another large area of painted plaster was found *in situ* on the (masonry) south wall. It had an overall length of 1.49 m. and an overall height from floor-level of 51 cm. The plaster was 4 to 6 cm. thick. The design and colour were similar to that on the north wall (Group 1), but here only one pair of vertical red stripes, each 6 mm. wide, survived. The stripes were only 21 cm. apart and did not taper as on the north wall. The full height of the dado was 48 cm. from floor-level to a point where it was bordered by a dark red dado band 2 cm. wide. Only 1 cm. of a white area above the dado band survived. The dado extended for a minimum of 76 cm. eastwards from the pair of stripes and westwards from the same stripes for a minimum of 50 cm., the distance in each case being less than the known intervening spaces on the (clay) north wall. A portion of this plaster still survives *in situ* and can be seen by visitors to the Roman Painted House. Some 28 fragments of dado directly associated with this group were retained.

THE FALLEN PLASTER

(1)   The Upper Demolition Deposits (DV–3030/9825/9971 and 9836).

These two deposits represented a final layer of clay and plaster debris which sealed the Clay Walled Building. They produced 147 fragments of painted plaster, of which only four are readily identifiable as South Corridor-type. Another two are of East Room-type, while the remainder are either uncharacteristic or unidentified.

(2)   Phase III Demolition. (DV–3031/9841, 9847, 9867 and 9868).

These four deposits represented the last horizon of demolition debris relating to the South Corridor and produced 1,058 fragments and articulated groups of painted plaster.
(i) The uppermost deposit consisted of two areas of articulated groups of plaster, much of which was recorded and lifted using a grid-system (Grid Areas A and B described below). The 899 fragments recovered had fallen from the (masonry) south wall.
Directly beneath this was a tumble of clay and plaster consisting of three deposits which contained much uncharacteristic or unidentified plaster, possibly dumped here from elsewhere.
(ii) The uppermost of these three deposits produced 42 fragments of painted plaster, four of which are of East Room-type and six of which are of Painted House-type showing parts of a painted column. The rest are either uncharacteristic or unidentifiable.
(iii) Below this was a deposit containing 91 fragments of which 28 are very weathered fragments of South Corridor dado. A further 14 fragments are of West Room-type while the remainder are either uncharacteristic or unidentifiable. One fragment of white has a graffito on it (Group 3).

Group 3 (Fig. 92) (DV–9867).

This white fragment has a graffito on it which may have formed part of an architectural drawing.

(iv) The lowest deposit contained 26 fragments of unidentifiable plaster.

GRID AREAS A AND B (Fig. 91).

These were areas where grid-systems were used to record and lift the articulated plaster which had fallen from the (masonry) south wall. The plaster lay face down adjacent to the south wall and extended 1.17 m. northwards from it. It is possible that this plaster had been stripped off in order to facilitate the dismantling of parts of the wall fabric for re-use elsewhere, probably in the construction of the shore-fort wall. The reconstruction of the South Corridor painted designs is largely based on the examination of this plaster.

GRID AREA A (DV–3031).

This area is located at the west end of the South Corridor on the east side of the shore-fort wall. It produced 144 articulated groups and fragments of painted plaster. Groups 4, 5 and 6 are important in the reconstruction. A further 457 fragments were found near Grid Area A. Of this total of 601 fragments 588 belonged to the South Corridor decorative scheme while 13 were either uncharacteristic or unidentified.

Group 4 (Figs. 92 and 95).

This was found near the shore-fort wall and is a maximum of 32 cm. in width by a maximum of 10 cm. in height. On the left side a corner formed by a thick red stripe (17 mm. wide at the top and 23 mm. wide at the side) encloses another corner formed by thin yellow stripes (4–5 mm. wide) on a white ground. The yellow stripe is 47 mm. away from the red stripe at the top and 43 mm. at the side. A diagonal row of four yellow pellets links the corners with the additional flourish of one pellet on either side of the yellow corner. This arrangement suggests the top right corner of a white panel with what shall be described as a RED/yellow border.

This panel is only 76 mm. away from a similar arrangement of stripes and pellets representing the top left corner of a YELLOW/green bordered white panel. Here the yellow stripe (21 mm. wide) encloses a thin green stripe (8 mm. wide) which is 32 mm. away from it along the top and 4 cm. at the side. In this case the pellets are green.

Group 5 (Figs. 92 and 95).

This was found to the east of Group 4 and has a maximum height of 155 mm. and a maximum width of 146 mm. It shows a thick red stripe (22 mm. wide) and a thin yellow stripe (6 mm. wide) which are 46 mm. apart, and which both meet a red stripe or zone (minimum 2 cm. wide) at right-angles on a white ground. It is known from the *in situ* plaster that the dado band is red and, therefore, this group could reasonably be interpreted as the lower right corner of a RED/yellow bordered white panel meeting the dado band.

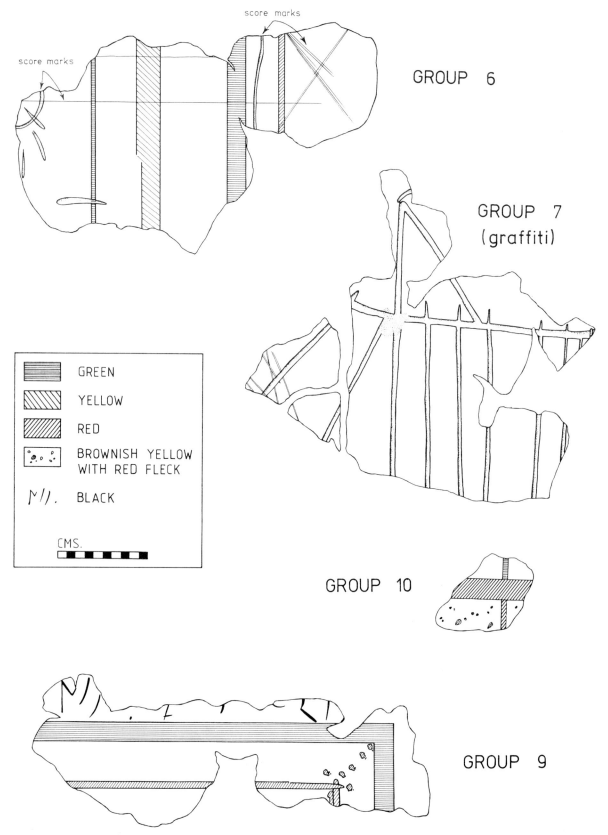

Fig. 93. *Drawing of assembled groups of painted wall-plaster and graffiti from the South Corridor of the Clay Walled Building C10 (Period VII), Groups 6, 7, 9 and 10.*

Group 6 (Figs. 93 and 95).

This was found east of Group 5 and has a maximum height of 23 cm. and a maximum width of 40 cm. Here, a thin green stripe (4 mm. wide) is beside a thick yellow stripe (26 mm. wide) and 4 cm. away from it on a white ground. Beside the thick yellow stripe and 75 mm. away from it is a thick green stripe (24 mm. wide) and then a thin red stripe (7 mm. wide) which is 36 mm. away from the green stripe. This could, therefore, be interpreted as a YELLOW/green bordered white panel next to the GREEN/red bordered white panel. The surface of the plaster has a number of deep scratches.

About 48% of all the plaster fragments lifted in Grid Area A were white and such a large amount suggests that the centres of the panels were undecorated. Much of this white plaster is very scratched, either accidentally or deliberately, with straight and curved lines which criss-cross each other in a seemingly random fashion. The following Group 7 has a definite graffito.

Group 7 (Fig. 93).

These ten articulated fragments of white plaster were found at the eastern end of Grid Area A and have a maximum height of 34 cm. by a maximum width of 38 cm. There is a rectilinear graffito, possibly of an architectural nature, deeply scratched into the surface of the plaster with a sharp instrument.
The remainder of the fragments lifted in Grid Area A are of red, yellow and green stripes (both thick and thin) on a white ground and fragments of South Corridor dado and dado band. One very small fragment has a red stripe or zone (minimum 6 mm. wide) painted along a concave surface and this could represent either a wall or a ceiling junction, although the evidence is inconclusive as no similar fragments were found in any other deposit.

THE FALLEN PLASTER ASSOCIATED WITH GRID AREA A (Fig. 91 shows approximate locations).

Surrounding Grid Area A and associated with it were a further 457 fragments and articulated groups of plaster. Of these, 180 fragments (42%) are white with scratch marks, 62 are fragments of South Corridor dado and 49 are fragments of a possible door-frame (Group 8). The rest were mainly fragments of red, yellow and green stripes (both thick and thin) including two panel corners, a GREEN/red one (Group 9) and a RED/yellow one, both on a white ground. There were 13 fragments which were uncharacteristic of the South Corridor and three of these probably derived from the East Room.

Group 8 (not illustrated).

This was found scattered near Grid Area A and consists of eight articulated fragments which have a maximum height of 16 cm. and a maximum width of 13 cm., plus 41 associated fragments. These display a broad dark red band (115 mm. wide) flanking a zone of white. The band has been painted beside a straight edge which perhaps formed part of a frame around a door opening. A thin skin of orange clay only 1 mm. thick is still adhering to the straight edge and may have functioned as a seal for a wooden door frame.

Group 9 (Figs. 93 and 95).

These three articulated fragments were also found scattered near Grid Area A and have a maximum height of 16 cm. and a maximum width of 44 cm. A corner formed by a green stripe (20–23 mm. wide) encloses a corner formed by a thin red stripe (7 mm. wide) which is 42 mm. away from it at the top and 37 mm. at the side. A diagonal row of four red pellets links the corners with an additional pellet on either side of the red corner and one within it. It seems likely that this could be interpreted as the top right corner of a GREEN/red bordered white panel. Above the green stripe are traces of lettering written in black pigment (see also Grid Area B, Groups 15 and 16).

Also associated with Grid Area A were 17 fragments of plaster which were found lying propped up vertically against the (masonry) south wall. One fragment shows a YELLOW/green panel corner of South Corridor-type. The rest are also South Corridor-type apart from two fragments which are again uncharacteristic, bringing the total number of uncharacteristic fragments associated with Grid Area A to 13.

GRID AREA B (Fig. 91).

This area was located towards the east end of the South Corridor. It produced 166 fragments and articulated groups of painted plaster. The following five Groups 10–14 are important in the final reconstruction. A further 132 fragments were found in association with Grid Area B. All of the 298 fragments formed part of the decorative scheme suggested by the *in situ* plaster.

Group 10 (Figs. 93 and 95)

This fragment was found near the (masonry) south wall at the western limit of Grid Area B and has a maximum height of 8 cm. and a maximum width of 10 cm. Here a thin green stripe (6 mm. wide) is shown meeting the red dado band (21 mm. wide) at right-angles on a white ground. This thin green line probably formed part of a YELLOW/green bordered white panel as seen in Grid Area A (Group 4). A vertical red dado stripe (6 mm. wide) meets the dado band exactly below the junction with the green stripe. It is thus probable that the thin red dado stripes seen in pairs *in situ* on both South Corridor walls (Groups 1 and 2) correspond with the thin internal panel stripes.

Group 11 (not illustrated).

This fragment was found near Group 10 and is only 30 mm. wide by 33 mm. high. It shows the internal angle of a thick yellow stripe (minimum 2 cm. wide) with one green pellet placed in the angle. This may have been the top left corner of the YELLOW/green bordered white panel described in Group 10.

Group 12 (Figs. 94 and 95).

This group consists of 13 fragments found near and to the north of Group 11. Ten fragments articulate (12a) and have a maximum height of 28 cm. and a maximum width of 31 cm. They show a thin green stripe (7 mm. wide) joining the red dado band (21 mm. wide) at right-angles on a white ground (see also Group 10). A plain white zone (presumably a panel centre) extends for a minimum of 29 cm. from the thin green stripe to the right as viewed. A further two fragments are of dado and show a thin red dado stripe (7 mm. wide) (12b) which probably joined the dado band below the junction with the thin green stripe. The remaining fragment (12c) is of dado and has graffiti on it which may relate to some graffiti which is scratched on the dado and dado band of the articulated fragments of this group.

Group 13 (not illustrated).

This shattered area of plaster was found near and to the east of Group 12 and was lifted in a plaster of Paris frame. It has a maximum height of 24 cm. and a maximum width of 25 cm. It shows a thick yellow stripe (minimum 15 mm. wide) and a thick red stripe (26 mm. wide) on a white ground, separated by a gap of 9 cm. On the other side of the red stripe and 39 mm. away from it is a thin yellow stripe (8 mm. wide). This group could be interpreted as a YELLOW/green bordered white panel adjacent to a RED/yellow bordered white panel.

Group 14 (not illustrated).

This is a large shattered area lifted in a plaster of Paris frame and has a maximum height of 30 cm. and a maximum width of 44 cm. It was found to the east of Group 13. Here a thick red stripe (23 mm. wide) and a thick green stripe (22 mm. wide) are separated by a gap of 73 mm. on a white ground. Beside the green stripe and 43 mm. away from it is a thin red stripe (6 mm. wide). A plain white area beside the thin red stripe extends away from it for a minimum of 27 cm. This group could be interpreted as a RED/yellow bordered white panel adjacent to a GREEN/red bordered white panel.

Two fragments and three large articulated areas of white plaster, possibly from panel centres, were also found in Grid Area B. A further 80 fragments are of South Corridor-type dado while the rest of the plaster is typically of thick and thin green, red and yellow stripes which seem to be from the South Corridor panel area above the dado.

THE FALLEN PLASTER ASSOCIATED WITH GRID AREA B (Fig. 91 shows approximate locations).

Surrounding Grid Area B and associated with it were 132 fragments and groups of painted plaster. Some 62 of these fragments are white and 24 fragments are of South Corridor-type dado and dado band. The following four groups of plaster are from this additional material.

Group 15 (Figs. 94 and 95).

These two associated fragments were found near Grid Area B. One fragment (15a) which is 9 cm. in height by 9 cm. in width shows a corner formed by a thick yellow stripe (2 cm. wide) enclosing another corner formed by a thin green stripe (5 mm. wide) on a white ground. The yellow corner is 32 mm. and 39 mm. above and beside the green corner, respectively. A descending diagonal row of four green pellets links the corners with an additional pellet on either side of the green corner. This may, therefore, represent the top right corner of a YELLOW/green bordered, white panel.

The second fragment (15b) which is 39 mm. in height by 73 mm. in width shows traces of letters painted in black pigment above a thick yellow stripe (2 cm. wide) on a white ground. As a group this could be interpreted as a YELLOW/green bordered white panel with black lettering above (see also Group 9 and Group 16).

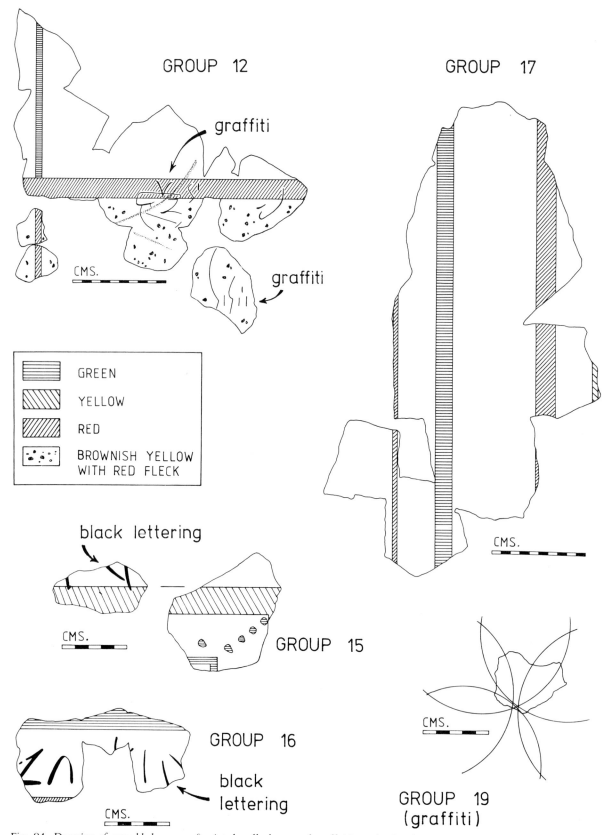

Fig. 94. *Drawing of assembled groups of painted wall-plaster and graffiti from the South Corridor of the Clay Walled Building C10 (Period VII), Groups 12, 15, 16, 17 and 19.*

Group 16 (Figs. 91 and 95).

This fragment found near Grid Area B is 7 cm. in height and 134 mm. in width. Here a thick green stripe (minimum 16 mm. wide) and a red stripe (minimum 3 mm. wide) are 51 mm. apart. On the white zone between the two stripes are black painted letters (see also Group 9 and Group 15). If this is interpreted as a GREEN/red bordered white panel, then the letters are below the thick green outer stripe and above the thin red inner stripe along the upper border of the panel.

Group 17 (Figs. 94 and 95).

This was also found near Grid Area B and the articulated fragments have a maximum height of 51 cm. and a maximum width of about 29 cm. Here a thick red stripe (21 mm. wide) and a thick green stripe (18 mm. wide) are 88 mm. apart on a white ground. Beside the red stripe and 39 mm. away from it is a thin yellow stripe (5 mm. wide), while beside the green stripe and 40 mm. away from it is a thin red stripe (5 mm. wide). This could be interpreted as a GREEN/red bordered, white panel adjacent to a RED/yellow bordered, white panel.

Group 18 (Fig. 95).

This large fragment of plaster has a maximum height of about 52 cm. and a maximum width of 38 cm. and was found near Grid Area B. Here a thick green stripe (2 cm. wide) is separated from a thick yellow stripe (18 mm. wide) by a space of 77 mm. on a white ground. Beside the green stripe and 43 mm. away from it is a thin red stripe (5 mm. wide) while beside the yellow stripe and 6 cm. away from it is a thin green stripe (6 mm. wide). This could be interpreted as a GREEN/red bordered white panel adjacent to a YELLOW/green bordered white panel.

(3) Phase III Occupation (DV–3032/9894).

This was a loam deposit containing occupational debris such as bone and pottery as well as 27 fragments of painted plaster. The only fragments identified as South Corridor-type were three small fragments of dado. The rest were either uncharacteristic or unidentifiable.

(4) The Phase III Floor (DV–9869/9895/3033/9978).

This deposit was sealed by the occupation debris of Phase III and was composed of orange clay and plaster fragments. The absence of Painted House-type plaster here suggests that demolition of that building may not yet have begun.

Some 959 fragments of painted plaster were recovered from this deposit, almost half of which (399 fragments or 42%) are plain white and can not be definitely assigned to the decorative scheme in the South Corridor. The design on the (masonry) south wall is reflected by 555 of the fragments suggesting that the north and south walls were similar. This number included 26 fragments of a dark red zone (minimum 68 mm. wide) beside a white zone and these may have formed part of either a door or window frame. The five remaining fragments appear to be uncharacteristic of the Clay Walled Building.

Fragments of painted plaster found in this deposit at the extreme eastern end of the South Corridor show subtle differences in the colours. The green and yellow border stripes are much paler while the dado band is 33 mm. wide instead of around 20 cm. wide and is a more pinky-brown colour than elsewhere.

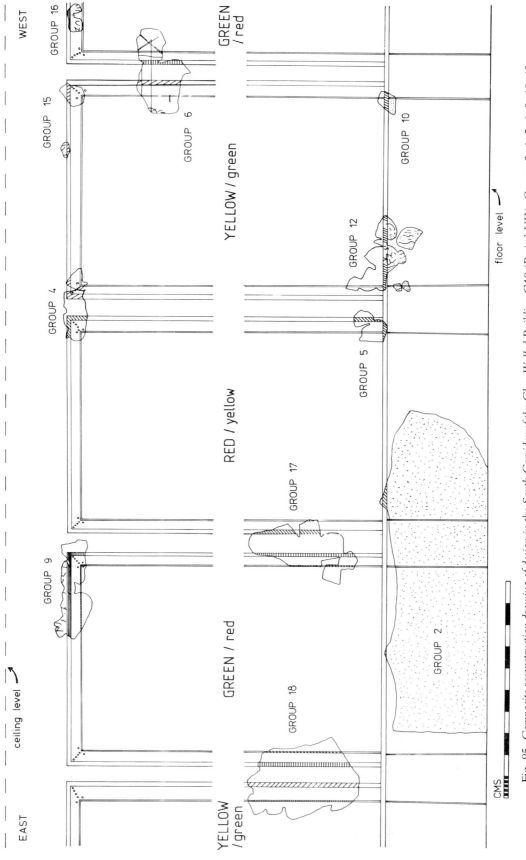

Fig. 95. Composite reconstruction drawing of design in the South Corridor of the Clay Walled Building C10 (Period VII), Groups 2, 4, 5, 6, 9, 10, 12 and 15–18.

Group 19 (Fig. 94).

Several of the white fragments from the extreme eastern end of the South Corridor have scratched compass-marks on them and one of these is illustrated.

RECONSTRUCTION OF THE PAINTED DESIGN IN THE SOUTH CORRIDOR (Fig. 95 and Plate XXXIV).

The reconstruction of the painted design in the South Corridor is largely based on the *in situ* plaster and on groups of plaster from Areas A and B. The final reconstruction is therefore of the (masonry) south wall although material derived from the (clay) north wall suggests that both sides of the corridor were similar in design. The scheme consisted of a dado and a dado band, surmounted by upright rectangular white panels with double-coloured borders on three sides (top and sides). There was no conclusive evidence for any design between the tops of the panels and the ceiling junction.

The Dado and Dado Band

The dado was the area of design painted on the zone of wall adjacent to the floor-level and, apart from any door-openings, it was probably continuous along both sides of the corridor. It had been painted a pale brownish-yellow colour and overflecked with random red splashes, possibly flicked at the wall with a loaded paintbrush. At 80 to 89 cm. intervals along the dado there were pairs of thin (6 mm. wide), vertical stripes varying from 21 to 30 cm. apart. Each of the three pairs of stripes seen *in situ* on the (clay) north wall (Group 1) tapered slightly inwards towards the floor while the only pair which survived *in situ* on the (masonry) south wall (Group 2) was upright.

The height of the dado as seen *in situ* on the (masonry) south wall was 48 cm. from floor-level to a point where it was bordered by a dark red horizontal stripe called the dado band which was about 2 cm. wide. Although the dado did not survive to its full height on the (clay) north wall, it would seem logical for both sides of the corridor to share similar design proportions.

The Panel Area

It is clear that above the dado there were large rectangular white panels with double-coloured striped borders on three sides, the fourth (lowest) side being formed by the dado band. Invariably the outer stripe was thick (about 2 cm.) and the inner stripe was thin (about 5 mm.).

Decorating the upper corners of the panels were descending diagonal rows of four pellets linking the inner and outer border stripe corners. An additional pellet was placed on either side of the inner (lower) corner as a further embellishment. The pellets were approximately round and may have been painted in with the point of a stick. They were always of the same colour as the thin internal stripe.

The articulated groups of painted plaster which had fallen from the (masonry) south wall (Areas A and B) suggested that there were three colour combinations which formed the panel borders:-

1)   A thick red outer stripe enclosing a thin yellow inner stripe (RED/yellow).
2)   A thick green outer stripe enclosing a thin red inner stripe (GREEN/red).
3)   A thick yellow outer stripe enclosing a thin green inner stripe (YELLOW/green).

The positions in which the various groups of painted plaster were found suggest the following colour sequence as viewed from right to left along the (masonry) south wall in Gridded Area A: a YELLOW/green panel near the shore-fort wall, followed by a RED/yellow panel and then a GREEN/red one. This sequence seems to have been repeated along the wall since the same succession of coloured borders is suggested for Grid Area B.

Plaster Group 12 (Figs. 94 and 95) shows a minimum panel width of 29 cm. If the pairs of thin red stripes on the dado correspond with the thin inner panel stripe on adjacent panels (as suggested by Group 10), then an average panel width of about 97 cm. can be calculated (including striped borders), with spaces of about 9 cm. between adjacent panels. The considerable variation in distances between the *in situ* dado stripes on the (clay) north wall suggest that the artist did not measure his design precisely. With the South Corridor being a minimum of 12.15 m. in length there would have been at least eleven panels along the (masonry) south wall.

The exact height of the panels is unknown. In the East Room, however, the space between the tops of the panels and the ceiling junction is known to be about 28 cm. The dado (including dado band) in the South Corridor is 50 cm. in height. The floor-to-ceiling height must have been at least 2 m. but is more likely to have been about 2.20–2.50 m. and the height of the panels could have been about 1.50 m. There is insufficient evidence to suggest that there was a design above the panels.

Plaster in Grid Area A (Group 8) suggests the presence of a door in the (masonry) south wall, perhaps destroyed in the 3.00 m. gap made during the construction of the later shore-fort wall. The broad dark red band here which is 115 mm. wide may have formed part of a door-frame. If such a painted door-frame replaced an entire bordered panel, then the door-opening could have been about 74 cm. wide by about 1.90 m. in height.

It should be noted that at the extreme eastern end of the South Corridor several fragments of painted plaster showed Corridor-type design elements in slightly paler colours and with a slightly wider dado band.

None of the fallen plaster in the South Corridor was identified as having come from the ceiling, nor was it possible to identify any fragments of window frame.

(B) THE WEST CORRIDOR OF THE CLAY WALLED BUILDING (Fig. 91).

The presumed West Corridor lay along the west side of the West Room. It seems to have formed a right angle with the South Corridor thus creating a continuous walkway along the south and west sides of the Clay Walled Building. A presumed clay wall had divided the West Corridor from the West Room, but the later construction of the shore-fort wall had totally destroyed it. Only part of the (masonry) west wall still survived and this was shared by both the West Corridor and the Tufa Block Building.

One small area of painted plaster was found *in situ* on the west wall (Group 20) although traces of plaster backing were noted along most of its length.

Although some 234 fallen fragments of painted plaster were recovered from six stratified deposits within the limits of the West Corridor, only 85 fragments from two of these deposits (Groups 21 and 22) seem to have been directly related to the phase represented by the *in situ* plaster. Three of the deposits consisted of later demolition debris and mainly contained plaster which is uncharacteristic of the Clay Walled Building. The remaining deposit was the fill of a medieval pit (Group 29) and among the 34 fragments found here were several which belonged to the Clay Walled Building and perhaps to the West Corridor.

A further 15 fragments of painted plaster which may have derived from the West Corridor dado were found elsewhere and only one of these fragments came from the Clay Walled Building (see Table H).

Group numbers 20–22 include an area of *in situ* plaster on the west wall of the Corridor and descriptions of all the fallen plaster fragments from the two key deposits mentioned above.

Where the deposit numbers are bracketed together in Table G, it means that the demolition debris was given more than one deposit number during excavation.

The only fragments of painted plaster which can be assigned to the West Corridor are fragments of dado of which there are two variants (see below) and it is these fragments which appear in the Tables.

Provenance	No. of fragments
Total plaster fragments found in the West Corridor	234
West Corridor-type fragments found elsewhere within the context of the Clay Walled Building.	1
From contexts other than the Clay Walled Building	14
Total fragments found in, or relating to the West Corridor	249

Table F. Derivation of all painted plaster fragments relating to the study of the decorative scheme in the West Corridor.

Provenance	Deposit No.	Belonging to W. Corridor decorative scheme.	Belonging to other areas of Clay Walled Building	Uncharacter-istic or unidentifiable	Total	Group
in situ on west wall (Area XV)	–	–	–	–		20
Medieval pit	DV–9850	3	13	18	34	
Later demolition	DV–9873	14	–	10	24	
Later demolition	DV–9862	–	–	1	1	
Later demolition	DV–3041 DV–9879	–	–	90	90	
Collapse of east (clay) wall	DV–9863	9	–	63	72	21
Pit sealed by collapse of east (clay) wall	DV–9865	2	–	11	13	22
Total plaster fragments found in West Corridor		28	13	193	234	

Table G. Analysis of painted plaster fragments found in the West Corridor of the Clay Walled Building.

Provenance	Deposit	No. of Fragments	Total
North side of West Room	DV–9890	1	
Total fragments found elsewhere within the Clay Walled Building		1	1
Tufa Block Building	DV–9866	1	
Shore-fort rampart dump	DV–9856	9	
Shore-fort rampart dump	DV–9882	4	
Total fragments from contexts other than Clay Walled Building		14	14
Total fragments found beyond the limits of the West Corridor			15

Table H. Fragments of painted plaster relating to the West Corridor decorative scheme which were found beyond the limits of the West Corridor.

West Corridor Plaster Fabric Type
Variant i (white dado with dark red and yellow speckle) = similar to Type G
Variant ii (pink dado with dark red and yellow speckle) = similar to Type G

THE *IN SITU* PLASTER

Group 20, West Wall (not illustrated).

The *in situ* plaster was a worn and discoloured area measuring only 34 cm. in length by 18 cm. in height. Traces of dark coloured flecks suggested that this was part of a dado similar to that in the South Corridor although conclusive identification was not possible due to its poor condition.

THE FALLEN PLASTER

Group 21 (not illustrated) (DV–9863).

This group of 72 fragments was recovered from a mass of orange clay which may have represented the collapse of the presumed east wall of the West Corridor.

Fifty of the fragments (69%) are white, most of which seem to derive from a clay wall as traces of orange clay still adhere to the backing. Nine fragments are of a dado and display random dark red and yellow flecks on a white ground (variant i). These dado fragments are a minimum of 35 mm. thick but as there is no trace of clay adhering to the backing they may have fallen from the masonry west wall.

Some five of the fragments, possibly from the panel area, show stripes on a white ground; three of these have a thin green stripe (5 mm. wide), the other two have a thick yellow stripe (21 mm. wide). The remaining eight fragments are small, unidentifiable pieces of red stripes or zones.

Group 22 (not illustrated). (DV–9865).

These 13 fragments were recovered from a pit sealed under the mass of collapsed clay east wall (Group 21). Two of the fragments are again of dado variant i (as seen in Group 21). The thick yellow and thin green stripes are also represented, two being of yellow and one of green. Four of the remaining fragments are white and four are unidentified stripes and zones which are not characteristic of the Clay Walled Building.

RECONSTRUCTION OF THE PAINTED DESIGN IN THE WEST CORRIDOR

Owing to the fragmentary nature of the small amount of *in situ* plaster it is not possible to offer much reconstructional evidence. All that can be said is that part of the dado may have been white flecked with dark red and yellow (variant i) and that it was at least 18 cm. in height. It is perhaps reasonable to suppose that the dado zone may have been about 50 cm. high, including a dado band of undetermined colour. Any other height would have produced an awkward discrepancy at the junction of the South and West Corridors, bearing in mind that the height of the dado, including the dado band, in the South Corridor is 50 cm.

The comparatively large quantity of white plaster from the presumed east wall suggests that there were fairly extensive areas of wall surface left white. The fragments showing thick yellow and thin green stripes could suggest YELLOW/green bordered white panels similar to those in the South Corridor. They may, however, be intrusions from the West Room where stripes in these colours are also known.

A later demolition deposit which sealed the West Corridor produced 14 fragments of a pale pink dado over-flecked with red and yellow (variant ii) which is similar to the variant i dado which has a white background. A 7 mm. wide grey stripe was noted on several of these variant ii fragments suggesting thin vertical grey stripes on the dado which are characteristic of the rest of the Clay Walled Building. The colour variation may have formed a part of the design in the West Corridor and the fragments have therefore been tentatively assigned to the decorative scheme there. Traces of orange clay were noted on the backing of one of the fragments. Another three fragments of dado variant ii were found in the medieval pit along with plaster of East Room (Group 29) and South Corridor-type designs.

(C) THE EAST ROOM OF THE CLAY WALLED BUILDING (Fig. 91).

Only the western part of this room survived, but parts of the clay walls on the north, west and south sides were found. There was one area of *in situ* painted plaster on the north wall (Group 23) and clear traces of plaster backing on all three walls suggesting that the whole room had been covered with painted designs.

Some 547 fragments and articulated groups of fallen plaster were recovered in nine stratified contexts within the limits of the East Room. Only five of these deposits proved to be of importance in the final reconstruction, with the remaining deposits being either:

a)   earlier than the Clay Walled Building
b)   deposits containing isolated fragments of either uncharacteristic or unidentifiable painted plaster
c)   general demolition scatter sealing the room and which contained largely uncharacteristic plaster

Thus only 220 fragments and articulated groups were directly related to the East Room during the phase represented by the *in situ* plaster, and only 104 of these could be attributed to the decorative scheme.

A further 31 fragments of East Room-type plaster were found elsewhere on the Bingo Hall site, and 25 of these were found in Clay Walled Building contexts. Thus the overall total of plaster fragments relating to the East Room is 578.

Table I gives the overall totals of painted plaster fragments relating to the East Room while Tables J and K explain the provenance of the fragments in more detail.

Group numbers 23–28 include one area of *in situ* plaster and descriptions of all the fallen plaster fragments from the five key deposits mentioned above. Group 29 is an assemblage of plaster found in the West Corridor containing plaster of East Room-type.

Where the deposit numbers have been bracketed together in Table J it means that the Phase II floor had been given more than one deposit number during the excavation. (The various phases in the life of the Clay Walled Building are dealt with more fully above, page 45.)

Provenance	No. of Fragments
Total plaster fragments found in the East Room	547
East Room-type fragments found elsewhere within the context of the Clay Walled Building	25
Found in contexts other than Clay Walled Building	6
Total fragments found in, or relating to the East Room	578

Table I. Derivation of all painted plaster fragments relating to the study of the decorative scheme in the East Room.

Provenance	Deposit No.	East Room Decorative Scheme	Other areas of Cl.-Wall. Bldg.		Uncharc. or Unident.	Total	Group No.
North wall *in situ* (Area XII)	DV–3062	–		–	–	–	23
Later demolition (Area I 'O')	DV–9819	–	4	South Corridor	43	47	–
Demolition scatter throughout East Room	DV–9824	14	14	5 West Room 9 South Corridor	220	248	26
Tumbled plaster in N.W. corner of room	DV–3061	5		–	35	40	24
Tumbled plaster under DV–3061	DV–3062	56		–	20	76	25A & B

Provenance	Deposit No.	East Room Decorative Scheme	Other areas of Cl.-Wall. Bldg.		Uncharc. or Unident.	Total	Group No.
Demo. of south wall (Area I 'N')	DV–9841	21	7	5 South Corridor 2 West Room	5	33	27
Demo. of west wall under DV–9819 Area (I 'O')	DV–9841	8		–	15	23	28
Phase II occupation	DV–9827	–		–	1	1	–
Phase II floor	DV–3079	–		–	33	33	–
	DV–9828	–		–	30	30	–
	DV–9829	–		–	3	3	–
	DV–9846	–		–	12	12	–
Phase I occupation	DV–9830	–		–	1	1	–
Total nos. of plaster fragments found in the East Room		104		25	418	547	

Table J. Analysis of painted plaster fragments found in the East Room of the Clay Walled Building.

Provenance	Deposit	No. of fragments	Total	Group
Medieval pit in West Corridor	DV–9850	12		29
Demolition of South Corridor	DV–9825	1		
	DV–9971	1		
	DV–9847	2		
General demolition scatter in West Room	DV–9837	9		
Total fragments found in other Clay Walled Building contexts		25	25	
late-Roman footing-trench, Shore-fort wall	DV–3021	2		
	DV–3029	4		
Total fragments from contexts other than Clay Walled Building		6	6	
Total fragments found beyond the limits of the East Room			31	

Table K. Fragments of painted plaster relating to the East Room decorative scheme which were found beyond the limits of the East Room

East Room Plaster Fabric = similar to Type C

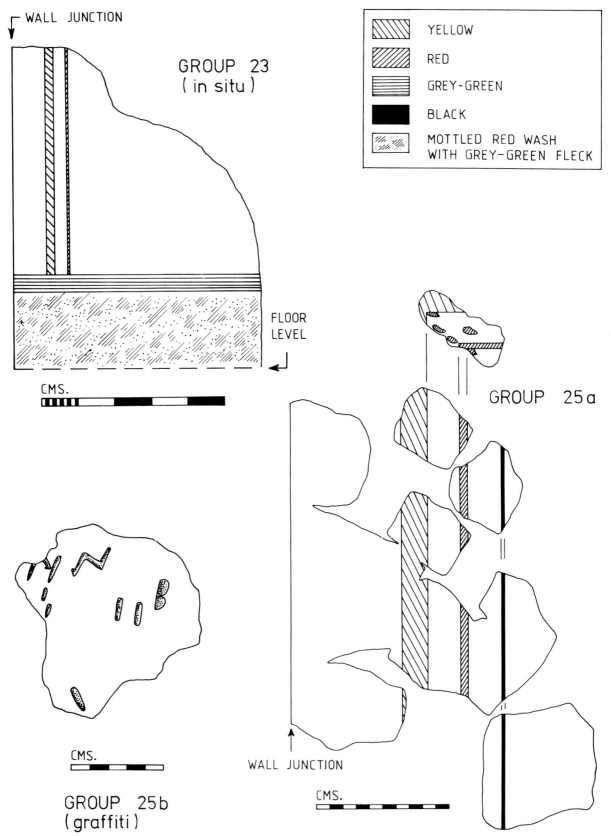

Fig. 96. *Drawing of assembled groups of painted wall-plaster from the East Room of the Clay Walled Building C10 (Period VII), Groups 23, 25a and 25b.*

THE *IN SITU* PLASTER

Group 23 (Figs. 96 and 98) (DV–3062).

This was on the north wall adjacent to, and marginally including, the north-west corner of the room. The maximum surviving height from the floor-level was about 85 cm. and the maximum surviving width from the wall junction was 67 cm. The plaster was 3 to 4 cm. thick applied directly to the clay wall.

The lower zone of the design was a dado 20 cm. high from floor-level. A white background had been mottled with a thin wash of red paint and then over-flecked with random splashes of grey-green probably flicked on with a loaded paintbrush. The upper limit of the dado was bordered by a horizontal grey-green dado band 4.5 cm. wide.

The area above this was white, apart from two coloured stripes which rose vertically from the dado band. The first was a thick yellow one (2 cm. wide) placed 9 cm. from the wall junction. Next there was a thin red stripe (5 mm. wide) which was 35 mm. from the yellow one. An area of plain white then extended for a minimum of 52 cm. to the east of the red stripe.

THE FALLEN PLASTER

The five deposits of importance to the reconstruction of the decorative scheme in the East Room (Groups 24–28) were all directly associated with the phase represented by the *in situ* plaster and formed part of the demolition of the clay walls. Group 29 is an assemblage of plaster fragments found in a medieval pit in the West Corridor.

Group 24 (not illustrated) (DV–3061).

This group was found in a deposit lying directly in front of *in situ* Group 23 and it probably represents an upper area of plaster which had fallen into the north-west corner of the room during demolition. The 40 fragments in this group include five fragments of a pink-red band (45 mm. wide) which is interpreted as the East Room ceiling band (see also Group 28). There are also nine fragments of green stripes (21 mm. and 15 mm. wide) which may be uncharacteristic. The remaining 26 fragments are white.

Group 25 (a and b) (Figs. 96 and 98) (DV–3062).

This was found directly underneath the deposit containing Group 24. It consists of 76 fragments, 56 of which can be assigned to the East Room. Some 44 of these are of the East Room dado, dado band and fragments of yellow-bordered panel as seen on the *in situ* plaster (Group 23). The remaining 12 East Room fragments are largely articulated and show part of a panel corner adjacent to the wall junction (Group 25A). The maximum height of the fragments is 40 cm. and the maximum width is 23 cm. A thick yellow and thin red stripe are in the same positions as seen on the *in situ* plaster, but with the addition of a black line (2 mm. wide) which is 25 mm. away from the red stripe. There is a pattern of inverted tear-shaped red pellets placed diagonally between the red and yellow corners.

Included in the deposit are two fragments of a possibly uncharacteristic red stripe (21 mm. wide). The remainder consists of 14 white fragments and four unidentifiable fragments of red stripes or zones. Two of the white fragments bore possible graffiti, one of which is illustrated (Group 25B, Fig. 35).

Group 26 (not illustrated) (DV–9824).

This group was recovered from a demolition scatter found throughout the East Room. It contains the largest amount of plaster found here with a total of 248 fragments. Only 14 of these (6%) can be readily identified as being East Room-type plaster and they include dado, dado band and the combination of thin red and thin black stripes which are interpreted as being part of a yellow bordered panel. Another 14 fragments are identifiable as South Corridor and West Room plaster. There are nine fragments of a dark pink-red stripe/zone (minimum 5 cm. wide) which may represent door or window edging. The group also contains 106 small fragments of plaster with distinctive pinks, blues, greens and browns which are uncharacteristic of the East Room and which may derive from an unexcavated structure to the north of the excavation. The remaining 105 fragments are mainly white, but include 27 unidentifiable fragments of red stripes or zones.

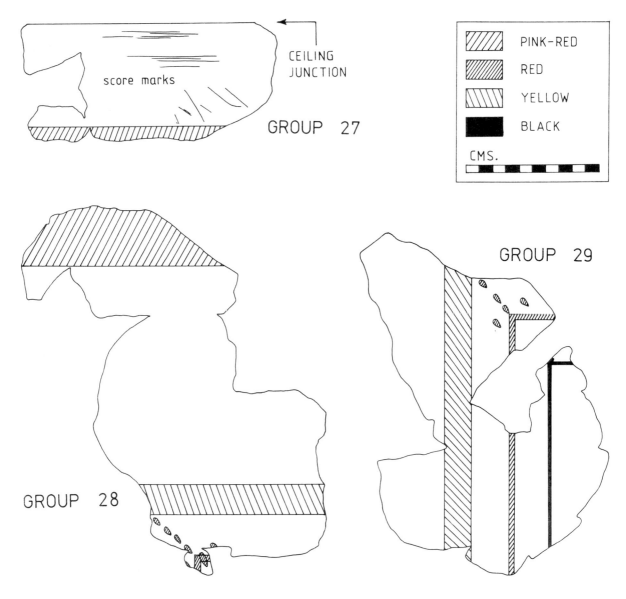

Fig. 97. *Drawing of assembled groups of painted wall-plaster from the East Room of the Clay Walled Building C10 (Period VII), Groups 27–29.*

Group 27 (Figs. 97 and 98) (DV–9841 Area I 'N').

These 33 fragments represent an area of fallen plaster in the south-west corner of the East Room. Of the 21 fragments which are identifiable as East Room-type, eight are of dado and dado band and four have a thick yellow stripe (minimum 14 mm. wide) possibly representing a yellow bordered panel.

Another six articulated fragments (maximum height 20 cm. by maximum width 15 cm.) show a yellow stripe (19 mm. wide) placed vertically 86 mm. from the wall junction. Next there is a red stripe (5 mm. wide) which is 27 mm. from the yellow stripe. The yellow stripe is discoloured to red at one end. Again this may represent part of a yellow bordered panel belonging to the East Room.

Three articulated fragments may represent a ceiling junction from the East Room (illustrated). An incomplete pink-red stripe/zone (minimum 12 mm. wide) is 78 mm. from a junction and this may be part of the broad ceiling band. The surface of the plaster appears to be scorched and is also scratched making it difficult to match the colour with that of the pink-red ceiling band as seen in Group 28.

The remaining twelve fragments are either uncharacteristic or unidentifiable. Five fragments of thin yellow stripe (7 mm. wide) and one fragment of red stripe/zone (minimum 14 mm. wide) may derive from the South Corridor. Two fragments showing a T-junction formed by two red stripes (4 mm. wide) are typical of the West Room. Another fragment shows a dark red stripe/zone (minimum 14 mm. wide) which may represent window or door-edging, while the remaining four fragments are white.

Group 28 (Figs. 97 and 98) (DV–9841 Area I 'O').

This group of 23 fragments seems to consist of plaster fallen from the central region of the west wall. An articulated mass of painted plaster, counted as one fragment, (maximum height 26 cm. and maximum width 24 cm.) represents the top left-hand corner of a yellow bordered panel (Fig. 98). This shows a horizontal pink-red ceiling band (minimum 44 mm. wide) which is 16 cm. above the outer yellow stripe (22 mm. wide) which frames the top of the panel. The corner of an inner red stripe (5 mm. wide) is approximately 30 mm. below the yellow stripe and a diagonal of four inverted tear-shaped red pellets is seen descending towards the red corner, with a further one either side of and within the red corner. Seven more of the fragments relate to this articulated mass.

All of the remaining 15 fragments are white apart from one which has a red stripe/zone (minimum 13 mm. wide).

Group 29 (Figs. 97 and 98) (DV–9850).

This group was found in a medieval pit in the West Corridor. The pit produced a total of 34 fragments, 12 of which are articulated (Fig. 98) and show yet another East Room-type panel top (maximum height 25 cm. and maximum width 18 cm.). A thick yellow stripe (21 mm. wide) is 30 mm. from a thin red stripe (5 mm. wide). The red stripe corner has a descending diagonal row of three inverted tear-shaped red pellets linking it with the yellow corner which has been broken away. A further red pellet lies on either side of the red corner, but no pellet is seen within it. Beside the red stripe and 26 mm. from it is a thin black line (3 mm. wide) forming the inner stripe corner of a triple border. There may be a black pellet embellishing the point of the corner, although the plaster is broken and whether or not this is an accidental smudge is uncertain. This design could derive from either corner of a panel top, although in the reconstruction (Fig. 98) it is placed in the top right-hand corner.

The remaining 22 fragments from the pit consist of one South Corridor-type fragment, three of West Corridor-type and 18 which are either unidentifiable or uncharacteristic of designs within the Clay Walled Building.

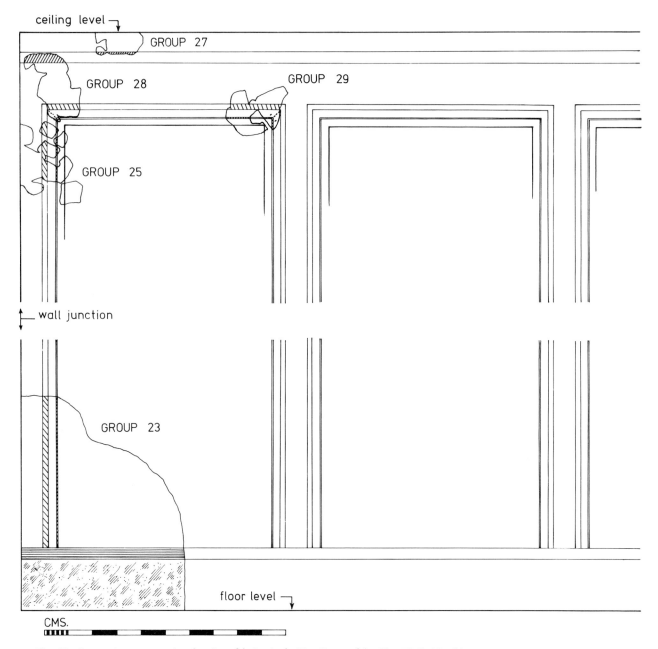

Fig. 98. *Composite reconstruction drawing of design in the East Room of the Clay Walled Building C10 (Period VII), Groups 23, 25 and 27–29.*

RECONSTRUCTION OF THE PAINTED DESIGN IN THE EAST ROOM (Fig. 98).

The reconstruction of the painted design in the East Room is based on the *in situ* plaster (Group 23) and on key assemblages of fallen plaster in Groups 24–29. The design consisted of a dado and a horizontal dado band surmounted by upright rectangular white panels with double or triple coloured borders on three sides. A broad horizontal ceiling band was placed above the panels near the junction with the ceiling.

The Dado and Dado Band

The dado was the area of design painted on the lower wall zone. Apart from any door-openings, it was probably continuous around the four walls of the room. A white background had been mottled with a wash of red paint and then over-flecked with random grey-green splashes flicked on with a loaded paint brush, thus creating a marbled effect. Fragments of dado found throughout the room were similar to the dado seen on the *in situ* plaster, suggesting a single colour scheme throughout the room. The dado was only 20 cm. high from the floor-level to where it was bordered by a horizontal grey-green dado band 45 mm. wide. Although vertical stripes were seen on the dados in both the South Corridor and the West Room, none was found in the East Room.

The Panel Area

Above the dado there were upright rectangular white panels with double or triple-coloured striped borders on three sides, the fourth (bottom) side being formed by the dado band. The outer stripe was invariably thick (about 20 mm. wide) and the inner stripe was thin (about 5 mm. wide). On the *in situ* plaster the thick outer stripe was yellow and the thin inner stripe was red and this colour combination was reflected on many fallen fragments. Although fragments of thick red and both thick and thin green stripes were also found in the room, possibly suggesting other border colours, there was insufficient evidence to prove this. It is therefore likely that most, if not all, of the panels were YELLOW/red bordered.

A thin black line was seen beside the thin red inner stripe on two of the panel tops (Groups 25 and 29) although it did not occur on the *in situ* plaster. It is possible that the thin black line did not extend down the entire panel, or alternatively, that perhaps it had been worn off the *in situ* plaster.

The tops of the panels were embellished with descending diagonal rows of three or four inverted tear-shaped red pellets linking the yellow and red stripe corners. An additional pellet was placed on either side of the red corner and sometimes one within the red corner. There was no suggestion of any decoration in the centre of the panels.

The width of the panels is unknown although a minimum width of 58 cm. including the border was seen on the *in situ* plaster (Group 23). It is clear, therefore, that the overall width of a panel and its borders must have been at least 65 cm. with a certain space of 9 cm. adjacent to the wall junction. If all the panels were 9 cm. apart, then four, five or six panels would fill the west wall which was 4.52m. in length. In view of the contemporary panels in the South Corridor being about 97 cm. in width, it seems likely that in fact there were only four panels along this wall, each about 1.02 m. wide. Any door opening would have replaced one of the panels and it seems clear that all four walls were probably treated in a similar manner.

The height of the panels is also unknown. The space to the ceiling above the bordered panels is calculated as about 283 mm. which is an aggregate of 160 mm. (panel to ceiling band), 45 mm. (ceiling band) and 78 mm. (ceiling band to ceiling). A probable floor-to-ceiling height is likely to have been about 2.20–2.50 m. in which case the panels would have been about 1.75 m. in height above the dado band.

Although there must have been at least one door-opening giving access to the room, the plaster does not provide evidence of which wall this was in. If door-openings corresponded with the inner black line of a panel border then they would have been about 85 cm. wide by about 1.90 m. in height.

The Ceiling Band

The articulated mass from Group 28 was interpreted as a horizontal band placed above the panels. It was pink-red in colour and was separated from the thick yellow top border stripe of the panel by a white zone 16 cm. wide. Five further fragments were found in Group 24 and although the join is poor they give an approximate width of 45 mm. for the band. The discoloured group of fragments found in Group 27 show the band to be 78 mm. from, and parallel to, a wall or ceiling junction. Broad pink-red bands such as this are not known to form part of a vertical pattern in this room and it is therefore likely that this was horizontal and above the panels as indicated in the West Room (Group 31). It should be noted that the dado band and ceiling band are of the same width and therefore balance each other in the overall decorative scheme.

The fallen plaster did not provide any information about windows in this room although it is tempting to visualise them as narrow rectangular openings at intervals above the panels. None of the fallen plaster was identified as having come from a ceiling.

(D) THE WEST ROOM (Fig. 91).

The excavation revealed that although the west side of this room had been destroyed by the construction of the shore-fort wall, portions of the north, east and south walls, which were of clay, had survived. Although there were traces of plaster backing on the surviving walls, the only good *in situ* plaster was in the south-east corner of the room (Group 30).

Some 785 fragments of fallen plaster were recovered from six stratified deposits within the room, five of which were demolition deposits directly relating to the *in situ* plaster. The sixth was a later Roman demolition deposit which sealed the Clay Walled Building and contained 287 fragments of uncharacteristic plaster which are not considered here. This leaves a total of 498 fragments which are discussed in Groups 31–35.

A further 24 fragments of West Room-type plaster were found elsewhere on the Bingo Hall site. Most of these were from the adjacent South Corridor and East Room which were contemporary with the West Room, while four were found in the shore-fort rampart dump. The overall total of fragments either found in, or relating to the East Room is 810.

Table L gives the overall totals of painted plaster fragments relating to the East Room while Tables M and N explain the provenance of the fragments in more detail.

Provenance	No. of Fragments
Total plaster fragments found in the West Room.	785
West Room-type fragments found elsewhere within the context of the Clay Walled Building.	21
From contexts other than the Clay Walled Building.	4
Total fragments found in, or relating to the West Room.	810

Table L. Derivation of all painted plaster fragments relating to the study of the decorative scheme in the West Room.

Provenance	Deposit	West Room Decorative Scheme	Other areas of Clay-Walled Bldg.		Uncharac. or Unident.	Total	Group No.
South and east wall *in situ* (Area X)	DV–3049	–		–	–	–	30
Later Roman demolition	DV–9887	–		–	287	287	–
Demolition scatter throughout West Room	DV–9837	96	28	19 South Corridor 9 East Room	199	323	33
Demolition of south wall	DV–3049	27		–	–	27	32
Demolition of north & east walls.	DV–9890	90	1	West Corridor	27	118	34
Uncharacteristic plaster, under DV–9890	DV–9891	–		–	7	7	35
Demolition of north wall, under DV–9891	DV–9892	23		–	–	23	31
Total nos. of plaster fragments found in the West Room		236		29	520	785	

Table M.   Analysis of painted plaster fragments found in the West Room of the Clay Walled Building.

Provenance	Deposit	No. of Fragments	Total
Demolition of South Corridor	DV–9867	14	
General demolition in East Room	DV–9824	5	
Near south wall of East Room	DV–9841	2	
Total fragments found in other Clay Walled Building contexts		21	21
Shore-fort rampart dump	DV–9835	2	
Shore-fort rampart dump	DV–9882	2	
Total fragments from contexts other than Clay Walled Building		4	4
Total fragments found beyond the limits of the West Room			25

Table N.   Fragments of painted plaster relating to the decorative scheme in the West Room
which were found beyond the limits of the West Room.

West Room Plaster Fabric Type = similar to Type K

THE *IN SITU* PLASTER

Group 30 (not illustrated). (DV–3049).

A small area of painted plaster was found *in situ* on both the south and east walls of the West Room adjacent to, and including, the south-east corner of the room. The east wall was displaced by some 5 cm. towards the west and this obscured the corner joint. The plaster survived for a maximum distance of 30 cm. along the east wall and 89 cm. from the displaced corner along the south wall. The maximum surviving height was 20 cm. from floor-level and the average thickness of the plaster was 8 cm. The surviving design was a cream coloured dado over-flecked with random splashes of yellow and black. No other design features survived. Two sections of the south wall were retained for study. One of these shows the West Room dado *in situ* on one side and the South Corridor dado *in situ* on the opposite side.

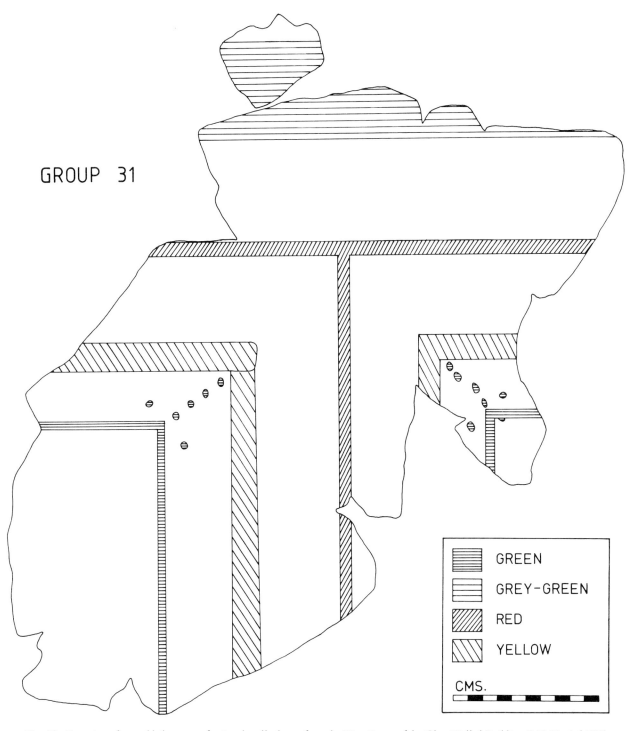

GROUP 31

GREEN
GREY-GREEN
RED
YELLOW

CMS.

Fig. 99. *Drawing of assembled groups of painted wall-plaster from the West Room of the Clay Walled Building C10 (Period VII), Group 31.*

THE FALLEN PLASTER

The five groups of plaster (Groups 31–35) described were directly associated with the *in situ* plaster and are interpreted as demolition from the upper wall areas, with the exception of Group 35 which may be intrusive. A considerable amount of white plaster was again found suggesting that the panel centres were undecorated.

Group 31 (Figs. 99 and 101). (DV–9892).

The reconstruction of the painted design in the West Room is largely based on this important group of 23 fragments. They were found lying face down under Group 35 and appear to have fallen from an upper area towards the middle of the north wall. The group apparently represents the tops of two adjacent rectangular panels within a red frame and below a broad green ceiling band. The maximum height of the group is 47 cm. and the maximum width is 40 cm.

The dominant panel border is a thick yellow stripe (14 to 20 mm. wide). Within each yellow border is a thin green stripe (5 to 6 mm. wide) which is spaced 31 to 45 mm. from the yellow. There is also a pattern of four round green pellets placed diagonally between the yellow and green corners, with a further pellet on either side of the green corner, similar to those in the East Room. The two YELLOW/green bordered panels are spaced 108 mm. apart with a vertical red stripe (8 mm. wide) placed centrally between them. This vertical red stripe rises to meet a horizontal red stripe (9 mm. wide) which lies 57 mm. above the thick yellow stripes. Higher still there is a grey-green ceiling band (approx. 65 mm. wide) which is itself 68 mm. above the horizontal red stripe. There is then a zone of white above the ceiling band which extends for a minimum distance of 16 mm. The average thickness of the plaster is 6 cm. and traces of orange clay still adhere to the backing showing that the group had once surfaced a clay wall.

It is clear from this group that a YELLOW/green bordered panel must have been a minimum of 170 mm. wide and a minimum of 245 mm. in height.

Group 32 (not illustrated) (DV–3049).

The 27 fragments in this group were found scattered close to the south wall of the West Room and are part of the West Room dado. One fragment shows a horizontal black band (6 cm. wide) above the dado. This group can be interpreted as demolition of the lower zone of the south wall of the room.

Group 33 (not illustrated) (DV–9837).

This represents a general demolition scatter found throughout the room. It is a large group containing 323 fragments of painted plaster, some 96 of which reflect the design in the West Room. Of these, 40 show a thick yellow stripe (18 mm. wide), 26 show a thin red stripe (5 mm. to 10 mm. wide) and 16 fragments have a thin green stripe (6 mm. wide). Another four of the fragments show the thick yellow stripe spaced between 29 and 50 mm. from the thin red stripe. There is also a fragment showing a thick yellow stripe corner with two green pellets. All these fragments are consistent with YELLOW/green bordered white panels within a red frame as seen in Group 31. A further nine fragments are West Room dado and dado band.

The remaining 227 fragments are either uncharacteristic or unidentifiable. Nineteen of them are of South Corridor-type, nine are of East Room-type, while 57 fragments are of the brightly coloured pigments which may derive from a structure to the north of the excavation. Another 27 fragments are unidentifiable red zones and stripes, some of which may represent South Corridor designs and some of which may have come from door or window surrounds. Finally, 115 fragments (36% of 323) are of scratched white plaster, some of which seem to have been scorched.

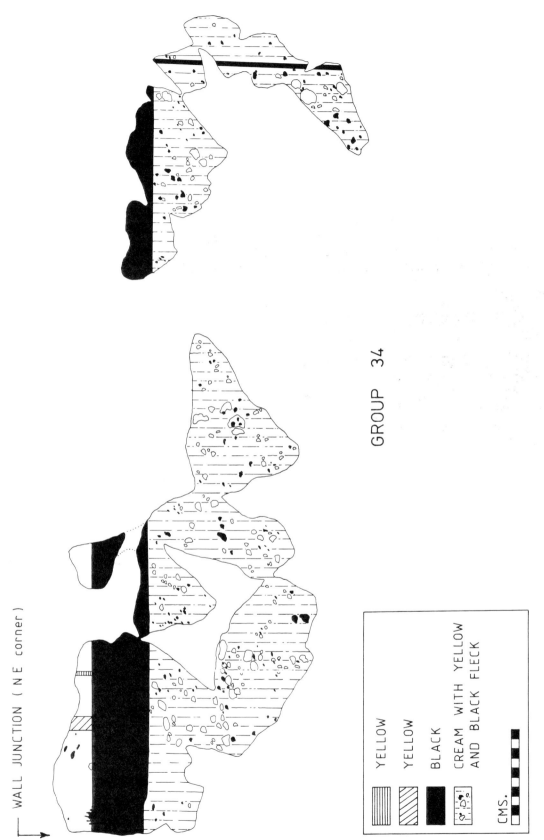

GROUP 34

WALL JUNCTION (N E corner)

YELLOW

YELLOW

BLACK

CREAM WITH YELLOW
AND BLACK FLECK

CMS.

Fig. 100. *Drawing of assembled groups of painted wall-plaster from the West Room of the Clay Walled Building C10 (Period VII), Group 34.*

Group 34 (Figs. 100 and 101) (DV–9890).

This group was found in the north-east area of the West Room and is interpreted as demolition of its north and east walls. It sealed Groups 31 and 35. Of the 118 fragments found, 33 are of West Room dado and this includes a largely articulated assemblage (maximum 790 mm. wide by 345 mm. in height) showing important design features (Fig. 101). This came from the east wall adjacent to, and including, the north-east corner of the room. It shows the minimum height of the dado to be 24 cm. Several of the fragments show a thin, black vertical stripe (5 mm. wide) on the dado but as these fragments do not join the rest it is not possible to determine how far it is from the wall junction. This dado stripe is a minimum of 21 cm. long.

Bordering the dado is a 6 cm. wide horizontal black dado band. Above this two vertical stripes on a white ground meet the dado band at right angles. The first stripe is yellow (15 mm. thick) and is 108 mm. away from the wall junction. Beside this is a green stripe (5 mm. wide) which is 44 mm. away from the yellow stripe. A zone of white extends for a minimum of 37 mm. from the green stripe. These stripes can be interpreted as the left hand lower corner of a yellow bordered panel immediately adjacent to the north-east wall junction on the east wall of the room. The thickness of the plaster varies from 18 mm. at the corner junction up to 55 mm. at the other end of the group.

Six more fragments of wall junction were also found which had fallen from the upper area of the wall. Five of these show a red stripe (minimum 5 mm. wide) running down the wall junction. The remaining fragment, together with the illustrated Group 34 (Figs. 100 and 101), has no such red stripe.

The thick yellow stripe is well represented on 13 fragments and the thin red corner stripe on five more. One fragment shows the thin red stripe to be 5 cm. away from the thick yellow stripe and the presence of one green pellet beside the yellow stripe suggests the top corner of a panel. Another fragment of thick yellow stripe corner is very worn and no pellets are visible. A further three fragments show the thick yellow stripe to be 4.3 cm. away from the thin green stripe. All the above fragments are consistent with the design on the large articulated Group 31 (Figs. 99 and 101).

Some 56 fragments are either uncharacteristic or unidentifiable and include the following:- one fragment which may have come from the West Corridor dado, nine fragments of unidentified stripes and zones of red, dark red and grey-green, (one of these was a red stripe or zone minimum 24 mm. wide on plaster applied to a fragment of box flue tile), and 18 fragments of the distinctive pigments and designs which seem to come from a structure to the north of the excavation. The remaining 28 fragments were white.

Group 35 (not illustrated) (DV–9891).

The seven fragments in this group were sealed between Group 34 (above) and Group 31 (below). All the fragments are of the distinctive pigments and designs which seem to have come from a structure to the north of the site.

RECONSTRUCTION OF THE PAINTED DESIGN IN THE WEST ROOM (Fig. 101).

The reconstruction of the painted design in the West Room is largely based on the *in situ* dado (Group 30) in the south-east corner of the room and the articulated fallen plaster (Groups 31 and 34). The composite reconstruction suggests a dado and dado band surmounted by upright rectangular white panels with YELLOW/green striped borders enclosed within an overall thin red stripe frame. Above the panels a wide white zone was divided horizontally by a broad ceiling band.

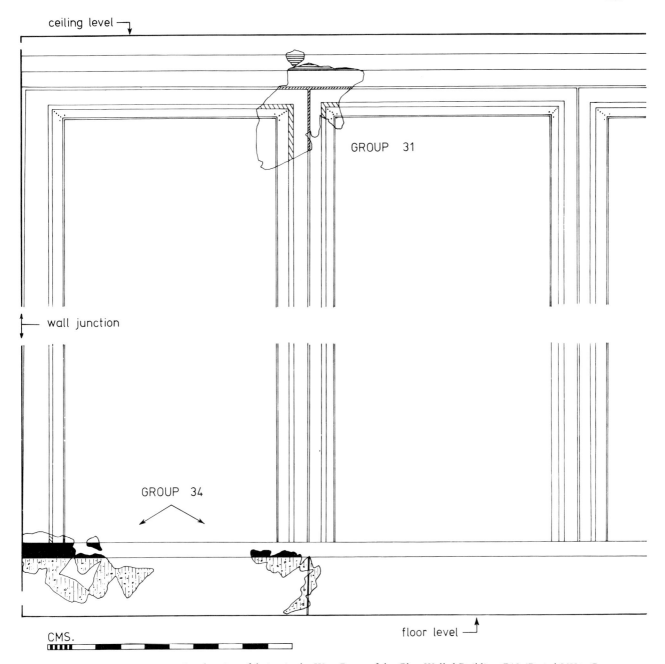

Fig. 101. *Composite reconstruction drawing of design in the West Room of the Clay Walled Building C10 (Period VII), Groups 31 and 34.*

The Dado and Dado Band

Fragments of dado found throughout the surviving area of the room were similar to the *in situ* dado (Group 30), i.e. a cream ground over-flecked with random splashes of black and yellow. This suggests a single dado colour scheme throughout the room.

A thin black vertical stripe (5 mm. wide) was seen on fallen fragments of dado, but did not appear below the dado band junctions of the thick yellow and thin green stripes seen in Group 34.

It is therefore possible that it emphasised the red framing stripe and not the panel borders as seen in the South Corridor.

The minimum height of the dado was 24 cm. to where it was bordered by a horizontal black dado band 6 cm. wide.

The Panel Area

Above the dado there were upright rectangular white panels with double coloured borders on three sides, the fourth (lower) side being formed by the dado band. The borders consisted of a thick yellow stripe (about 20 mm. wide) enclosing a thin green stripe (about 5 mm. wide). Both panel borders were then enclosed within an overall red stripe (about 10 mm. wide) which framed the top and sides of the panels. Several fragments of wall junction showed this stripe running down the wall junctions towards the dado band. The red stripe was not seen on Group 34 (Fig. 100), although possibly it had wandered slightly from its designated path at that point.

It is clear that two YELLOW/green bordered panels were adjacent to each other towards the centre of the north wall (Group 31) and that there was another YELLOW/green bordered panel beside the northern corner of the east wall (Group 34). It seems reasonable to suppose that the rest of the panel borders were also YELLOW/green and the large quantity of stripes reflecting these colours found throughout the surviving area of the room seems to support this.

The top corners of the panels were embellished with a diagonal row of four round green pellets linking the yellow and green angles. An additional pellet was placed on either side of the green corner. The centre of the panels seems to have been undecorated.

The actual width of the panels is unknown although a minimum width of 17 cm. is clear (Group 31). If all the panels were 108 mm. apart (this distance occurs in Groups 31 and 34), then four panels with an overall width of about 1.00 m. each would fit the east wall of the West Room which was 4.52 m. long. This largely agrees with the South Corridor where an average panel width of 97 cm. is established. All four walls were probably similar and any door openings would have replaced one of the panels.

The height of the panels is not known, although a minimum height of 245 mm. is clear (Group 31). With a possible floor-to-ceiling height of about 2.30–2.50 m. the panels could have been about 1.75 m. in height from the dado band as calculated for the East Room.

There must have been at least one door-opening in this room, but its position is not known. If door-openings corresponded with the inner green stripe of the panel borders, as seems likely, then they would have been about 86 cm. wide and about 1.90 m. in height.

The Ceiling Band

The broad 65 mm. wide grey-green band found (Group 31) is interpreted as a ceiling band. It was separated from the thick yellow border stripe of the panels by a gap of 134 mm. The distance above to the ceiling was at least 16 mm., but this may have been about 5–10 cm. to correspond with the East Room. It is interesting to note that the dado band and the ceiling band were roughly the same width as noted in the East Room. None of the fallen plaster was identified as having come from a ceiling.

3) DISCUSSION

The Roman painted plaster found during the Bingo Hall site excavation consisted of 6,427 scattered fragments and collapsed sections, as well as several *in situ* areas. The *in situ* plaster, together with some 2,161 (34%) of the fallen fragments formed part of the decoration of Phase II of the Clay Walled Building. The remaining 4,266 (66%) fragments await further study. About 300 of these form a distinctive group displaying blues, greens, pinks and browns which may derive from unexcavated structures north of the site. The remainder largely consists of material dumped on this site from elsewhere in Roman Dover.

The key groups of painted plaster described (Groups 1–35) include both the *in situ* areas and the fallen fragments relating to Phase II of the Clay Walled Building. These provided sufficient information for the reconstruction of two rooms (the East Room and the West Room) to ceiling-level and also the South Corridor to panel-top level. Reconstruction of the design in the West Corridor is uncertain.

The Painted Plaster Design in the Clay Walled Building

The overall design was a simple, repetitive scheme throughout the known rooms and corridors of the building, although it varied in detail from area to area. The basic scheme consisted of a marbled dado surmounted by a horizontal dado band. The white field above this, which extended to ceiling-level, was divided into symmetrical, upright rectangular panels by coloured stripes and lines, with the lowest side of each panel being formed by the dado band. Both of the rooms found had a broad, horizontal ceiling band above the panels, but this was not seen in the corridors. Door and window surrounds may have been outlined in broad bands of dark red. No evidence of ceiling decoration was found.

The dados differed slightly in each of the rooms and corridors although they were basically similar in technique. In each a background colour was stippled with one or two other colours to produce a zone of marbled appearance, limited by a horizontal dado band and sometimes embellished with vertical stripes. The colours, proportions and decorative elements varied from area to area. The dado in the East Room was narrow, being only 30 cm. in height, including the dado band, above floor level while the dado in the South Corridor was 50 cm. in height, again including the dado band. Also, the four areas studied produced four different combinations of colour as follows:-

1) pale brownish-yellow flecked with red and limited by a dark red dado band in the South Corridor
2) either white or pale pink flecked with dark red and yellow and limited by a dado band of unknown colour in the West Corridor
3) mottled red wash with grey-green fleck and limited by a grey-green dado band in the East Room
4) cream flecked with black and yellow and limited by a black dado band in the West Room.

In the South Corridor and the West Room the dados were further embellished with occasional narrow vertical stripes either singly (West Room), or in pairs (South Corridor). In both cases these stripes were the same colour as the dado band. None was seen in the East Room and their presence in the West Corridor remains uncertain. In the South Corridor they respect the inner panel border stripes whereas in the West Room they appear to respect a continuous red framing stripe which encloses the panels.

The widths of the dado bands also varied, being about 4 cm. and 6 cm. wide in the East and West Rooms, respectively, but only 2 cm. wide in the South Corridor. It should be noted that in these areas the dado bands (and vertical dado stripes where applicable) were always in one of the colours used for the marbled overfleck.

In the South Corridor and in both of the rooms the panel decoration was achieved by varying arrangements of thick and thin stripes. In the South Corridor each panel had a double border formed by a thick stripe (about 2 cm.), enclosing a thinner stripe (about 5 mm.) which was of a different colour and which was about 4 cm. away from it. The three colour combinations which followed in sequence along the wall were RED/yellow, GREEN/red and YELLOW/green. In the West Room similarly proportioned panel borders were in turn enclosed by a third stripe in red (about 1 cm. wide) which was presumably continuous around the room both above and between the panels and about 5–6 cm. away from them, including the wall junctions. In the East Room the proportions of the panel borders were again similar although here the double border enclosed a thin black line (about 2 mm. wide) at least in the upper zone of the panels. This was 25 mm. away from the inner stripe. Other colour combinations may have followed in sequence here as in the South Corridor.

In both of the rooms and also in the South Corridor the panel tops were embellished with diagonal, descending rows of three or four pellets linking corresponding corners within each panel border. A further pellet was positioned on either side of the inner corner and sometimes another within it. These pellets always took the colour of the inner, narrower stripe. In the East Room, where a third inner black line was present, the pellets did not extend down as far as the corner of the line. The pellets were roughly round in the South Corridor and West Room, but were an inverted tear-shape in the East Room.

The East and West Rooms both had broad ceiling bands which were about 45 mm. wide (East Room) and 60 mm. wide (West Room) and which were above the panel area, but below the ceiling junction. These broad bands appeared to compliment the broad dado bands in each of the two rooms as they were of the same width. No such decorative element was noted in the South Corridor.

The panels, including the coloured border stripes, are calculated as about 97–100 cm. in width and were probably spaced about 9–11 cm. from each other. This would allow four panels per wall in each of the two rooms and at least eleven panels along the known length of the south wall of the South Corridor.

The height of the panels is unknown, but is calculated as about 1.50 m. from the dado band in the South Corridor and about 1.75 m. from the dado band in the rooms. This is based on a presumed floor-to-ceiling height of about 2.20–2.50 m.

One group of fallen plaster found in the South Corridor (Group 8) displays a broad, dark red band 115 mm. wide which is interpreted as the frame of a door-opening. Such frames exist around door-openings in the adjacent Painted House and were probably also part of the design in the Clay Walled Building. It seems reasonable to suppose that a door-opening could replace a panel and that small, rectangular windows would have been sited above the panel areas without affecting the continuity of the design.

Two types of graffiti occur in the Clay Walled Building. The first type appears to be letters painted in black onto the wet plaster along the tops of GREEN/red panels and YELLOW/green panels in the South Corridor. Some of the letters have 'dragged' the wet plaster surface. In two cases the lettering is above the panels and in one case it is between the panel border stripes. It has not yet been deciphered.

The other type of graffiti has been scratched into the dry surface of the plaster with a sharp instrument and this varies from fragments of writing, to small 'doodles' and also parts of larger drawings. In some cases, particularly in the South Corridor, the plaster was scored by innumerable random lines as if it had been 'keyed' ready for a new plaster surface that was never applied. Some of the fragments, again particularly those from the South Corridor, also showed considerable weathering and plant-pitting as if the structure had been exposed to the elements for some time before demolition.

Colours and Painting Technique in the Clay Walled Building

Five basic colours were used being red, green, yellow, black and white although there were variations in colour tones, possibly achieved by mixing pigments.

There were three reds:-
1) a deep red used for the stripes in all areas
2) a darker red used for the dado band in the South Corridor and for the door surrounds
3) a deep pink-red used for the ceiling band in the East Room.

There were two greens:-
1) a deep leaf green used for the stripes
2) a grey-green used for the ceiling band in the West Room and also for the dado band and fleck in the East Room

There were two yellows:-
1) a strong canary yellow used for the stripes
2) a pale brownish yellow used as a background colour for the dado in the South Corridor

The application of the paint varied from a thin wash (East Room dado) to a thick opaque layer of paint (door surrounds). Apart from the over-flecking of the dados the pigments were generally applied singly. In several places it is possible to see score-marks in the plaster under the paint, presumably to act as guide lines for the artist. The black lettering along the top of the panels in the South Corridor was done when the plaster was still wet, indicating a true fresco technique. Some of the stripes have smudge marks beside them where a rule may have been pulled away carelessly, thus smearing the paint. In fact, various smudge marks, drips of paint, slight overlaps, poorly executed corners and generally imprecise measuring of the design elements combine to create a somewhat casual appearance. This may in part be accounted for by the speed at which the painting was necessarily carried out in fresco, but judging by the simplicity of the design it may also be possible that these two rooms and corridors were not considered important enough to merit a more elaborate (and expensive) decorative scheme.

Parallels

The geometric design scheme in the Clay Walled Building is perhaps one of the simplest of a range of Roman wall-painting styles found during excavations in Dover and is dated A.D. 210–270. It contrasts with the *in situ* design scheme in Rooms 2–4 of the Painted House which is far more elaborate.

The general concept of the Clay Walled Building wall-plaster (i.e. a stippled dado, limited by a dado band and surmounted by rectangular panels formed by coloured lines and stripes on a white ground) is, however, similar to other groups of wall-plaster found in Dover:-

1) *in situ* in the North Passage of the Painted House (see above)
2) fallen fragments from the Tufa Block Building
3) fallen fragments from the Painted House (see above Subject 36) which seem to have derived from the external walls and which are composed of plaster fabric Type C
4) the collapsed clay wall of a large Roman timber-framed building on the Gaol Lane site (publication pending). There, too, a graffito in black paint had been applied along the tops of the panels as in the South Corridor of the Clay Walled Building.

The first three of the above four groups all pre-date the Clay Walled Building.

Geometric decorative schemes based on upright, rectangular panels above a dado and dado band have been found on other sites in Britain, notably at Verulamium (Ref. 112) where they are represented in all periods. In general they are far more elaborate than the designs in the Clay Walled Building.

One of the simplest forms that such geometric decorative schemes can take consists of coloured lines on a white ground above a dado and dado band as found in Dover. A fourth century example of this type of simple, linear decoration was found in a Roman villa at Iwerne Minster, Dorset (Ref. 113). A photograph of the *in situ* wall-plaster there taken in 1897, however, shows that the decoration was slightly more elaborate than in the Clay Walled Building with the addition of foliage between the panels.

A Roman villa at Druten, near Nijmegen in the Netherlands (Ref. 114) has good parallel designs. There, it would appear that three decorative schemes, reconstructed from fallen fragments recovered from different areas of the excavation, shared similar design characteristics. In each case a stippled dado, limited by a dado band, was surmounted by a white field divided into upright, rectangular panels by varying arrangments of coloured lines and stripes. Apart from the pelleted upper panel corners in at least one case, the panels were otherwise undecorated, as in the Clay Walled Building. The villa had fallen into decay by the late-second century A.D. indicating that the wall decoration was earlier.

Fragments of fallen plaster recovered from both the Legionary Fortress and the *Canabae Legionis* at Nijmegen (Ref. 115) also appear to have formed part of such simple decorative schemes and may be late-first to early-second century. At Herculaneum, in Italy, an example of a simple, linear panel design on a white ground above a dado band and stippled dado was found in an upstairs room at the Casa de bicentenario (Ref. 116). There, however, the panel centres were embellished with coloured roundels whereas in the Clay Walled Building the panel centres were undecorated.

In Kent, the linear type of painted scheme found in the Clay Walled Building, has recently been published from the Lullingstone Roman Villa. There, the panel area was subdivided into smaller rectangles by yellow, green and red lines. Each rectangle so created was also embellished, as at Dover, with pellet decoration in both the upper and lower corners. Although there are minor differences in concept between the two sites, it is just possible that the panels in the Clay Walled Building could be reconstructed in a similar manner.

D). THE WALL-PLASTER AND PIGMENT ANALYSES FROM THE ROMAN HOUSE

By Graham Morgan, Dip. Cons., M.Phil., FIIC.

(a) THE MORTAR SAMPLES

Some 13 small mortar samples (lettered A-K) were collected from Dover and subjected to analysis. Each sample was necessarily below 100 gms. (the British Standard minimum weight requirement), but the results are none-the-less of considerable comparative value. Visual separation produced four basic groups, ignoring the paint and intonacco, as follows:-

Mortar Group 1   A white mortar on a white mortar: Samples A, G and probably E1 and E2
Mortar Group 2   A white mortar on a buff mortar: Samples B, C, F, K
Mortar Group 3   A buff mortar with chalk, a single layer: Samples D1 and D2.
Mortar Group 4   A group of fairly similar mortars with quantities of tile: Samples H, I and J.

This grouping partly confirms the earlier classification of mortars carried out by Peter Keller, where Sample A is identified as the mortar from the internal walls of the Painted House; Sample B is the mortar from the ceilings of the Painted House and Sample D the mortar used on the external walls of the House. Most of the other samples seem to be mortars introduced onto the site in fairly small quantities. These samples were subject to analysis of lime content and the residues left, after the dissolution of the lime, used for particle size distribution and geological identification.

The particle size distribution curves, with the exception of D, show general similarity, of only partly sorted mainly angular material. This may be beach deposit, but local material actually from Dover beaches has not been examined. The material present in the larger particles (2 mm. and over) is mainly; flint, quartz, 'iron stone', silica fossils, and tile. The finer particles are mainly; quartz sand, flint, glauconite and silica/silt. The glauconite may have come from lower chalk deposits, either from the beach sand or from chalk used in the aggregate. Varying quantities of chalk were noticed in all samples, usually not more than 10% and grass or straw was also used in varying amounts. There were traces of a lower mud layer on sample F, with a widely spaced grooved impression. Sample I had a grooved box tile impression on the rear.

Description of mortar samples

paint	intonacco	first layer	second layer
A) red on yellow on	white	off white	coarse white
	0.5–0.75 mm.	8 mm.	38 mm.
% lime	81%	68%	51%
B) burnished red	white	white	buff with straw
	0.75–1.0 mm.	12 mm.	15 mm.
% lime	90%	82%	45%
C) yellow & green	white	white	buff
	0.75 mm.	10 mm.	25 mm.
% lime	76%	47%	41%
D) red	white	off white	buff with chalk
	0.5–.75 mm.	1.5–3.0 mm.	25 mm.
% lime	93%	88%	73%
D2) 1 grey & yellow	white	off white	buff with chalk
	1 mm.	6 mm.	25 mm.
lime %	96%	88%	75%
E1) red	white	coarse buff	none ?
	3.5–8.5 mm.	18 mm.	
lime %	94%	43%	combined layers ?
E2) 1 white on red	white	coarse buff	none
	0.25 mm.	11 mm.	
lime %	——	48%	
F) red, yellow, white on pink, 0.3 mm.	white	off white	buff with chalk on a mud layer
	1 mm.	16 mm.	18 mm.
lime %	98%	67%	35%

paint	intonacco	first layer	second layer	
G) red, yellow, dark red, pale green	white 1 mm.	white 8 mm.	coarse white 18 mm. + 15 mm.	
lime %	90%	66%	52%	52%
H) white 0.1 mm.	white 0.2 mm	white with tile 20 mm.	none —	
lime %	——	35%		
I) red/brown, yellow	white 0.75 mm.	off white 4 mm.	pink/tile 24 mm	
lime %	93%	43%	39%	
J) none	white 0.75 mm.	chalky white 3.5 mm.	pink/tile 28 mm.	
lime %	——	72%	48%	
K) pink traces	white 1 mm.	coarse white 26 mm	none —	
lime %	69%	63%	—	

b) THE PIGMENT SAMPLES

These were subject to visual description for colour and order of paint application, as well as mortar type and layer thickness. The pigments were then analysed by micro chemical tests, being confirmed by X-ray diffraction where necessary.

1) DV 2307 71 pink
   burnished red on pink on white int. on buff mortar on buff mortar.
   0.3–0.5mm   0.75mm   10mm   50mm
   red ochre or brick dust and lime, the upper surface may be richer in ochre but the burnishing also has a darkening affect.

2) DV 2308 104 blue
   blue on grey on white int. on white mortar.
               0.75mm   9mm
   Egyptian blue on lime + carbon.

3) DV 2306 92 dark red/maroon
   red on white int. white mortar on buff mortar with straw.
       1mm   11mm   17mm
   red ochre. The white mortar contains fragments of oyster shell.

4) DV 4381 62 vermilion
   red on pink (int.?) on white/grey mortar with straw.
   0.1mm   0.3mm   18mm
   cinnabar on red ochre + lime

5) DV 2342 34 orange
   orange on white int. on white mortar.
           1mm   17mm
   red/yellow ochres

6) DV 1158 17 orange red
   orange red on buff sandy int. on white interface on white mortar.
             1mm   0.1–0.2mm   18mm
   red ochre or brick dust

7) DV 2307 76 black
pale green/grey on black on pale pink on white int. on white
0.75mm
mortar on white mortar.
15mm   8mm
green earth + lime + carbon on lime + red ochre

8) DV 2307 76 pale pink
burnished pale pink on white int. on white mortar on white mortar.
                0.75mm   9mm   15mm
lime + red ochre with possible traces of cinnabar.

9) DV 2307 76 mustard/yellow
brown/grey on cream with blue specks on pink on white int.
                            0.1mm   0.5mm
on white mortar on white mortar.
    7mm   16mm
red ochre + carbon on lime + yellow ochre + Egyptian blue (pale green ?)
on lime + red ochre and possible traces of cinnabar.

10) DV 9607 119 yellow
burnished yellow on white int. on white mortar on white mortar.
        0.15mm   0.5mm   12mm   30mm
yellow ochre

11) DV 2307 71 pink
burnished dull pink on white int. on white mortar on white mortar.
        0.1mm   0.5mm   12mm   30mm
red ochre or brick dust.

12) DV 2308 195 cream
white on white int. on white mortar on white mortar.
        0.5mm   7mm   8mm
lime with traces of brick dust

13) DV 2350 38 lime green adjacent to maroon
pale green on pale grey/blue on red on white int. on white mortar
                            0.5mm   15mm
on white mortar.
        18mm
lime + green earth + traces of Egyptian blue on lime + carbon + Egyptian blue on red
ochre.

14) DV 2350 38 light grey
pale grey/blue on white int. on white mortar
        0.5mm   15mm
lime + carbon + Egyptian blue

15) DV 2366 112a green
green on pale grey on white int. on white mortar on buff mortar.
        0.5mm   8mm   10mm
green earth + some carbon on lime + carbon + some Egyptian blue traces.

The pigments are natural materials, with the exception of Egyptian blue which is manufactured and quite common. Red ochre or haematite, or in a very impure form brick or tile dust, varies in colour from dark brown to red, yellow ochre or limonite varies from yellow to brown. The carbon may be soot or charcoal, usually only being distinguishable if in large particles. The green is glauconite or green earth, and particles were found in the mortar itself, probably from the lower chalk. White was here pure lime, probably made from chalk. It was also used to dilute the darker colours. The cinnabar (vermilion in its artificial form) is mercury sulphide, usually imported from Spain and considered to be very expensive. It was originally considered to be very rare in Roman Britain, but the present study has already shown that it was used on at least a dozen British sites. It tends to be purer in the earlier periods, being diluted with red ochre towards the third and fourth centuries. Here it is pure suggesting an earlier date. The presence of an intonacco layer suggests that the true fresco technique was used, pigments being applied to the wet plaster, intonacco. Most of the samples show brush marks but some were burnished on, before the plaster had completely set. The mortar backings of the pigment samples correspond with the mortar samples, being of the same general type; pigment on intonacco on off-white mortar on coarser white mortar or white on buff mortar. However DV 4381 62 and DV 1158 17 are neither exactly comparable with the fabric types shown amongst the mortars.

ANALYTICAL RESULTS

1) INTONACCO

Lab. No.	Mortar Type	Thickness in mm.	% lime	Aggregate/filler.
18	A	0.5–0.75	81	Chert
21	B	0.75–1.0	90	
26	D	0.5–0.75	93	quartz grain
29	D	1.0	96	Chert
35	F	1.0	98	
38	G	1.0	90	
42	I	0.75	93	quartz grain
47	K	1.0	69	Chert

2) UPPER MORTAR LAYER

19	A	8	68	flint/sand
22	B	12	82	
24	C	10	47	
27	D	3	88	
30	D	6	88	
33	E	18	43	
34	E	11	48	
36	F	16	66	
38	G	8	66	
41	H	20	35	flint/tile
43	I	4	43	flint/sand
45	J	3.5	72	flint/tile
48	K	26	63	flint/sand

3) LOWER MORTAR LAYER

20	A	38	51	flint/sand
23	B	15	45	
25	C	25	41	
28	D	25	73	
31	D	25	75	
37	F	18	35	
40	G	18 + 15	52	
44	I	15 + 9	39	flint/tile
46	J	28	48	flint/tile

Samples of mortar from the Painted House wall, floor 'opus signinum' and samples of chalk were also analysed. The results were as follows.

Wall Mortar

This was composed of large flint pebbles with flint and sand gravel. It contained 75% lime, including perhaps up to 50% hard chalk or lime. The very high silt/silica content (37% of the insoluble) suggests a lower chalk or lias limestone source for the lime, although it may be due to the presence of large amounts of chalk in the aggregate.

Floor Mortar

This was mainly coarse tile with 31% lime.

Chalk

Unstratified samples of chalk from the excavation were analysed. They contained about 97.5% calcium carbonate, with the remainder being grey silt. This chalk analysis compares favourably with the intonacco lime content and may well have been the source of the lime.

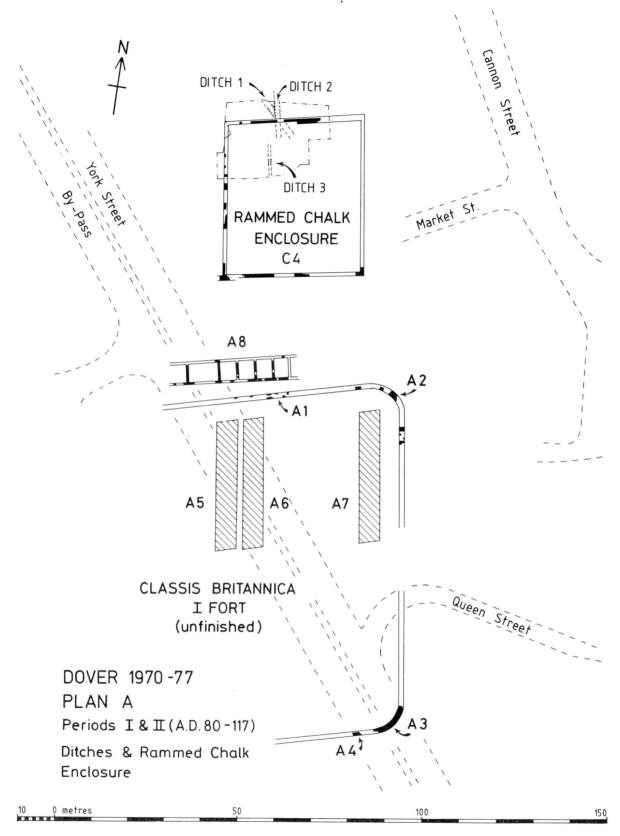

Fig. 102. *Period Plan A showing features and structures (Periods I and II).*

CHAPTER V

DISCUSSION OF PERIODS I–VIII

The extensive excavations on the Bingo Hall and Painted House sites at various times between 1970 and 1977 disclosed a long and complicated history of structural development, from the early-second century to the fourth century A.D. This included the construction of large sections of several prime buildings situated north of the *Classis Britannica* forts (Ref. 117). Indeed the overall programme of work by the Unit over a wider area has revealed more major buildings and to these extra-mural buildings can be added glimpses of at least five others seen at various times over the past 200 years. The first was seen under St. Mary's Church in 1778 (Ref. 118); the second in Market Square in 1881 (Ref. 119); a third close by in 1950 (Ref. 120); a fourth near Adrian Street in 1949 (Ref. 121) and a fifth found by the Unit east of the fort in 1974 (Ref. 122). From this it is certain that an area of at least five hectares (12½ acres) contains Roman buildings, several of first quality, in what may be regarded as a large civil settlement, or *vicus*, attached to the fort.

It seems clear that this settlement was bordered on the west side by the principal road running out of the north gate of the *Classis Britannica* II fort inland towards Canterbury and London. The east side was marked by the banks of the tidal River Dour, but the north side has not yet been fully defined while the southern limit clearly extended as far as Snargate Street. Collectively, these fine buildings taken with the naval fort, the extensive harbour and the two masonry lighthouses on its flanking cliffs, constituted a great new naval base, very probably to be identified with the *Novus Portus* of Ptolomy (Ref. 123). No later than the mid-second century Dover had superceded Richborough (Ref. 124) and become the Gateway of Roman Britain.

PERIOD I.

The earliest features on the Bingo Hall and Painted House sites were the three small ditches (p. 13), which date from the late-first and early-second centuries. These probably correspond with a small ditch traced for 36 m. on the Battle of Britain Homes site in 1971, beneath the *Classis Britannica* II fort (Kent Monograph series 3, page 56) and which contained several sherds of mid-first century pottery. These shallow ditches, with perhaps others yet to be found, probably served both drainage and boundary purposes. They demonstrate limited use of the slopes above the west bank of the tidal River Dour during the second half of the first century and also prior to the construction of the *Classis Britannica* I and II forts.

One or more of these ditches on the Bingo Hall and Painted House sites could have served as the western boundary of an area containing several early chalk-block buildings, mostly found on the Cannon Street West site in 1983–85 (report pending).

PERIOD II. (Fig. 102 Plan A).

Sometime in the opening decades of the second century the rammed chalk foundations of a large walled enclosure were built across much of the Bingo Hall and Painted House sites (page

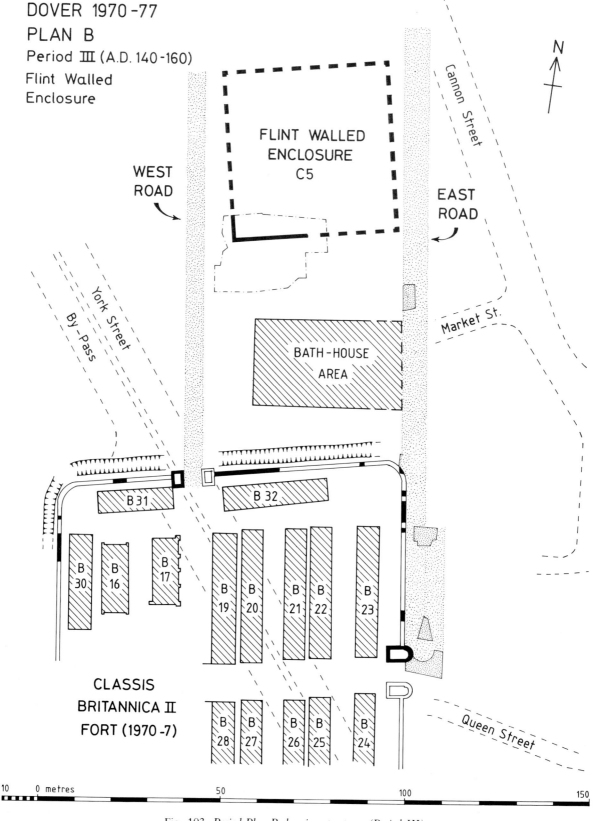

Fig. 103. *Period Plan B showing structures (Period III).*

14). This seems to have enclosed an overall area about 41.70 by 38.50 m. This enclosure corresponds in date with that for the layout of the adjacent *Classis Britannica* I fort (A1–A7) and the large unfinished building on its north side (A8). Early work has shown that the *Classis Britannica* I fort was hurriedly abandoned with only the foundations laid (perhaps in A.D. 117) and it seems likely that the (Period II) enclosure was also never finished. Certainly there was a general lack of demolition rubble on most of the sites where the rammed chalk foundations were found (Plan A) and this implies a lack of related buildings at that time.

Whilst the intended function of the unfinished *Classis Britannica* I fort is clear, thanks largely to what is built over it, it is less clear what was the intended function of the enclosure to its north. Nor is it at all clear why the foundations to the north side should be so massive, for with a width of more than 3.00 m. it was more than twice as wide as the foundations for the walls (only 1.18–1.45 m. wide) of the unfinished fort. Whilst walled compounds are known on some Roman military sites it is likely that continuing work on adjacent sites will throw more light on this interesting structure.

What seems clear, however, is that the enclosure was not laid out parallel to the north wall of the fort, which itself had been constructed as a modest parallelogram. Instead its axis seems to correspond with the grid inside the fort and to a lesser extent the external building (A8) on the north side. In this respect it would have been parallel to any conjectured road running northwards out of the unfinished fort. In detail its south-west corner lay about 31.80 m. from the fort wall and its south-east corner about 29.30 m. giving an average distance of about 30.50 m. This corresponds well with 7/8ths of an Actus p.m. (about 105 Roman feet), calculated at 30.80 m. The enclosure itself is rather less exact with its overall measurements falling close to 1⅛th Actus p.m. (about 135 Roman feet), calculated at 39.70 m. (Ref. 125)

PERIOD III (Fig. 103 Plan B).

At about A.D. 140–160 the rammed chalk foundations of the unfinished enclosure were totally superceded by other structures. The south side was buried beneath a large new military bath-house; the centre by a new road and an open area; and on the Bingo Hall and Painted House sites by a pair of integral flint walls (page 15). The latter joined at right-angles and seemed to have formed the south-west corner of another substantial walled enclosure, this time built much further to the north. It seems likely that this had an entrance on the south side which, if centrally placed, suggests an east-west width of about 45 m. It may be significant that this is only slightly greater than the width of the earlier and (unfinished) Rammed Chalk Enclosure, which it so clearly replaced, but at a point some 40 m. further north. The suggested similarity in size and form could indicate a similar function.

Whatever the precise function of the two joining flint walls they seem to correspond in date with the Period I occupation within the *Classis Britannica* II fort (A.D. 130–140 to A.D 155). Importantly, the north wall of this fort had been constructed some 10 m. further north than that intended for the north wall of the unfinished *Classis Britannica* I fort. Beyond this new wall the next 15 m. were occupied by the fort ditch and a wide east-west road and the next 23 m. by the garrison's new external bath-house. The north side of the bath-house was flanked by another road and an open area, totalling another 21.50 m. The south wall of the Flint Walled Enclosure was thus some 59.60 m. north of the completed fort wall. This was almost twice the distance of the Rammed Chalk Enclosure from the unfinished *Classis Britannica* I fort, recorded as about 31 m. (see above). At 59.60 m. this corresponds roughly with 1¾ Actus p.m. (a distance of 210 Roman feet) calculated at 61.80 m. and this hints at regulated planning.

It must also be significant that the line of the north wall of the Period II enclosure was followed very closely by the line of the south wall of the Period III enclosure, the two being almost superimposed. On the general assumption that the enclosures were similar, as the limited evidence could suggest, then the Flint Walled Enclosure may also have been roughly square with

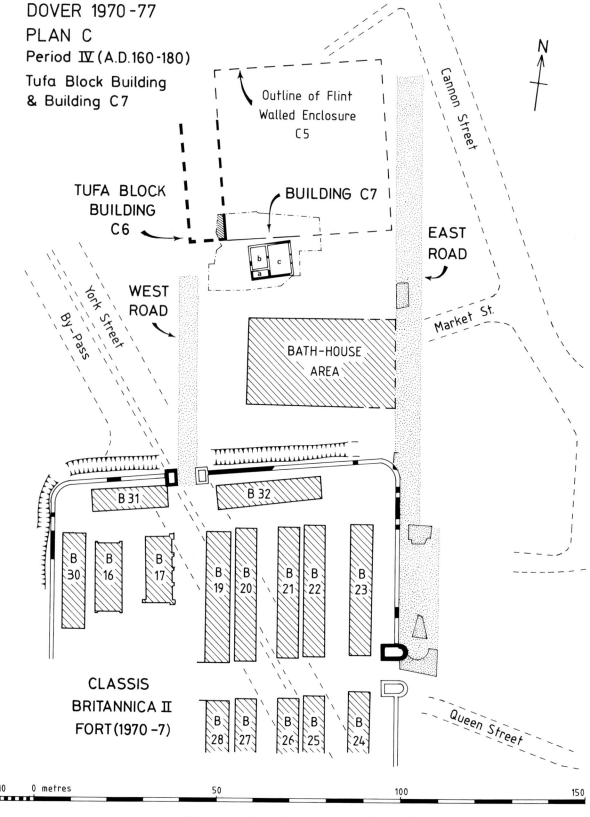

Fig. 104. *Period Plan C showing structures (Period IV).*

dimensions of say 40 or 45 m. (Plan B). The line of the west wall of the Period II enclosure was not precisely followed by the Period III enclosure, as the latter was built about 3.0 m. to the east. Presumably this change was caused by the revised layout for the completed *Classis Britannica* II fort. Nor do the west walls of the respective enclosures appear parallel. Whilst the details of the Flint Walled Enclosure are less clear, it does seem that it was swung several degrees to the north-west. This seems to have placed its south wall parallel to the fort wall, but asymmetrically to the adjacent bath-house and the two flanking roads. Coincidentally, or not, the suggested reconstructed width of the enclosure, at 45.00 m. still fits evenly between the two roads with a comfortable space on each side.

The construction of the Period III enclosure seems to have fortuitously dictated most of the subsequent planning across much of the site. Its function is also a matter of some doubt, but a walled compound is again one of the better possibilities. Only full excavation of the area to the north is likely to resolve this problem.

What is also of special interest here, in terms of regulated planning, is the position of the two Roman roads leading northwards from the fort area. The main East Road, first found in 1985, seems to project from the east wall of the fort. The main West Road, very largely destroyed by the great West Ditch of the later shore-fort, appears to have continued the *via principalis* out of the north gate of the fort. Predictably these roads appear parallel and significantly their centres lie about 60.0 m. apart. Hence, with the north wall of the fort also being about 60.0 m. from the south wall of the Flint Walled Enclosure, a neat parallelogram some 60.0 m. sq. is created. This effectively formed a small *insula* of about 1¾ Actus p.m. (210 Roman feet), calculated at 61.80 m. between these four major elements and into which the Roman military bath-house was comfortably fitted (publication pending).

PERIOD IV (Fig. 104 Plan C).

About A.D. 160–180 radical changes took place on the Bingo Hall and Painted House sites (page 17) and these appear to correspond with the Period II rebuilding work inside the *Classis Britannica* II fort. The Flint Walled Enclosure was swept away, wholly or in part, and replaced by at least two buildings. One (C7) was a good quality, rectangular building about 11.50 m. by 9.00 m. and consisted of three rooms, one probably much bigger than the other two. The walls were mortared, some internal surfaces were painted red or white and the floors were of trodden soil.

The precise function of this building is not entirely clear, but the painted walls suggest a degree of refinement and perhaps domestic use. The actual Painted House which eventually replaced it clearly had a domestic function and this could support a domestic function for building C7. Elsewhere, at Silchester (Ref. 126) and Verulamium (Ref. 127) buildings of broadly similar size and form have been located and are variously described as shops, workshops or small houses.

The second building to be constructed on this site after the removal of the Flint Walled Enclosure, was the Tufa Block Building (C6), largely cut away by the later shore-fort ditch. This was built about 6 m. north-west of Building C7, constructed in similar materials, but strangely not on the same axis. Only one heated room, later sub-divided, was found at the northern edge of the site and it is highly probable that one or more additional rooms of this structure remain to be found further north.

The calculations for the size of Room 5 of the later Painted House (see below) suggest that the Tufa Block Building may have had an east-west width of about 10 m. The presence of the great shore-fort ditch makes details uncertain, but the absence of any masonry or robber-trenches west of its western lip, provides a maximum space of about 20 m.

Most significantly, the south wall of the new Tufa Block Building coincides exactly with the line of the largely removed south wall of the Flint Walled Enclosure! Equally, the new east wall of the Tufa Block Building closely follows and over-rides the west wall of the same enclosure. Very clearly the existence of the latter determined the position of the former!

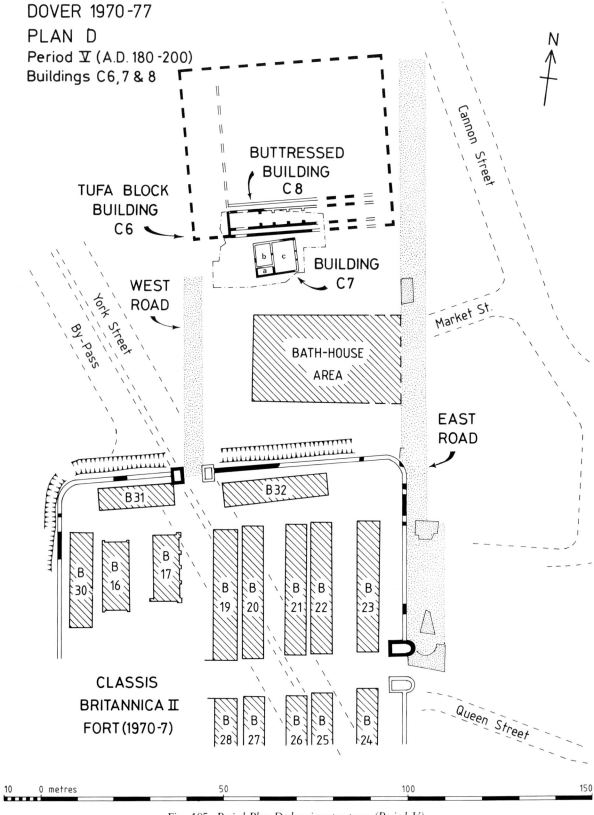

DOVER 1970-77
PLAN D
Period V (A.D. 180-200)
Buildings C6, 7 & 8

N

BUTTRESSED BUILDING C8

TUFA BLOCK BUILDING C6

BUILDING C7

Cannon Street

WEST ROAD

Market St.

York Street

By-Pass

BATH-HOUSE AREA

EAST ROAD

B31

B32

B 30

B 16

B 17

B 19

B 20

B 21

B 22

B 23

CLASSIS BRITANNICA II FORT (1970-7)

B 28

B 27

B 26

B 25

B 24

Queen Street

10   0 metres   50   100   150

Fig. 105. *Period Plan D showing structures (Period V).*

It seems likely that any connecting rooms in the Tufa Block Building followed a north-south axis, as partially dictated by the pre-existing enclosure wall and that the hypocausted room formed the south end of a large north-south range. Considering that both the Period V (Buttressed Building) and the Period VI (Painted House) structures were later butted to the Tufa Block Building, a major north-south building does seem to be implied. As such it has been conjectured on the outline plan (Fig. 104) with the same estimated length as the Flint Walled Enclosure (Period III) of 45 m. This reconstruction does, however, have the unfortunate effect of partially cutting across the line of the presumed main road into the fort. This is caused by the extended Tufa Block Building following (outside) the west wall of the earlier Flint Walled Enclosure. However, as the total north-south lengths of neither the Flint Walled Enclosure or the Tufa Block Building is known, the precise effect on the road cannot be gauged.

PERIOD V (Fig. 105 Plan D).

At about A.D. 180–200 a major new structure was built across the Bingo Hall site and this took the form of a large, internally buttressed building (C8). It lay on an east-west axis and sprang neatly from the east wall of the Period IV Tufa Block Building (C6). It was traced eastwards for a minimum of 23.62 m. Its width as found was about 7.50 m. whilst a conjectured north aisle and a fourth wall to the north would have increased the width to about 9.70 m.

Such an internally buttressed building is difficult to parallel in Britain, but it seems likely that the buttresses would have supported masonry piers and these a high and presumably heavy roof. If the walls linking the lines of buttresses were in fact sleeper-walls and the external walls (be it one or two) were solid, then an unusual basilican-type structure begins to emerge. The central 'nave' would thus have been about 4.00 m. wide and the side aisles each about 1.55 m. wide internally. It is difficult to see this building other than as a somewhat pretentious range on one side of a large courtyard, perhaps giving access from one important building, or area, to another. If so, it must have continued eastwards, perhaps to join another major building not yet found.

It seems clear from all this that the Tufa Block Building of Period IV was itself significantly large and important for this major addition to be made. The Buttressed Building was laid out to form a rough right-angle with the Tufa Block Building and this created two large linking ranges, with the original rooms forming a west range and the new Buttressed Building forming a south range. The new south range, so created, largely followed the line of the demolished south wall of the Period III enclosure and it clearly bypassed building C7, which was thus left isolated barely 1.0 m. to the south on its misaligned axis.

All this strongly suggests that the focal point of all the building work on the site (during Periods III, IV and V) was to the north beyond the limit of the excavation. Indeed there is every likelihood, Period VI considered, that the two ranges here identified formed part of either a three-sided, or even four-sided, complex of considerable size. If the Buttressed Building did serve as a link to another major building then there is a good chance that such a building was in fact the east range of such a complex. Here again the Flint Walled Enclosure of Period III may have predetermined the overall dimensions. Its presumed east wall (at 45 m.) appears too close to the East Road to allow any new (east) range to be inserted beyond it. Hence, such a conjectured east range is rather more likely to have been inserted inside the enclosure's east wall and it has been shown in this position on the reconstructed plan (Fig. 105). Whilst much of this must remain a matter of considerable conjecture it none-the-less conveniently fits the evidence for the reconstruction of the (later) newly found block eastwards of the Painted House (see Period VI, below).

It is clear that the Period V work on the Bingo Hall and Painted House sites corresponds with the *Classis Britannica* II fort (Period III) dated to A.D. 190–208.

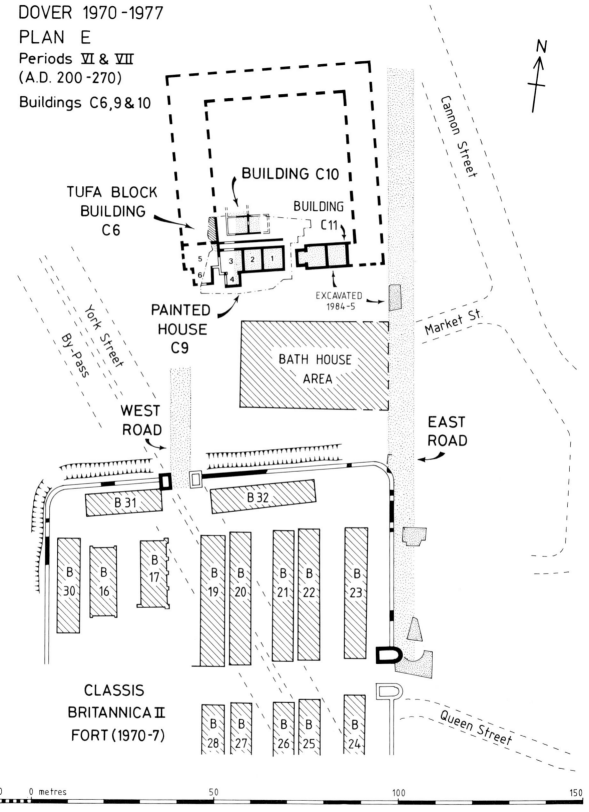

DOVER 1970 -1977
PLAN E
Periods VI & VII
(A.D. 200 -270)
Buildings C6,9 & 10

Fig. 106. Period Plan E showing structures (Periods VI and VII).

PERIOD VI (Fig. 106 Plan E).

At about A.D. 200, again corresponding with the *Classis Britannica* II fort Period III (A.D. 190–208), another major programme of building work was carried out on the Painted House and Bingo Hall sites. This saw the removal of Building C7 and also of the short-lived Buttressed Building (C8) and the construction of a major new east-west range (now known as the Painted House) in place of both. Even so the grand new range was attached to the (by then) much older Tufa Block Building (Period IV) and this again reinforces the view that the latter was a major structure in its own right. Indeed it seems highly unlikely that either the Buttressed Building (Period V) or the Painted House (Period VI) would have been attached to a minor, or lesser, structure.

The new range probably had a total length of about 28 m. and consisted of four main rooms, with a north passage and two smaller rooms attached on the south side, thus having a maximum width of about 12 m. The whole was built as part of a single operation with thick mortared walls, elaborate underfloor and wall heating, strong concrete floors and grand perspective paintings in every room. The structure probably had an upper-storey and was clearly a building of the very highest quality. Tiles stamped CLBR built new into the structure help support the view, implied by the continued occupation of the adjacent fort, that it was built by the men of the *Classis Britannica*.

It seems clear from both the scale and quality of the building and also the resources required in its construction, that the Painted House was an official building provided for some very special domestic, or social, purpose. On its own merits it seems likely that it was built either for a leading official attached to the major naval base, or more likely, as a transit residence for important officials passing to and from the Continent. The presence of the major fortified naval base with its harbours and lighthouses, highlights Dover's role, at the end of Watling Street, as the Gateway of Roman Britain. It must be that it also formed a vital link in the *cursus publicus*, the imperial posting service, with the *Classis Britannica* fleet providing the ferry-service from Dover to Boulogne. In this respect then the Painted House seems to have served the same broad function as a *mansio* and indeed some of the main structural elements could correspond. The main heated rooms may have been reception rooms and the smaller, attached rooms may have been bedrooms.

It must be worth mentioning here that the governor's transport officer, one Olus Cordius Candidus, was stationed at Dover itself! Clearly he lived at the port, either in the naval fort or in the extra-mural settlement. It is just possible, depending on his precise date, that he lived in either the building below the Painted House (C7), in the Tufa Block Building (C6), or even in the Painted House itself! Indeed his altar and shrine dedicated to the Mother Goddess of Italy, was found within only several metres of all these buildings, though in a re-used context!

The construction of the Painted House range also provides additional clues to what may lie further north and indeed greatly enhances the view that the focal point of most building operations was in that direction. Whilst the Painted House range butted to the south end of the Tufa Block Building it also extended beyond it for about 17.50 m. to the east.

After a space of about 2.50 m. another almost identical range of rooms (still under excavation) extended eastwards again (C11). The opening between the two ranges was metalled and seems to represent a minor entrance between the buildings. The probability is, the general symmetry of the main structures considered, that this entrance was centrally placed and that the newly found range of rooms also ran for about 17.50 m. before joining a conjectured east range. Coincidentally, or not, this position is largely that of the east range postulated under the Period V reconstruction and this is also shown on the Period VI building reconstruction (Fig. 106). Here the east wall of the new building is shown as being in line with the conjectured east wall of the Flint Walled Enclosure (Period III) and thus still within the limits set by the East Road. This produces a total east-west length of 55 m. for the overall range of which the Painted House seems to have formed the south-west part.

In effect this created a rather grand south range for the complex postulated in Period V and indeed goes a long way to support the idea that the complex had three or four ranges, perhaps of roughly equal length. If so, an overall rectangle of some 50–55 m. could be suggested for Period VI and this is also shown on the reconstruction (Fig. 106). Indeed a large structure of these dimensions would still fit comfortably between the main East and West Roads, though again this still leaves a problem, caused by the positioning of the Period III enclosure, of some encroachment onto the road out of the fort. Allowing for the probable widths of both the known west range and the conjectured east range (say 8–10 m. each) an internal area of about 37 m. could be suggested.

Exactly what such a grand courtyard building might represent is, until further excavation takes place, open to speculation. However, the probable role of the Painted House block as part of a *mansio* could equally apply to the whole complex. Elsewhere, as at Silchester (Ref. 128), Chignall St. James, Chelmsford (Ref. 129) and Lower Wanborough (Ref. 130), *mansiones* as official accommodation blocks for officials on the *cursus publicus*, are mostly large courtyard buildings, often 40–60 m. in size, with ranges of rooms and passages on most sides. The nearest useful parallel is only 19 km. (12 miles) away at Richborough, another major military site, where a large courtyard building has been identified as a long-established *mansio* (Ref. 131). At Richborough the *mansio*, perhaps originally at least some 50.00 m. sq., lay north-east of the known first century military installations and this is also the position at Dover. The Richborough site served as a major port-of-entry in the first and early-second centuries until its role was largely superceded when the *Classis Britannica* base was built at Dover in Hadrianic times (Ref. 132). The Richborough building was strangely never aligned on the military buildings, but its conjectured counterpart at Dover was very largely on the same axis as the two *Classis Britannica* forts! Notwithstanding these differences an official *mansio* at each site is both reasonable and likely. More than this cannot yet be said, though it must be stated that the respective plans differ in detail.

PERIOD VII (Fig. 106 Plan E).

Sometime about A.D. 210–230 an additional structure, of modest proportions, was constructed on the Bingo Hall site and altered on at least two subsequent occasions. This was a timber-framed building with clay walls, an earth floor and almost certainly of only one storey, consisting of at least three rooms and two corridors. It was built within the angle formed by the Tufa Block Building and the Painted House range. Its walls were later brightly decorated with large coloured rectangular panels.

This building underwent a partial rebuild perhaps about A.D. 230–250 (Phase II) and minor work, perhaps even as late as A.D. 250–270 (Phase III). On balance it is likely, the late date of the Painted House considered, that Period VII entirely post-dates the *Classis Britannica* II fort (abandoned in about A.D. 208) and equates with the latter's decay and gradual burial through the middle decades of the third century.

The Clay Walled Building seems to have been domestic in nature and may have served as offices or accommodation. Its total size is unknown, but its length was greater than 12.58 m. and its width much greater than 6.85 m. The insertion of such a modest building in the angle between two large masonry ranges, in an area originally intended to be open, is at once unusual. It suggests at least two things. The first is that there was a real need for extra rooms, or accommodation, or both, and secondly that space elsewhere was rather limited. In addition the rebuilding of part of this structure and the continued use of the Painted House, both through the middle decades of the third century show continued use right up until the construction of the late-Roman shore-fort, nominally in about A.D. 270. It is most interesting to note such activity during this time for the *Classis Britannica* had pulled out of Dover in about A.D. 208 and seems not to have returned. It is likely that the abandonment of the adjacent naval fort in that year caused a loss of rooms and accommodation space which was, in part, resolved by the construction of the Clay Walled Building and the continued use of the Painted House.

PERIOD VIII

Sometime between about A.D. 250–270 the biggest redevelopment of Roman Dover was carried out by army units, newly arrived in the port. Their task was to construct a major four-acre fort close to the harbour, as part of the coastal system of defences being greatly extended to combat the activities of sea-borne Saxon raiders. The scale of the defensive response, along the Channel and East Coast, highlights the large-scale of these raids already noted as a major threat in the early-third century.

The old *Classis Britannica* II fort lay in ruins and partly buried on the lower slopes of the Western Heights and was clearly identified as unsuitable. The area chosen instead lay largely to the north-east and much closer to the tidal estuary and harbour installations. Even so, the new south and west defensive walls still cut the north-east corner of the ruined naval fort and also through other intact buildings that lay in the extra-mural settlement. The main victims, so far known, were the Painted House, the Clay Walled Building and the Tufa Block Building, all of which were substantially destroyed by the west wall and ditch of the new shore-fort.

Exactly when this major event took place at Dover is of some not inconsiderable interest. The corresponding fort at Richborough (Ref. 133) seems to have been constructed about A.D. 275–280. At Dover, precise dating may eventually come from the hundreds of late-Roman coins found during the ongoing excavations within the shore-fort limits, but these await cleaning and detailed study. On the Painted House site the latest coin sealed by the fort's rampart is one of Gordianus III (A.D. 238–244) and on the Bingo Hall site, one of Severus Alexander (A.D. 222–235). However, the pottery evidence and building work suggest activity up to at least about A.D. 230–250 (Period VII Phase II) and perhaps even as late as A.D. 250–270 (Period VII Phase III). What must be highly significant, however, is the absence here of certain coins of the radiate type that are so common over most areas within the shore-fort itself. Those of Claudius II (A.D. 268–70), Tetricus I (A.D. 270–3) and Tetricus II (A.D. 270–3) are particularly common and their total absence from Period VIII deposits strongly argues a closing date before about A.D. 265–270. Indeed whilst radiates of Philip I and II (A.D. 244–9), Valerian (A.D. 254–260) and Gallienus (A.D. 253–68) are less common at Dover and elsewhere, their total absence from Period VIII deposits could also be used to argue a date prior to about A.D. 250–260! On the available evidence from these two sites, both circumstantial and material, it seems likely therefore that the demolition and fort-construction took place sometime between about A.D. 250 and A.D. 270. However, until the total evidence from the site has been studied a nominal date of A.D. 270 has been adopted.

Painted House and Bingo Hall Sites (1970–77)			Classis Britannica Fort Sites (1970–77).	
Period	Structure or Feature	Date Assigned A.D.	Structure or Feature	Date Assigned A.D.
I	Three Small Ditches (C1–C3)	Late-1st to Early-2nd centuries	One Small Ditch	Mid-1st century
II	Rammed Chalk Enclosure (C4) (unfinished)	Early-2nd century	CL.BR. I Fort (A1–A8) (unfinished)	117 ?
III	Flint Walled Enclosure (C5)	140–160	CL.BR. II Fort (B1–B95) Period I	130–140 to 155
IV	Tufa Block Building (C6) The Building Beneath the Painted House (C7)	160–180	CL.BR. II Fort Period II	163–180
V	Buttressed Building (C8)	180–200		
			CL.BR II Fort Period III	190–208
VI	Painted House (C9)	200		
VII	Clay Walled Building (C10) (Phase I–III)	210–270	Soil Forming Over Ruins Of CL.BR. II Fort	210–270
VIII	West Defences of Shore Fort. Cuts all earlier structures	270	South-West Corner of Shore Fort Cuts Ruins of CL.BR. II Fort	270

Table listing principal features and structures, in period and date order, on part of the *Extra-mural* settlement (Painted House and Bingo Hall sites) and also on the *Classis Britannica* fort sites.

BIBLIOGRAPHICAL REFERENCES

REF. NO.	SUBJECT	AUTHOR	PUBLICATION
1	Richborough superceded	Cunliffe, B. (ed)	*Excavation of the Roman Fort at Richborough, Kent V* (1968), p. 243.
2	Novus Portus	Ptolemaeus, C.	*Geography*, Books I–VIII.
3	The Classis Britannica Fort	Philp, B.J.	*The Excavation of the Roman Forts of the Classis Britannica at Dover, 1970–1977* (1981)
4	Timber-framed Sea Wall, 1855	Elstead, W.P.	*Arch. Jnl.*, 13 (1856), p. 101.
5	*Classis Britannica* Base	–	See Ref. No. 3.
6	Floor Mosaics	Neal, D.S.	*Roman Mosaics in Britain* (1981), p. 19.
7	Late-Roman shore-forts	Johnson, D.E.	*The Saxon Shore, C.B.A. Research Report No. 18* (1977), p. 1–6.
8	Richborough earlier Roman buildings	–	See Ref. No. 1, p. 240.
9	Classis Britannica abandonment	–	See Ref. No. 3, p. 2.
10	Stamped Tiles	–	See Ref. No. 3, p. 123.
11	Copper alloy writing stylus	Wheeler, R.E.M.	*London in Roman Times* (1980) p. 58, Pl. XX.
12	Copper alloy pin	Crummy, N.	*The Roman Small Finds from Excavations in Colchester 1971–9, Colchester Arch. Rept. 2*, p. 29, Fig. 27.
13	Copper alloy brooch	–	See Ref. No. 11, p. 90, Fig. 24,8.
14	Copper alloy mount	Bushe-Fox, J.P.	*Excavation of the Roman Fort at Richborough, Kent*, Vol. II (1928), p. 50, Pl. XXIII, 64. (Repts. Res. Comm. Soc. Antiqs. No. X).
15	Bone pins	–	See Ref. No. 12, p. 21–22, Fig. 19.
16	Bone pins	–	See Ref. No. 12, p. 20, Fig. 17.
17	Bone pins	–	See Ref. No. 12, p. 21, Fig. 18.
18	Samian	Stanfield, J.A. and Simpson, G.	*Central Gaulish Potters*, (1958).
19	Samian	Knorr, R.	*Terra-sigillata – gefässe des Ersten Jahrunderts mit Töpfernamen.* (1952).
20	Samian	Hartley, B.R.	In *Verulamium Excavations I*, (1972), p. 216–262, (Repts. Res. Comm. Soc. Antiqs. No. XXVIII).
21	Samian	Hermet, F.	*La Graufesenque (Condatomago)*, (1934).
22	Samian	Oswald, F.	*Index of Figure-types on Terra Sigillata (Samian Ware)* (1936–37).
23	Samian	Rogers, G.	*Poteries Sigillées de la Gaule Centrale, I: Les Motifs Non-figurés*, Gallia Supp. No 28, (1974).
24	Samian	Vernhet, A. and Vertet, H.	*T. Flavius Secundus of La Graufesenque, Figlina, no. 1* (1976), p. 29–38.
25	Samian	Grimes, W.F.	*Holt, Denbighshire: the Works-depot of the Twentieth Legion at Castle Lyons, Y Cwmmrodor 41*, (1930).
26	Samian	Terrisse, J.R.	*Les Céramiques Gallo-Romaines des Martres-de-Veyre*, Gallia Supp. No. 19, (1968).
27	Samian	Fölzer, E.	*Die Bilderschüsseln der Ostgallischen Sigillata Manufakturen*, (1913).
28	Samian	Oswald, F. and Pryce, T.D.	*An Introduction to the Study of Terra Sigillata*, (1920).

29	Samian	Oswald, F.	Decorated Ware from Lavoye, *Jnl. Roman Studies*, No. 35, (1945) p. 49–57.
30	Mortars	Young, C.J.	*The Roman Pottery Industry of the Oxford Region* (1977), B.A.R. 43.
31	Mortars	Bushe-Fox, J.P.	*Excavations on the site of the Roman Town at Wroxeter, Shropshire in 1912* (1913). (Repts. Res. Comm. Soc. Antiqs. No. I).
32	D.O.E. Report	Frere, S.S.	*Principles of Publication in Rescue Archaeology (D.O.E. 1975).*
33	Coarse pottery	Bushe-Fox, J.P.	*Excavation of the Roman Fort at Richborough, Kent.* Vol I (1926), p. 88–106. (Repts. Res. Comm. Soc. Antiqs. No. VI).
34	Coarse pottery	Sheldon, H. et al	*Southwark Excavations 1972–74,* (1978).
35	Coarse pottery	Frere, S.S.	*Arch. Cant.,* LXVIII (1954), p. 101–143.
36	Coarse pottery	–	See Ref. No. 3, p. 207–249.
37	Coarse pottery	Hull, M.R.	*The Roman Potters' Kilns at Colchester* (1963).
38	Coarse pottery	Gillam, J.P.	*Types of coarse pottery in Northern Britain* (1970).
39	Coarse pottery	Seillier, C. and Thoen, H.	*Septentrion,* Vol 8 (1978), pp. 65–75.
40	Coarse pottery	Bushe-Fox, J.P.	*Excavation of the Roman Fort at Richborough, Kent,* Vol. III (1932), p. 166–187. (Repts. Res. Comm. Soc. Antiqs. No. X).
41	Coarse pottery	Bushe-Fox, J.P.	*Excavation of the Roman Fort at Richborough, Kent,* Vol. IV (1949), p. 258–272. (Repts. Res. Comm. Soc. Antiqs. No. XVI).
42	Coarse pottery	Anderson, A.	A Guide to Roman Fine Wares, Vorda Research Series 1 (1980).
43	Coarse pottery	Jenkins, F.	*Arch. Cant.,* LXXIV (1960) p. 151–161.
44	Coarse pottery	Philp, B.J.	*Excavations at Faversham, 1965* (1968), p. 76–84.
45	Coarse pottery	Philp, B.J.	*Arch. Cant.,* LXXI (1957), p. 177–184.
46	Coarse pottery	Philp, B.J.	*Excavations in the Darent Valley, Kent* (1984), p. 98–107.
47	Coarse pottery	Frere, S.S.	*Verulamium Excavations I* (1972), p. 265–364, (Repts. Res. Comm. Soc. Antiqs. No. XXVIII).
48	Coarse pottery	Cunliffe, B.	*Excavations at Fishbourne 1961–1969* (1971), pp. 159–259, (Repts. Res. Comm. Soc. Antiqs. No. XXVII).
49	Coarse pottery	Catherall, P.D.	*Britannia,* XIV (1983), pp. 103–141.
50	Coarse pottery	Woods, P.J.	*Brixworth Excavations* (1971).
51	Coarse pottery	Bushe-Fox, J.P.	*Excavation of the Roman Fort at Richborough, Kent,* Vol. II (1928), p. 97–105. (Repts. Res. Comm. Soc. Antiqs. No. VII).
52	Coarse pottery	Hawkes, C.F.C. and Hull, M.R.	*Camulodunum,* (1947), p. 170–286, (Repts. Res. Comm. Soc. Antiqs. No. XIV)
53	Coarse pottery	Jones, D. and Rhodes, M.	*Excavations at Billingsgate Buildings, Lower Thames Street, London, 1974* (1980), p. 42–43. (Special Paper No. 4, Lon. & Middx. Arch. Soc.).
54	Coarse pottery	Richardson, B. and Tyers, P.	*Britannia, XV* (1984), p. 133–141.
55	Coarse pottery	Cunliffe, B.	*Britannia,* XI (1980), p. 227–288.
56	Coarse pottery	Cunliffe, B.	*Excavations at Portchester Castle, Vol. I, Roman* (1975), p. 270–367, (Repts. Res. Comm. Soc. Antiqs. No. XXXII).
57	Coarse pottery	–	*Verulamium Excavations, Vol. II* (1983), p. 294–341. (Repts. Res. Comm. Soc. Antiqs. No. XLI).
58	Coarse pottery	Young, C.J.	*The Roman Pottery Industry of the Oxfordshire Region* (1977), B.A.R. No. 43.

59	Tile fabric 2, *Classis Britannica*	–	See Ref. No. 3, p. 125–126.
60	Voussoir tile, Fishbourne	Cunliffe, B.	*Excavations at Fishbourne 1961–1969* (1971) Vol. II p. 45 and Fig. 24 (Repts. Res. Comm. Soc. Antiqs. No. XXVII).
61	Voussoir tile, Reculver.	Cramp. G.	*Kent Arch. Review* No. 4 (1966), p. 69.
62	'The Painted House' Underfloor Heating System.	Willson, J.	*Kent Arch. Review* No. 47 (1977), p. 165–169.
63	Beauport Park box-flue tiles.	Brodribb, G.	*Britannia* Vol. X (1979), p. 148–9.
64	Plastering	Vitruvius	*De Architectura* Book VII.
65	Mosaics	–	See Ref. No. 6.
66	Tombstone Relief	Liversidge, J.	*Britain in the Roman Empire* (1968), p. 85, Fig. 31.
67	Red and Yellow Schemes	Joyce, H.	*The Decoration of Walls, Ceilings and Floors in Italy in the 2nd and 3rd Centuries* (1981), p. 19.
68	Combe End Plaster	Lysons, S.	*Arch. XVIII* (1817), p. 113.
69	Iwerne Minster Plaster	Hawkes, C.F.C.	*Arch. Jnl.*, CIV (1947), p. 50.
70	Leicester Plaster	Toynbee, J.M.C.	*Art in Britain under the Romans* (1964), p. 215–219.
71	Southwark Plaster	Yule, B.	*Britannia* XV (1984), p. 311.
72	York Minster Plaster	Davey, N.	*Britannia* III (1972), p. 266.
73	Lullingstone Plaster	Meates, G.W.	*The Lullingstone Roman Villa* (1955), p. 129
74	Verulamium Plaster	–	See Ref. No. 57. p. 239, Pl. XXXIX.
75	Caerwent Plaster	Ashby, T. et al.	*Arch.* LVIII. (1902–3), p. 141.
76	Rudston Plaster	Stead, I.M.	*Rudston Roman Villa* (1980), p. 141.
77	Winchester Plaster	Biddle, M.	*Antiq. Jnl.* XLIX (1969), p. 315
78	Sparsholt Plaster		Unpublished
79	Wiggington Plaster	Greenfield, E.	*J.R.S.* LVI (1966), p. 208.
80	Dorchester Plaster	Green, C.J.S.	*P.D.N.H.A.S.* XCI (1969), p. 184.
81	Kingscote Plaster	Swain, E.J.	*Britannia* VIII (1977), p. 412.
82	Southwell Plaster	–	See Ref. No. 70, p. 219.
83	Winterton Plaster	–	See Ref. No. 72, p. 268.
84	Dover Parallels	Toynbee, J.M.C.	*Kent Arch. Review*, No. 29 (1971), p. 264.
85	Pompeii Parallels	Carpiceci, A.C.	*Pompeii* (1977).
86	Rome and Ostia Parallels	–	See Ref. 67.
87	Mildenhall Finds	Painter, K.S.	*The Mildenhall Treasure* (1977), p. 26.
88	Bacchus	Davey, N. and Ling, R.	*Wall-Painting in Roman Britain*, (1981) p. 111.
89	Bacchus	Hutchinson, V.	*Bacchus in Roman Britain*, B.A.R. No. 151 (1986), p. 381.
90	Subject 3	Frere, S.S.	*Verulamium Excavations*, Vol. III (1984), p. 125, Pl. XIVa.
91	Subject 4	Abatte, F, (ed.), Sutton, A.J. (trans.)	*Roman Art* (1972), p. 60, Pl. 38.
92	Subject 4	Hanfmann, G.M.	*Roman Art : A Modern Survey of the Art of Imperial Rome* (1964), Pl. IX.
93	Subject 6	Liversidge, J. (ed.)	*Roman Provincial Wall Painting in the Western Empire, B.A.R. Int. Ser. 140* (1982), p. 103, abb. 5.16–18.
94	Subject 6	–	See Ref. No. 93, p. 92, abb. 5.3.
95	Subject 6	–	See Ref. No. 88.
96	Subject 8	–	See Ref. No. 71.
97	Subject 9	Pearce, B.W.	*Arch. Cant.* XXXIX (1927), p. 153.
98	Subject 31	Zienkiewich, J.D.	*The Legionary Fortress Baths at Caerleon* (1986), Pl. XCVIIa, Fig. 87.
99	Subject 36	Philp, B.J.	Forthcoming volume.
100	Roman Wall-Plaster	–	See Ref. No. 71.
101	Roman Wall-Plaster	Liversidge, J.	*Cirencester : Romano-British Wall Paintings from the Dyer Court Excavations, 1957.* Bristol and Gloucestershire Arch. Society, Vol. 81 (1962), p. 41–50.

102	Roman Wall-Plaster	–	See Ref. No. 93, Pl. 2.3.
103	Roman Wall-Plaster	–	See Ref. No. 71.
104	Roman Wall-Plaster	Croisille, J.M.	*Les Natures Mortes Campaniennes* (1965), Pl. XII:24.
105	Roman Wall-Plaster	–	See Ref. No. 89, p. 143.
106	Roman Wall-Plaster	–	See Ref. No. 92, Pl. XXII.
107	Roman Wall-Plaster	–	See Ref. No. 89, p. 130.
108	Roman Wall-Plaster	–	See Ref. No. 67, p. 69–80.
109	Roman Wall-Plaster	–	See Ref. No. 6, Cat. Nos. 25c, 52 and 58.
110	Roman Wall-Plaster	–	See Ref. No. 99.
111	Roman Wall-Plaster	–	See Ref. No. 93, p. 183–192.
112	Roman Wall-Plaster	–	See Ref. No. 88, p. 171–191.
113	Roman Wall-Plaster	R.C.H.M.	*Dorset Vol. IV* (1972), p. 41, pl.48
114	Roman Wall-Plaster	Peters, W.J.Th., Swinkels, L.J.F. and Moormann, E.M.	*Die Wandmalereien der römischen Villa von Druten und die Frage der Felderdekoration in den europäischen römischen Provinzen*, B.R.O.B. 28 (1978), p. 153–197
115	Roman Wall-Plaster	Peters, W.J.Th.	*Mural Painting Fragments found in the Legionary Fortress and the Canabae Legionis at Nijmegen*, B.R.O.B. 29 (1979) p. 373–402.
116	Roman Wall-Plaster	–	See Ref. No. 115, p. 379–381.
117	*Classis Britannica* Fort, Dover	–	See Ref. No. 3, p. 1.
118	St. Mary's Church, 1778	Lyon, J.	*Archaeologia V* (1779), p. 325.
119	Market Square, 1881	Watkin, W.T.	Arch. Jnl., 38 (1881), p. 432.
120	Market Square, 1950	Threipland, L.M.	Arch. Cant. LXXI (1957), p. 14.
121	Adrian Street, 1949	–	See Ref. No. 120, p. 21.
122	B.M.W. site, 1974	Philp, B.J.	Forthcoming.
123	Novus Portus	–	See Ref. No. 2.
124	Richborough	–	See Ref. No. 1, p. 243.
125	Roman Standardization, Actus	Walthew, C.V.	*Britannia IX* (1978), p. 333.
126	Workshop at Silchester	Ward, J.	*Romano-British Buildings and Earthworks* (1911), p. 183.
127	Building at Verulamium	–	See Ref. No. 47, Fig. 25.
128	Mansio at Silchester	Wacher, J.	*The Towns of Roman Britain, London* (1975), p. 263.
129	Mansio at Chignall St. James, Chelmsford	Going, C.J.	*Britannia VIII* (1977), p. 406, Fig. 23.
130	Mansio at Lower Wanborough	Phillips, B. and Walters, B.	*Britannia VIII* (1977), p. 223–227.
131	Mansio at Richborough	Bushe-Fox, J.P.	See Ref. No. 51, p. 13–22, Pl. XXXIX.
132	Richborough, major port of entry, 1st to early-2nd centuries	–	See Ref. No. 1, Vol. V (1968).
133	Richborough, late-Roman shore-fort	–	See Ref. No. 1, Vol. V (1968), p. 245.
134	Roman Coins	Mattingly, H. and Sydenham, E.A.	The Roman Imperial Coinage, Vols II (1926), III (1930) and IV (1936 and 1938)

Index

PLATES

Plate II *View of Painted House site from the south-west, just before excavations began in 1970.*

Plate III *Section of the broad Rammed Chalk Foundation (under foreground rod) (Period II), from the east, Bingo Hall site.*

Plate V *Detail showing damaged hypocaust with rubble filling of Tufa Block Building (Period IV), from the north, Bingo Hall.*

Plate IV *South-east corner of Tufa Block Building (Period IV), with part of surviving hypocaust, inserted flue-arch (foreground rod) and late-Roman shore-fort in background, Bingo Hall site.*

Plate VII *Detail of internal buttress S2 of Buttressed Building (Period V), beneath wall-stubs of Clay Walled Building (Period VII), Bingo Hall site.*

Plate VI *Foundation of centre wall of Buttressed Building (Period V), showing internal buttresses S4 and S5 and north wall of Painted House passage in background, Bingo Hall site.*

Plate VIII *Room 2 of the Painted House (Period VI) showing external masonry and flue and surviving internal walls and floor.*

Plate X *Detail of south respond of door-opening between Rooms 2 and 3, with socket for door-sill, Painted House (Period VI).*

Plate IX *Room 3 of the Painted House (Period VI) showing surviving walls and floor and Room 2 in background.*

Plate XII *Detail of tile capping over hypocaust channel in Room 1, Painted House (Period VI).*

Plate XI *Detail of external flue-arch feeding hypocaust of Room 3, Painted House (Period VI), with wall of earlier building C7 (Period IV) in foreground.*

Plate XIV Detail of chalk-block plugs closing hypocaust channels in Room 3, Painted House (Period VI).

Plate XIII Detail of central chamber of hypocaust-system in Room 2, Painted House (Period VI).

Plate XV *Rubble fill in north-west corner of Room 2, Painted House (Period VI).*

Plate XVIII *Room 6 of the Painted House (Period VI) showing east and south walls and floor as cut by the shore-fort ditch.*

Plate XVII *Detail of south wall of Room 5, Painted House (Period VI) as cut by shore-fort ditch and with base of later bastion above.*

Plate XVI *Room 4 of the Painted House (Period VI), showing east wall and floor, the latter cut by the late-Roman shore-fort foundations.*

Plate XX *Detail of plastered wall of Clay Walled Building (Period VII), over buttress S2 of Buttressed Building (Period V), Bingo Hall site.*

Plate XIX *Section of plastered clay wall (under small scales) of Clay Walled Building (Period VII), over foundations of Buttressed Building (Period V), with late-Roman shore-fort wall in background, Bingo Hall site.*

Plate XXII Detail of fallen wall-plaster in South Corridor of Clay Walled
Building (Period VII), Bingo Hall site.

Plate XXI Detail of in situ painted plaster on north wall of East Room of Clay
Walled Building (Period VII), Bingo Hall site.

Plate XXIII *Panels 2, 3 and 4, south wall, Room 2, Painted House.*

Plate XXIV *Detail showing vine across Panel 3, south wall, Room 2, Painted House.*

Plate XXV *Detail showing fronds and basket of fruit, Panel 4, south wall, Room 2, Painted House.*

Plate XXVI *Panels 9, 10 and 11, west and north walls, Room 2, Painted House.*

Plate XXVII *Detail showing large frond under Panel 9, west wall, Room 2, Painted House.*

Plate XXVIII *Detail of thyrsus across Panel 10, west wall, Room 2, Painted House.*

Plate XXIX *Detail showing torch across Panel 11, north wall, Room 2, Painted House.*

Plate XXX *Panels 16 and 17, east wall, Room 2, Painted House.*

Plate XXXI *Panels 20 to 23, north and east walls, Room 3, Painted House.*

Plate XXXII *Detail of tympanon beneath Panel 22, east wall, Room 3, Painted House.*

Plate XXXIII *Panels 26 and 27, east wall, Room 4, Painted House.*

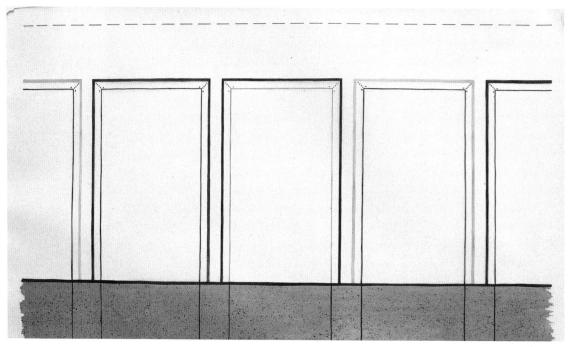

Plate XXXIV *Painted design on south wall, south corridor, Clay Walled Building, as reconstructed from in situ and fallen plaster fragments.*

Plate XXXV *Painted design on south wall, Room 2, Painted House, as reconstructed from in situ and fallen plaster fragments.*

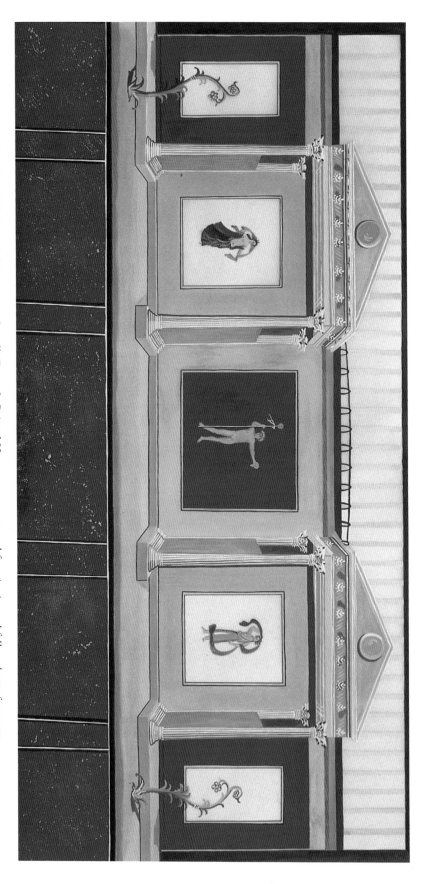

Plate XXXVI *Painted design on north wall, Room 3, Painted House, as reconstructed from in situ and fallen plaster fragments.*